The IUCN Species Survival Commission

2004 IUCN Red List of Threatened Species™

A Global Species Assessment

Edited by

Jonathan E.M. Baillie, Craig Hilton-Taylor and Simon N. Stuart

Liberté • Égalité • Fraternité
RÉPUBLIQUE FRANÇAISE

MINISTÈRE DES AFFAIRES
ÉTRANGÈRES

Direction générale
de la Coopération internationale
et du Développement DgCiD

The Rufford
Maurice Laing
Foundation

CRITICAL ECOSYSTEM PARTNERSHIP FUND

Gordon and Betty
MOORE
FOUNDATION

Natural Resources   Ressources naturelles
Canada   Canada

Ministerie van
Buitenlandse Zaken

WETLANDS
INTERNATIONAL

IUCN
Water and Nature Initiative

WWF

The Red List Consortium

IUCN
The World Conservation Union

SSC
Species Survival Commission

BirdLife
INTERNATIONAL

CONSERVATION
INTERNATIONAL

CENTER
FOR APPLIED
BIODIVERSITY
SCIENCE
at CONSERVATION
INTERNATIONAL

NatureServe

The IUCN Species Survival Commission

2004 IUCN Red List of Threatened Species™

A Global Species Assessment

Edited by
Jonathan E.M. Baillie, Craig Hilton-Taylor and Simon N. Stuart

Authors
Jonathan E.M. Baillie, Leon A. Bennun, Thomas M. Brooks,
Stuart H.M. Butchart, Janice S. Chanson, Zoe Cokeliss,
Craig Hilton-Taylor, Michael Hoffmann, Georgina M. Mace,
Sue A. Mainka, Caroline M. Pollock, Ana S.L. Rodrigues,
Alison J. Stattersfield and Simon N. Stuart

Foreword by
Hamdallah Zedan

Preface by
David Brackett

IUCN – The World Conservation Union
2004

This publication has been made possible by funding from the French Ministry for Foreign Affairs (DgCiD – Direction générale de la Coopération internationale et du Développement) and the Rufford Maurice Laing Foundation.

Published by: IUCN, Gland, Switzerland and Cambridge, UK.

Citation: Baillie, J.E.M., Hilton-Taylor, C. and Stuart, S.N. (Editors) 2004. *2004 IUCN Red List of Threatened Species. A Global Species Assessment*. IUCN, Gland, Switzerland and Cambridge, UK. xxiv + 191 pp.

ISBN: 2-8317-0826-5

Cover design: McHale Ward Associates, Ware, UK

Cover photos: © Robert Puschendorf, Anthony G. Miller, Dai G. Herbert, John E. Randall, Jack Jeffrey Photography and Troy Inman (see inside back cover for details).

Layout by: McHale Ward Associates, Ware, UK

Produced by: IUCN Publications Services Unit, Cambridge, UK

Printed by: Thanet Press Limited, Margate, UK

Available from: IUCN Publications Services Unit
219c Huntingdon Road, Cambridge CB3 0DL, UK
Tel: +44 1223 277894, Fax: +44 1223 277175
E-mail: info@books.iucn.org
www.iucn.org/bookstore

A catalogue of IUCN publications is also available

The text of this book is printed on Fineblade Smooth 115gsm made from low-chlorine pulp

To Brian Groombridge
in recognition of his major
contribution to the *IUCN Red List*,
and to the broader field of
biodiversity assessment

Contributions to the IUCN Species Survival Commission and the *2004 IUCN Red List of Threatened Species™*

The IUCN Species Survival Commission gratefully recognizes its extensive network of volunteers who make production of the *IUCN Red List* possible. Those individuals who have contributed time and expertise are listed in the Acknowledgements. SSC also wishes to acknowledge those donors whose major financial contributions support a wide variety of SSC activities, as well as development and production of the *IUCN Red List*.

The French Ministry for Foreign Affairs (DgCiD – Direction générale de la Coopération internationale et du Développement) promotes the international implementation of the main environmental conventions that came out of the Rio Summit, notably the CBD. In general, DgCiD provides two main types of financial support: (1) le Fonds de Solidarité Prioritaire (FSP), to finance the support institutions in developing countries, especially in Africa; and (2) le Fonds Français pour l'Environnement Mondial (FFEM), to finance development projects that have a significant impact upon biodiversity, the greenhouse effect, international water resources, desertification, etc. DgCiD provides support to the work of international conservation NGOs, and in particular to IUCN in all its capacities (headquarters, regional offices, and commissions) but especially for the publication of reference material on the state of the environment. This is why DgCiD has supported the publication of this Red List analysis.

The Rufford Maurice Laing Foundation came into being in August 2003 as a result of a merger between The Maurice Laing Foundation, founded by Sir Maurice Laing in June 1972 and The Rufford Foundation founded in June 1982 by John Hedley Laing. The Foundation is a private grant-making trust. This programme supports registered charities whose work is concerned with nature conservation, the environment, and sustainable development, with approximately half of the Foundation's funding going to these areas. Through a grant to the Institute of Zoology in the UK, the Rufford Maurice Laing Foundation provides support for the annual compilation and production of the *IUCN Red List*, and in particular the compilation of this publication.

BirdLife International is a partnership of people for birds and the environment. The BirdLife Partnership is the leading authority on the status of birds and their habitats. BirdLife International is a partner in the Red List Programme and is also the Listing Authority for birds on the *IUCN Red List* and through its Partnership, works closely with the IUCN/SSC Specialist Groups in this capacity. For over 20 years, BirdLife has published information on globally threatened bird species in regional Red Data Books and global Red Lists, such that birds are recognized as the best-documented group of species. Over ten million people support the BirdLife Partnership of national non-governmental conservation organizations and local networks. Partners work together on shared priorities, programmes, and policies, learning from each other to achieve real conservation results. The BirdLife Partnership promotes sustainable living as a means of conserving birds and all other forms of biodiversity.

Conservation International (CI) has been actively involved the Red List Programme for over ten years. CI's mission is to conserve the Earth's living heritage, our global biodiversity, and to demonstrate that human societies are able to live harmoniously with nature. CI believes that the Earth's natural heritage must be maintained if future generations are to thrive spiritually, culturally and economically. CI supports the Red List Programme in particular through its Center for Applied Biodiversity Science, but also through its regional Centers for Biodiversity Conservation.

The Center for Applied Biodiversity Science (CABS) at Conservation International works to strengthen the ability of CI and other institutions to identify and respond to emerging threats and pressures affecting the Earth's biological diversity. As a partner in the Red List Programme, CABS collects and compiles the baseline data needed to address the extensive gaps in our knowledge about biodiversity and its threats. To this end, CABS has established a joint biodiversity assessment unit with the IUCN Species Survival Commission, which is coordinating the Global Amphibian Assessment and the Global Mammal Assessment. CABS also provides direct support to a number of IUCN/SSC Specialist Groups.

NatureServe is a non-profit conservation organization that plays an active role in the Red List Consortium, in particular by helping to coordinate the Global Amphibian Assessment in the western hemisphere. NatureServe serves as the secretariat for the network of natural heritage programmes and conservation data centres that now include 76 independent biodiversity inventory programmes operating throughout the Americas. NatureServe and its member programmes have been assessing the condition and distribution of species and ecosystems, and maintain comprehensive databases on North American vertebrates, vascular plants, and selected invertebrate groups. They also have significant data holdings for selected regions and species in Latin America.

The Critical Ecosystem Partnership Fund (CEPF) is a joint initiative of Conservation International, The Global Environment Facility, the Government of Japan, the John D. and Catherine T. MacArthur Foundation and the World Bank. CEPF provides strategic assistance to non-governmental organizations, community groups and other civil society partners to help safeguard Earth's biodiversity hotspots. A fundamental goal is to ensure civil society is engaged in biodiversity conservation. The CEPF is providing major financial support to the Global Mammal Assessment.

Together with the ***Moore Family Foundation***, the ***Gordon and Betty Moore Foundation*** has generously funded the Center for Applied Biodiversity Science's Biodiversity Assessment Unit, and thereby supports the *IUCN Red List of Threatened Species™*.

Natural Resources Canada (NRCan) is a federal government department specializing in energy, minerals and metals, forests and earth sciences. NRCan deals with natural resource issues that are important to Canadians, looking at these issues from both a national and international perspective, using its expertise in science and policy. How land and resources are managed today will determine the quality of life for Canadians both now and in the future. NRCan hosts the web server for the *IUCN Red List*.

Wetlands International (WI) is a leading global non-profit organization dedicated solely to the work of wetland conservation and sustainable management. Well-established networks of experts and close partnerships with key organizations provide Wetlands International with the essential tools for catalysing conservation activities worldwide. Its activities have been carried out in over 120 countries. WI's mission is to sustain and restore wetlands, their resources and biodiversity for future generations through research, information exchange and conservation activities, worldwide. WI managed the Dutch Ministry of Foreign Affairs (DGIS) funding for the IUCN/SSC Eastern Africa freshwater assessment project, a regional Red List assessment of many aquatic taxa. WI has jointly with SSC resurrected the Global Freshwater Fish Specialist Group that will continue to assess freshwater fish for the *IUCN Red List*.

The IUCN Water and Nature Initiative (WANI) is a 5-year action programme to demonstrate that ecosystem-based management and stakeholder participation will help solve the water dilemma of today – bringing rivers back to life and maintaining the resource base for many. WANI provides support to the SSC Freshwater Biodiversity Assessment Programme to collect the base-line species data.

The World Wide Fund for Nature (WWF) provides significant annual operating support to the SSC. WWF's contribution supports the SSC's minimal infrastructure and helps ensure that the voluntary network and Publications Programme are adequately supported. WWF aims to conserve nature and ecological processes by: (1) preserving genetic, species, and ecosystem diversity; (2) ensuring that the use of renewable natural resources is sustainable both now and in the longer term; and (3) promoting actions to reduce pollution and the wasteful exploitation and consumption of resources and energy. WWF is one of the world's largest independent conservation organizations with a network of National Organizations and Associates around the world and over 5.2 million regular supporters. WWF continues to be known as World Wildlife Fund in Canada and in the United States of America.

Contents

Foreword

The evolution of life forms and their interaction with each other and with the environment has made Earth a uniquely habitable place. Species and the ecosystems they are part of provide a large number of goods and services that sustain our lives. This biodiversity is essential to our planet, human well-being and to the livelihood and cultural integrity of people. Yet biodiversity is currently being lost at unprecedented rates due to human activities. Species extinction is a commonly used measure of biodiversity loss. As is documented in this publication, some 12% of bird species and about a quarter of mammal species are globally threatened. Species extinction rates currently exceed the background rates by two to four orders of magnitude. In effect, this amounts to the sixth great extinction of life on Earth.

To address the challenge of biodiversity loss, the Conference of the Parties of the Convention on Biological Diversity, in 2002, adopted the target of achieving by 2010 a significant reduction in the current rate of biodiversity loss at the global, regional and national level as a contribution to poverty alleviation and to the benefit of all life on Earth. The world's leaders at the World Summit on Sustainable Development subsequently endorsed this target. The Summit also highlighted the essential role of biodiversity in meeting the Millennium Development Goals, especially the targets of halving the incidence of poverty and hunger by 2015.

The *IUCN Red List of Threatened Species*™, prepared and updated under the leadership of the Species Survival Commission of IUCN – The World Conservation Union, has for four decades provided global assessments of the status of species and other taxa in order to highlight those threatened with extinction, and therefore promote their conservation. It is widely recognized as the most objective and authoritative listing of species that are globally at risk of extinction.

Until recently, however, it has been difficult to measure changes in the status of threatened species in an objective and scientifically rigorous way. At its meeting in February 2004, the Conference of the Parties of the Convention on Biological Diversity called for the development of a Red List indicator as part of a set of indicators to assess progress towards the 2010 target. This *Global Species Assessment* applies Red List data to calculate a Red List Index. This Index combines global representativeness with a fine ecological resolution to provide information on changes in relative aggregate extinction risk across entire taxonomic groups. The Red List Index is an important tool that complements other indicators to assess progress towards the 2010 target.

I would like to congratulate the IUCN Species Survival Commission and its partner organizations – BirdLife International, Conservation International, and NatureServe – for compiling the new issue of the *IUCN Red List* and this *Global Species Assessment* and extend my appreciation to all those who are working around the world to monitor biodiversity and help build the necessary capacity and political will to ensure its conservation and sustainable use.

Hamdallah Zedan
Executive Secretary
United Nations Convention on Biological Diversity

Preface

The world is facing a global extinction crisis. Perhaps the most eloquent expression of this I have heard was a comment by then Prime Minister of Norway, Gro Harlem Brundtland, to the opening of a session of one of the Trondheim Conferences on Biodiversity, when she said "The library of life is burning, and we don't even know the titles of the books". It remains for me a powerful image of the damage we are doing to the Earth and to our future options as humankind.

Our lives are inextricably linked with the library of life – or biodiversity – and ultimately its protection is essential for our very survival. It is the complex interactions of life's many forms that provide the basic essentials for human existence such as the air we breathe or the food we eat. We experience the benefits of biodiversity every day, from its role in decomposing waste, pollinating crops, filtering water, or helping to reduce floods or erosion, to mention but a few. Yet we continue to watch the mounting flames with little understanding of what is being lost, how fast the library of life is disappearing or what impact the loss will have on our lives, or on future generations, or on our planet.

The *IUCN Red List of Threatened Species*™ is one attempt to increase the world's store of knowledge about our biological resources before they are lost. Providing information about the status of biodiversity is a critical first step in both highlighting the severity of the problem and encouraging societies to begin to assume accountability for their actions, so that we can maintain at least current levels of biodiversity.

Globally, the heads of governments have made a start at recognizing the crisis. At the World Summit on Sustainable Development they adopted a global biodiversity target to "…significantly reduce the rate of loss of biodiversity by 2010…" The countries of the world are beginning to consider how they will achieve that target. The conservation community at large is beginning to focus its efforts towards the same end. One of the key challenges all are facing is how to measure progress, how to know whether what is being done is having an impact, and whether that impact is positive or negative with respect to the target. This document begins to offer some answers about how we can monitor trends in biodiversity.

Although analyses of the *IUCN Red List* have been carried out on a regular basis, the 2004 *Global Species Assessment* (GSA) is the first to be conducted by the Red List Consortium (IUCN Species Survival Commission, BirdLife International, the Center for Applied Biodiversity Science at Conservation International, and NatureServe), resulting in broader coverage and new in-depth analyses. It is the first assessment to include the Red List Index that measures trends in extinction risk for all bird and amphibian species. It is the first time that complete assessments of amphibians, cycads and conifers have been included, and it is also the first analysis to use distribution maps for all mammals and amphibians. The new data, new analyses and broader expertise result in this document being one of the most comprehensive assessments of the conservation status of the world's species ever conducted.

This document addresses biodiversity at the species level. Species are in the middle of the biodiversity continuum from genes to ecosystems. They are readily recognized, and offer an opportunity to measure and communicate changes at other levels of complexity. While species-based conservation cannot and should not replace efforts to conserve genetic diversity or ecosystem functioning, it is often the most readily available surrogate for conservation of biological diversity.

The data from the *IUCN Red List* are often used in setting priorities for conservation, but it is wrong to think that they can do so on their own. Setting conservation priorities is a sensitive policy exercise which normally includes the assessment of the conservation status of a species, but also takes into account other factors such as ecological, phylogenetic, historical, or cultural preferences for some taxa over others, as well as the probability of success of conservation actions, availability of funds or personnel to carry out such actions, and legal frameworks for conservation of threatened taxa.

The *IUCN Red List* is intended to be policy-relevant, but not policy-prescriptive. That is, the *IUCN Red List* provides the best available information about the conservation status of the listed species, and the relative risk of extinction, often including information on the drivers of that risk, but it is not intended to provide specific recommendations on the appropriate policy response to that information.

The existence of the *IUCN Red List of Threatened Species*™ and the *Global Species Assessment* depends in large part on the contributions of an extraordinary network of experts brought together through the convening power of the IUCN Species Survival Commission and the partners in the Red List Consortium. It tells a powerful story of the assault of humankind on the biodiversity of this planet, but it also offers a collection of information that can help turn us in a more sustainable direction. I commend it to your attention.

David Brackett
Chair
IUCN Species Survival Commission

Acknowledgements

The publication of this *Global Species Assessment* has been made possible through funding from the French Ministry for Foreign Affairs (DgCiD – Direction générale de la Coopération internationale et du Développement). The DgCiD support included some funding for one of the editors (CHT). The Rufford Maurice Laing Foundation also provided funding for one of the editors (JEMB), for the Red List Programme intern and for the annual update of the *IUCN Red List* web site. The Moore Family Foundation and the Gordon and Betty Moore Foundation provided funding for another editor (SNS). Jean-Christophe Vié and Georgina Mace assisted with the fund raising.

Undertaking and producing this analysis would not have been possible without the dedicated help and willingness of a large number of people. The editors would like to thank in particular all the authors of the sections for their extremely hard work, for keeping to the deadlines, and for their constructive comments in reviewing the drafts. The completion of this analysis would not have been possible without the dedication of the whole writing team and the backup provided by all the members of the Red List Consortium. The writing team comprised: Jonathan Baillie, Leon Bennun, Thomas Brooks, Stuart Butchart, Janice Chanson, Zoe Cokeliss, Craig Hilton-Taylor, Michael Hoffmann, Georgina Mace, Sue Mainka, Caroline Pollock, Ana Rodrigues, Alison Stattersfield, and Simon Stuart.

In addition to the section authors, a number of people provided information or wrote case studies to illustrate particular issues. The editors and section authors warmly thank the following people for their contributions: Hilary Aikman, Luciano Andriamaro, Peter Best, Bastian Bomhard, Arabella Bramley, Amie Bräutigam, Martin Brooks, Rebecca Cairns-Wicks, Rachel Cavanagh, Trevor Coote, Neil Cox, William Darwall, Nicholas Dulvy, Dominique Fiedler, Nicholas Goodwin, Richard Griffiths, Rod Hitchmough, Elodie Hudson, Larry Master, Joan Mayol Serra, Rory McAuley, Don Merton, Alan Millar, Tony Miller, Paul Pearce-Kelly, Nigel Pitman, Zo Lalaina Rakotobe, Harison Randrianasolo, John Reynolds, Harison Rabarison, Hugh Robertson, Paul Salaman, Ed Saul, Wes Sechrest, Mary Seddon, Colin Simpfendorfer, Astrid Vargas, Jean-Christophe Vié, and Bruce Young.

The editors thank David Brackett (Chair of SSC), and the IUCN Species Programme Officers: Mariano Gimenez Dixon, Anna Knee, and Wendy Strahm for commenting on various drafts and providing assistance.

To help bring the document to life, a number of people and institutions very generously provided photographs: Ross Alford, Tim Allen, Henk Beentje, Dean Biggins, S.D. Biju, BirdLife International, Philip Bishop, Rebecca Cairns-Wicks, Vickie Caraway, Dave Clarke, Colin Clubbe, Harold Cogger, Tony Comacho, Dave Currie, de Saix, Antonio Di Croce, Digital Vision, John Donaldson, Cristian Echeverria, Endangered Wildlife Trust, Michael and Patricia Fogden, Nigel Forshaw, Fundacion ProAves, Glenn Gerber, Justin Gerlach, Janice Golding, Wendell Haag, Mandy Heddle, Nick Helme, Wolcott Henry, Dai Herbert, Craig Hilton-Taylor, Troy Inman, Jack Jeffrey, Zhigang Jiang, Chan Ah Lak, Malcolm Largen, Suzanna León-Yánez, Tasso Leventis, Paul Loiselle, Anna Lushchekina, Chris Magin, Sue Mainka, Ferne McKenzie, Alan Miller, Anthony Miller, R. Mitchell, David Moyer/Wildlife Conservation Society, David Mudge, Piotr Naskrecki, Anna Nekaris, Fabio Olmos, Tony Palliser, Vic Peddemors, Juan Pratginestós/WWF-Brazil, Robert Puschendorf, Asad Rahmani, John Randall, Michael Samways, Christoph Scheidegger, Roland Seitre, Guy Shorrock/RSPB Images, Jeremy Stafford-Deitsch, P.J. Stephenson, Wendy A. Strahm, Bernard Suprin, Frank Todd, Michael Tyler, Peter Paul van Dijk, Jean-Christophe Vié, Richard Wainwright, Henk Wallays, David Weller, Jacob Wijkema, WWF-Canon/David Hulse, WWF-UK, Zoological Society of London, and Sterling Zumbrunn. The photographs were researched by Amie Bräutigam, Zoe Cokeliss, Anna Knee, Craig Hilton-Taylor, Andrew McMullin, Simon Stuart and Richard Thomas. The graphics for this publication were produced mainly by Janice Chanson, Mike Hoffmann and Ana Rodrigues.

The data on which this analysis was based was compiled by staff at BirdLife International (for details see Birdlife 2004b), the Global Amphibian Assessment coordinating team: Neil Cox, Janice Chanson, Simon Stuart, and Bruce Young (see details below), the Global Mammal Assessment coordinating team: Jonathan Baillie, Mariano Gimenez Dixon, and Wes Sechrest (see details below), the IUCN Freshwater Biodiversity Assessment Programme staff: Will Darwall and interns Thomas Lowe and Kevin Smith (see details below) and the IUCN Red List Programme staff: Craig Hilton-Taylor, Caroline Pollock and the Red List intern Tristan Tyrrell. We also note the contributions of past interns: Matthew Linkie and Tracy Dickinson, and the Plants Officer Alain Mauric. The Red List Programme is especially grateful to all the Species Programme Officers for encouraging and supporting Specialist Groups to contribute to the Red List.

Producing this analysis would not be possible were it not for the extraordinary enthusiasm, dedication and willingness of many people around the world who contribute an enormous amount of time and effort to supply Red List assessments and the supporting documentation required for the *IUCN Red List*. In particular, we must acknowledge all the SSC Specialist Group Chairs, Red List Authority focal points, Specialist Group members, and the many field scientists who have been involved in contributing to the *IUCN Red List*. In the lists below we have tried to highlight all the individuals, groups of individuals, organizations, and participants at particular workshops who's contributions appear on the *2004 IUCN Red List of Threatened Species™*. With such a long list of names, it is highly probable that we have inadvertently forgotten someone or spelt your names incorrectly; please forgive us.

Assessors (this list excludes the amphibian assessors, these are listed separately below):

T. Abbott, A. Acero, P. Acevedo-Rodríguez, E. Acuña, W.F. Adams, F. Adema, E.M.G. Agoo, B. Agwanda, V. Ahlman, M. Alais, A. Alberts, C. Aldan, G. Allen, M. Allet, P. Almada-Villela, R. Alonso, G. Amori, A.F. Amorim, E.F. Anderson, A. Angerbjörn, M.L.G. Araújo, A.E. Areces-Mallea, C.A. Arfelli, A.J.S. Argolo, A.G. Arredondo, C.S. Asa, P. Ashton, G.S.M. Asmat, A. Assi, A. Assogbadjo, R.P.D. Atkinson, S. Aulagnier, L. Averyanov, G.A. Awan, V. Bachraz, J. Baillie, M.I. Bampi, N.T. Ban, A. Bañares, S. Bandeira, P. Barratt, P Barriga, G.M. Barroso, H. Bauer, R. Baxter, G. Bazante, K.R. Beaman, G. Bearzi, I. Beasley, M.D. Beccaceci, H.J. Beentje, D. Belitsky, T. Bell, C.L. Bellamy, P. Bellingham, G. Benavides, P. Benda, M.B. Bennett, J. Benzie, W. Bergmans, R. Bernal, R.S. Bérnils, A. Beyer, R. Bills, V. Birstein, D. Blair, R.J. Blakenmore, D.A. Blank, V.C. Bleich, B.R. Blood, P. Bloomer, A.E. Bogan, L. Bohs, L. Boitani, R. Bonfil, K. Bonham, C. Bonifaz, R. Boonratana, A. Boratynski, P. Bouchet, W.R. Branch, S. Branstetter, J. Brash, G.T. Braulik, M. Breuil, D. Bridson, D.A. Broughton, D.S. Brown, R.L. Brownell Jr., B. Bruce, M.M. Bruegmann, T. Brule, S.D. Buckner, X. Buitrón, G.H. Burgess, P.M. Burgoyne, A. Burke, J. Burrows, F.J. Burton, T. Butynski, P. Bygrave, A. Cabanban, S. Cable, G.M. Cailliet, R. Cairns-Wicks, E. Calderon, M. Camhi, R. Cantley, J.P.P. Carauta, V. Caraway, A. Carlstrom, C.M.S. Carrington, D.S. Carroll, G. Carron, R.L. Carter, S. Carter-Holmes, L. d'A.F Carvalho, A. Castellanos, G. Castley, P. Catling, T.B. Cavalcanti, R.D. Cavanagh, A. Cedeño, C. Cerón, S. Chakraborty, P. Charvet-Almeida, A.A. Chaudhry, M. Cheek, G.E. Chiaramonte, A.G. Chiarello, W. Chitaukali, M. Chong, L.S.L. Chua, R.C.K. Chung, D. Clark, J.L. Clark, C. Clarke, G.P. Clarke, G. Cliff, E. Cloete, C. Clubbe, N. Coetzee, N. Cole, K. Collins, L.J.V. Compagno,

J.G. Conran, C. Conraths, C.J. Conroy, E. Constantino, L. Contreras, S. Contreras-Balderas, J. Conyers, J.A. Cook, S.F. Cook, J. Cootes, L.K. Corbett, X. Cornejo, A.S. Cornish, J.P.S. Correia, E. Cortés, L. Cortés-Oritz, M. Corti, M. Cosse, E.D. Cossíos, F.W. Cotterill, E. Cotton, O. Courtenay, R.H. Cowie, K.A. Crandall, P. Craven, Q.C.B. Cronk, L. Csiba, B. Csuti, A.D. Cuarón, N. Cumberlidge, F. Cuzin, B.L. Cypher, G.A.B. da Fonseca, J. Dalponte, I. Darbyshire, G.S. Davis, S.E. Dawson, M. Day, M.P. de Almeida., P.C. de Grammont, J.J. de Granville, P.J. de Lange, E.F. de Vogel, W.J.J.O. de Wilde, A.J. de Winter, J. Decher, T.D. Defler, T. Delgado, C. Dellafiore, J.R. Demboski, J. Denham, M. Di Bernardo, J.C. Di-Bernardo, R.F. Dicht, F. Dieterlen, W. Dittus, T. Dold, L. Dollar, J.S. Donaldson, J.L. Dowl, R.C. Dowler, T. Down, C. Downer, J. Dransfield, M. Drioli, D. Du Puy, J.M.B. Duarte, W. Duckworth, C.A.J. Duffy, S. Duke, M.E. Dulloo, N.K. Dulvy, L.S. Durbin, R. East, J. Easton, A. Eastwood, D.A. Ebert, P.J. Eddowes, C.W. Edwards, A.-M. Eklund, L.G. Eldredge, J. Ellis, K.C. Emberton, S. Endrody-Younga, R. Erickson, C. Espinoza, F.B. Essig, J. Estes, M. Etuge, A. Eudey, G. Evans, R. Evans, L. Fagundes, J. Fahr, N. Fairall, D. Fairclough, A. Farjon, C. Faulkes, C. Feh, S. Fennessy, I.K. Fergusson, M. Festa-Bianchet, Y. Finet, D. Finnie, G.A. Firsov, B. Fitz Maurice, W.A. Fitz Maurice, A. Flaherty, J. Florence, D. Florens, G. Folkerts, S. Fordham, G. Foster, S.L. Fowler, M.P. Francis, F.L. Franco, A. Freire-Fierro, T. Frest, A. Frias-Martin, R.A. Fridell, K.D. Friedland, D. Frodin, C. Frost, Fu Likuo, D. Fuller, T.K. Fuller, M. Furtado, O.B.F. Gadig, J. Ganzhorn, J.E. Garcia, M. Garcia, R.J. Garcia, G. Garcia-Moliner, R. Gardner, G. Garfi, A. Gasgoigne, E. Geffen, T. Geissmann, C. Gemmill, S. George, G. Gerber, J. Gerlach, S.A. Ghazanfar, R. Gibson, M. Gimenez Dixon, J.R. Ginsberg, S. Gippoliti, F. Giusti, D. Gledhill, B. Goettsch, A. Golamco Jr., J. Golding, K.J. Goldman, C. Gómez-Hinostrosa, M. González, S. González, M. González-Espinosa, I. Gordon, G. Gosline, J. Grady, L. Granjon, A. Gray, M. Griffin, H.I. Griffiths, O. Griffiths, J. Groenendijk, P. Grubb, D.L. Guadagnin, A., Güner, A. Guttman, M. Haase, M.A. Hack, M. Hadfield, L. Hadway, T. Haevermans, D.J. Hafner, J.C. Hafner, N. Hahn, W.P. Haines, F. Hajek, M. Hamer, J. Hammond, J. Hare, M. Harmelin-Vivien, J.H. Harris, R.B. Harris, D. Harrison, W. Hawthorne, W.K. Hayes, L. Heaney, M.L. Heddle, S. Hedges, R. Hefner, J. Heller, A. Henderson, R. Henderson, S. Henley, D.G. Herbert, J. Herbert, C. Hernández, H,M. Hernández, P. Hersteinsson, W.J. Hess, M.R. Heupel, E.W. Heymann, N.T. Hiep, D. Hill, K.D. Hill, C. Hilton-Taylor, G.B. Hinton, G.S. Hinton, A. Hofer, M. Hoffmann, Z.S. Hogan, C. Hong-Wa, A. Hoock, J. Horrocks, M. Hounsome, K. Howell, N. Hozbor, C. Hughes, B. Human, G. Huntsman, J. Hurter, S.A. Hussain, A. Hutson, R. Hutterer, C. Huveneers, M. Ibanez, P.L. Ibisch, T.M. Iliffe, H. Is-haquou Daouda, H. Ishihara, N. Ishii, J.B. Iverson, D. Jacobs. T. Jaffré, G. Jakubowsky, T. Jaramillo, P. Jenkins, Y.V. Jhala, N. Jiddawi, J.E. Jiménez, A.J.T. Johnsingh, D. Johnson, C. Jones, P. Jørgensen, J. Juste, D. Kahwa, C. Kalkman, B. Kanchnasaka, A.B. Katende, L. Kaufman, E. Kaunda, K. Kawanishi, Kazunari Yano, M. Keith, B.T. Kelly, D.L. Kelly, J. Kerbis Peterhans, V. Kessner, R. Kiesling, R.N. Kilburn, N. Kingston, S. Kingswood, G.L. Kirkland Jr., L.K. Kiwi, C.R. Knapp, K.M. Kochummen, G. Köhler, J.E. Kotas, M. Kottelat, D. Kreb, S. Krentz, M. Krose, M. Kulbicki, F.E. Kurczewski, R. Kyambadde, P.M. Kyne, H. Labat, S. Laegaard, J. Lamilla, A.F. Lamónaca, B. Lang, C.N. Lange, P. Last, L. Lavrenchenko, M. Lawes, Le Xuan Canh, G. Leach, L. Leandro, D.M. Lenain, S. León-Yánez, R. Lessa, Li Zhenyu, T.J. Lisney, R. List, Liu Zhengyu, S. Llamozas, N. Lloyd, P. Lloyd, J. Lockyear, P. Loiselle, S. Loots, A.J. Loveridge, J. Lovett, J. Loving, A. Lowrie, S.Y. Lu, M. Lucherini, R. Ludovic, A.D. Lüthy, A. Lyenga, B. Maas, D.W. Macdonald, S.O. MacDonald, N.A. Madhyastha, D. Madulid, A.M. Maeda-Martinez, Z.L.K. Magombo, A. Mailosi, D.P. Mallon, G. Manganelli, C. Mannheimer, M.C.D. Mansur, M. Mantuano, J.M. Manzanares, M. Marcelino, S. Maree, J. Marino, S. Marjinissen, A.L. Markezich, M. Marks, O.A.V. Marques, M.B. Martins, A. Massa, S. Matola, C. Matthee, A. Mauchamp, J. Mauricio, R. Mazzoleni, N. Mbeiza Mutekanga, J.H. McAdam, D. McAllister, R. McAuley, E. McCance, K. McCreery, K.P. McDonald, R.M. McDowall, C. McGaugh, D. McGinnity, C.A. McGuinness, J.W. McNutt,

L.D. Mech, S.L. Mendes, S. Mickleburgh, A.J.K. Millar, A.G. Miller, M.G.L. Mills, N. Mitchell, M. Mitré, P. Moehlman, H. Mogollón, A. Monadjem, R. Montúfar, M. Moraes, S.A.A. Morato, P. Moreno, J.C. Moura-Leite, C. Moya, P. Muriel, P. Murugaiyan, J.A. Musick, S.G. Mycock, S. Myers, M. Mylonas, F. Naggs, D.W. Nagorsen, A. Nakazono, M. Nambou, R.C. Namora, H. Navarrete, G.G. Ndiritu, M.B. Ndjele, J.A. Neer, D. Neill, J.A.J. Nel, R. Nel, D. Nellis, C. Nelson, K. Nelson, J. Nerz, T.R. New, C. Ngereza, N.H. Nghia, Nguyen Tien Hiep, F. Nicayenzi, G. Nichols, F. Nicolalde, T. Nikolic, K. Nixon, L. Noblick, B. Norman, G. Notarbartolo di Sciara, A.J. Novaro, K. Nowell, D. Nyberg, M.R. Oates, R.A. Odum, M.I. Oetinger, S.F. Oetinger, M.J. O'Farrell, N. Oguge, P. Oguge, N. Oleas, R.B. Oliveira, W. Oliver, S. Othman, J. Ottenwalder, N. Ovsyanikov, W. Page, S. Palazzi, G. Palmer, D. Pan, F.J., Pan, C.M. Pannell, F.M. Parauka, C. Parent, A.J. Paton, M. Patten, L. Paul, M. Pawson, P. Pearce-Kelly, O. Pearson, G. Pedralli, T. Peguy, A.L. Peixoto, J. Perälä, J.P. Pereira, A. Perera, M.B. Peres, A.M. Perez, N. Perez, O. Pergams, M. Perrin, R. Pethiyagoda, F. Petrovic, B. Peyton, M.F. Pfab, Phan Ke Loc, S. Pheeha, K.A. Phillips, M.K. Phillips, P.S.M. Phiri, S.J. Pierce, R. Pillans, U. Piovezan, J. Pires O'Brien, N. Pitman, J. Pogonoski, B. Pokryseko, B.J. Pollard, D.A. Pollard, C.M. Pollock, W.F. Ponder, R. Powell, A. Poyarkov, M.S. Pradhan, D. Prado, R.C. Preece, J. Ptolemy, Z. Pucek, A. Punt, H.J. Quero, C. Quintana, E.A. Rahman, N. Ramirez-Marcial, F.M. Randriantafika, G. Rasmussen, G.B. Rathbun, M. Reardon, J.W. Reid, D.C.F. Rentz, C. Reuther, J.C. Reynolds, G. Rincon, T. Ripken, H. Rischer, F. Rivera, R. Robbins, E. Robbrecht, C. Roberts, L. Robinson, C.F.D. Rocha, W.A. Rodrigues, J.V. Rodríguez-M., G.W. Roemer, A.I. Roest, J.G. Rohwer, W. Rojas, M. Romero, H. Romero-Saltos, K. Romoleroux, R.S. Rosa, J.P. Ross, B. Roth, J.P. Roux, D.I. Rubenstein, A. Runstrom, K. Rushforth, B. Russell, R. Rutty, S. Ryan, A.B. Rylands, Y. Sadovy, C. Safina, M. Saleh, M. Samoilys, M.J. Samways, B. Sánchez, M. Sandiford, J. Santiana, F. Santos Motta, A.L. Sarti Martinez, L.G. Saw, I. Sazima, G.B. Schaller, C. Scheidegger, P.J. Schembri, C. Schenck, M. Schilthuizen, D. Schlitter, P.A. Schmidt, D. Schnell, R. Scott-Shaw, E.R. Secchi, M.B. Seddon, S. Semesi, J.A. Seminoff, B. Séret, T.L. Serfass, H.S. Shellhammer, G. Sherley, K. Sidiyasa, C. Sillero-Zubiri, J.C.S. Silva, N.M.F. Silva, M. Simons, C. Simpfendorfer, R.K. Sinha, A. Situ Yingyi, P. Skelton, B. Sket, L.E. Skog, S. Slack-Smith, L. Slooten, M.J. Smale, A.T. Smith, B.D. Smith, G. Smith, R. Smith, S.E. Smith, J. Smith-Abbott, H. Snell, J. Snoeks, J. Sobel, A. Solem, B. Sonké, J.M.R. Soto, M.M. Sotomayor, C. Spence, R. St. Pierre, C. Stamm, J. Stanisic, F. Starmühlner, F. Stauffer, D.T. Steele, J. Steffek, G. Sternberg, J. Stevens, P.F. Stevens, M. Stiassny, W. Strahm, C. Stuart, T. Stuart, W. Stuppy, K.A. Subramanian, L. Suin, J.M. Sulentich, R.M. Sullivan, W. Sun, L.F. Sundström, B. Suprin, C. Surprenant, M. Tannerfeldt, T. Tarifa, P. Tattersfield, E. Tavares, A. Taylor, B.L., Taylor, N.P. Taylor, P. Taylor, A. Tchabovsky, C. Tenberg, V. Tezoo, C.S. Thaeler Jr., M. Thulin, J. Timberlake, S.D. Tirira, D. Tiu, P. Tolson, K. Tomiyama, R.B. Torres, A. Tye, M. Tyson, M. Uhart, C.U. Ulloa, Y. Uozumi, C. Valdespino, J.C. Valenzuela, A. van Jaarsveld, E. van der Straeten, H. van Rompaey, N. van Strien, C.A.M. van Swaay, P.C. van Welzen, D. Varela, I. Vargas, R. Varman, N. Varty, A.M.S. Vaz, L.A. Velez-Espino, A. Venkataraman, J. Vermeulen, J. Victor, J.-C. Vié, A. Vincent, J.L. Vivero, G.M. Vogel, R. Von Cosel, C.M. Vooren, A.P. Vovides, Vu Ngoc Thanh, R. Wager, H. Wai, H.F. Waldemarin, S. Waldren, P. Walker, R. Walker, T.I. Walker, J.Y. Wang, M.S. Warren, R.K. Wayne, D. Weller, S. Wells, A. Whistler, L. White, W.T. White, I. Whyte, T. Wiewandt, M.J. Wigginton, M. Wikelski, G. Wiles, S.A. Williams, D. Wingate, A. Witsuba, G. Wong, N. Woodfield, R. Woodroffe, P. Wright, W. Wuster, Xiang Qiaoping, R. Yahr, S. Yahya, K. Yano, E. Yensen, D.C. Zappi, J. Zielinski, S. Zoerner, S. Zona, and G. Zorzi.

Assessors (Groups and Organizations):

Often, instead of individuals being named as the assessors, the name of the Specialist Group is used instead, especially in cases where assessments are agreed by consensus amongst the members of a group. Hence we record our thanks to all the members of the following Specialist Groups:

African Elephant Specialist Group, African Rhino Specialist Group, Antelope Specialist Group, Asian Elephant Specialist Group, Asian Rhino Specialist Group, Australasian Marsupial and Monotreme Specialist Group, Australasian Reptile and Amphibian Specialist Group, Bear Specialist Group, Bison Specialist Group, Bryophyte Specialist Group, Canid Specialist Group, Caprinae Specialist Group, Cat Specialist Group, Cetacean Specialist Group, China Plant Specialist Group, Chiroptera Specialist Group, Conifer Specialist Group, Crocodile Specialist Group, Deer Specialist Group, Edentate Specialist Group, Equid Specialist Group, European Reptile and Amphibian Specialist Group, Hippo Specialist Group (now the Pig, Peccary & Hippo SG), Hyaena Specialist Group, Hyrax Specialist Group (now under the Afrotheria SG), Inland Water Crustacean Specialist Group, Insectivore Specialist Group, Lagomorph Specialist Group, Lepidoptera Specialist Group, Mollusc Specialist Group, Mustelid, Viverrid and Procyonid Specialist Group (now the Small Carnivore SG), New World Marsupial Specialist Group, Odonata Specialist Group, Orthopteroid Specialist Group, Pangolin Specialist Group, Pig, Peccary & Hippo Specialist Group, Polar Bear Specialist Group, Primate Specialist Group, Rodent Specialist Group, Seal Specialist Group, Shark Specialist Group, Sirenia Specialist Group, Social Insects Specialist Group, South American Camelid Specialist Group, Sturgeon Specialist Group, Temperate Broadleaved Tree Specialist Group (now under the Global Tree SG), Tortoise & Freshwater Turtle Specialist Group, West Indian Iguana Specialist Group (now the Iguana SG), and Wolf Specialist Group.

Additional organizations involved in providing Red List assessments include:

American Fisheries Society Endangered Species Committee, ANZECC Endangered Fauna Network, BirdLife International Red List Authority, Makerere University Institute of Environment and Natural Resources, Nature Protection Trust of Seychelles, Project Seahorse, and the UNEP–World Conservation Monitoring Centre.

Assessors (Workshops)

A number of Red List assessments are generated through workshops. In many instances, the assessors are simply recorded as "Participants of xxx workshop". This is the first attempt to record such workshops and their participants, so we apologise for any workshops or participants that have been omitted.

Tree Assessment Workshops:

African Regional Workshop (Conservation & Sustainable Management of Trees, Zimbabwe, July 1996): S.O. Achieng', S. Bandeira, L. Boulos, B. Campbell, G.P. Clarke, R. Drummond, S. Edwards, C. Geldenhuys, C. Hilton-Taylor, C. Jenkins, S. Kanyamibwa, A.B. Katende, A. Maroyi, N. Marshall, N. Mianda-Bungi, T. Müller, D. N'Sasso, J.C. Okafor, S. Oldfield, A.-S. Ouédraogo, P.S.M. Phiri, J. Reay, C. Rogers, N.C. Songwe, and J. Timberlake.

Americas Regional Workshop (Conservation & Sustainable Management of Trees, Costa Rica, November 1996): T. Ammour, X. Buitron, E. Calderon, J.J. Campos, A.J. Coombes, L. Corrales, E. Dalcin, J. de Koning, F.B. Gandara Mendes, A.-M. Giulietti, W. Hess, C. Jenkins, M. Kanninen, S. Keel, S. Llamozas, N. Marshall, M. Mitre, D.E. Mora de Retana, C.H. Nelson Sutherland, A. Newton, K. Nixon, A.-S. Ouédraogo, S. Oldfield, C.N. Pereira, J. Pires-O'Brien, D. Prado, M. Rodriguez, W.G. Sanchez, M.S. Sandison, M. Sneary, N.E. Ventura Centeno, P. Wellner, and N. Zamora.

Asian Regional Workshop (Conservation & Sustainable Management of Trees, Viet Nam, August 1996): C.R. Babu, J. Benson, Cao Van Sung, Chu Tuan Nha, L. Chua, Dang Huy Huynh, Doan Diem, Duong Thi To, D. Frodin, Fuh-Juinn Pan, C. Jenkins, D.V. Johnson, Le Dinh Kha, Le Trong Cuc, D. Madulid, J.P. Mogea, Nguyen Hoang Anh, Nguyen Hoang Nghia, Nguyen Tien Ban, Nguyen Thanh Phong, Nguyen Van Truong, Ninh Khac Ban, S. Oldfield, Pham Hoai Duc, J. Reay, M. Sneary, T. Soehartono, W. Strahm, Thai Van Trung, Tran Lien Phong, Vongxay Manivong, Vu Van Dzung, Weibang Sun, C. Williams, and Yong Shik Kim.

Freshwater Turtles:

Asian Turtle Trade Working Group (Cambodia, December 1999): S. Bhupathy, K.A. Buhlmann, B. Chan, T.-H. Chen, B.C. Choudhury, I. Das, D.B. Hendrie, D.T. Iskandar, R. Kan, S.M. Munjural Hannan Khan, M. Lau, H. Ota, T. Palasuwan, S.G. Platt, S.M.A. Rashid, A.G.J. Rhodin, D.S.K. Sharma, C.R. Shepherd, Shi Haitao, B.L. Stuart, R.J. Timmins, P.P. van Dijk, and Y. Yasukawa.

CAMP Workshops:

CAMP Workshop, Kenya (November 1996): A.H. Boga, C. Clubbe, B. Dawa, A. Githitho, C. Hankamer, P. Ipulet, P. Kahumbu, J. Kibugi, Q. Luke, M. Maunder, A.J. Mengereni, N. Muthiga, P. Muthoka, M. Olwell, and H.M. Siwa.

CAMP Workshops on Medicinal Plants, India (January 1997): M. Ahmedullah, B.S. Aswal, V.P. Bhatt, S. Chatterjee, L.B. Chaudhary,B. Datt, G.S. Giri, T. Husain, S.K. Kashyap, C.P. Kala, M.K. Kaul, P.C. Kotwal, A. Kumar, J.H. Lalramnghinglova, J.K. Maheshwari, S.K. Mamgain, S. Molur, M.S. Mondal, P.K. Mukherjee, R. Nayar, D.C. Pal, G. Pandey, N. Pradham, V. Prakash, T.S. Rana, R.R. Rao, A.K.S. Rawat, K.A. Sahoo, A. Saklani, A.R.K. Sastry, S.K. Sen, N.C. Shah, G.P. Sharma, M.P. Shiva, J. Singh, K.K. Singh, P.B. Singh, S.J.B. Srivastava, V. Tandon, V. Uppal, D.K. Ved, and S. Walker.

CBSG/ANGAP CAMP Faune de Madagascar Workshop (May 2001): D. Anderson, F. Andreone, V.E. Andrianjaka, J. Behler, Q. Bloxam, A. Britt, J. Cadle, K. Glander, S. Goodman, R.B. Iambana, A. Jolly, G. Kuchling, J.M. Lernould, P. Loiselle, E.E. Louis, M.I. Mayor, R.A. Mittermeier, M. Nicoll, I. Porton, F.C. Rabemananjara, S. Rabesihanaka, N. Rabibisoa, J.R. Rafaliarison, G. Rafomanana, P. Rahagalala, F. Raharison, E. Raholimavo, A. Rajarison, J. Rakotoarimanana, G. Rakotoarisoa, D. Rakotomalala, E. Rakotomavo, B.H. Rakotondratsima, M. Rakotondratsima, D. Rakotondravony, R. Rakotondravony, J.B. Ramanamanjato, M.A. Ramanantsoa, J. Ramanarana, O. Ramilison, R. Raminosoa, H. Randriamahazo, J. Randrianirina, V. Randrianjafy, V. Randriantsizafy, A.P. Raselimanana, R. Rasoloarison, B. Rasolonandrasana, J. Ratsimbazafy, H.N. Raveloson, R. Ravolanaivo, C.C. Raxworthy, J. Razafindrakoto, R. Razafindrasoa, M. Razanahoera-Rakotomalala, O.C. Razandrimamilafiniarivo, Saïndou, V. Soarimalala, A. Vargas, and P.C. Wright.

CBSG CAMP Workshop, India (August 1997): N.V.K. Ashraf, G.K. Bhat, M.R. Borges, A.K. Chakravarthy, S. Chattopadhyay, D.K.L. Choudhury, G. Christopher, J.C. Daniel, P.S. Easa, N. Gopalakrishna, E.A. Jayson, G.K. Joseph, R. Krishnan, M. Krishnappa, M.M. Mansoor, G. Marimuthu, V. Menon, M.K. Mishra, R.S.L. Mohan, S. Molur, D. Mudappa, M. Muni, P.O. Nameer, P. Padmanabhan, S. Paulraj, M.S. Pradhan, K.K. Ramachandran, G. Ramaswamy, M.V. Ravi Kumar, K. Shankar, C.K. Shivanna, Y.P. Sinha, N. Sivaganeshan, V.V. Sivam, K. Srihari, K.A. Subramanian, R. Sukumar, K.S. Sundar, W. Sunderraj, M.H. Swaminath, A. Udhayan, G. Utkarsh, S. Varma, A. Venkataraman, and S. Walker.

CBSG CAMP Workshop: Status of South Asian Chiroptera, India (January 2002): M.A. Ali, P.J.J. Bates, A.R. Binu Priya, B.A. Daniel, J.C. Daniel, H. de Boer, P.M.C.B. Digana, D.P.S. Doss, V. Elangovan, A.C. Girish, N. Gopukumar, A. Hutson, Khin Muang Swe, J. King Immanuel, V.S. Korad, D. Kranti Yardi, D.S. Joshi, S. Kandula, A.J. Koilraj, G.H. Koli, A. Madhavan, G. Marimuthu, S. Mistry, S. Molur, M. Muni, P.T. Nathan, K. Nathar, A. Noble, K. Padma Priya, P. Padmanabhan, P.J.E. Pandaranayaka, M.S. Pradhan, E.Y.S. Priya, H. Raghuram, B. Ravichandran, L.G. Ravikumar, S.P.R. Solomon, R. Rajasekar, K. Seedikkoya, K.R. Senacha, J. Sheela, T.K. Shrestha, E.A.A. Shukkur, N. Singaravelan, Y.P. Sinha, K.S. Sreepada, C. Srinivasulu, A. Thabah, J. Vanitharani, S. Walker, and W.B. Yapa.

CBSG CAMP Workshop: Status of South Asian Primates, India (March 2002): R. Ali, H. Andrews, H.R. Bhat, J. Biswas, J. Bose, D. Brandon-Jones, M.K. Chalise, B. Chakravarthy, K.N. Changappa, D. Chetry, J. Das, J. Dela, W. Dittus, A. Eudey, M.M. Feeroz, S. Ganapathiappan, S.C. Ghimire, M.K. Ghimire, S. Gunatilake, G.K. Joseph, J.B. Karki, N.K. Kodithuwakku, R. Krishnamani, Ajith Kumar, Awadesh Kumar, H.R. Kumar, K.R. Liyanage, N.S. Manoharan, R. Medhi, M.K. Misra, S. Mitra, P.O. Nameer, K.S. Neelakantan, M.S. Pradhan, K. Pushkar, S. Ram, K.K. Ramachandran, V. Ramakantha, G. Ramaswamy, S.K. Sahoo, A.K. Sharma, M. Singh, G.S. Solanki, R.K. Somaweera, P. Srivatsava, P.C. Tyagi, A. Watson, A.N. Weerasinghe, and S. Wijeyamohan.

Mammal Workshops:

Brazil Threatened Species Workshop (December 2002) [primate group only]: J.C. Bicca-Marques, A.A. Biedzicki de Marques, A.G. Chiarello, B. Cozenza, R. Cunha de Paula, G.A.B. da Fonseca, F. de Camargo Passos, F.R. de Melo, J. de Sousa e Silva, Jr., M. Gordo, C.E. Grelle, M. Iolita Bampi, S. Lucena Mendes, M. Marcelino, R.V. Marques, A.R. Mendes Pontes, R. Moura, F. Olmos, and A.B. Rylands.

Fourth International Conservation Workshop for the Threatened Fauna of Arabia: Arabian Ungulates Working Group (February 2003): F. Al Baroudi, S. Al Dhaheri, M.A. Al Dosary, M.H. Al Jahdhami, H.S. Al Khalifa, M.A. Al-Mutairi, T. Bailey, I. Barcello, C. Drew, P.B. Giridas, F. Launay, D. Mallon, P. McKinney, P. Mésochina, I.A. Nader, J. Newby, D. O'Donovan, P. Phelan, M. Qarqaz, Saleh Naghmoosh Thani Ali Saadi, A. Spalton and M. van Delft.

African Elephant Specialist Group – Red List Task Force, AfESG Meeting, Namibia (December 2003): D. Balfour, J. Blanc, C. Craig, H. Dublin, C. Foley, D. Gibson, J. Hart, S. Kasiki, S. Lahm, M. Litoroh, J. Mshelbwala, L. Mubalama, L. Niskanen, G. Nomba, P. Omondi, J.R. Onononga, C. Papa Conde, M. Tchamba, A. Tehou, C. Thouless, C., and I. Whyte.

GMA African Small Mammals Workshop, London (January 2004): E. Abdel Rahman, B. Agwanda, G. Amori, A. Assogbadjo, S. Auglanier, J. Baillie, R. Baxter, P. Benda, W. Bergmans, J. Bielby, L. Boitani, G. Catullo, W. Chitaukali, C.G. Coetzee, Z. Cokeliss, B. Collen, M. Corti, F.W. Cotterill, J. Decher, F. Dieterlen, J. Fahr, M. Gimenez-Dixon, L. Granjon, M. Griffin, P. Grubb, C. Hilton-Taylor, M. Hoffman, K. Howell, R. Hutterer, A. Hutson, H. Is-haquou Daouda, N. Isaac, D. Jacobs, P. Jenkins, J. Juste, J. Kerbis Peterhans, D. Knox, L. Lavrenchenko, J. Long, S. Maree, I. Marzetti, A. Monadjem, N. Oguge, C. Rondinini, D. Schlitter, W. Sechrest, P.J. Taylor, and E. van der Straeten.

Shark Workshops:

Shark Specialist Group Australia and Oceania Regional Red List workshop (March 2003): P. Barratt, M.B. Bennett, G.H. Burgess, R.D. Cavanagh, L.J.V. Compagno, C.A.J. Duffy, A. Flaherty, S.L. Fowler, M.P. Francis, I. Gordon, M.R. Heupel, P.M. Kyne, T.J. Lisney, R. McAuley, J.A. Musick, L. Paul, S.J. Pierce, R. Pillans, J. Pogonoski, D.A. Pollard, M. Reardon, C. Simpfendorfer, J. Stevens, T.I. Walker, W.T White, and S.A. Williams.

Shark Specialist Group Deep-sea Chondrichthyan Red List workshop (November 2003): E. Acuña, J.P. Caldas, R.D. Cavanagh, C.A.J. Duffy, S. Fordman, S.L. Fowler, M.P. Francis, K. Graham, J.A. Holtzhausen, C. Huveneers, P.M. Kyne, J. Lamilla, J.A. Musick, F. Serena, W.T. White, and K. Yano.

Shark Specialist Group South American Regional Red List workshop (June 2003): E. Acuña, A.F. Amorim, M.A.R. Camarena, R.D. Cavanagh, G.E. Chiaramonte, P. Charvet-Almeida, M.P. de Almeida, M.L.G. de Araújo, A. Domingo, V. Faria, M. Furtado, M.M.B. Gonçalez, N. Hozbor, J. Lamilla, L. Leandro, R. Lessa, P.L. Mancini, A. Massa, J.A. Musick, S.G. Mycock, G. Rincon, R.S. Rosa, J.M.R. Soto, J. Stevens, C.M. Vooren, and T.I. Walker.

Shark Specialist Group Subequatorial Africa Regional Red List workshop (September 2003): J. Bell, J. Brash, G.H. Burgess, R.D. Cavanagh, G. Cliff, L.J.V. Compagno, A. Cooke, M. Dicken, M. Ducrocq, S. Dudley, D.A. Ebert, S.L. Fowler, C. Hilton-Taylor, H. Holtzhausen, B. Human, N. Jiddawi, M. McCord, R. Nel, A.J. Pegado, S. Pheeha, H. Rasolonjatovo, L. Robinson, S. Semesi, M.J. Smale, M. van Tienhoven, S. Wintner, and S. Yahya.

Evaluators

All the assessments submitted for inclusion in the *IUCN Red List* since 2000 have undergone a peer review process through the appointed Red List Authorities. Each assessment is required to be reviewed and approved by at least two named people. We thank the following for their valuable time spent reviewing assessments:

A. Abreu, A.H. Abuzinada, E.M.G. Agoo, I. Alados, A. Alberts, D.M.H. AL-Eisami, R. Ali, M. Amer, G. Amori, Z.T. Ashenafi, E. Baard, V. Bachraz, D. Balfour, B. Bassano, P. Bates, R. Baxter, J. Behler, M. Bekoff, P. Benstead, S. Bestelmeyer, C. Birkinshaw, J. Blanc, A.E. Bogan, P. Bouchet, R. Bour, D. Bramwell, D. Brandon-Jones, C. Breitenmoser, U. Breitenmoser, C. Breitenmoser-Wursten, M. Brooke, T. Brooks, T. Brule, K. Buhlmann, I. Burfield, S. Butchart, T. Butynski, R. Cairns-Wicks, D. Callaghan, D. Capper, O. Carrillo, R.D. Cavanagh, F. Cervantes, M.K. Chalise, S. Chan, J. Chemnick, D. Chetry, S. Cilliers, V. Clausnitzer, R. Clay, C. Clubbe, N. Collar, L.J.V. Compagno, L. Contreras, S.F. Cook, E. Coppejans, G. Coppois, A. Cornish, O. Courtenay, R. Cowie, K. Crandall, P.J. Cribb, Q. Cronk, M. Crosby, D. Crouse, J. Croxall, F. Cuzin, S. Daniels, W. Darwall, J. Das, P. Davidson, E.F. de Vogel, R. Dekker, J. Dela, T. Dickinson, W. Dittus, F.S. Dobson, M. Domeier, J.S. Donaldson, J.M.B. Duarte, H.T. Dublin, J.W. Duckworth, M.E. Dulloo, G. Dutson, R. East, D.A. Ebert, A.-M. Eklund, J. Ekstrom, R. Emslie, R. Estes, A. Eudey, M. Evans, A. Farjon, F. Feh, S. Fennessy, M. Festa-Bianchet, L. Fishpool, C. FitzGibbon, D. Florens, S.J. Foster, S.L. Fowler, J. Fox, M.P. Francis, G. Garcia-Moliner, M. Gardner, S. Garnett, P. Garson, D. Geiger, P. Geissler, E.M. Gese, W. Gibbons, M. Gimenez Dixon, S. Gippoliti, J. Golding, S. González, D. Gottelli, K. Graham, M. Griffin, M. Groves, P. Grubb, P. Haaker, W. Haberl, M.A. Hack, D.J. Hafner, T. Hallingbäck, M. Hamer, M. Harmelin-Vivien, R. Harris, F. Hawkins, R. Hecky, B. Hedges, S. Hedges, D.G. Herbert, M. Hernández, K.D. Hill, C. Hilton-Taylor, N. Hodgetts, H. Hofer, M. Hoffmann, R. Hudson, B. Human, S.A. Hussain, A. Hutson, R. Hutterer, S.J. Incháustegui, N. Ishii, J. Iverson, P. Jackson, P. Jenkins, C. Jermy, Y.V. Jhala, P.M. Jørgensen, G.K. Joseph, L. Kaufman, K. Kauhala, T. Kawamicki, G.L. Kirkland Jr., L. Kohorn, W.R. Konstant, M. Kottelat, P. Krausman, T. Kristensen, M. Kulbicki, D. Kulka, P.M. Kyne, J.N. Labat, P. Lafrance, M.K. Laurenson, M. Lawes, R. Lea, M.R.P. Leite, S. Léon-Yánez, P. Lindsey, S. Lourie, S. Lovari, P.P. Lowry, Q. Luke, N.D.T. Luu, G.M. Mace, D.A. Madulid, L. Maffei, J.R. Malcolm, D.P. Mallon, I. Malombe, T. Maran, A.D. Marsden, D. Marsden, T.S. Masoud, M. Maunder, J. Mauremootoo, A. Mauric, R. McAuley, R. McClellan, P. Medici, J, Mickel, S. Mickleburgh, P. Mikkelsen, S. Miller, G. Mills, E.J. Milner-Gulland, S. Mitra, R.A. Mittermeier, P. Moehlman, P.D., Moehlman, A. Moehrenschlager, R. Moran, J.A. Musick, A. Nakazono, D. Nel, Nguyen Duc To Luu, K. Nowell, A. O'Brien, W.L.R. Oliver, J. Paxton, H. Payne, R. Peckover, N. Peet, W.F. Perrin, N. Pilcher, J. Pilgrim, D. Pillay, N. Pitman, A. Plowman, J. Pogonoski, C.M. Pollock, W.F. Ponder, R. Pople, R. Porter, M. Pourkazemi, M.S. Pradhan, I. Prakash, Hai-Ning Qin, P. Racey, A.R. Rahmani, C. Rajeriarison, D. Randall, A. Randrianasolo, E. Randrianjohany, T. Ranker, G. Rathbun, G.B. Rathbun, R.R. Reeves, C. Reuther, A. Rhodin, D. Roberts, M. Rodden, F. Rodrigues, B. Roth, D.I. Rubenstein, B. Russell, A.B. Rylands, Y. Sadovy, M. Saeki, S.K. Sahoo, M. Samoilys, M.J. Samways, C. Scheidegger, M. Schilthuizen, D. Schlitter, P. Scott, G. Sedberry, M.B. Seddon, B. Seret, D. Shackleton, A.K. Sharma, A. Shoemaker, S. Shutes, C. Sillero-Zubiri, L. Silveira, C.A. Simpfendorfer, A.T. Smith, C. Smith, R. Smith, G.S. Solanki, M. Sovada, J.S. Sparks, R. St. Pierre, S. Stankovic, A. Stattersfield, M. Stehmann, J. Stevens, D.W. Stevenson, M.L.J. Stiassny, W. Strahm,

C. Stuart, T. Stuart, W. Stuppy, M. Swarner, L. Tallents, B. Tan, L. Tatin, P. Tattersfield, B.L. Taylor, N.P. Taylor, S. Taylor, P. Thomas, F.G. Thompson, J. Tobias, S. Todd, R. Valencia, P.P. van Dijk, H. van Rompaey, J.E. Victor, A.C.J. Vincent, B. von Arx, A. Vovides, T.I. Walker, A. Watson, D. Wege, P. Wegge, W.T. White, R.S.R. Williams, S. Williams, R. Wirth, P.A. Wolseley, J. Wood, K.R. Wood, Z. Xianchun, E. Yensen, Y. Yuqun, L. Zapfack, S. Zona, and G.L Zuercher.

Evaluators (Groups and Organizations)

All the above evaluators are members from one or more of the following Red List Authorities:

African Elephant Red List Authority, African Rhino Red List Authority, Afrotheria Red List Authority, Antelope Red List Authority, Arabian Plants Red List Authority, Asian Wild Cattle Red List Authority, BirdLife International Red List Authority, Bryophyte Red List Authority, Cacti and Succulent Plant Red List Authority, Canid Red List Authority (including the Ethiopian Wolf Working Group), Caprinae Red List Authority, Carnivorous Plants Red List Authority, Cat Red List Authority, Cetacean Red List Authority, China Plants Red List Authority, Chiroptera Red List Authority, Conifer Red List Authority, Cycad Red List Authority, Deer Red List Authority, East African Plants Red List Authority, Ecuador Plants Red List Authority, Equid Red List Authority, Grouper & Wrasse Red List Authority, Hyaena Red List Authority, Iguana Red List Authority, Indian Ocean Island Plant Red List Authority, Inland Water Crustacean Red List Authority, Insectivore Red List Authority, Lagomorph Red List Authority, Lichen Red List Authority, Macaronesian Plants Red List Authority, Madagascar Plants Red List Authority, Marine Turtle Red List Authority, Mollusc Red List Authority, Mustelid, Viverrid and Procyonid Red List Authority (now the Small Carnivore RLA), Odonata Red List Authority, Orchid Red List Authority, Otter Red List Authority, Palm Red List Authority, Philippine Plants Red List Authority Pig, Peccary and Hippo Red List Authority, Primate Red List Authority, Pteridophyte Red List Authority, Rodent Red List Authority, Shark Red List Authority, South Atlantic Island Plants Red List Authority, Southern African Invertebrate Red List Authority, Southern African Plant Red List Authority, Sturgeon Red List Authority, Syngnathid Red List Authority, Tapir Red List Authority, and Tortoise and Freshwater Turtle Red List Authority.

Some evaluators were from outside of the appointed Red List Authorities; the organizations represented include:

American Museum of Natural History: New York, Australian Museum, BirdLife Seabird Programme, Birds Australia, British Antarctic Survey, Conservation International: Dominican Republic, Grupo Jaragua: Dominican Republic, Guyra Paraguay: Conservación de Aves, IUCN Freshwater Biodiversity Assessment Programme, IUCN Red List Programme Office, Megapode Specialist Group, Pennsylvania State University: US, SSC Plant Conservation Committee, University of Cambridge, University of Gent: Belgium, Wild Bird Society of Japan, and the World Pheasant Association.

Global Amphibian Assessment Acknowledgements:

The Moore Family Foundation and the Gordon and Betty Moore Foundation, through Conservation International, provided the core financial support for the GAA. The MAVA Foundation, the US Department of State, the Regina Bauer Frankenberg Foundation for Animal Welfare, the National Science Foundation (DEB-0130273 and INT-0322375), the Critical Ecosystem Partnership Fund, George Meyer, Ben Hammett, and the Disney Foundation provided additional major support. The Kadoorie Farm and Botanic Garden, WWF Australia, the Taipei Zoological Foundation, the Chicago Zoological Society, the Society for Wildlife and Nature, and the Columbus Zoo also provided generous support. Claude Gascon and Jorgen Thomsen in particular assisted us with fundraising. Any opinions, findings, and conclusions or recommendations expressed in this material are those of the authors and do not necessarily reflect the views of the National Science Foundation.

Darrel Frost of the American Museum of Natural History provided extensive assistance on taxonomic and nomenclatural issues, without which it would have been much more difficult to implement the GAA.

David Wake of the Museum of Vertebrate Zoology at the University of California at Berkeley gave us privileged access to the AmphibiaWeb database. We are most grateful to both of these people for their unfailing support.

We received assistance and advice in ways too numerous to mention from the IUCN/SSC Declining Amphibian Populations Task Force (DAPTF), in particular from Tim Halliday, Jim Collins, Jim Hanken and John Wilkinson.

The following people provided local logistical support for the GAA workshops: Jean-Marc Hero (Australia), Zhong Shengxian (China), Barasa Johnson (Kenya), Sanjay Molur and Sally Walker (India), Rosa Mary Saengsanthitham (Thailand), Enrique Lahmann (Costa Rica), Sabrina Cowan and Allen Allison (Hawaii), Adriano Paglia, Jose Maria Cardoso da Silva and Luis Paulo de Souza Pinto (Brazil), Paul and Sara Salaman and José Vicente Rodriguez (Ecuador), Doreen Zivkovic (Switzerland), Esteban Lavilla (Argentina), Juan Carlos Ortiz (Chile), David Gower and Mark Wilkinson (UK) and Sixto Inchaustegui (Dominican Republic). We also thank Craig Hilton-Taylor, Michael Wei-Neng Lau, Sanjay Molur, Bob Inger, Arvin Diesmos, Matt Foster, Mike Hoffmann, Penny Langhammer and Don Church who assisted in facilitating working groups during GAA workshops.

Gustavo da Fonseca, Claude Gascon, Russell Mittermeier, Tom Brooks, Larry Master and Georgina Mace provided guidance and encouragement throughout the project, and we wish to express a special debt of gratitude to them. We are particularly thankful to Ana Rodrigues, Resit Akçakaya, Georgina Mace, Stuart Butchart and Tom Lacher for their advice on statistical analysis. Rob Waller, Debra Fischman, Sonia Krogh, Vineet Katariya and Mark Denil provided extensive, high-quality GIS support. Xie Feng provided invaluable assistance in many ways, and in particular by helping us with the Chinese data, and giving us access to scientific literature in Chinese. Don Church and Allison Parker did a very large amount of work locating missing bibliographic references and entering them into the database. Laara Manler, Caryn Simmons and Andrew Mitchell gave us the logistical and administrative support that we needed.

The majority of the distribution maps used for US species were adapted from distribution data and maps assembled at Ball State University by Priya Nanjappa, Laura M. Blackburn,. and Michael J. Lannoo. Development of the "United States Amphibian Atlas Database" was supported in part by grants and/or matching funds from the National Fish and Wildlife Foundation, United States Fish and Wildlife Service, and Disney Wildlife Conservation Fund.

The GAA was entirely dependent on the more than 500 herpetologists who generously gave their time and knowledge. The enthusiasm and commitment of these people has enabled us to generate a comprehensive global picture of amphibian status and trends for the first time. We record our thanks to the following people, asking for forgiveness from anyone whose name is inadvertently omitted or misspelled: M. Acevedo, A. Acosta, F. Acuña Juncá, M. Adams, S. Adoor, L. Afuang, C. Aguilar Puntriano, R. Albornoz, A. Alcala, R. Alford, M. Ali Reza Khan, A. Allison, D. Almeida, A. Almendariz, A. Amezquita, J.-L. Amiet, N.B. Ananjeva, S.C. Anderson, G. Andrade, F. Andreone, A. Angulo, B. Anthony, M. Ao, K. Aplin, V. Arachchilage Samarawickrama, M.C. Ardila-Robayo, W. Arizabal, N. Arnold, J.W. Arntzen, C. Arzabe, C. Austin, B. Ayyasamy Daniel, C. Azevedo-Ramos, W. Babik, M. Bailey, R. Bain, A. Balasubramanian, D. Baldo, E. Balletto, C. Bambaradeniya, G. Baorong, U. Barrantes, L. Barreto, N.G. Basso, C. Beachy, D. Beamer, T. Beebee, P. Beerli, M. Beier, P. Beja, B.D. Bell, J. Bertoluci, D. Bhagwanrao Sawarkar, G. Bhatta, S. Bhupathy, D. Bickford, S.D. Biju, P. Bishop, S. Blomquist, B. Blotto, R. Boistel, F. Bolaños, W. Bolivar, D.M. Borges-Nojosa, M. Born, J. Bosch, D. Bradford, A. Braswell, R. Brereton, M. Breuil, D. Brown, P. Brown, R. Brown, G. Buddhe, M. Burger, B. Bury, M. Bustamante, P. Cabral Eterovick, A. Cadena, J.E. Cadle, D. Cannatella, L. Canseco, U. Caramaschi, F. Casteñeda, F. Castro, R. Cedeño Vázquez, J.A. Cespedez, B. Chan, T. Chanard, Y. Changyuan, A. Channing, G. Chavez, S. Chelmala, L. Cheng, P. Chippindale,

S. Choudhury Bordoloi, Y. Chuaynkern, D. Church, D.F. Cisneros-Heredia, J. Clarke, D. Cogalniceanu, Hal Cogger, Harold Cogger, G.R. Colli, L. Coloma, M. Considine, J.H. Cordova Santa Gadea, C. Cortez Fernandez, R. Crombie, M. Crump, G. Cruz, M. Cunningham, J. Daltry, R. Daniels, C.F.D. da Rocha, I. Das, Y. Datong, T. Davenport, C. Davidson, P.C. de Anchietta Garcia, G. Degani, I.J. de la Riva, M. Denoel, A. De Silva, N. Dharmapriya Rathnayake, L.M. Diaz, H. Díaz-Páez, I.E. di Tada, A.C. Diesmos, A. Disi, N. Doak, K. Dodd, C. Dolino, D. Donaire-Barroso, M.A. Donnelly, L. Dovey, R. Drewes, A. Dubois, W.E. Duellman, T. Dujsebayeva, S. Dutta, T. Eamkamon, P. Edgar, G. Eken, E.H. El Mouden, E. Elron, Z. Ermi, A.R. Estrada, R.A. Estupinan, J. Fa, J. Faivovich, G. Fellers, X. Feng, E. Fernández-Badillo, M. Firoz Ahmed, O. Flores, J. Formas, R. Formas, T. Fretey, Q. Fuenmayor, S. Gafny, U. Galatti, L. Gang, I. García, M. Garcia Paris, J.E. Garcia-Perez, A. Gardner, T. Garner, M. Gartshore, C. Gascon, A. Gasith, P. Gaucher, G. Gee, E. Gem, J. Gerlach, G. Gillespie, V. Giri, F. Glaw, C.A. Gonçalves da Cruz, A.V. Gour-Broome, D. Gower, T. Grant, R. Griffiths, R. Grasso, W. Guanfu, R. Guenther, B. Gutierrez, C. Haddad, S. Haitao, T. Halliday, G.A. Hammerson, K. Hampson, J. Hardy, James Harrison, Julian Harrison, B. Hedges, A. Herman, J. Hernández, M. Hernandez, J.-M. Hero, M.I. Herrera, R. Herrington, R. Heyer, H. Hines, M.S. Hoogmoed, P. Horner, C. Hoskin, K. Howell, S. Hraoui Bloquet, D. Huacaz, G. Hui-qing, D. Hunter, R. Ibanez, B. Ibéné, J. Icochea Monteza, P. Imbun Yambun, S. Inchaustegui, R. Inger, K. Irwin, V. Ischenko, D. Iskandar, D. Jackson, J. Jaeger, C. Jaramillo, R. Jehle, R. Jennings, J. Jensen, J. Jianping, U. Joger, R. Joglar, K.-H. Jungfer, T. Kahn, H. Kaiser, M.D. Kamrul Hasan Dolon, Y. Kaneko, R. Khalikov, W. Khonsue, T. Kiliç, I. Kiss, S. Koenig, G. Köhler, J. Köhler, T. Kovács, F. Kraus, L. Kuangyang, B. Kubicki, T. Kumar Shrestha, P. Kumara, A. Kupfer, H. Kurniati, S. Kuzmin, A. Kwet, L. LaClaire, R. Lajmanovich, M. Lakim, E. La Marca, J.A. Langone, B. Lanza, M. Largen, E.O. Lavilla, D. Lawson, R. Lecis, J. Lee, F. Lemckert, E. Lehr, M. Leonida Diesmos, J. Lescure, F. Liang, K. Lips, M. Littlejohn, M. Lizana Avia, S. Loader, J. Loman, S. Lötters, O. Luiz Peixoto, J. Lynch, R.D. MacCulloch, C. Magin, M. Mahony, R.A. Maldonado-Silva, A. Mallari, K. Manamendra-Arachchi, T. Mann, J. Manzanilla, J.L. Martinez Ruiz, I. Martínez-Solano, C. Marty, I. Maslova, S. Mass, Y. Matamorros, M. Matsui, S. May, J. Mayol Serra, L.C.J. Mazibuko, R. McCranie, R.W. McDiarmid, K. McDonald, J. Measey, J. Meerman, P. Menendez, M. Menegon, J. Menzies, A. Merino-Viteri, E. Meyer, M. Mohan Borah, P. Moler, V.R. Morales, S. Morey, C. Morrison, D. Moyer, C. Miaud, A. Mijares-Urrutia, L. Minter, A. Miranda Leiva, J. Mitchell, V. Molina, S. Molur, M. Morales, G. Moreira Drummond, C. Msuya, H. Muller, A. Muñoz Alonso, E. Muths, J. Nabhitabata, P. Narvaes, Nascimento, D.R. Neira Herrera, R. Neves Feio, D. Newell, F. Nogales, A.M. Nistri, H. Nuñez, J. Nuñez, R.A. Nussbaum, P. Nyström, A. Ogielska, A. Ogrodowczyk, A.M. Ohler, K. Olgun, P. Ong, O.V. Oommen, N. Orlov, J.C. Ortiz, W. Osborne, M. Osorno, K. Ovaska, A. Padhye, L. Paguntalan, C. Painter, J. Palden, J. Palis, S. Panha, T. Papenfuss, F. Parker, G. Parra, M. Parris, A.M. Paulino Telles de Carvalho e Silva, D. Pavan, C. Pearl, M. Pedregosa, R. Pereira Bastos, J.-L. Perret, R. Pethiyagoda, C. Phillips, M. Pickersgill, B. Pimenta, L. Pipeng, J.P. Pombal Jr., S. Potsch de Carvalho e Silva, J.C. Poynton, V.A. Prasanna Samarawickrama, D. Price, A. Pounds, R. Powell, M. Puky, R. Puschendorf, N. Quang Truong, A.C. Queiroz Carnaval, A. Quevedo Gil, M.P. Ramirez, N. Rastegar-Pouyani, M.S. Ravichandran, C.J. Raxworthy, P. Ray, E. Recuero Gil, S. Reichle, J.M. Renjifo, R. Retallick, R.P. Reynolds, S. Richards, S. Richter, D. Roberts, P. Robertson, A. Rodríguez, L. Rodriguez, A. Rodríguez Gómez, M.-O. Roedel, S. Ron, J. Rorabaugh, D. de C. Rossa-Feres, D. Roy, J.V. Rueda Almonacid, T. Ryan, R.A. Sadek, A.W. Salas, A. Salvador, S. Santiago, G. Santos Barrera, P. Sanyal, S.M.D. Sarkar Uddin, J. Savage, R. Schabetsberger, A. Schiotz, B. Schmidt, R. Schulte, T. Schwaner, E. Scott, N. Scott, M.V. Segalla, C. Senaris, S. Sengupta, B. Shaffer, K. Shanker, M. Sharif Khan, Mumpuni, L. Shengquan, D. Shepard, L. Shoo, L. Shunqing, R. Siegel, D. Silvano, U. Sinsch, G. Skuk, T. Slimani, E.N. Smith, F. Solís, M. Sparreboom, M. Sredl, C. Srinivasulu, M. Stoeck, B. Stuart, R. Stuebing, N. Suhaina Yaakob,

J. Sukumaran, R. Swain, S. Swan, S.R.M Swarnapali Samaradiwaka, M. Tandy, D. Tarkhnishvili, M. Tejedo, K. Thirakhupt, R. Thomas, H. Thu Cuc, R. Tinsley, M. Tocher, E. Toral, J. Townsend, M. Trefaut Rodrigues, L. Tzi Ming, B. Tuniyev, D. Ubaldo, C.A. Ubeda, I.H. Ugurtas, K. Ukuwwela, T. Uzzell, D. Vallan, P.P. Van Dijk, M. Van Sluys, K. Vasudevan, A. Veloso, M. Vences, V. Verdade, S.P. Vijayakumar, P. Vogel, M. Vogrin, J. Vonesh, J. Vörös, V. Vredenburg, R. Vyas, D. Wake, M. Wake, B. Waldman, P. Walker, D. Watling, A. Weerasinghe, S. Weerawardhena, M. Wei Neng Lau, H. Welsh, Z. Wenge, C. Wenhao, Y.L. Werner, D. Wickramasinghe, E.R. Wild, J. Wilkinson, M. Wilkinson, B. Wilson, L.D. Wilson, G. Wogan, A. Wong, E.M. Xavier Freire, W. Xiuling, M. Yánez-Muñoz, B. Young, W. Yuezhao, Y. Zhigang, Z. Zhonghua, G. Zug, and R. Zweifel.

Global Mammal Assessment (GMA):

The contribution of the GMA to the 2004 *IUCN Red List* has been limited largely to the assessments conducted at the African Small Mammals Workshop (see list of participants above under workshops). We wish to record our thanks to the coordinators of this project: Jonathan Baillie, Mariano Gimenez Dixon, Wes Sechrest and their support staff Zoe Cokeliss and Cody Schank. We thank in particular the Critical Ecosystem Partnership Fund for funding the African Small Mammals Workshop, the Central African Regional Program for the Environment (CARPE), Instituto di Ecologia Applicata, and the Zoological Society of London for helping to fund the African Small Mammals Workshop. We would also like to acknowledge the helpful collaboration of Elsevier and their Mammals of Africa (MoA) initiative edited by David Happold, Jonathan Kingdon, and Thomas Butynski.

IUCN Freshwater Biodiversity Assessment Programme:

The IUCN Freshwater Biodiversity Assessment Programme has contributed assessments to the 2004 *IUCN Red List* as a result of regional assessment projects they have conducted. Will Darwall, the Programme Officer, and his interns Thomas Lowe and Kevin Smith are thanked for their help in running the projects and processing these assessments and the supporting documentation for the Red List. The East African Freshwater Biodiversity Assessment project was carried out with financial support from the Dutch Ministry of Foreign Affairs (DGIS) under the Partners for Wise Use of Wetlands Programme, managed by Wetlands International. Conservation International Madagascar provided funding for a project to evaluate the conservation status of endemic freshwater fish of Madagascar (assessed initially at a CBSG CAMP Workshop, see above) and to map their distributions. The IUCN Water and Nature Initiative (WANI) also provides support to this Programme.

Executive Summary

The Status of Globally Threatened Species

• **The 2004 *IUCN Red List* contains 15,589 species threatened with extinction.** The assessment includes species from a broad range of taxonomic groups including vertebrates, invertebrates, plants, and fungi. However, this figure is an underestimate of the total number of threatened species as it is based on an assessment of less than 3% of the world's 1.9 million described species.

• **Among major species groups, the percentage of threatened species ranges between 12% and 52%.** The *IUCN Red List* identifies 12% of birds as threatened, 23% of mammals, and 32% of amphibians. Although reptiles have not been completely assessed, the turtles and tortoises are relatively well reviewed with 42% threatened. Fishes are also poorly represented, but roughly a third of sharks, rays and chimaeras have been assessed and 18% of this group is threatened. Regional case studies on freshwater fishes indicate that these species might be more threatened than marine species. For example, 27% of the freshwater species assessed in eastern Africa were listed as threatened. Of plants, only conifers and cycads have been completely assessed with 25% and 52% threatened respectively.

• **The first complete assessment of amphibians reveals that they are likely to be the most threatened vertebrates.** Not only are amphibians significantly more threatened than other assessed vertebrate groups, but they also have a higher proportion of species on the verge of extinction. In total, 21% of amphibians are Critically Endangered or Endangered, whereas the proportions for mammals and birds are only 10% and 5% respectively. This high level of threat might be an underestimate, as 23% of amphibians could not be assessed because sufficient data were not available. These poorly known species are often rare and have small distributions.

• **There are major gaps in our knowledge of the status of threatened species.** While the status of vertebrates is relatively well documented (roughly 40% assessed), we know little about non-terrestrial systems (freshwater and marine), or many species-rich habitats (such as tropical forests or the ocean depths), or species-rich groups such as invertebrates, plants and fungi (which together compose the overwhelming majority of species).

• **Threatened species are not randomly distributed across orders and families.** A number of families have significantly more threatened species than would be expected on average, while others have far less. This non-random distribution of threats across the tree of life means that entire evolutionary lineages are liable to go extinct very quickly. For example, of the birds, the albatrosses, cranes, parrots, pheasant, and pigeons are significantly more threatened than other groups. Of the mammals, the ungulates, carnivores, primates, dugongs and manatees are particularly at risk. The salamanders, true toads, Asian tree frogs, Cameroonian stream frogs and typical tropical American frogs among the amphibians are more threatened than would be expected.

Extinction in Recent Times

• **As we learn more about the status of species, the world's list of extinctions continues to increase.** The *IUCN Red List* now contains 784 documented extinctions and 60 extinctions in the wild since 1500 AD. Over the past 20 years, 27 documented extinctions or extinctions in the wild have occurred. These numbers certainly underestimate the true number of extinctions in historic times as the majority of species have not been described, most described species have not been comprehensively assessed, and proving that a species has gone extinct can take years to decades.

• **Recent extinction rates far exceed the rates of extinction in the fossil record.** Extinction rates based on known extinctions of birds, mammals and amphibians over the past 100 years indicates that current extinction rates are 50 to 500 times higher than extinction rates in the fossil record. If Possibly Extinct species are included this increases to 100 to 1,000 times natural (background) extinction rates. This is an extremely conservative estimate, as it does not account for undocumented extinctions. Although the estimates vary greatly, it appears that current extinction rates are at least two to four orders of magnitude above background rates.

• **Extinctions are becoming increasingly common on continents.** While the vast majority of extinctions since 1500 AD have occurred on oceanic islands, continental extinctions are now as common as island extinctions. An assessment of recent extinctions indicates that roughly 50% of extinctions over the past 20 years occurred on continents. This trend is consistent with the fact that most terrestrial threatened species are continental.

Trends in the Status of Threatened Species

• **The Red List Indices show that the status of birds and amphibians continues to deteriorate.** The Red List Indices (RLIs) are an important new development, which measures trends in extinction risk by comparing the conservation status of specific groups over time. For birds the RLI demonstrates that their status has deteriorated steadily since 1988, which was the year that birds were first completely assessed. A preliminary assessment of amphibians demonstrates similar rates of decline since 1980. However, amphibian species closest to extinction have shown a much steeper rate of decline in status.

• **The limited information available for other taxonomic groups indicates that declines may be widespread.** Population trends are available for 260 Cycads (Cycadopsida, 288 species in total), and of these, 79.6% (207 species) are declining, 20.4% (53 species) are stable and none are considered to be increasing.

Geography of the Red List

• **Most threatened species occur in the tropics, especially on mountains and on islands.** Most threatened birds, mammals, and amphibians are located on the tropical continents: Central and South America; Africa south of the Sahara; and tropical South and Southeast Asia. These realms contain the tropical and subtropical moist broadleaf forests that are believed to harbour the majority of the earth's living terrestrial and freshwater species. Therefore, the patterns evident for mammals, birds and amphibians are likely to be representative of most terrestrial taxonomic groups.

• **The distribution of threatened marine species is poorly known.** Of the limited number of marine species that have been assessed, initial findings indicate that threatened marine mammals are concentrated in the northern Pacific Ocean and threatened seabirds, chondrichthyan fishes (sharks, rays and chimaeras) and seahorses (the latter two not completely assessed) in the eastern Indian Ocean and southwest and west-central Pacific.

• **The uneven distribution of threatened species means that a number of countries have a disproportionate number of species at risk of extinction.** Countries with the most threatened and threatened endemic species tend to lie within the continental tropics and countries with the highest proportion of threatened species are mostly tropical island nations. Countries with both a high number of threatened and threatened endemic species include Australia, Brazil, China, Indonesia, and Mexico. Other countries or territories holding particularly large numbers of threatened species include Colombia, India, New Caledonia, Peru, South Africa, and Viet Nam (all of these are among the top three countries for at least one taxonomic group) while Colombia, India, Malaysia, Myanmar, New Caledonia, Papua New Guinea, the Philippines, South Africa, and the United States are all among the top three countries for numbers of threatened endemics for at least one taxonomic group. Additional countries characterized by particularly high proportionate threat in multiple taxa include Madagascar, São Tomé and Principe, and the Seychelles.

• **Patterns of distribution of threatened species are relatively congruent between the taxonomic groups analysed.** Differences are primarily driven by underlying range-size distributions among taxonomic groups (e.g., birds tend to have much larger range sizes than amphibians) and by ecological limitations of specific taxa (e.g., birds are better able to disperse over saltwater than amphibians). Greater variation in the distribution of threatened species is expected as more diverse groups of species are completely assessed. For example, threatened reptiles or cacti will likely have much greater representation in arid areas.

The Many Causes of Threat

• **Habitat destruction and associated degradation and fragmentation are the greatest threats to assessed terrestrial species.** Habitat loss appears to be by far the most pervasive threat, impacting 86% of threatened birds, 86% of threatened mammals and 88% of threatened amphibians. Habitat loss will remain a dominant threat, as there is no sign that human transformation of the landscape is slowing.

• **Threat processes vary both within and between taxonomic groups.** Although habitat destruction is universally the most dominant threat process, birds, mammals, and amphibians are particularly vulnerable to specific threat processes. Over-exploitation is a major threat to mammals, impacting 33% of threatened species. For birds, over-exploitation and invasive alien species are of similar importance, both impacting about 30% of threatened species (although invasives are impacting 67% of threatened birds on islands). For threatened amphibians, the major threats are different, with 29% of species being affected by pollution (including climate change) and 17% by disease (particularly chytridiomycosis). The interaction between disease and extreme climatic events (drought) is the leading hypothesis for widespread amphibian declines.

- **Threat processes in the marine and freshwater systems are poorly understood.** However, it appears that over-exploitation is presently the greatest threat to marine species, followed by habitat loss. Incidental mortality as a result of fisheries is an increasing threat, affecting seabirds, marine mammals, and other marine species. Habitat loss is likely the most severe threat to freshwater species followed by pollution and invasive species.

- **Threat processes are dynamic and change over time.** Invasive alien species were historically the greatest threat to birds, followed by over-exploitation and habitat loss. Today, habitat loss has emerged as the dominant threat to birds, followed by invasive species and finally over-exploitation. This order may change again if predictions of global warming are correct.

The Social and Economic Context of the Red List

- **People and threatened species are often concentrated in the same areas.** This is especially true in much of Asia (in particular southeast China, the Western Ghats of India, the Himalayas, Sri Lanka, Java (Indonesia), the Philippines and parts of Japan), and in parts of Africa (especially the Albertine Rift in Central Africa and the Ethiopian Highlands).

- **The number of threatened species is likely to rapidly increase in regions where human population growth rates are high.** Future conflicts between the needs of threatened species and rapidly increasing human populations are predicted to occur in Cameroon, Colombia, Ecuador, India, Madagascar, Malaysia, Peru, Philippines, Tanzania, and Venezuela.

- **Countries that currently have a low human population density but a high rate of population growth could be opportunistic places for pre-emptive conservation initiatives.** For example, Bolivia, Papua New Guinea, Namibia, Angola, and the countries of North Africa.

- **Countries that have the most threatened species tend to be those that are least able to invest significant resources into conservation.** Examples of countries with high numbers of threatened species and relatively low Gross National Incomes (GNI) are Brazil, Cameroon, China, Colombia, Ecuador, India, Indonesia, Madagascar,

Peru, and the Philippines. Countries with relatively strong economies but a large number of threatened species include Argentina, Australia, Malaysia, Mexico, United States, and Venezuela. Other countries, particularly those of Europe, have significant financial resources but generally very few globally threatened species.

Conservation Responses

- **Globally threatened species frequently require a combination of conservation responses to ensure their continued survival.** These responses encompass research, species-specific actions, site and habitat based actions, policy responses and communication and education.

- **The majority of threatened species require substantially greater action to improve their status.** While many species already receive some conservation attention, many others do not.

- **Species can be, and many already have been, saved from extinction.** However, this requires a combination of sound research, careful co-ordination of efforts, and, in some cases, intensive management.

- **Improving the effectiveness of conservation action** requires a better understanding of the needs for such action across species, the extent to which it is being applied, and the effects it has had in preventing species extinctions.

- **The *IUCN Red List* information can be used in many different ways as a conservation tool.** The Red List can be used to: provide information on the conservation status of individual species; guide the listing of individual species in national or international legislation; aid in conservation planning and priority setting; help to identify priority species for conservation action and recovery planning; and support educational programmes.

Introduction

Photo: © Bernard Suprin.

Photo 1.1
First discovered in 1988, the beautiful *Pittosporum tannianum* (Critically Endangered) from New Caledonia was thought to have gone Extinct in 1992. But in 2002 it was rediscovered. Three plants are now known to exist, giving this species a tenuous lifeline to avoid extinction for a second time. This story epitomizes that of so many species on the *IUCN Red List of Threatened Species™*.

What is the overall status of biodiversity, what rate is it being lost at, where is it being lost, and what are the causes of decline? As the world begins to respond to the current crisis of biodiversity loss, this information is needed to design and implement effective conservation strategies and to communicate the scope and severity of the problem. The ability to monitor changes in the status of biodiversity is also essential for measuring our success or failure in halting biodiversity loss. However, providing this information is a large and complex task and will require multiple measures to assess the status and trends of the many aspects of biodiversity. For example, different measures may be necessary to assess genes, populations, species, and ecosystems.

The *IUCN Red List of Threatened Species™*, known as the *IUCN Red List*, is one approach for assessing and monitoring the status of biodiversity. The *IUCN Red List* is supported by the Red List Consortium, comprised of the IUCN – The World Conservation Union (in particular the Species Survival Commission), BirdLife International, Conservation International (in particular the Center for Applied Biodiversity Science), and NatureServe. Together these organizations provide the world's largest knowledge base on the global status of species. The 2004 Red List contains the global status and supporting information on 38,047 species and is available on the web at http://www.iucnredlist.org.

This analysis of the information contained in the 2004 *IUCN Red List* aims to provide insight into the status and trends of the world's species, with a focus on those at greatest risk of extinction. Specifically, we highlight: the taxonomic groups that are at the greatest risk of extinction; recent documented extinctions; trends in the status of threatened species; regions of the world where threatened species tend to be found; the threats that are driving species towards extinction; the social and economic context in which extinctions are taking place; and the conservation responses that are available.

The aim of the IUCN Red List Programme is to provide the general public, conservationists, non-governmental organizations, the media, decision makers and policy makers with the most comprehensive scientifically rigorous information on the conservation status of the world's species, so that informed decisions and actions can be taken. The *IUCN Red List* is intended to be policy-relevant, and it can be used to inform conservation planning and priority setting processes, but it is not intended to be prescriptive.

IUCN has been producing lists of threatened species since the 1960s (Scott *et al.* 1987; Burton 2003) and the first Red Data Book was published in 1966 (Simon 1966), although prototypes were in circulation from 1962 (Burton 2003). The earlier Red Lists were produced to highlight specific species that were believed to be threatened with extinction and therefore in need of conservation attention. The mandate of the *IUCN Red List* has now expanded to identify large-scale patterns and trends in the status of species. Identifying taxonomic groups or regions that tend to have species that are facing a high or low probability of extinction can be accomplished by conducting multi-species analyses. These patterns are explored in Sections 2 and 5. Identifying trends in the status of species is more complicated and requires the re-assessment of a group of species at regular intervals and the identification of genuine changes. Section 4 presents the first Red List Indices, showing the trends in the status of threatened birds and amphibians.

Fundamental to the objectivity and the scientific rigour of the *IUCN Red List* are the Red List Categories and Criteria developed in 1994 (IUCN 1994a) and revised in 2001 (IUCN 2001). There are nine categories: Extinct, Extinct in the Wild, Critically Endangered, Endangered, Vulnerable, Near Threatened, Least Concern, Data Deficient, and Not Evaluated (see Appendix 2a). Every species falls into one of these categories. Quantitative criteria have been developed for the categories Critically Endangered, Endangered and Vulnerable (see Appendix 2a). Species listed within each of these categories are believed to share a similar probability of extinction risk. However, the Red List Categories and Criteria are coarse and do not reflect precise probabilities of extinction risk.

Species falling into the categories of Critically Endangered, Endangered and Vulnerable are collectively described as 'threatened', and are the focus of much of the analysis and discussion presented in this *Global Species Assessment*. However, not all of the species listed on the *IUCN Red List* are threatened with high risk of extinction. The *IUCN Red List*, albeit not yet comprehensively, also includes information on conservation successes, and as data collection and reporting efforts expand, it will also record more completely the status of species listed as Least Concern.

The information contained in the *IUCN Red List* is provided principally by the Specialist Groups of the IUCN Species Survival Commission (SSC) and from BirdLife International's network, with additional information coming from other members of the Red List Consortium, and partner organizations. The SSC Specialist Group Network comprises nearly 8,000 specialists with representatives in almost every country of the world. Two recent initiatives, both implemented under the umbrella of the SSC, in collaboration with the Center for Applied Biodiversity Science of Conservation International, and NatureServe, have helped to greatly improve the coverage of the 2004 Red List. These are the Global Amphibian Assessment (GAA) and the Global Mammal Assessment (GMA). These are large-scale assessments that aim to determine the status of all species within a taxonomic group as well as to provide baseline information, for example, on species' distribution and ecology (for more information on these global assessment processes see Appendix 1).

In addition to providing information on the conservation status of individual species, the information from the *IUCN Red List* is used in a variety of ways. These include: the use of Red List data for guiding the listing of individual species in national or international legislation (e.g., the Convention on the Conservation of Migratory Species of Wild Animals (CMS) and the Convention on International Trade in Endangered Species of Wild Fauna and Flora (CITES)); incorporation of the IUCN Red List Categories and Criteria into national and regional Red List programmes; the development of conservation planning and prioritization tools, including the identification of important sites for biodiversity (e.g., protected areas, Ramsar or World Heritage sites, Key Biodiversity Areas, Important Bird Areas, Important Plant Areas, and Alliance for Zero Extinction sites); the identification of priority species for conservation action and recovery planning; and the use of Red List data for educational programmes.

The *2004 IUCN Red List of Threatened Species*™ features a far more extensive analysis of the patterns and trends of threatened species than ever before, and this is presented here as the first *Global Species Assessment*. Staff members of IUCN, BirdLife International, Conservation International, and the Zoological Society of London have prepared this document. The 13 authors have reviewed and commented on all of the sections here. The lead authors of the sections are as follows: Jonathan Baillie, Craig Hilton-Taylor and Simon Stuart (Section 1); Craig Hilton-Taylor and Caroline Pollock (Section 2); Jonathan Baillie and Zoe Cokeliss (Section 3); Stuart Butchart and Alison Stattersfield (Section 4); Thomas Brooks and Michael Hoffmann (Section 5); Simon Stuart, Stuart Butchart, Alison Stattersfield, Georgina Mace and Janice Chanson (Section 6); Janice Chanson (Section 7); Ana Rodrigues (Section 8); and Sue Mainka, Leon Bennun and Simon Stuart (Section 9). The data underlying this analysis are available at http://www.iucnredlist.org.

Photo: © Antonio Di Croce.

Photo: © Jeremy Stafford-Deitsch.

Photo: © Anthony G. Miller.

Photo: © Jack Jeffrey Photography.

Photo: © Michael Samways.

Photo: © Piotr Naskrecki.

The *IUCN Red List* includes more than 38,000 species of plants and animals including **Photo 1.2** (top left) the Scimitar-horned Oryx *Oryx damah* (Extinct in the Wild) formerly from North Africa and now part of a major reintroduction programme; **Photo 1.3** (top right) the Akepa *Loxops coccineus* (Endangered) a honeycreeper endemic to Hawaii; **Photo 1.4** (middle left) the Basking Shark *Cetorhinus maximus* (Vulnerable), a widely distributed cold-water pelagic species that is vulnerable to overfishing; **Photo 1.5** (middle right) the Harlequin Sprite Damselfly *Pseudagrion newtoni* (Vulnerable) which disappeared from its type locality in South Africa, has since been found at another site where cattle grazing of river banks and the spread of invasive alien trees has been curbed; **Photo 1.6** (bottom left) the Dragon Tree *Dracaena cinnabari* (Vulnerable) forming characteristic woodlands on the island of Soqotra, Yemen, but under threat due to possible over-utilization and climate change; and **Photo 1.7** (bottom right) the Mount Nimba Viviparous Toad *Nimbaphrynoides occidentalis* (Critically Endangered) occurs only in a small area of Mount Nimba in Guinea and Cote d'Ivoire, where it lives in montane grassland, a habitat that is in grave danger as a result of plans to mine iron ore.

Globally Threatened Species

Photo: © WWF-UK.

Photo 2.1
The magnificent Iberian Lynx *Lynx pardinus* (Critically Endangered) found in Portugal and Spain, may be the first wild cat species to go extinct in recent times, if habitat loss, persecution, and loss of its main food source continues.

2.1 Introduction: the Current Status

The 2000 update of the *IUCN Red List* (Hilton-Taylor 2000) included global conservation assessments for 16,507 species, 11,406 of which were listed as threatened. Since 2000, the taxonomic coverage of the *IUCN Red List* has substantially increased (for further details on the taxonomic expansion, see description of the Red List Programme in Appendix 1). In addition, there has been a concerted effort to record and document Least Concern species (i.e., species with low extinction risk). Appendix 2a provides a summary of the IUCN Red List Categories and Criteria (IUCN 2001).

The 2004 update of the *IUCN Red List* includes assessments for 38,047 species:

- 15,589 are threatened with extinction (listed as Critically Endangered, Endangered or Vulnerable),
- 844 are Extinct or Extinct in the Wild,
- 3,700 are listed as Near Threatened or Conservation Dependent,
- 3,580 are Data Deficient, and
- 14,334 are Least Concern.

In addition to the species level assessments, the 2004 *IUCN Red List* also includes 2,140 assessments of infra-specific taxa (i.e., taxa below the level of a species) or discrete subpopulations, of which 1,383 are listed as threatened. In total, assessments for 40,187 taxa are included on the *2004 IUCN Red List of Threatened Species*™ thus enhancing the reputation of the *IUCN Red List* as the most comprehensive assessment of the status of the world's 'species'.

The 15,589 species threatened with extinction, although only just over one per cent of the world's described species, includes 12% of all bird species, 23% of all mammal species, 32% of all amphibian species and 34% of all gymnosperms (mainly conifers and cycads). In other words, one in every eight birds, one in every four mammals, and one in every three amphibians and gymnosperms is facing a high to extremely high risk of extinction in the near future (see Table 2.1).

2.2 How Little is Known: the Number of Described Species and the Number Evaluated

Although the number of species assessed has increased substantially in recent updates of the *IUCN Red List*, the conservation status of most of the world's species remains poorly known. Only a very small proportion (2.5%) of the world's described species have been evaluated for the *IUCN Red List* (see Table 2.1), and there is a strong bias in this sample towards terrestrial vertebrates and plants and in particular to those species found in biologically well-studied parts of the world.

The true proportion of species evaluated is certainly higher than the figures given in Table 2.1 because of the under-reporting of Least Concern assessments. This problem is being addressed by the Red List Programme (see Appendix 1).

The proportion of species evaluated is further confounded by the increasing numbers of species being described in the major taxonomic groups (see Box 2.1). There is also considerable uncertainty about how many of the published names are accepted and how many are synonyms.

For most of the major taxonomic groups, the discovery of entirely new species contributes significantly to the increases in species numbers. However, for birds, the discovery of new species is now rare, a recent exception being the discovery of a new flightless rail, the Calayan Rail *Gallirallus calayanensis,* on a remote island in the Philippines (the status of this has not yet been evaluated). The discovery of new species of large mammals is also now very unusual, but there are exceptions, most notably the discovery of the Soala *Pseudoryx nghetinensis* and the Giant Muntjac Deer *Muntiacus vuquangensis* in Viet Nam in the 1990s. A number of 'cryptic' new mammal species are also being discovered through the resolution of species complexes using new molecular or advanced morphological techniques. However, many of the changes in mammal species numbers are due to subspecies being raised to species as a result of a change in species concept (i.e., a shift from the biological species concept to the phylogenetic species concept), a phenomenon that has been termed 'taxonomic inflation' (Isaac *et al.* 2004). There are currently a number of mammal subspecies included on the *IUCN Red List*, which may be treated as full species in the third edition of *Mammal Species of the World* (Wilson and Reeder in press), and so the true number of mammal species evaluated is probably higher than the 4,853 indicated in Table 2.1.

Table 2.1 Numbers of threatened species by major taxonomic group

(See Appendix 2b for details on sources of numbers of described species and Appendix 3a for changes in the numbers of threatened species since 1996)

	Number of described species	Number of species evaluated	Number of threatened species in 2004	Number threatened as % of species described	Number threatened as % of species evaluated*
Vertebrates					
Mammals	5,416	4,853	1,101	20%	23%
Birds	9,917	9,917	1,213	12%	12%
Amphibians**	5,743	5,743	1,856	32%	32%
Reptiles	8,163	499	304	4%	61%
Fishes	28,500	1,721	800	3%	46%
Subtotal	**57,739**	**22,733**	**5,274**	**9%**	**23%**
Invertebrates					
Insects	950,000	771	559	0.06%	73%
Molluscs	70,000	2,163	974	1%	45%
Crustaceans	40,000	498	429	1%	86%
Others	130,200	55	30	0.02%	55%
Subtotal	**1,190,200**	**3,487**	**1,992**	**0.17%**	**57%**
Plants					
Mosses***	15,000	93	80	0.5%	86%
Ferns and allies***	13,025	210	140	1%	67%
Gymnosperms	980	907	305	31%	34%
Dicotyledons	199,350	9,473	7,025	4%	74%
Monocotyledons	59,300	1,141	771	1%	68%
Subtotal	**287,655**	**11,824**	**8,321**	**2.89%**	**70%**
Others					
Lichens	10,000	2	2	0.02%	100%
Subtotal	**10,000**	**2**	**2**	**0.02%**	**100%**
Total	**1,545,594**	**38,046**	**15,589**	**1%**	**41%**

* Apart from the mammals, birds, amphibians and gymnosperms (i.e., those groups completely or almost completely evaluated), the figures in the last column are gross over-estimates of the percentage threatened due to biases in the assessment process towards assessing species that are thought to be threatened, species for which data are readily available, and under-reporting of Least Concern species. The true value for the percentage threatened, lies somewhere in the range indicated by the two right-hand columns. In most cases this represents a very broad range. For example, the true percentage of threatened insects lies somewhere between 0.06% and 73%. Hence, although 41% of all species on the *IUCN Red List* are listed as threatened, this figure needs to be treated with extreme caution given the biases described above.

** It should be noted that for certain species endemic to Brazil, there was not time to reach agreement on the Red List Categories between the Global Amphibian Assessment (GAA) Coordinating Team, and the experts on the species in Brazil. The Red List Categories displayed in the 2004 *IUCN Red List* (http://www.iucnredlist.org) are those that were agreed at the GAA Brazil workshop in April 2003. However, in the subsequent consistency check conducted by the GAA Coordinating Team, many of these were found to be inconsistent with the approach adopted elsewhere in the world, and a "consistent Red List Category" was also assigned to these species. There was not time to agree these "consistent Red List Categories" with the Brazilian experts. However, in order to retain comparability between the results for amphibians with those for other taxonomic groups, the data summarized in this table, and used for the analysis in the remainder of this publication, are based on the "consistent Red List Categories", not categories shown against each of these species in the *IUCN Red List*.

*** Mosses include the true mosses (Bryopsida), the hornworts (Anthocerotopsida), and liverworts (Marchantiopsida); while the ferns and allies include the club mosses (Lycopodiopsida), spike mosses (Sellaginellopsida), quillworts (Isoetopsida), and true ferns (Polypodiopsida).

Box 2.1

Numbers of Species in the Major Taxonomic Groups

- The number of mammal species has increased from 4,629 in the second edition of *Mammal Species of the World* (Wilson and Reeder 1993) to 5,416 in the third edition (Wilson and Reeder in press);

- The number of reptile species has increased from 7,970 in 2000 to 8,163 (data derived from the EMBL Reptile Database: Uetz 2004);

- The number of amphibian species has increased from 4,950 in 2000 to 5,743 species (data from Amphibian Species of the World (Frost 2004), Amphibia Web (2004) and the Global Amphibian Assessment);

- The number of fish species has increased from 25,000 in 2000 to 28,500 species (data derived from FishBase: Froese and Pauly 2004).

- The birds are the only vertebrate group where the numbers of accepted species have remained fairly stable since 1996, although there have been marked changes within certain groups, e.g., the albatrosses (Diomedeidae) where the number of species has increased from 14 to 21.

- The numbers of species in the invertebrate groups are based on the work of Hammond (1992) and are recognized to be highly provisional, with perhaps as much as 20% uncertainty (Hammond 1995).

- The number of seed plant species is highly debated. A conservative estimate of almost 259,000 species is used here following Thorne (2002). However, there are many alternative estimates with numbers ranging from 223,300 to 422,127 species (see Mabberly 1997; Schmid 1998; Bramwell 2002; Govaerts 2001, 2003; and Scotland and Wortley 2003).

See Appendix 2b for further details on sources.

Photo: © WWF-Canon / David Hulse.

Photo 2.2
The Saola *Pseudoryx nghetinhensis* (Endangered) is generally considered to be the greatest mammal discovery in recent times, and is so different from any currently known species that a separate genus had to be created. It was only 'discovered' by western science in 1992 and described in 1993. Occurs in Lao PDR and Viet Nam.

The lack of stability in the numbers of described species, and the high degree of uncertainty surrounding some of the numbers, need to be borne in mind when examining the results for what has been evaluated. Figure 2.1 shows the proportion of species evaluated in all the major taxonomic groups.

The vertebrates (Figure 2.1a) are the best evaluated group, with almost 40% of the species recorded on the *IUCN Red List*, while the plants and invertebrates are poorly evaluated by comparison. Within the vertebrates, the birds and amphibians are fully evaluated (Figure 2.1b) (though the analysis excludes a few new amphibian species that were described in 2004 after the completion of the Global Amphibian Assessment project, e.g. *Phyllodactylus punctatus, Philautus petilus, Tomopterna luganga*, etc.), while the number of mammals evaluated has declined from 100% in 1996 (Baillie and Groombridge 1996) to almost 90%. This decline is because of the increasing number of described mammal species (but see the discussion above about 'taxonomic inflation'). Reptiles and fishes are currently poorly represented on the *IUCN Red List*, but plans are in place to address this (see Appendix 1).

For the invertebrate groups (Figure 2.1c), relatively few species have been evaluated, and the evaluations that have been done have tended to focus on molluscs (particularly freshwater and terrestrial species) and on crustaceans (primarily inland water crustaceans). Among the insects, the only groups that have received noteworthy attention are the swallowtail butterflies (Papilionidae) and the dragonflies and damselflies (Odonata). The other invertebrates are very poorly represented on the *IUCN Red List*, but the following phyla are represented at least by a few species: Annelida (segmented worms); Cnidaria (e.g., sea anemones); Echinodermata (e.g., sea urchins, starfish, etc.); Nemertinia (unsegmented worms); Onychophora (velvet worms); and

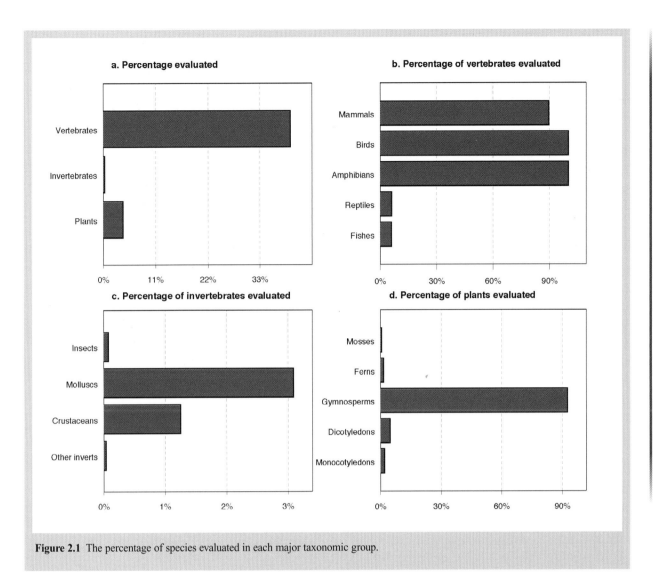

Figure 2.1 The percentage of species evaluated in each major taxonomic group.

Platyhelminths (flatworms). There are other significant invertebrate groups (in terms of species numbers and their role in ecosystem function) that are not yet represented on the *IUCN Red List* such as the Porifera (sponges) and the Nematoda (roundworms). There are plans to increase the number of invertebrate evaluations particularly for freshwater dependent taxa (see Appendix 1).

Although almost 12,000 species of plants are now recorded on the *IUCN Red List*, this represents only 4% of the world's plant diversity. The species evaluated now include representatives from all the major plant taxonomic groups. But the only major plant group almost fully evaluated is the gymnosperms (conifers and cycads; Figure 2.1d). In considering plants it is also important to note the 33,798 species listed as threatened in the *1997 IUCN Red List of Threatened Plants* (Walter and Gillett 1998). This work in effect remains a companion Red List that should be used in conjunction with the annual updates of the *IUCN Red List of Threatened Species*™, until such time as all taxa

in the 1997 Plants Red List have been reassessed under the 2001 IUCN Red List Categories and Criteria (IUCN 2001; see further discussion under section 2.4 below).

In addition to the taxonomic groups discussed above, the *IUCN Red List* also includes representatives from two other Kingdoms. The Protista (comprising approximately 80,000 described species) are represented by one Extinct species of red alga (a seaweed from Australia), while the Fungi (comprising approximately 72,000 described species) are represented by only two threatened species of lichen (numbers of described species from Hammond 1995) (see Section 2.5).

Despite the relatively low number of species evaluated and the biases towards the better known taxonomic groups, the 2004 *IUCN Red List* provides clear evidence that there is cause for conservation concern (see Sections 2.3 and 2.4 and Section 4), and it is likely that the situation is similar for taxonomic groups not yet evaluated.

2.3 How Many Threatened Animal Species are There?

The 2004 *IUCN Red List* includes 7,266 animal species threatened with extinction compared to 5,435 in 2000 (see Tables 2.1 and 2.2 and Appendix 3a). Comparing the numbers of threatened species in the major taxonomic groups reported for the 2000 and 2004 updates of the Red List (see Appendices 3a and 3b), it is clear that the overall number of threatened species has increased in all groups, with the exception of the mammals (see details below). Most of the increase in numbers of threatened animals is due to the incorporation of assessments for all amphibian species for the first time (the number of threatened amphibians increased from 146 in 2000 to 1,856). Although there are more threatened species, the proportions of each taxonomic group threatened, with the exception of that for the amphibians, has remained much the same as in 2000. This is because the increases have been either relatively small (e.g., for the reptiles a net gain of 10 threatened species) or they have been offset by increases in the number of described species (e.g., for fishes a net gain of 48 threatened species and a gain of 3,500 described species). The birds are the only taxonomic group for which since 2000 there has been a decrease in the number of recognized species (9,946 to 9,917) and an increase in the number threatened (1,130 to 1,213). In most cases these 'apparent' increases in numbers of threatened species are not genuine deteriorations in status, but the result of better knowledge or changes in taxonomy. Any extrapolation of trends from the numbers of threatened species in 2000 versus 2004 should only take into account the genuine changes (see Section 4 for further details).

The IUCN Red List Categories and Criteria (IUCN 2001, p. 7) state that species listed as Data Deficient (DD) "should not be treated as if they were non-threatened". In reality, many Data Deficient species are likely to be threatened, so we are generally under-estimating levels of threat, particularly in comprehensively assessed groups like the amphibians and mammals with relatively large numbers of DD species (1,290 and 380 respectively). However, a proportion of the DD species are also likely to be listed as Least Concern or even as Extinct once the relevant data become available. How many DD species are threatened and how many are not, is difficult to estimate. In this analysis we take an evidentiary rather than a precautionary approach, and so are under-estimating the levels of threat. Hence the 2,882 animal species listed as DD on the 2004 *IUCN Red List* are not included in the number considered to be threatened (Table 2.1).

In addition to the species listed as threatened, 2,302 are listed as Near Threatened (NT). This category has no quantitative criteria, and is used for species that come close to meeting the thresholds for a threatened category (see Appendix 2a). The vast majority of Near Threatened animal species are mammals (587) and birds (773). If the numbers in this category were combined with those listed as threatened, then the percentage of birds, mammals and amphibians that are threatened or near threatened would rise to 20%, 35% and 39% respectively (based on numbers of evaluated species).

There is an additional category – LowerRisk/conservation dependent (LR/cd) that was used in an earlier version of the Red List Categories (IUCN 1994a) but has subsequently been dropped (IUCN 2001). This category was used to indicate species that would be listed as threatened were it not for species-specific conservation programmes. There are still 111 animal species listed as LR/cd (Table 2.2), and until such time as these are all re-evaluated, this category will persist as an artefact of the previous classification system. The LR/cd category was rarely used for animals except for mammals, which still have 64 species in this category, 39 of which are hoofed mammals or artiodactyls, and 14 are cetaceans (whales and dolphins) (see Figure 2.2a).

2.3.1 Threatened Vertebrates

2.3.1.1 Mammals, Birds and Amphibians

The 1996 *IUCN Red List* (Baillie and Groombridge 1996) featured complete evaluations for all of the world's bird and mammal species. Since then, the birds have been re-evaluated twice by BirdLife International and its partners (BirdLife International 2000, 2004a). A major advance for 2004 is the inclusion of a third completely evaluated group of vertebrates, namely the amphibians. The amphibians were evaluated as part of the Global Amphibian Assessment (GAA) project that started in 2001 (IUCN, CI and NatureServe 2004). As discussed above in Section 2.2, the number of described mammal species has increased and as a result there are 563 'new' mammal species that have not yet been evaluated. In addition, many of the mammal assessments were done eight years ago and might no longer be a true reflection of the status of the species concerned (3,472 of the mammal species assessments, 737 of which are threatened, date from the 1996 *IUCN Red List*, but a third of the threatened species have been re-evaluated since 1996). Nevertheless given that almost 90% have been evaluated, the results for mammals can still be compared to those for the birds and the amphibians (see Figures 2.2 a, b, c and Table 2.1).

Table 2.2 Summary of Red List Category classifications by class of animals

Class*	EX	EW	Subtotal	CR	EN	VU	Subtotal	LR/cd	NT	DD	LC	Total
Mammalia	73	4	77	162	352	587	1,101	64	587	380	2,644	4,853
Aves	129	4	133	179	345	689	1,213	0	773	78	7,720	9,917
Amphibia**	34	1	35	427	761	668	1,856	0	359	1,290	2,203	5,743
Reptilia	21	1	22	64	79	161	304	3	74	60	36	499
Cephalaspidomorphi	0	0	0	0	1	2	3	0	5	4	1	13
Elasmobranchii	0	0	0	9	19	38	66	1	70	139	93	369
Holocephali	0	0	0	0	0	0	0	0	0	1	3	4
Actinopterygii	81	12	93	161	140	429	730	12	105	290	104	1,334
Sarcopterygii	0	0	0	1	0	0	1	0	0	0	0	1
Echinoidea	0	0	0	0	0	0	0	0	1	0	0	1
Arachnida	0	0	0	0	1	9	10	0	1	7	0	18
Chilopoda	0	0	0	0	0	1	1	0	0	0	0	1
Crustacea	7	1	8	56	79	294	429	9	2	32	18	498
Insecta	59	1	60	47	120	392	559	3	74	49	26	771
Merostomata	0	0	0	0	0	0	0	0	1	3	0	4
Onychophora	0	0	0	3	2	4	9	0	1	1	0	11
Hirudinoidea	0	0	0	0	0	0	0	0	1	0	0	1
Oligochaeta	1	0	1	1	0	4	5	0	1	0	0	7
Polychaeta	0	0	0	1	0	0	1	0	0	1	0	2
Bivalvia	31	0	31	52	28	16	96	5	60	12	9	213
Gastropoda	260	12	272	213	193	472	878	14	186	531	69	1,950
Enopla	0	0	0	0	0	2	2	0	1	3	0	6
Turbellaria	1	0	1	0	0	0	0	0	0	0	0	1
Anthozoa	0	0	0	0	0	2	2	0	0	1	0	3
Total	697	36	733	1,376	2,120	3,770	7,266	111	2,302	2,882	12,926	26,220

*Mammalia (mammals), Aves (birds), Reptilia (reptiles), Amphibia (amphibians), Cephalaspidomorphi (lampreys and hag fish), Elasmobranchii (sharks, skates and rays), Holocephali (chimaeras), Actinopterygii (bony fishes), Sarcopterygii (coelacanth), Echinoidea (sea urchins, starfish, etc.), Arachnida (spiders and scorpions), Chilopoda (centipedes), Crustacea (crustaceans), Insecta (insects), Merostomata (horshoe crabs), Onychophora (velvet worms), Hirudinoidea (leeches), Oligochaeta (earthworms), Polychaeta (marine bristle worms), Bivalvia (mussels and clams), Gastropoda (snails, etc.), Enopla (nemertine worms), Turbellaria (flatworms), Anthozoa (sea anemones and corals).

**Note that the numbers for Amphibia are derived from a consistency check of the Global Amphibian Assessment results (see footnote to Table 2.1). The *IUCN Red List* website, however, shows different numbers as agreement on the results of the consistency check has not yet been reached: 34 EX, 1 EW, 412 CR, 725 EN, 633 VU, 360 NT, 1,338 DD and 2,240 LC.

IUCN Red List Categories: EX – Extinct, **EW** – Extinct in the Wild, **CR** – Critically Endangered, **EN** – Endangered, **VU** – Vulnerable, **LR/cd** – Lower Risk/conservation dependent, **NT** – Near Threatened (includes LR/nt – Lower Risk/near threatened), DD – Data Deficient, LC – Least Concern (includes LR/lc – Lower Risk/least concern). Note: the numbers for Not Evaluated (**NE**) are not presented.

The proportions of species in the different Red List Categories differ markedly between these three vertebrate groups. Comparing the threatened categories (CR, EN and VU), 12% of bird species are considered threatened, versus 23% of mammals and 32% of amphibians. The amphibians have more than twice as many species listed as Critically Endangered or Endangered (1,188 in total) than the birds and mammals (see Table 2.2 and Figure 2.2) and are currently the most threatened class of vertebrates on the *IUCN Red List*. In addition, 12% of mammals, 8% of birds and 6% of amphibians are listed as Near Threatened. The situation for the amphibians may be even worse than the figures indicate, because 23% of them are listed as Data Deficient (i.e., there is inadequate information to assess the extinction risk).

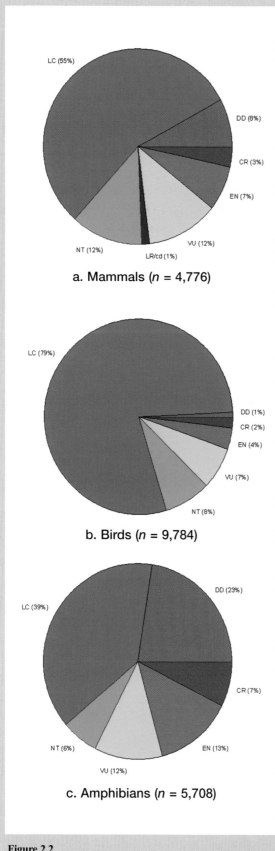

LC (55%)

DD (8%)

CR (3%)

EN (7%)

VU (12%)

NT (12%)

LR/cd (1%)

a. Mammals (*n* = 4,776)

LC (79%)

DD (1%)

CR (2%)

EN (4%)

VU (7%)

NT (8%)

b. Birds (*n* = 9,784)

DD (23%)

LC (39%)

CR (7%)

NT (6%)

EN (13%)

VU (12%)

c. Amphibians (*n* = 5,708)

Figure 2.2
Percentages of extant mammal, bird and amphibian species in
each Red List Category. The pie charts exclude the categories
Extinct, Extinct in the Wild and Not Evaluated.

Once further information is obtained on these species it is probable that many will be listed in one of the threatened categories or even as Extinct. Mammals are better known than the amphibians, with only 8% listed as Data Deficient, while the birds are extremely well known with only 1% as Data Deficient. It was mentioned in section 2.2 that the mammals were the only group where the number of threatened species had declined. The decline (from 1,130 in 2000 to 1,101 species) is not due to successful conservation actions followed by a genuine recovery. This change is the result of new listings for a number of African rodent species as a result of taxonomic changes and better information and knowledge being made available through the Global Mammal Assessment project (see Appendix 1).

The proportion of species considered not threatened also differs markedly with 78% of birds, 56% of mammals and 39% of amphibians being listed as Least Concern. The relatively large numbers of Least Concern bird species is, however, no reason to be complacent as many common bird species are in decline across the world (BirdLife International 2004b).

Figure 2.2 clearly indicates that a large number of mammal, bird and amphibian species are close to extinction, with 27% of the species evaluated listed as globally threatened because they have small and/or rapidly declining populations and/or small ranges. In total, 405 mammal, bird and amphibian species are Critically Endangered and face an extremely high risk of extinction in the immediate future. The prospect of a major extinction event raises questions about which groups of species are most likely to be lost, and which are more susceptible to decline than others. A number of studies in recent years have analysed the *IUCN Red List* data to determine which orders and families of birds and mammals are most susceptible to extinction (Bennett and Owens 1997; Mace and Balmford 2000; Purvis *et al.* 2000a). As we now have updated information for all threatened birds and, for the first time, all amphibians, this analysis has been repeated here (see Appendix 2b for details of the methodology and Appendices 3c-h for the detailed results), and the main findings are presented in Figure 2.3 (for mammals), Figure 2.4 (for birds) and Figure 2.5 (for amphibians).

Care is needed in interpreting the results in Figures 2.3 to 2.5. That a given order or family has a significantly lower percentage of threatened or extinct species than average does not mean that it has "low threat". Indeed, the 'expected' levels of threat in the absence of human activities are presumably close to zero, and therefore most taxa are highly threatened in relation to what would be expected in a natural situation. The results in Figures 2.3 to 2.5 are all comparisons in relation to the average situation amongst species in the same group. For example, a family with 33% threatened species is not significantly different from the average threat levels in amphibians but it is very significantly more threatened than the average amongst birds. It should also be noted that the low percentage of threatened and extinct species is in some cases artificially low because of lack of knowledge on the species' threatened status. For example, only two out of 109 species of the amphibian family Caeciliidae are listed as threatened (Figure 2.5), but 66 species are Data Deficient, many of which might turn out to be threatened.

The results in Figure 2.3a (see Appendix 3c for detailed results) show that the Rodentia (rodents) is the only mammalian order with significantly fewer than expected threatened or extinct species, despite having the largest number of threatened mammal species on the Red List. Five orders have significantly more threatened species than would be expected, namely the Sirenia (dugongs and manatees), Perissodactyla (equids, rhinos and tapirs), Artiodactyla (deer, antelope, cattle, sheep, goats, etc.), Primates, and the Carnivora (cats, dogs, weasels, bears, etc.). These results are similar to those found by Mace and Balmford (2000).

The mammalian families that are highlighted as having significantly higher numbers of threatened species than average (Figure 2.3b; see Appendix 3d for detailed results) include the Hominidae (great apes); Tapiridae (tapirs); Nesophontidae (West Indian shrews); Indridae (avahi, sifakas and indri); Equidae (zebras and wild horses); Peramelidae (bandicoots); Lemuridae (lemurs); Chrysochloridae (golden moles); Capromyidae (hutias); Felidae (cats); Cercopithecidae (Old World monkeys); Bovidae (wild cattle, antelope, sheep and goats); and Pteropodidae (fruit bats). Many of these families are the same as those identified by Mace and Balmford (2000), but there are some new additions (e.g., the Felidae and Cercopithecidae). While the results confirm Mace and Balmford's (2000) observation that most of the highly threatened families are species poor, the Bovidae, Cercopithecidae and Pteropodidae are relatively species rich. Some of the differences could be artefacts of the statistical methods used. The major threats to the Bovidae and Cercopithecidae include habitat loss (primarily due to agricultural expansion) and hunting (for food and medicinal purposes), while for the Pteropodidae (a group which is fairly restricted in its geographic range), habitat loss due to extraction of timber, hunting for food, and general human disturbance are the main threats.

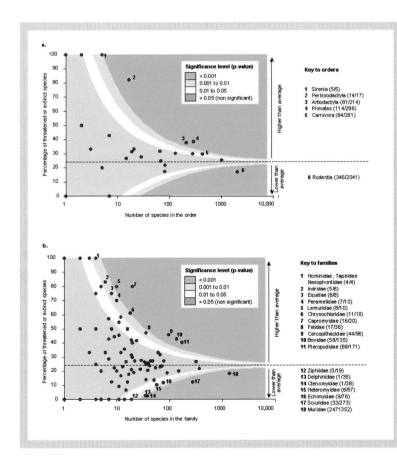

Figure 2.3
The percentage of threatened or extinct mammal species: a) in each mammalian order; and b) in each mammalian family. Each circle corresponds to an order or family, positioned according to the number of species in the order and the percentage of those species that are threatened (Vulnerable, Endangered or Critically Endangered) or extinct (Extinct or Extinct in the Wild). The horizontal dashed line indicates to the percentage of threatened or extinct species among mammals as a whole (24%). Orders or families with higher levels of relative threat are depicted above this line, orders or families with lower levels are represented below. The coloured bands indicate the level to which the percentage of threatened or extinct species in each order or family is significantly different from the average. Orders or families with threat levels that are very significantly different from the average (p <0.01) are listed individually on the right section of the figure. Values between parentheses indicate number of threatened or extinct species/total number of species (e.g., 84 out of 281 species of Carnivora are threatened or extinct). For the summary data, see Appendices 3c and 3d.

Photo: © Troy Inman

Photo: © Anna Lushchekina

Photo: © Richard Wainwright

Photo's 2.3, 2.4, and 2.5 (top to bottom)
Representatives of mammalian families with more threatened species than average include: Western Gorilla *Gorilla gorilla* (Endangered) from Central Africa; Saiga Antelope *Saiga tartarica* (Critically Endangered) from Central Asia; and the Comoro Black Flying Fox *Pteropus livingstonii* (Critically Endangered).

The mammalian families identified as having significantly fewer threatened species than expected include the Ziphiidae (beaked whales); Delphinidae (dolphins); Ctenomyidae (tuco-tucos); Heteromyidae (pocket and kangaroo mice); Echimyidae (spiny rats); Sciuridae (squirrels, marmots, prairie dogs); and the Muridae (mice, rats, gerbils). The Delphinidae are generally widely distributed species and as a result although relatively well-known locally they are very poorly known globally; hence seven subpopulations are listed as threatened on the IUCN Red List, compared to only one species globally, while 20 species are listed as Data Deficient. The level of extinction risk in the Ctenomyidae and Sciuridae might be underestimated because these families are poorly known in terms of their taxonomy and population biology. The Muridae is by far the largest mammalian family and it dominates the mammals in the Red List numerically with 227 threatened and 20 Extinct species. It is possible that the extinction risk for this group has been underestimated because many of the species are poorly known. In addition many apparently widespread murid species might be species complexes, which, once resolved, could result in an increased number of range-restricted species that are under threat. However, many of the murid genera are highly adaptable to habitat loss and have become commensal with people.

A significant finding from this analysis and that of Mace and Balmford (2000) is that in general, most of the threatened orders and families of mammals are species-poor. This, coupled with observations from other groups that threatened higher taxa tend to be phylogenetically unique, strongly suggests that impending extinctions will lead to a disproportionate loss of evolutionary novelty.

Mace and Balmford (2000) found no clear-cut relationships between the percentage of threatened species in a group and either its species richness or its average body mass or body size. Mace and Balmford (2000) suggest that much more detailed analyses of life history traits and extinction risk are required to disentangle the causes and constraints. Some progress in this regard has been made in a recent study of the impacts of human population density on extinction risk in carnivores (Cardillo *et al.* 2004). They demonstrated that extinction risk in carnivores was more strongly predicted by intrinsic biological traits than exposure to high-density human populations.

Figure 2.4 shows that extinction risk is not distributed evenly, or randomly, across bird orders and families. Certain orders and families contain a large proportion of threatened species, while others contain a smaller proportion than expected. Nine bird orders contained significantly more threatened species than average (Figure 2.4a; see Appendix 3e for detailed results): Apterygiformes (kiwis); Sphenisciformes (penguins); Pelecaniformes (cormorants, pelicans, etc.); Procellariiformes (albatrosses and petrels); Ciconiiformes (storks, ibises and spoonbills); Galliformes (pheasants, partridges, quails, etc.); Gruiformes (cranes, bustards, rails, etc.); Columbiformes (doves and pigeons); and the Psittaciformes (parrots). The Piciformes (woodpeckers, toucans, barbets, etc.); Apodiformes (swifts and hummingbirds); and Passeriformes (songbirds) are the orders with significantly fewer threatened species than average (Figure 2.4a).

There are 15 extinction prone families (Figure 2.4b; see Appendix 3f for detailed results): the Mesitornithidae (mesites); Apterygidae (kiwis); Gruidae (cranes); Spheniscidae (penguins); Megapodiidae (megapodes); Diomedeidae (albatrosses); Drepanididae (Hawaiian honeycreepers); Phalcrocoracidae (cormorants); Cracidae (cracids); Procellariidae (petrels); Zosteropidae (white-eyes); Rallidae (rails); Phasianidae (pheasants, partridges, etc.); Columbidae (doves and pigeons); and Psittacidae (parrots). Ten families contain significantly fewer than expected threatened species: Bucconidae (puffbirds); Dendrocolaptidae (woodcreepers); Paridae (tits); Capitonidae (barbets); Nectariniidae (sunbirds); Picidae (woodpeckers); Trochilidae (hummingbirds; Tyrannidae (tyrant flycatchers); Emberizidae (buntings); and the Muscicapidae (thrushes, warblers and flycatchers).

The results generally match those reported by Bennett and Owens (1997) as all eight families identified by them as having significantly more threatened species appear here again as do many of the other families with unusually high numbers of threatened species. Differences in the results obtained by Bennett and Owens (1997) and those shown in Figure 2.4 can largely be explained by the different classification systems used for the families. For example, the Hawaiian honeycreepers are treated here as a distinct family separate from the Fringillidae, and have significantly more threatened species than expected with 31 out of 34 listed as threatened. The situation in this family is symptomatic of the levels of habitat loss and the impacts of invasive species on the native fauna and flora of Hawaii. The cormorants, however, are a new addition to the list of families with more threatened species than expected because four additional species have now been added to the Red List. Three of the additions were due to improved knowledge, but in the case of the Bank Cormorant *Phalacrocorax neglectus*, there has

Photo: © Ferne McKenzie

Photo: © Troy Inman

Photo: © Jack Jeffrey Photography

Photo's 2.6, 2.7, and 2.8 (top to bottom) Representatives of avian families with more threatened species than average include: Brown Kiwi *Apteryx mantelli* (Endangered) from New Zealand; Waved Albatross *Phoebastria irrorata* (Vulnerable) from the Galápagos, Ecuador; and the 'Akiapola'au *Hemignathus munroi* (Endangered) a honeycreeper from Hawaii.

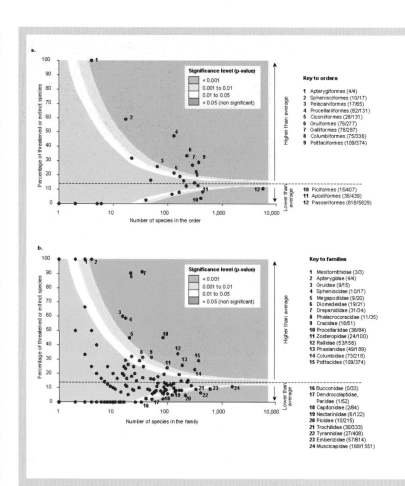

Figure 2.4

The percentage of threatened or extinct bird species: a) in each avian order; and b) in each avian family. Each circle corresponds to an order or family, positioned according to the number of species in the order and the percentage of those species that are threatened (Vulnerable, Endangered or Critically Endangered) or extinct (Extinct or Extinct in the Wild). The horizontal dashed line indicates to the percentage of threatened or extinct species among birds as a whole (12%). Orders or families with higher levels of relative threat are depicted above this line, orders or families with lower levels are represented below. The coloured bands indicate the level to which the percentage of threatened or extinct species in each order or family is significantly different from the average. Orders or families with threat levels that are very significantly different from the average (p <0.01) are listed individually on the right section of the figure. Values between parentheses indicate number of threatened or extinct species/total number of species (e.g., 16 out of 51 species of the family Cracidae are threatened or extinct). For the summary data, see Appendices 3e and 3f.

been a genuine deterioration in status as a result of human disturbance, competition with seals for breeding sites, a decreasing food supply and the impacts of oil spills. Among the most threatened families are those that suffer particularly from exploitation for food (megapodes, pheasants, pigeons) or as pets (parrots).

The analysis by Bennett and Owens (1997) further showed that increased extinction risk is associated with increases in body size and low fecundity rates and it is suggested that the evolution of low fecundity many millions of years ago predisposed certain lineages to extinction. Purvis *et al.* (2000) have also shown that bird extinctions are phylogenetically non-random. While some of the orders and families that are more threatened than expected have relatively few species (e.g., the mesites and kiwis), many are relatively species rich (e.g., the parrots). In other words, we stand to loose not only unique phylogenetic lineages, but also lineages of large and charismatic groups.

The analysis of amphibian orders (Figure 2.5a; see Appendix 3g for detailed results) is not particularly informative as there are only three orders. The results indicate that the Gymnophiona (caecilians, or limbless amphibians) are significantly less threatened than average

(only two threatened out of 168 species), but this is misleading because 111 of the species are listed as Data Deficient. With better information these species could prove to be as threatened as the average for amphibians. The Caudata (salamanders and newts) have significantly more threatened species than average, as the species tend to have small ranges and are very sensitive to habitat loss. The average number of threatened species is determined by the Anurans (frogs and toads), by far the largest amphibian group with over 5,000 species.

The results of the family level analysis are much more informative (see Figure 2.5b; see Appendix 3h for detailed results). The families with significantly more threatened species than average include: Astylosternidae (Cameroonian stream frogs); Hynobiidae (Asian salamanders); Rhacophoridae (Asian tree frogs); Plethodontidae (lungless salamanders); Bufonidae (true toads); and the Leptodactylidae (Neotropical typical frogs). The Astylosternidae are confined to West and Central Africa, with the highest diversity being centred on Cameroon, where they tend to have small ranges at mid-elevations. The mid-elevation habitats in this region are being heavily impacted through expanding agriculture and deforestation.

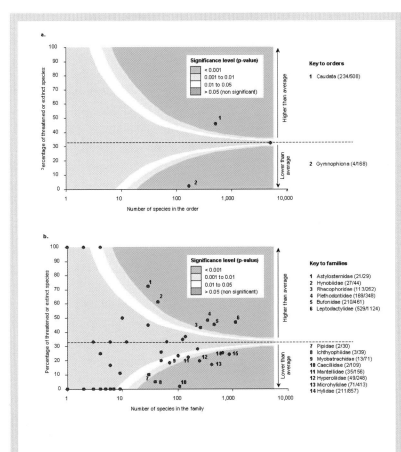

Figure 2.5
The percentage of threatened or extinct amphibian species: a) in each amphibian order; and b) in each amphibian family. Each circle corresponds to an order or family, positioned according to the number of species in the order and the percentage of those species that are threatened (Vulnerable, Endangered or Critically Endangered) or extinct (Extinct or Extinct in the Wild). The horizontal dashed line indicates to the percentage of threatened or extinct species among amphibians as a whole (32%). Orders or families with higher levels of relative threat are depicted above this line, orders or families with lower levels are represented below. The coloured bands indicate the level to which the percentage of threatened or extinct species in each order or family is significantly different from the average. Orders or families with threat levels that are very significantly different from the average (p <0.01) are listed individually on the right section of the figure. Values between parentheses indicate number of threatened or extinct species/total number of species (e.g., 27 out of 44 species of the family Hynobiidae are threatened or extinct). For the summary data, see Appendices 3g and 3h.

Photo: © S.D. Biju

Photo 2.9
The announcement in 2003 of the discovery of a new family of frogs, the Nasikabatrachidae, from the Western Ghats of India took the scientific world by surprise. The only species, *Nasikabatrachus sahyadrensis* (Endangered), is known from only two localities, and spends most of its time deep underground.

The Hynobiidae are very sensitive to habitat loss, which is severe in parts of their range, and hence have more threatened species than expected. The high level of threat in the Rhacophoridae is mainly a reflection of the large number of threatened species in the genus *Philautus*. The members of this large genus tend to have very small ranges, especially in India and Sri Lanka, where they are easily impacted by habitat loss. Many species in the Plethodontidae also tend to have very small ranges. The Mexican and Central American members of this family are particularly threatened because of habitat loss. The Bufonidae has the largest number of species that appear to be rapidly declining due to the impacts of chytrid fungus (see Sections 3.7, 3.8 and 6.5 for further

Photo 2.10
The Maud Island Frog *Leiopelma pakeka* (Vulnerable) is one of four members of the primitive New Zealand frog family, Leiopelmatidae, all of which are threatened. This species is confined to a 16 ha forest remnant on Maud Island, although an introduced population was established on Motuara Island in 1997.

Photo 2.11
The Seychelles Palm Frog *Sooglossus pipilodryas* (Vulnerable) is restricted to Silhouette Island in the Seychelles, where it is closely associated with the palm *Phoenicophorium borsigianum* (Near Threatened). All four members of the frog family Sooglossidae, endemic to the Seychelles, are threatened.

details). Most dramatically, 74 of the 77 species in the genus *Atelopus* (harlequin toads) are threatened or extinct. Other high-profile toad genera with high percentages of threatened species include the viviparous toads of Africa (*Nectophrynoides* and *Nimbaphrynoides*). The Leptodactylidae is the largest amphibian family, more than half of which are considered threatened. The family is dominated by the 700 members of *Eleutherodactylus* (the largest genus of vertebrates), which typically have very small ranges and so are particularly susceptible to habitat loss. Some members of the family have also suffered from the impacts of the chytrid fungal disease, chytridiomycosis.

The results in Figure 2.5b do not show a number of very small but phylogenetically significant families where all the species are listed as threatened or extinct. These include: Rheobatrachidae (gastric-brooding frogs; both species listed as Extinct); the recently described Nasikabatrachidae from India comprising a single evolutionarily unique, threatened species (Biju and Bossuyt 2003); Rhinodermatidae (Darwin's frogs; one species possibly extinct, the other in decline); Leiopelmatidae (New Zealand frogs; all four species threatened, one in serious decline); and Sooglossidae (Seychelles frogs; all four species threatened). The giant salamanders (Cryptobranchidae) are also worthy of mention, with one of the three species being Critically Endangered, and the other two being Near Threatened.

The families with significantly fewer threatened species than average include: Pipidae (tongueless frogs) a group that appears to be generally resistant to disturbance and disease; Ichthyophiidae (Asian caecilians; but many species listed as Data Deficient); Caeciliidae (typical caecilians; but many Data Deficient species); Myobatrachidae (Australian water frogs); Mantellidae (Madagascan frogs); Hyperoliidae (African tree frogs and reed frogs); Microhylidae (narrow-mouthed toads); and Hylidae (typical tree frogs). Although the species in these families are less threatened than expected, nearly all of them include a number of very seriously threatened species.

The results for the amphibians differ from those for the mammals and birds in that many of the families with largest percentages of threatened species are species rich (notably Leptodactylidae, Bufonidae, Rhacophoridae and Plethodontidae). However, the amphibian results are similar to mammals and birds in that there are several small, highly threatened families that are phylogenetically unique. It is possible that the massive decline and increasing number of extinctions being observed in the amphibians will lead to a disproportionate loss of evolutionary novelty.

Photo: © Glenn Gerber

Photo 2.12
The Anegada Ground Iguana *Cyclura pinguis* (Critically Endangered) was once distributed over the entire Puerto Rico Bank, but today is confined to the island of Anegada, British Virgin Islands. Vulnerability to predation by humans and their dogs and cats may have resulted in the contraction in range. A reintroduction programme is in place for this species.

2.3.1.2 Reptiles

The reptiles are an under-represented vertebrate group on the *IUCN Red List* as only 6% of the 8,163 described species have been evaluated so far (see Tables 2.1 and 2.2). The evaluations have tended to focus on particular taxonomic groups that are well known (the crocodilians, turtles, iguanas and tuataras) or on species in the more poorly known groups (lizards and snakes) that are considered to be under threat. Of the species evaluated, 61% are listed as threatened.

Two reptile orders have been completely evaluated, namely the Crocodylia (crocodiles, alligators and caimans) and the Rhynchocephalia (tuataras). The Crocodylia have ten (43%) of their 23 described species listed as threatened. The Chinese Alligator *Alligator sinensis* is considered the most threatened crocodilian in the world, but there is a large population in captivity and an Action Plan has been drafted to reverse the long trend of habitat loss and population decline for this alligator (Ross 2001). The tuataras from New Zealand are the only surviving members (two extant species) of their order (all other members of the order (and family Sphenodontidae) are known only from the fossil record). One species is listed as threatened and the other is considered to be Least Concern.

The Testudines (turtles and tortoises) are relatively well covered on the *IUCN Red List*, with 205 (67%) of the 305 described species evaluated, 128 (42%) of which are listed as threatened (see Box 2.2).

Other reptile groups such as the Amphisbaenia (worm lizards) have not been evaluated at all, and likewise very few snakes and lizards have been evaluated. Within the lizards, the main focus has been on the Iguanidae and other closely related families. Many snakes and lizards are cryptic, hard to

find and poorly known. However, the Global Reptile Assessment (see Appendix 1) started in 2004 will greatly improve our knowledge of this group of vertebrates.

The Decline of Turtles

The very rapidly deteriorating status of tortoises and freshwater turtles in Southeast Asia has resulted in an increasing number of these species being listed as threatened on the *IUCN Red List*. Globally, 42% of turtle and tortoise species are threatened.

Photo: © Peter Paul van Dijk

Photo 2.13
The Painted Terrapin *Callagur borneoensis* (Critically Endangered) inhabits southern Thailand, Peninsular Malaysia and Borneo. The species has suffered loss of some populations and reduction of remaining populations, caused by direct exploitation of adults, harvesting of eggs, and habitat degradation and loss.

continued overleaf...

Box 2.2 *continued*

Table Box 2.2

Numbers of threatened species by turtle and tortoise family

Testudine families*	Number of described species	Number of species evaluated	Number of threatened species in 2004	Number threatened as % of species described
Bataguridae	69	57	42	61%
Carettochelyidae	1	1	1	100%
Chelidae	51	27	13	25%
Cheloniidae	6	6	5	83%
Chelydridae	3	2	2	67%
Dermatemydidae	1	1	1	100%
Dermochelyidae	1	1	1	100%
Emydidae	41	28	13	32%
Kinosternidae	25	10	4	16%
Pelomedusidae	18	6	1	6%
Podocnemididae	8	7	6	75%
Testudinidae	51	38	25	49%
Trionychidae	30	21	14	47%
Total	305	205	128	42%

*Bataguridae (Asian river turtles, leaf and roofed turtles, Asian box turtles), Carettochelyidae (pignose yurtles), Chelidae (Austro-American sideneck turtles), Cheloniidae (sea turtles), Chelydridae (snapping turtles), Dermatemydidae (river turtles), Dermochelyidae (leather-back turtles), Emydidae (pond turtles/box and water Turtles), Kinosternidae (mud and musk turtles), Pelomedusidae (Afro-American sideneck turtles), Podocnemididae (Madagascan big-headed and American sideneck river turtles), Testudinae (tortoises), Trionychidae (softshell turtles).

Source: Family names and numbers of described species are from the EMBL Reptile Database compiled by Peter Uetz: http://www.embl-heidelberg.de/~uetz/LivingReptiles.html.

The turtle families completely assessed include the two marine turtle groups, Cheloniidae and Dermochelyidae, with six of the seven species listed as threatened. Other speciose turtle families with high numbers of threatened species include the Bataguridae, Chelidae, Emydidae, Kinosternidae and Trionychidae (see Table).

Freshwater turtles are being heavily exploited for food, and in some cases medicine, and the harvest levels are highly unsustainable, and unregulated. As populations are disappearing in Southeast Asia, there are disturbing signs that the focus of the harvest will shift to the Indian Subcontinent, and perhaps even further afield to the Americas and Africa. The tortoises are impacted by collection for the pet trade.

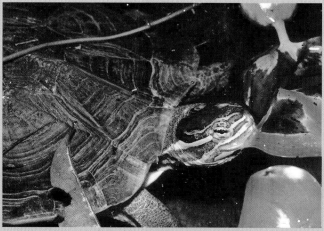

Photo: © Peter Paul van Dijk

Photo 2.14
The Annamese Pond Turtle *Mauremys annamensis* (Critically Endangered) is known only from a small area of central Viet Nam, where its exact habitat remains undiscovered. It is threatened by intensive collection to supply the Asian turtle consumption trade, the pet trade and by habitat degradation. The species does well in captivity and re-introduction may be feasible in the future.

Photo: © Sterling Zumbrunn

Photo: © John E. Randall

Photo 2.16
Nassau Grouper *Epinephelus striatus* (Endangered) is found from Bermuda and Florida throughout the Bahamas and Caribbean Sea. The species is fished commercially and recreationally, with much of the catch coming from spawning aggregations.

Photo 2.15
The Pacific Seahorse *Hippocampus ingens* (Vulnerable) is traded for traditional medicine, curios and aquaria, and is incidentally caught as bycatch by fisheries along the Pacific coast of Central and South America.

Photo: © Tim Allen

Photo 2.17
Yellow-crowned Butterflyfish *Chaetodon flavocoronatus* (Vulnerable) is endemic to the Mariana Islands. This relatively rare species appears irregularly in the aquarium trade. Little is known about its biology.

2.3.1.3 Fishes

Just over 6% of the world's fish species have been evaluated for the *IUCN Red List* (Tables 2.1 and 2.2). Of the species evaluated, 487 are considered to be purely marine, 1,139 are confined to inland water systems (mainly freshwater) and 96 occur in both marine and inland water systems.

Because marine species have long been considered resilient to extinction, they have, until recently been neglected by extinction risk assessments (but see Boxes 3.8, 4.2 and 6.1). The *IUCN Red List* includes 131 threatened marine fish species. Amongst the species included are the seahorses and pipefishes (Syngnathidae), groupers (Sarranidae), wrasses (Labridae), damselfishes (Pomacentridae), angelfishes (Pomacanthidae) and the chondrichthyan fishes (sharks, skates and rays). While a number of these species are restricted-range coral reef fishes, some are widespread, commercially valuable species subject to fisheries. As there are so few marine fishes on the *IUCN Red List* it is premature to analyse the information any further. However, Box 2.3 on the chondrichthyan fishes illustrates some of the issues and the extent to which some marine species are threatened.

Box 2.3

Disappearing from the Depths: Sharks on the Red List

Early days in the global assessment of chondrichthyan fishes (sharks, rays and chimaeras) lists 18% as threatened
The slow life histories and low population growth rates of sharks, skates, rays and chimaeras limits their capacity to withstand over-fishing and habitat destruction (Fowler *et al.* in press). To date, the IUCN/SSC Shark Specialist Group (SSG) has assessed one third (373 species) of the world's chondrichthyans (out of a total of approximately 1,100 species) and 17.7% are listed as threatened (Critically Endangered, Endangered or Vulnerable), 18.8% Near Threatened, 37.5% Data Deficient and 25.7% Least Concern (see Box 8.10 on the Whiskery Shark). Restricted-range species occupying heavily fished areas, such as sawfishes and deep-sea dogfishes, typify some of the more seriously threatened species. Least Concern species share a number of features; they are abundant

continued overleaf...

21

Box 2.3 *continued*

and/or widespread, occur in protected areas or areas with limited fishing, are not particularly susceptible to fisheries or are taken by well-managed fisheries. The SSG aims to have all the species assessed by 2006.

All seven species of sawfishes (Pristidae) are listed as Critically Endangered or Endangered

Sawfishes inhabit coastal tropical, subtropical and warm-temperate regions, often in estuaries and freshwater. Their unique 'saw' - a long rostrum studded with 'teeth' - makes them extremely vulnerable to capture in nets, and difficult to remove alive. With highly priced fins and 'saws', some fisheries target these species, but most mortality is as bycatch of other fisheries, compounded by the effects of extensive coastal development. While both the United States and Australia are working on recovery of their populations, an international programme is needed to address species elsewhere in the world.

Photo: © R. Mitchell

Photo 2.18
A juvenile Largetooth Sawfish *Pristis microdon* (Endangered) caught as part of a tag and release programme. The distinctive rostrum that gives the species its name is highly sought after, but is also often responsible for the species becoming entangled in fishing nets as bycatch. It is a wide-ranging Indo-west Pacific species.

Deepwater species are highly threatened

Lack of information from the little-studied depths has resulted in many deep-sea sharks (>50%) being listed as Data Deficient. Where information is available, species have undergone rapid declines in abundance. Severely threatened species include the Australian endemic species, Harrisson's Dogfish *Centrophorus harrissoni* and the Southern Dogfish *C. uyato* with declines of >99% in two decades due to commercial fishing (Cavanagh *et al.* 2003; Graham *et al.* 2001). Deep-sea data collection is challenging, and the SSG is encouraging the precautionary approach to management as a matter of urgency.

Regional Red List workshops are facilitating comparisons around the world.

For example, the assessment for the Tope Shark *Galeorhinus galeus* lists it as Endangered (South America), Vulnerable (southern Australia), and Near Threatened (New Zealand and southern Africa). This species has valuable flesh, but it has particularly low biological productivity, and comparing the situation across regions demonstrates how inadequately managed species can be severely depleted. Four species of guitarfishes (Rhinidae and Rhynchobatidae) - the fins of which are among the most valuable in the world - have been listed as threatened due to high levels of exploitation and evidence of local population depletions in some regions.

Assessing skates

Work on the flat, winged chondrichthyans – the skates and rays – has started. A workshop to assess the skates (Rajidae) was held in September 2004 in Cape Town, South Africa. Skates comprise a quarter of all chondrichthyans and many have restricted geographic ranges and are potentially highly vulnerable to overexploitation (Dulvy and Reynolds 2002). Skates typify the problems we have assessing chondrichthyans - lack of species-specific data in many regions, taxonomic difficulties, and poor knowledge of distributions and exploitation patterns.

For further information visit the SSG website: http://www.flmnh.ufl.edu/fish/organizations/ssg/ssg.htm

Based on information provided by Rachel Cavanagh and Nicholas Dulvy (IUCN/SSC Shark Specialist Group)

For freshwater fish species, because many more have been evaluated, it is not surprising that the number listed as threatened (631 purely freshwater species or 670 that occur in both freshwater and marine) is much higher than for the marine fish. However, the species evaluated are a biased sample as they tend to come from discrete geographic areas: the East African Great Lakes; western Europe; Madagascar; Mexico; South Africa; and the United States. As with the marine species it is premature to analyse these data. However, some of the issues and an indication of the degree of threat faced by freshwater species are presented by means of a case study from East Africa (Box 2.4).

Photo: © Paul Loiselle

Photo 2.19
Damba Mipentina *Paretroplus maculatus* (Critically Endangered) endemic to Madagascar, has undergone severe declines due to severe fishing pressure, impact of introduced inavsive species, and habitat destruction.

This East African case study indicates that 27% of the freshwater fishes evaluated in that region are listed as threatened. This figure is comparable to that for North America (United States and Canada) where a recent analysis by NatureServe of the status of 801 species of freshwater fish indicated that 20% are threatened (based on the NatureServe Global Heritage Ranks of G1 – Critically Imperilled and G2 – Imperilled; L. Master pers. comm.; see Box 3.7). It is highly probable that increased attention on freshwater fish species by the SSC over the next few years will confirm a global crisis among these species.

Freshwater Species Assessments in Eastern Africa

The SSC is currently conducting global and regional assessments of entire taxonomic groups (see Appendix 1). This case study outlines some benefits of this approach and highlights the danger of extrapolating from assessments based on sub-samples to provide estimates for the threatened status of entire taxonomic groups. The danger arises from the likely bias in those species currently assessed for the Red List. Very often species assessed may be those *a priori* thought to be threatened, those species for which there are abundant data, and species in those geographic areas where research has been more active. The geographic bias is particularly clear for freshwater dependant taxa with an estimated 29% of species on the 2003 *IUCN Red List* coming from North America. An additional source of bias comes from the under-reporting of Least Concern species making it difficult to know the true proportion of species threatened. These sources of bias can be eliminated when complete taxonomic groups are assessed either at the global or regional scale.

The first regional assessment of freshwater dependant taxa was completed in 2004 in East Africa. The Red List status was assessed for a large majority of the freshwater fishes, molluscs, crabs and Odonata (dragonflies and damselflies) (in total 1,700 taxa were assessed). A summary of the preliminary results demonstrates the disparity in the perceived levels of threat to these taxonomic groups before and after the assessment (Figure Box 2.4.1). For fish, molluscs and Odonata, the number of species assessed increased dramatically, but the percentage of threatened species declined.

Focusing on freshwater fish, it is apparent that previous assessments targeted the Lake Victoria fish community following the apparent large-scale decline and loss of many cichlid species due to the combined impacts of invasive species, eutrophication and possibly over-fishing. From Figure Box 2.4.1 it is evident that this picture is not representative of the status of fish in other parts of the region. It should be noted though that, given the high levels of endemism in the Rift Valley lakes, a similar catastrophe could arise elsewhere within the region if the appropriate conservation measures are not put in place.

continued overleaf...

Box 2.4 *continued*

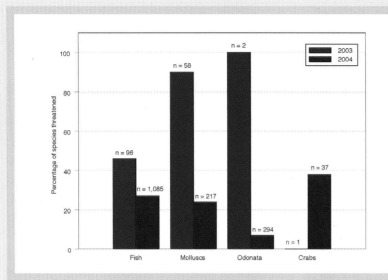

Figure Box 2.4.1
Percentages and numbers of taxa assessed as threatened in the 2003 *IUCN Red List* and in the more recent East Africa assessment (including regional assessments) in 2004

Assessments of threatened status combined with species distribution maps for extent of occurrence provide a useful tool to identify areas with high numbers of threatened species within the region (see Figure Box 2.4.2). Similar analyses can be employed to identify centres of species richness and of restricted range species (see Section 5).

Such outputs provide useful tools to assist in regional prioritization for conservation funding and site-based conservation actions. This approach can also be scaled down to the river basin level, providing biodiversity information to guide both the site selection of water development projects, and the minimization or mitigation of any subsequent impacts. The assessment also provides an essential baseline for long-term monitoring purposes.

An additional benefit of the regional approach is increased regional capacity for biodiversity assessment through training in assessment tools such as for the Red List, and through direct involvement of regional scientists in the assessment process. Forty eight regional scientists and decision makers were involved in this particular project.

Multi-taxonomic regional assessments not only provide a more realistic picture of the threatened status of taxonomic groups but through assessment of taxa from a range of trophic levels, they can provide a more holistic picture of biodiversity status within an ecosystem.

Based on information provided by William Darwall, IUCN Freshwater Biodiversity Assessment Programme

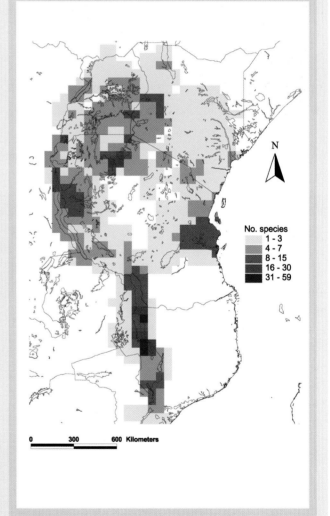

Figure Box 2.4.2
Preliminary map showing density of threatened fish species in East Africa

2.3.2 Threatened Invertebrates

Despite the apparently large numbers of evaluated (3,487 species) and threatened (1,992 species) invertebrates on the *IUCN Red List*, these numbers are proportionally extremely small when one considers that 95% of all known animals are invertebrates (Hammond 1995). Less than 0.3% of invertebrates are known to have been evaluated, but there is significant under-reporting of Least Concern species, and hence any analysis of the numbers threatened would be misleading (see Tables 2.1 and 2.2). Among those invertebrates that have received the most attention there are some groups with apparently large numbers of threatened species, including 429 primarily inland water crustaceans, 559 insects (mainly butterflies, dragonflies and damselflies), and 974 molluscs (predominantly terrestrial and freshwater species).

The need for a stronger focus on the invertebrate groups has long been recognized, and the SSC is developing a strategy to address this problem (see Appendix 1). In the interim, the list of evaluated invertebrates is slowly increasing, with the most significant changes taking place among the molluscs. Less than five per cent of molluscs have been evaluated and these assessments have largely been confined to terrestrial and freshwater species. The majority of the assessments relate to the better-known regions such as North America, Europe, Australia, as well as recognized areas of endemism on islands.

The East African case study (Box 2.4) includes three freshwater invertebrate groups, the crustaceans, molluscs, and Odonata (dragonflies and damselflies). Based on the species evaluated, 7% of Odonata, 23% of molluscs and 38% of the crabs were listed as threatened. A more comprehensive regional survey of the status of invertebrates has been conducted in North America (Canada and United States), the results of which are presented as a case study (Box 2.5).

Photos: © Dai G. Herbert

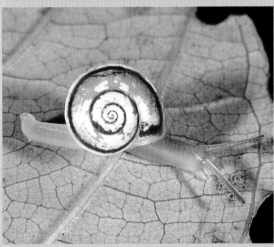

Photos 2.20, 2.21 and 2.22 (top to bottom) South Africa is home to some remarkable threatened molluscs, for example: **Photo 2.20** the Dlinza Forest Pinwheel *Trachycystis clifdeni* (Critically Endangered); **Photo 2.21** Purcell's Hunter Slug *Laevicaulis haroldi* (Endangered); and **Photo 2.22** *T. haygarthi* (Endangered). Many of these species have highly restricted distributions and are therefore sensitive to any habitat disturbance. .

Box 2.5

Threatened North American Invertebrates

The proportion of threatened North American (excluding Hawaii) invertebrates varies considerably across taxonomic groups, with butterflies, dragonflies, moths and tiger beetles being those least threatened, while the freshwater mussels, snails, crayfishes and grasshoppers are amongst those most threatened. Almost one-third (29%) of the world's known freshwater mussel species occur in North America (Stein *et al.* 2000), hence the 41% listed as threatened in this region has global significance. The most threatened invertebrates in North America are what are termed 'cave obligates'; these include terrestrial species known as troglobites and subterranean aquatic species known as stygobites. Most of these invertebrates are flatworms, arachnids, insects, crustaceans and segmented worms. These obligate cave dwellers are characterized by extreme rarity and endemism, with many species known only from a single location (Stein *et al.* 2000). Most cave obligates are yet to be described, hence only about 15% of the possible 6,000 species found in North America have been evaluated. The obligate cave dwellers are all from groups that are poorly represented on the *IUCN Red List*, and are clearly a component of the invertebrate fauna that requires closer attention worldwide.

A study factoring in the described but unassessed species (Master and Wilcove in prep.) indicates that the actual number of threatened invertebrates in North America is conservatively at least five times that shown in the table below (L. Master pers. comm.).

Photo: © Wendell R. Haag.

Photo 2.23
The Fine-lined Pocketbook *Lampsilis altilis* (Endangered) is an example of a freshwater mussel endemic to the United States. The species is found at sites in five river drainages in Alabama. It has been eliminated from most of its range through habitat modification, sedimentation, and degradation of water quality.

Table Box 2.5

Numbers of threatened North American invertebrates

Invertebrate group	Number of species evaluated	Number of threatened species in 2004*	% threatened
Freshwater mussels	306	126	41%
Snails (land and freshwater)	1,669	943	57%
Crayfishes	340	111	33%
Fairy, clam, and tadpole shrimps	79	13	16%
Butterflies and skippers	634	43	7%
Tiger beetles	104	9	9%
Stoneflies	629	119	19%
Mayflies	596	130	22%
Grasshoppers	749	229	31%
Dragonflies and damselflies	463	37	8%
Four moth groups (Saturniidae, Sphingidae, *Papaipema*, *Catocala*)	270	21	8%
Cave obligates (not snails or crayfishes)	896	735	82%
Invertebrates total	6,735	2,516	37%

* The numbers threatened are based on the Global Heritage Ranks of G1 (Critically Imperilled) and G2 (Imperilled).
Data Source: NatureServe analysis (September 2004).

Based on information provided by Larry Master, NatureServe

2.4 How Many Threatened Plants are There?

The 2004 *IUCN Red List* includes assessments for 11,824 species of plants, 8,321 of which are listed as threatened (Table 2.3). However, only just over 4% of described plant species (see comments under section 2.2 about the debate on the number of species) have been evaluated, and almost 3% of these are threatened (see Table 2.1).

In considering the numbers of threatened plants it is important to take into account the 33,798 species listed as threatened and extinct in the *1997 IUCN Red List of Threatened Plants*; almost 13% of the world's flora at that time (Walter and Gillett 1998). The 1997 Red List was compiled from a database containing information on 139,719 plant taxa (including subspecies, varieties and synonyms). Determining exactly how many species were evaluated for that Red List is difficult, but it is known that 14,861 of these species were not synonyms, were threatened in at least one country, but were not considered to be globally threatened (H. Gillett pers. comm.). Hence the number evaluated for the 1997 Red List probably exceeds 48,659 species. Although an incomplete sample of the global flora, and despite geographic biases (91% of the species listed are single-country endemics, with the largest numbers in Australia, South Africa and the United States), the 1997 Plants Red List stands as the single largest compilation of information on the conservation status of any taxonomic group.

The assessments for the 1997 Plants Red List were done using the pre-1994 qualitative Red List Categories. That system is not strictly comparable to either the 1994 or 2001 versions of the IUCN Red List Categories and Criteria (IUCN 1994a, 2001). Hence the 1997 results are not incorporated into this analysis, but they are used for illustrative purposes.

Since the amalgamation of the plant and animal Red Lists in the *2000 IUCN Red List of Threatened Species*™ the number of plant assessments has steadily increased (Table 2.1 and Appendix 3a). Of the 11,824 plants evaluated, 70% (8,321 species) are listed as threatened (Tables 2.1 and 2.3). This partially reflects a bias amongst the botanical community to focus primarily on the threatened species, but there is also a tendency to under-report Least Concern assessments. The focus on threatened species is clearly illustrated by the assessments of bryophytes (mosses, liverworts and hornworts) in Table 2.3, where the subset of 93 species was specifically chosen in order to "provide the

Table 2.3 Summary of Red List Category classifications by class of plants

Class*	EX	EW	Subtotal	CR	EN	VU	Subtotal	LR/cd	NT	DD	LC	Total
Bryopsida	2	0	2	10	15	11	36	0	0	0	1	39
Anthocerotopsida	0	0	0	0	1	1	2	0	0	0	0	2
Marchantiopsida	1	0	1	12	16	14	42	0	0	0	9	52
Lycopodiopsida	0	0	0	1	2	8	11	0	1	0	1	13
Sellaginellopsida	0	0	0	0	0	1	1	0	1	0	0	2
Isoetopsida	0	0	0	2	0	1	3	0	0	0	0	3
Polypodiopsida	3	0	3	29	36	60	125	0	12	45	7	192
Coniferopsida	0	0	0	17	43	93	153	26	53	59	327	618
Cycadopsida	0	2	2	47	39	65	151	0	67	18	50	288
Ginkgoopsida	0	0	0	0	1	0	1	0	0	0	0	1
Magnoliopsida	78	20	98	1,228	1,825	3,972	7,025	196	807	439	908	9,473
Liliopsida	2	2	4	144	261	366	771	17	107	137	105	1,141
Total	86	24	110	1,490	2,239	4,592	8,321	239	1,048	698	1,408	11,824

*Bryopsida (true mosses), Anthocerotopsida (hornworts), Marchantiopsida (liverworts), Lycopodiopsida (club mosses), Sellaginellopsida (spike mosses), Isoetopsida (quillworts), Polypodiopsida (true ferns), Coniferopsida (conifers), Cycadopsida (cycads), Ginkgoopsida (ginkgo), Magnoliopsida (dicotyledons), Liliopsida (monocotyledons).

IUCN Red List Categories: EX – Extinct, **EW** – Extinct in the Wild, **CR** – Critically Endangered, **EN** – Endangered, **VU** – Vulnerable, **LR/cd** – Lower Risk/conservation dependent, **NT** – Near Threatened (includes LR/nt – Lower Risk/near threatened), DD – Data Deficient, LC – Least Concern (includes LR/lc – Lower Risk/least concern). Note: the numbers for Not Evaluated (**NE**) are not presented.

public with general information as to which bryophytes are threatened with extinction" (Tan *et al.* 2000). The same is partly true of the assessments for ferns and fern allies (includes club mosses, spike mosses, quillworts and true ferns), but in this case the 210 species evaluated (although only 1% of the species) represent a widely distributed geographic sample and so might be more representative of the threats faced by this plant group. Certainly the figures of 15% Critically Endangered and 18% Endangered (see Table 2.3) may well be indicative of the degree of threat faced by this plant group.

A strong bias in the plant assessments in the 2000 *IUCN Red List* was towards threatened tree species because of the inclusion of the 7,388 species (includes species in all categories from Data Deficient to Extinct) listed in *The World List of Threatened Trees* (Oldfield *et al.* 1998). That bias has been slightly reduced through the inclusion of non-tree assessments. However, the trees are still dominant with 7,996 species (68%) included on the 2004 *IUCN Red List*, 5,637 of which are listed as threatened. Many of the recent plant assessments have, however, introduced a geographic bias as they are single country or sub-country endemics (e.g., Cameroon, China, Ecuador, Madagascar, Mauritius, Namibia, Saint Helena, South Africa, Yemen (Soqotra), and the United States (Hawaii)).

As with the invertebrates, the seemingly very large figure of 8,321 threatened plant species is proportionally very small relative to the total number of plant species worldwide (see Table 2.1). The proportion threatened may well be even smaller if the estimated higher numbers of seed plants is shown to be correct (1.84% versus 2.89%). It is therefore premature at this stage to attempt any detailed analysis of the plants as the low numbers evaluated and the strong biases towards trees and certain geographic areas misrepresents the overall picture for plants. For further details on the numbers of plants in each category, see Tables 2.1 and 2.3, and the detailed order and family results in the Summary Statistics tables on the Red List web site (www.iucnredlist.org).

Despite the low numbers evaluated and the biases, some trends are evident for plants. Two classes of plants have been fully evaluated, namely the cycads and the conifers (with the exception of two species of conifer). Whether these gymnosperm groups are representative of what is happening to plants generally is debatable. However, both are relatively ancient lineages and clearly illustrate very different threats and trends (see Figures 2.6a and b). Although there are almost equal numbers of threatened conifers and cycads

Photo: © Henk Beentje

Photo 2.24
Ossiculum aurantiacum (Critically Endangered) is a highly attractive epiphytic orchid endemic to the Cameroon. It has not been seen again in the wild since it was first collected in 1980, despite intensive searching in the area.

Photo: © Vickie L. Caraway

Photo 2.25
Maui *Hesperomannia arbuscula* (Critically Endangered) is a small shrubby tree known only from the Hawaiian Islands of Maui and Oahu. Main threats are habitat degradation by pigs, competition with alien plant species, predation by rats, and from trampling or collecting by humans.

Photo: © Colin Clubbe

Photo 2.26
The Pokemeboy *Acacia anegadensis* (Critically Endangered) is endemic to Anegada, British Virgin Islands. Few mature trees now survive because of past exploitation for resin from these trees.

(153 and 151 respectively), the proportion of cycads that are threatened is considerably higher. For the conifers, 25% of the species are listed as threatened (17 Critically Endangered, 43 Endangered and 93 Vulnerable). The *1997 IUCN Red List of Threatened Plants* (Walter and Gillett 1998) lists 30% of conifers in the old Endangered (E) and Vulnerable (V) categories. For cycads, 52% of the species are listed as threatened (47 Critically Endangered, 39 Endangered and 65 Vulnerable). In addition, a further 23% of cycad species are considered Near Threatened. The cycads are listed as threatened because they have small and declining populations and/or small ranges. At present the cycads are the most threatened plant group known, and are one of the most threatened taxonomic groups on the Red List. As with many of the threatened vertebrates, the conifers and cycads are unique phylogenetic lineages indicating that perhaps non-random extinction (as demonstrated for the mammals, birds and amphibians in section 2.3.1.1) is also happening in the plant kingdom. The cycads in particular are a unique lineage of plants that survived the last extinction spasm and which are now facing imminent extinction in the wild as a direct result of human activities.

Photo: © Craig Hilton-Taylor

Photo 2.28
The Drakensberg Cycad *Encephalartos ghellinckii* (Vulnerable) although well-protected in the northern parts of its range in KwaZulu-Natal, South Africa, has suffered declines in the southern parts of its range due to human exploitation for the horticultural market.

Photo: Cristian Echeverria

Photo 2.27
The Monkey Puzzle *Araucaria araucana* (Vulnerable) ranges from the Coastal Cordillera of Chile to the Andes in Argentina. The timber is widely used and many trees are illegally felled.

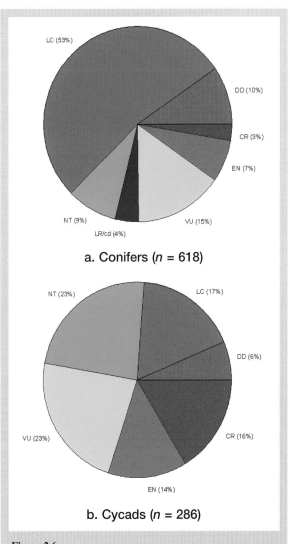

a. Conifers (*n* = 618)

b. Cycads (*n* = 286)

Figure 2.6
Percentages of extant species in each Red List Category for conifers and cycads. The pie charts exclude the categories Extinct, Extinct in the Wild and Not Evaluated.

Box 2.6

A Comparison between the Threatened Plants of Mainland Ecuador and the Island of Soqotra (Yemen)

Mainland Ecuador

Ecuador is a small but highly diverse country with a unique flora. It falls within one of the recognized tropical hotspots of biodiversity, having a flora of approximately 15,492 native species, 26% of which (4,011 species) are considered to be endemic (Valencia *et al.* 2000). In 2000 the first of a series of reports on the conservation status of Ecuador's endemic plants was published (Valencia *et al.* 2000). For this report the conservation status of 3,825 of the 4,011 endemics were evaluated using the IUCN Red List Categories and Criteria (IUCN 2001). To-date, some 2,159 species (56% of those evaluated) have been incorporated into the *IUCN Red List*. The remaining 1,666 species, primarily orchids and species endemic to the Galapago, will be incorporated in future updates.

Valencia *et al.* (2000) list 2,884 mainland Ecuadorian endemics as threatened (268 Critically Endangered, 823 Endangered and 1,793 Vulnerable). In other words 72% of the endemics and 19% of the total native flora is threatened. With such a high proportion listed as threatened it is surprising that none were listed as Extinct in mainland Ecuador. It is believed that 53 species are possibly extinct, but surveys are required to confirm this. In addition to the threatened species, 385 mainland endemics are listed as Near Threatened, 297 as Data Deficient and only 160 as Least Concern.

Soqotra Archipalago

The floras of oceanic islands are often particularly rich in species and show a high degree of endemism. The archipelago of Soqotra (located between the Horn of Africa and the Arabian Peninsula) with a dry tropical flora is no exception. It has one of the richest island floras in the world - on a par with those of the Galapagos, Mauritius, Juan Fernandez and the Canary Islands. The flora comprises 825 native flowering plant species, 306 of which are endemic. Many of the endemics are remnants of ancient floras that disappeared long ago from the African and Arabian mainlands. They create unusual vegetation formations and make the archipelago the world's tenth richest island group for endemic plant species.

All of the Soqotran endemics have been evaluated, and all except one (a Least Concern species) are on the 2004 *IUCN Red List*. Three of the endemics are listed as Critically Endangered, 26 as Endangered and 120 as Vulnerable, giving a total of 149 threatened species. Hence 49% of the endemics and 18% of the native flora are threatened. Three species are listed as Extinct, 14 are Near Threatened, 27 are Data Deficient and 112 are Least Concern.

Photo: © Suzanna León-Yánez

Photo 2.29
Centropogon erythraeus (Endangered) is an endemic shrub from Ecuador where it is known from two subpopulations in the southern Andes.

Photo: © Anthony G. Miller.

Photo 2.30
The Pomegranate Tree *Punica protopunica* (Vulnerable), a close relative of the cultivated pomegranate, is endemic to Soqotra. Although the population is apparently stable at present it has evidently declined in the past, for reasons that are not certain.

Based on information provided by Nigel Pitman and Tony Miller

The proportions of threatened monocotyledons (Liliopsida) and dicotyledons (Magnoliopsida) are very similar (Table 2.3). However, it is clear that the 10,614 flowering plants that have been evaluated so far are very much a biased sample towards those that are more threatened. Interestingly though, the families that emerge as having the most threatened species are also some of the most speciose and cosmopolitan e.g., Araceae (118); Compositae (324); Dipterocarpaceae (369); Euphorbiaceae (359); Gramineae (64); Leguminosae (589); Orchidaceae (146); Palmae (238 species); and Rubiaceae (369). These families include many plants of major economic importance as food crops, sources of timber and building materials, medicines, and as ornamentals. The loss of these plant species will have major socio-economic implications in the future.

There is much debate about the size of the world's threatened flora. Pitman and Jørgensen (2002) consider the commonly cited figure of 13% (derived from Walter and Gillett 1998) too low and suggest that the true figure may be closer to 50% of all known plants. Bramwell (2003) argues that a figure of 50% exaggerates the scale of potential plant extinction, and that the true figure is probably about 21%. A case study comparing comprehensive assessments of plants endemic to two areas, namely mainland Ecuador - a biodiversity hotspot (Myers *et al.* 2000) and the islands of Soqotra - a recognized Center of Plant Diversity (Miller and Guarino 1994), is presented (Box 2.6). In both instances the percentage of the total flora threatened is 18-19%, figures very close to the estimate proposed by Bramwell (2003).

The SSC has an ambitious programme to increase the coverage of plants on the *IUCN Red List* over the next few years, as it strives to meet the 2010 CBD target of obtaining a preliminary conservation assessment of the world's described plant species (see Appendix 1). As the assessments increase it will be interesting to determine whether or not the patterns observed in mainland Ecuador and in Soqotra are repeated elsewhere in the world.

2.5 Other Taxonomic Groups

The fungi, lichens and the seaweeds (red algae) have traditionally been considered members of the plant kingdom, but are now treated under separate kingdoms. These taxonomic groups have not been the focus for any Red List activity; however, there are probably many species in these groups that are facing extinction. In 2003, three species from these groups were evaluated and entered into the *IUCN Red List* for the first time, thereby expanding the Red List coverage to four kingdoms. These were two threatened lichens and an Extinct red alga from Australia (Table 2.4; see also Box 3.5). While these species pose particular challenges on how to apply the Red List Criteria, it is hoped that this small start will lead to a greater focus on these neglected but important organisms.

Key Findings

- **15,589 species are threatened with extinction. This includes 12% of all bird species, 23% of mammals evaluated, 32% of all amphibians, and 31% of all gymnosperms.**

- **Although a significant proportion of the world's biodiversity faces extinction, it is not possible to quantify how many species are at risk because we have not yet named all the species, the baseline checklists are constantly changing, and we have yet to assess the bulk of the world's species.**

- **The risk of extinction is best known for the vertebrates, in particular the amphibians, birds and mammals.**

Table 2.4 Summary of Red List Category classifications by class of other organisms

Class*	EX	EW	Subtotal	CR	EN	VU	Subtotal	LR/cd	NT	DD	LC	Total
Lecanoromycetes	0	0	**0**	1	1	0	**2**	0	0	0	0	**2**
Rhodophyceae	1	0	**1**	0	0	0	**0**	0	0	0	0	**1**
Total	1	0	**1**	1	1	0	**2**	0	0	0	0	**3**

*Lecanoromyctes (discolichens), Rhodophyceae (red algae)

IUCN Red List Categories: EX – Extinct, **EW** – Extinct in the Wild, **CR** – Critically Endangered, **EN** – Endangered, **VU** – Vulnerable, **LR/cd** – Lower Risk/conservation dependent, **NT** – Near Threatened (includes LR/nt – Lower Risk/near threatened), DD – Data Deficient, LC – Least Concern (includes LR/lc – Lower Risk/least concern). Note: the numbers for Not Evaluated (**NE**) are not presented.

- The numbers of threatened species are increasing across virtually all the major taxonomic groups.

- Amphibians have been completely assessed for the first time, and have a higher percentage of threatened species, particularly Critically Endangered ones, than either the birds or the mammals.

- The extinction risk for amphibians may be under-estimated as 23% of them are listed as Data Deficient.

- Threatened species are not randomly distributed across orders and families. A number of families have significantly more threatened species than would be expected on average, while others have far less. The non-random distribution means that entire evolutionary clades are liable to go extinct very quickly.

- While reptiles are generally under-represented on the *IUCN Red List*, the turtles and tortoises are relatively well represented with 42% threatened with extinction.

- The increasing number of sharks, rays and chimaeras on the Red List demonstrates that these marine species might be as threatened as some terrestrial groups, especially because of their slow life histories, low population growth rates and their inability to withstand the increasing fishing pressures around the world.

- A freshwater case study from East Africa shows the value of multi-taxa regional assessments for conservation planning and provides an insight about the degree of threat faced by freshwater species.

- Invertebrates are poorly represented on the Red List, with assessments confined to the better-known groups such as butterflies, inland water crustaceans, dragonflies and molluscs. A case study from the United States indicates that some invertebrate groups are likely to be highly threatened globally.

- Plants are also poorly represented on the Red List, despite being the taxonomic group with the largest numbers evaluated.

- Two classes of plants have been completely assessed, the conifers and the cycads. The cycads are one of the most threatened groups of species on the Red List with 52% listed as threatened.

- A case-study comparing evaluations of all endemic plants from mainland Ecuador and the island group of Soqotra, supports the argument that approximately 21% of the world's flora may be threatened.

- The *IUCN Red List* now includes three representatives from two other kingdoms – the Protista and the Fungi.

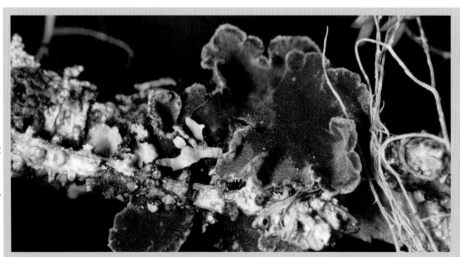

Photo 2.31
The Boreal Felt Lichen *Erioderma pedicellatum* (Critically Endangered) is one of only two species of fungi on the *IUCN Red List*. This lichen has completely disappeared from New Brunswick (Canada), Norway and Sweden. The only remaining populations are in Nova Scotia and Newfoundland, Canada. Major threats are habitat destruction through logging and air pollution.

Extinctions in Recent Time

Photo: © Michael and Patricia Fogden.

Photo 3.1

The Golden Toad *Bufo periglenes* (Extinct) has become the flagship species of the amphibian decline phenomenon. This photo of males congregating at a breeding pool in the Monteverde Cloud Forest in Costa Rica gives an indication of its former abundance within its tiny range. It last bred in normal numbers in 1987. In 1988, only eight males and two females could be located. In 1989, a single male was found, this being the last record of the species.

3.1 Introduction

The global extinction of a species usually represents an end point in a long series of population extinctions. During this process of extinction unique evolutionary history is lost at every stage, but the death of the last individual of a species represents the permanent and irreversible loss of one of life's unique evolutionary and functional forms. Creating an inventory of recent extinctions helps to highlight the long list of unique species that have been lost forever. Understanding the extent of recent extinctions provides insight into historic extinction rates, which in turn can be compared to the rates over geological time to determine if current trends are normal or a cause for concern. An insight into the process of extinction can help us to identify species that are at risk of extinction and enable us to highlight taxonomic groups or species from specific regions that are or will be particularly prone to extinction. This section focuses on defining the extent of recent extinctions as well as identifying patterns of extinction. These patterns are discussed further in Section 6 where the dynamic process of extinction is addressed.

3.2 Current Extinctions

The *IUCN Red List* documents extinctions that have occurred on a global scale during historic times (for population extinctions see Box 3.1). A species qualifies for the IUCN Red List Category of Extinct (EX) when there is no reasonable doubt that the last individual has died (IUCN 2001, see Appendix 2a). At least 784 documented extinctions have occurred since 1500 AD, but this almost certainly represents a very small proportion of species that have become extinct during this time period. Many historic extinctions have either not been detected, or have taken place in taxonomic groups that have not yet been evaluated for the *IUCN Red List*.

Identifying the actual number of historic extinctions is difficult because only *c.* 1.9 million of the world's estimated 5 – 30 million species (see Erwin 1982; Hodkinson and Casson 1991; Novotny *et al.* 2002) have been described. Recent extinctions may be even more prevalent among undescribed species due to the sheer number and the fact that the discovery and description of species tends to be biased toward more broadly distributed and abundant taxa (see Collen *et al.* 2004).

Among the *c.* 1.9 million described species, only a few taxonomic groups have recently undergone thorough

Box 3.1

Population Extinction

While the focus of the *IUCN Red List* is on global extinctions, it is also important to consider all the population or local extinctions that occur on the path towards the final end point of a species. Significant biodiversity may be lost with the extinction of each population as they tend to carry unique genetic material and are often distinct in terms of morphology or behaviour. Population extinctions that are not followed by re-colonization also result in the loss of functional biodiversity, as the species no longer plays a functional role in the local ecosystem (such as decomposition or pollination). Such species are described as functionally or ecologically extinct. When species have been reduced to a fraction of their former range they become ecologically extinct on a global scale. Although the *IUCN Red List* captures some population extinctions during the documentation process, population extinctions are not specifically listed. This is because the quality and resolution of data required to assess populations simply does not exist for most species. However, as data quality improves, the documentation of population extinctions will play an increasingly important role in monitoring both biodiversity trends and ecosystem function.

conservation assessments to determine whether or not all taxa are still extant (see Table 2.1). The Global Amphibian Assessment is an example of where a recent assessment of all species has resulted in the listing of an additional 29 Extinct species. Similar assessments of large and poorly known groups such as insects, spiders, crustaceans, plants, fungi or species from poorly studied regions will undoubtedly result in significant increases in the list.

Even where assessments have been conducted it can take years or decades to prove that a species is truly Extinct. The basic paradox of "documenting" extinctions is that absence of evidence is not necessarily evidence of absence (Stine and Wagner in press). IUCN has begun to highlight species that are believed to be Extinct, but have not yet been included in the list because appropriate surveys are still required to confirm that the last individual has died (see Box 3.2). Systematically flagging these Possibly Extinct species will help to provide a much clearer picture of the true extent of recent extinctions.

Box 3.2

Critically Endangered (Possibly Extinct) Species

The Red List Programme is currently developing criteria for the identification of some Critically Endangered species as "Possibly Extinct" (see Appendix 2c for further details). For birds the tag of "Possibly Extinct" is applied to those species listed as Critically Endangered "which are, on the balance of evidence, likely to be Extinct, but for which there is a small chance that they may still be extant" (Butchart *et al.* in prep). For other taxa, the tag has been applied more generally to species that may possibly be Extinct. Listing species as Extinct when there is a chance that they are still extant can have significant conservation implications, because conservation funding is rarely targeted at species believed to be Extinct. It is therefore suitably precautionary to retain species in threatened categories if there is any reasonable possibility that they may still be extant. The "Possibly Extinct" tag has only been applied to amphibians and birds and a few representatives of other taxonomic groups and is therefore not indicative of the total number of CR (Possibly Extinct) species on the Red List. However, for amphibians and birds it provides a good indication of the number of extinctions that may be confirmed in the not too distant future. In total, 208 species have been identified as CR (Possibly Extinct), 122 of which are amphibians. Many of these amphibians have disappeared relatively rapidly and recently, including 18 species of harlequin toad in Central and South America from the genus *Atelopus*. Eighteen species of bird are CR (Possibly Extinct), including the Nukupu'u *Hemignathus lucidus* (last seen in Hawaii in 1996) and Spix's Macaw *Cyanopsitta spixii* (last seen in Brazil towards the end of 2000). Incomplete assessments of other groups such as mammals, reptiles, fishes, molluscs and plants account for the remaining 69 Possibly Extinct species.

The total number of extinctions listed by IUCN has increased from 766 in 2000 (Hilton-Taylor 2000) to 784 in 2004 (Table 3.1; Appendix 3i). However, because the documentation of the number of extinctions remains very incomplete, this increase does not provide much information on the rate at which extinctions are occurring, or the number of extinctions between 2000 and 2004. In fact all but one of the extinctions that have been added to the *IUCN Red List* in 2004 (the exception being the St. Helena Olive *Nesiota elliptica*, see Box 3.3) probably occurred before 2000. However, the new additions do highlight groups that have recently been investigated and have experienced significant numbers of extinctions. The taxonomic group with the largest increase in the number of documented extinctions is the amphibians with 29 additions. In the case of amphibians the increase of documented extinctions reflects both high rates of decline over the past 50 years (Houlahan *et al.* 2000; Alford *et al.* 2001) and a greater focus on the conservation status of this taxonomic group as a result of the Global Amphibian Assessment (see Appendix 1). Further information on amphibian extinctions is provided in Box 3.4. The 13 additional plant listings in the *IUCN Red List* (Appendix 3i) are primarily the result of recent work on the Hawaiian, Ascension and Soqotran islands. This represents just the beginning of a long documentation process of extensive island plant extinctions. A recent assessment of the Hawaiian flora alone regarded 82 species as presumed or possibly extinct (Wagner *et al.* 1999). Regardless of recent additions, we know that 85 plant extinctions is a gross under-representation, as many of the 380 species listed as Extinct in the *1997 IUCN Red List of Threatened Plants* (Walter and Gillett 1998) have not yet been added to the 2004 *IUCN Red List*. This is because new standards have been applied in the documentation process and many of the 1997 Extinct plant species are still under review (see Appendix 1). The addition of Bennett's Seaweed (*Vanvoorstia bennettiana*) represents an entirely new kingdom in the Red List (see Box 3.5).

Table 3.1

The numbers of Extinct (EX) and Extinct in the Wild (EW) species by taxonomic group in 2004

	2004		
	EX	EW	Total
Vertebrates			
Mammals	73	4	77
Birds	129	4	133
Reptiles	21	1	22
Amphibians	34	1	35
Fishes	81	12	93
Subtotal	**338**	**22**	**360**
Invertebrates			
Insects	59	1	60
Crustaceans	7	1	8
Molluscs	291	12	303
Others	2	0	2
Subtotal	**359**	**14**	**373**
Plants			
Mosses	3	0	3
Ferns and allies	3	0	3
Gymnosperms	0	2	2
Dicots	78	20	98
Monocots	2	2	4
Subtotal	**86**	**24**	**110**
Protista			
Red algae	1	0	1
Subtotal	**1**	**0**	**1**
Total	**784**	**60**	**844**

Box 3.3

The St. Helena Olive

The St. Helena Olive *Nesiota elliptica* (Rhamnaceae) was a small tree (up to 4 (perhaps as high as 7) m tall) that grew on the highest parts of the island's eastern central ridge. It became very rare in the 19th century, probably as a consequence of habitat loss, and by 1875 only 12 to 15 trees were recorded as growing on the northern side of Diana's Peak. It had been thought to have become Extinct until a single tree was discovered in August 1977. The tree was found to suffer from numerous systemic fungal infections, which may have been exacerbated by damage sustained during attempts to conserve it. It was found dead on 11 October 1994 and the species became Extinct in the Wild.

The St. Helena Olive continued to survive in cultivation, but ensuring its survival proved difficult, as cuttings were difficult to root (of hundreds attempted, success was only achieved with one). The species very rarely set good seed as it was 99% self-incompatible, and it was susceptible to fungal infections. The last seedling surviving showed signs of ill health due to fungal infections and in 2003 deteriorated extremely quickly following a dry winter. In December 2003, despite extensive efforts to rejuvenate the species, we witnessed the extinction of the St. Helena Olive.

Photo: © Rebecca Cairns-Wicks

Photo 3.2
The St. Helena Olive *Nesiota elliptica*.

Based on information provided by Rebecca Cairns-Wicks, IUCN/SSC South Atlantic Islands Plant Specialist Group

Box 3.4

The Discovery of Amphibian Extinctions

Until recently, there has been little focus on amphibian extinctions. Only 34 amphibian species are recorded as having become Extinct, 20 of these being endemics to Sri Lanka, most of which disappeared over 100 years ago. It is likely that there have been many undetected amphibian extinctions over the last two centuries, and the concentration in Sri Lanka, although real, is also a reflection of the detailed taxonomic studies of frogs that have taken place there. Nine of the 34 amphibian extinctions have taken place since about 1980, these being the species listed in Table 3.4, plus two others from northeastern Australia, the Southern Gastric Brooding Frog *Rheobatrachus silus* and the Southern Day Frog *Taudactylus diurnus*. Eight of these nine recent extinctions were sudden disappearances in suitable habitats, and are probably the result of the fungal disease, chytridiomycosis, probably operating in conjunction with climate change (Laurance *et al.* 1996; Berger *et al.* 1998; Ron *et al.* 2003; Burrowes *et al.* 2004).

However, these figures are probably a very large under-estimate of the level of amphibian extinctions since 1980. A total of 122 amphibian species are listed as Critically Endangered (Possibly Extinct), and 113 of these could have disappeared since 1980. Most of these took place in Central and South America, in particular from southern Mexico south to Ecuador, with others recorded from Puerto Rico, Hispaniola, Jamaica, Venezuela, and southern Brazil. Other possible extinctions have been noted in Australia, Indonesia, China, Kenya, and Tanzania. Most of the disappearances happened very suddenly, and it seems increasingly likely that chytridiomycosis, linked to climate change, is the main cause (see Section 6.5). Proving extinction beyond reasonable doubt is often very difficult. A few species that were thought to be Extinct were subsequently rediscovered in remnant populations. For example, *Atelopus cruciger* was not seen in its native Venezuela after 1986, until a tiny population was found in 2003 (Manzanilla and La Marca 2004). Thus, the true number of amphibian extinctions since 1980 is somewhere between nine and 122 species. These dramatic amphibian declines appear to be spreading, with recent reports from Dominica (Magin 2003), Spain (Bosch *et al.* 2001) and New Zealand (Bell *et al.* 2004).

The current catastrophic wave of amphibian extinctions is taking out major evolutionary lineages. Already, one entire family, the Gastric-brooding Frogs from Australia (Rheobatrachidae), has been lost, and another, the Darwin's Frogs from Chile and Argentina (Rhinodermatidae) is at severe risk, as are the primitive New Zealand Frogs (Leiopelmatidae). Among the larger families, the toads (Bufonidae) have been hit particularly

Photo: © Michael J. Tyler

Photo 3.3
The Southern Gastric-brooding Frog *Rheobatrachus silus* (Extinct) from northeastern Australia is one of only two members of the family Rheobatrachidae, both of which are now extinct. The name of this species comes from its breeding behaviour: the females brood the larvae in their stomachs, and they give birth to froglets through the mouth.

continued overleaf...

Box 3.4 *continued*

hard, most notably the beautiful harlequin toads (*Atelopus* spp.). Of 77 *Atelopus* species, three are Extinct (two since 1980), and 18 are Possibly Extinct (all since 1980). Amphibian extinctions are happening so rapidly, and so

few scientists are monitoring them that it is hard to gain a clear, current picture of their status. But the indications are that this is the most serious wave of all extinctions currently taking place.

Photo 3.4
Atelopus chiriquiensis (Critically Endangered), a species of harlequin toad, has, like other members of its genus, undergone a catastrophic decline, probably due to the fungal disease chytridiomycosis. The species occurred in the lower montane zone of Costa Rica and western Panama, but it is now believed to have disappeared from Costa Rica (last record in 1996), and might also have gone from Panama (last record in the late 1990s).

Based on information provided by Bruce Young and the contributors to the IUCN Global Amphibian Assessment

Box 3.5

Bennett's Seaweed

One addition to the Red List that deserves mention is a species of red algae, Bennett's Seaweed (*Vanvoorstia bennettiana*). It was only ever known from two sites in Australia: Spectacle Island in Parramatta River (New South Wales) in 1855; and the seabed between Point Piper and Shark Island in Port Jackson (Sydney Harbour) in 1886. No specimens have been recorded in the intervening 117 years despite numerous surveys and it has therefore been declared Extinct. This species is a member of the kingdom Protista (or Protoctista) which is a diverse assemblage that are united based on the lack of characteristics expressed in members of other kingdoms. They are defined as eukaryotic organisms that are distinct from plants, animals and fungi. It is unfortunate that the first, and so far only, representative of an entire kingdom enters the Red List as Extinct. However, this addition represents an important first attempt at documenting the extinction of smaller life forms that are fundamental to the survival of life on this planet.

Based on information provided by Alan J.K. Millar

Photo 3.5
Bennett's Seaweed *Vanvoorstia bennettiana*.

Although the numbers of recent extinctions are stable or increasing for most taxonomic groups, both mammals and insects show a decline in the number of recorded extinctions in the 2004 Red List (Appendix 3i). This is primarily because of taxonomic revision and the removal of erroneous listings (species previously listed that went extinct before 1500 AD) rather than the rediscovery of species declared as Extinct. Only one mammal, the Bavarian Pine Vole *Microtus bavaricus*, has been rediscovered over the past four years. It had not been seen since 1962, but a small population was found on the German-Austrian border in 2000. Other recent rediscoveries include: the New Zealand Storm Petrel *Oceanites maorianus*, a seabird rediscovered in 2003; Miller Lake Lamprey *Lampetra minima*, a fish endemic to a small area in Oregon, United States, and thought to have become Extinct in 1958, but its continued existence was confirmed after thorough surveys in the late 1990s; *Gulella thomasseti*, an endemic snail from the Seychelles rediscovered in August 2002; the Fabulous Green Sphinx Moth *Tinostoma smaragditis* from Hawaii, rediscovered in 1997 but only recently brought to the attention of the IUCN Red List office; the Pitt Island Longhorn Beetle *Xylotoles costatus*, rediscovered on South East Island in the Chatham Islands group; the Lord Howe Island Stick Insect *Dryococelus australis*, rediscovered in 2001 on Balls Pyramid, a rocky outcrop 23km from Lord Howe Island (Australia); and *Pittosporum tanianum*, a tree endemic to New Caledonia, rediscovered in May 2002 but only known from three remaining individuals.

Photo: © Tony Palliser / BirdLife International.

Photo 3.6

The New Zealand Storm Petrel *Oceanites maorianus* (Critically Endangered) was assumed to be Extinct following the lack of records since specimens were collected in the 1800s. However, it was rediscovered in 2003, with two separate observations of birds identified as this species, followed by further sightings in 2004.

Photo: © Mandy Heddle.

Photo 3.7

The Fabulous Green Sphinx Moth *Tinostoma smaragditis* (Endangered) was listed as Extinct in 1996, but in February 1998 a single male was attracted to a light trap on the island of Kauai, Hawaii. Since 1998, further individuals have been trapped, but the species is threatened due to the impacts of invasive species on its habitat.

3.3 Extinct Species that Survive *Ex Situ*

In addition to Extinct species, IUCN also records species that are Extinct in the Wild (EW). This includes species that are now only found in captivity, cultivation or as naturalized populations (IUCN 2001, see Appendix 2a). Extinct in the Wild species are in many respects Extinct, as they no longer play a functional role in their ecosystems. Also, because successful re-introductions are rare (see Box 3.6), it cannot be assumed that most of these species will be restored to the wild.

The number of EW species has increased from 50 in 2000 to 60 in 2004 (Table 3.1; Appendix 3i). The growth in the number of EW species is easier to document because these species are usually well monitored and conservationists are usually involved in keeping the species alive in captivity or cultivation. However, proving that a species is EW can take years, as it requires confirmation that the last wild individual has died. Three species appear to have genuinely moved from Critically Endangered to Extinct in the Wild since 2000, all of them from the Hawaiian Islands. These include two plants, the 'Oha Wai *Clermontia peleana* and Haha *Cyanea pinnatifida*, and one bird, the Hawaiian Crow *Corvus hawaiiensis*. The Po'ouli *Melamposops phaeosoma*, a bird also from the Hawaiian island of Maui, looks set to become the next addition to this list. Efforts are underway to take the last three known individuals into captivity as they are failing to breed in the wild.

Box 3.6

Successful Re-introductions are Rare

Re-introduction of Extinct in the Wild species to their original habitat can only be successful if sufficient habitat remains to support the re-introduced populations, and if the factors which caused the initial extinction in the wild have been addressed (see IUCN 1995). The Taiwanese endemic *Rhododendron kanehirai*, for example, cannot be re-introduced to its native habitat because this was entirely destroyed by the construction of a dam at its only known site (Lu and Pan 1997). Conversely, although sufficient habitat remains on Guam to allow the re-introduction of the Guam Rail *Gallirallus owstoni* into its native habitat, it will always require protection due to the continued presence of the predatory Brown Tree Snake *Boiga irrelgularis*. However, not all re-introduction programmes are doomed to failure. The recent re-introduction of the Scimitar-horned Oryx *Oryx dammah* to Tunisia has so far run smoothly (Mallon and Kingswood 1999), and once two generations of the re-introduced animals have bred successfully this species will be downlisted. Other promising re-introductions include the Black-footed Ferret *Mustela nigripes* (see Box 8.8), Red Wolf *Canis rufus*, California Condor *Gymnogyps californianus*, Mallorcan Midwife Toad *Alytes muletensis* (see Box 8.7) and the Redwood *Trochetiopsis erythroxylon* on St. Helena (see Box 8.6).

Photo 3.8
The last two known wild individuals of the Hawaiian Crow *Corvus hawaiiensis* (Extinct in the Wild) disappeared in 2002. Some individuals remain in captive breeding facilities and a reintroduction plan is being developed.

3.4 What is the Rate of Extinction?

The evolution of new species and the extinction of others is a natural process. This is evidenced by the fact that species present today only represent between two and four per cent of all species that have ever lived (May *et al.* 1995). Over geological time there has been a net excess of speciation over extinction that has resulted in the diversity of life that we experience today. However, the high number of recent extinctions suggests that the world might now be facing a rapid net loss of biodiversity. This can be tested by comparing recent extinction rates to average extinction rates over geological time.

The fossil record appears to be punctuated by five major mass extinctions (Jablonski 1986), the most recent of which occurred 65 million years ago. However, the majority of extinctions have been spread relatively evenly over geological time (Raup 1986), enabling estimates of the average length of species' lifetimes through the fossil record to be made. Studies of the marine fossil record indicate that individual species persist from one million to ten million years (May *et al.* 1995). These data probably underestimate background extinction rates, because they are necessarily largely derived from taxa that are abundant and widespread in the fossil record. Using a conservative estimate of five million as the total number of species on the planet, we would therefore expect anywhere between five extinctions per year to roughly one extinction ever two years (for all five million species on the planet). Bird, mammal and amphibian extinctions over the past 100 years total to roughly 100 species which in itself would appear similar to background extinction rates, but these groups represent only 1% of described species. Over the same time period, one would therefore assume that 100 times this number of species (i.e., 10,000 species) were lost over the past 100 years (assuming that the susceptibility to extinction of birds, mammals and amphibians is similar to species as a whole, which of course, is not known). Given the uncertainty over the total number of species on the planet it is more meaningful to convert these data into a relative extinction rate, measured as the number of extinctions per million species per year (E/MSY) (Pimm *et al.* 1995). A background extinction rate of 0.1–1 E/MSY corresponds to average fossil species lifetimes.

Measuring recent extinction rates is difficult, not only because our knowledge of biodiversity is limited, but also because even for the best studied taxa there is a time-lag between the decline towards extinction and actual loss of species. In the case of extinctions caused by habitat loss, in particular, it may take thousands of years before a restricted remnant population is finally driven to extinction (Diamond 1972). With this in mind it is possible to use recent documented extinctions to make a very conservative estimate of current extinction rates, though this is limited because only a few taxonomic groups have been reasonably well analysed for extinctions. Recent extinctions have been best studied for birds, mammals and amphibians. With a total of approximately 21,000 described species of birds, mammals and amphibians (see Table 2.1), the E/MSY for

Photo: © John S. Donaldson.

Photo 3.9
Only a single individual of Wood's Cycad *Encephalartos woodii* (Extinct in the Wild) was ever found in Kwa-Zulu-Natal, South Africa.
Its extinction may have been a natural event, although the final end of the wild population may have been hastened by over-exploitation for medicinal purposes by local people. There is no likelihood of ever reintroducing the species back into the wild as there are only male plants in existence, and the risk of theft would be too great.

these groups is 48 to 476 times greater than the background extinction rate. If Possibly Extinct species are included in this analysis, the total number of extinctions and possible extinctions over the past 100 years for these groups is 215 species, which results in an E/MSY that is 102 to 1,024 times higher than background rates.

A range of other techniques has been used to estimate contemporary extinction rates more generally, involving the measurement of a range of proximate (e.g., habitat destruction) and ultimate (e.g., human energy consumption) drivers of extinction. These studies give rise to estimates of E/MSY that are 1,000 to 11,000 times higher than background rates (Pimm and Brooks 1997), generally higher than the very conservative estimate for birds, mammals and amphibians given here. However, because the *IUCN Red List* is very conservative in recording species as Extinct, or even Possibly Extinct, and because many extinctions have probably been missed due to limited survey effort for most taxonomic groups, the result presented here is believed to underestimate extinction rates very significantly. Whatever the exact rate of species loss, it is clear that contemporary extinction rates are vastly higher than those typical over the planet's history, and are probably much too fast to be balanced by speciation. It is therefore likely that the world is experiencing a net loss of species, perhaps for the first time in millions of years.

3.5 Which Taxonomic Groups are Most Prone to Extinction?

Recorded extinctions are not randomly distributed across taxonomic groups. However, sampling biases confound the extent to which some groups are more or less susceptible to extinction than others. For example, molluscs (291 Extinct species) and birds (129 species) are the groups with the most recorded recent extinctions, but their comparatively high levels of extinction reflect the interests of early collectors and observers, and do not necessarily indicate that these groups are unusually extinction prone. The relatively low number of Extinct species reported in species-rich groups such as insects (59 extinctions), crustaceans (7 extinctions) and other invertebrates (2 extinctions) is most certainly the consequence of their being poorly studied, and does not indicate that they are more resilient in the face of threats. What is certain is that all groups that have been relatively well assessed, such as birds, mammals, amphibians, trees, and molluscs, have all experienced high numbers of extinctions.

Although it is not possible to compare the extent to which different major taxonomic groups vary in their susceptibility to extinction, it is possible to make comparisons within groups that have been completely or almost completely assessed. Analyses of bird and mammal taxa have found extinctions to be 'selective', with clustering in certain genera and families (Russell *et al.* 1998). Similar patterns have now also been identified in amphibians (see Box 3.4). In addition, birds and mammals in species-poor genera tend to have higher probabilities of extinction than those in more species-rich genera (Bennett and Owens 1997; Purvis *et al.* 2000b and c), which in turn increases the likelihood that entire genera will go extinct. This, coupled with the tendency for extinction-prone taxa to be evolutionarily "old" (Gaston and Blackburn 1997), indicates that extinction is non-random and that we are losing a disproportionate number of evolutionarily unique species.

3.6 Where have Extinctions Occurred?

The majority of documented extinctions have been of terrestrial species (582), followed by freshwater (226), and marine (15) (a few of these species are classified in more than one of these systems). While the extinction record of terrestrial species is incomplete, the documentation of freshwater and marine extinctions is virtually non-existent. Freshwater extinctions have been best documented in the United States, where 105 such species are known to have been lost (17 fishes, 2 amphibians, 78 molluscs, 8 insects and 2 crustaceans). Whether or not this is representative of other regions is unknown (see Box 3.7). Until recently, there were very few documented extinctions of marine species, and this was generally interpreted as these taxa being more resilient, rather than extinctions taking place unnoticed. However, a consensus is now emerging that there is no *a priori* reason to consider marine species to be necessarily less susceptible to extinction than terrestrial species (see Box 3.8).

The majority of recorded species extinctions since 1500 AD have occurred on islands. A total of 72% of recorded extinctions in five animal groups (mammals, birds, amphibians, reptiles, and molluscs) was of island species. Furthermore, for each individual taxonomic group the percentage of recorded extinctions occurring on islands was greater than that occurring on continents. In total, 62% of mammals, 88% of birds, 54% of amphibians, 86% of reptiles, and 68% of molluscs were island species. Nevertheless, there are major differences in the extinction

Box 3.7

Box 3.7

Freshwater Extinctions in North America

The southeastern United States is a world centre of diversity for freshwater species and accounts for most of the diversity summarized in Box 2.5. But this area also stands out in another way as well: species that depend on riverine habitats are, as a whole, faring the worst of any groups of North American organisms (Chaplin *et al.* 2000). Molluscs in particular have been seriously impacted. NatureServe data identifies 39 species of freshwater mussels and snails are presumed extinct and another 76 species are possibly extinct, having not been seen in many years despite searches (Master *et al.* 2000).

The leading cause for these freshwater mollusc extinctions is thought to be habitat destruction and alteration due primarily to dam construction, which has turned most large free-flowing rivers in the United States into a series of impoundments. However, point and non-point pollution, invasive alien species (e.g., zebra mussels), and altered hydrologic regimes have also impacted mollusc populations and continue to threaten many species (Richter *et al.* 1997; Master *et al.* 1998). These problems are not restricted to the United States, and are likely having significant impact on freshwater faunas worldwide.

Based on information provided by Larry Master, NatureServe

Box 3.8

Extinction of Marine Species

Like marine mammals, birds and turtles, marine fishes and invertebrates are coming under increasing pressure from human activities and face the threat of extinction, as indicated by severe and widespread declines (Casey and Myers 1998; Davis *et al.* 1998; Baum *et al.* 2003; Myers and Worm 2003; Sadovy and Cheung 2003; Hutchings and Reynolds 2004) and fisheries management failures (Hutchings and Myers 1994), as well as emerging science that is revealing the inherent vulnerability to over-exploitation and extinction of many species and species groups (Hoenig and Gruber 1990; Grimes and Turner 1999; Huntsman *et al.* 1999; Reynolds *et al.* 2001; Dulvy *et al.* 2003) and the complexity of species' and ecosystems' responses to severe depletions (e.g., Dayton *et al.* 1995; Jackson *et al.* 2001; Hutchings and Reynolds 2004).

As a phenomenon, extinction in the sea has been a contentious issue. One reason for this is the fact that there are many fewer examples of recent extinctions in the marine environment than on land or in fresh waters, which has led to the belief that marine extinctions have been and are uncommon. Yet the work of several authors in recent years (Carlton *et al.* 1999; Dulvy *et al.* 2003) suggests and provides evidence that marine extinctions are occurring but are simply not being detected in the same way that they are in other environments. Another factor in the debate is the widespread and persistent perception that marine species are more resilient to extinction because they are – or are presumed to be – highly fecund, wide-ranging, and/or fast-growing, and, thus, should be capable of withstanding high levels of exploitation, and of recovering rapidly from low numbers. However, a growing body of scientific evidence indicates that marine species are characterized by the same attributes that account for vulnerability in terrestrial and freshwater species (see section 6.10.3). Many marine species are long-lived and are late to reach sexual maturity, which puts them at an inherent disadvantage when subjected to exploitation (Camhi *et al.* 1998; Coleman *et al.* 1999; Musick *et al.* 2000a; Parker *et al.* 2000). Many marine species are not as widespread as is commonly believed but are restricted by the heterogenous nature of the marine environment and/or limited dispersal capabilities to small, in some instances very small, ranges (Hawkins *et al.* 2000; Smith *et al.* 2002). Further, high fecundity has been shown not to be associated with higher rates of reproduction (Denney *et al.* 2002) or to ensure against over-exploitation (Sadovy 2001). Finally, there is increasing evidence that marine populations do not recover from severe depletion even when fishing ceases (Hutchings 2000; Hutchings and Reynolds 2004).

Dulvy *et al.* (2003) document 133 local and global extinctions in marine species (21 of which are global), including 3 global and 62 local fish extinctions. Exploitation is the most important factor in causing extinction in marine species. In addition, while it may once have been true that commercial extinction would precede biological extinction, such that fishing would cease once it became unprofitable, the multi-species nature of most current fisheries and the high value of others (Sadovy and Cheung 2003; Sadovy *et al.* 2003) result in the persistence of fishing effort that can lead to biological extinction. The currently available evidence indicates that extinction in the sea is, and will become, a much larger problem than is currently recognized.

Based on information provided by Elodie Hudson and Amie Bräutigam

patterns between the five taxonomic groups mapped in Figure 3.1. Bird extinctions are overwhelmingly biased towards oceanic islands (including New Zealand), whereas the largest concentration of mammal extinctions is in Australia. Documented amphibian extinctions are focused on Sri Lanka, but this might be an artefact of under-recording extinctions elsewhere. Mollusc extinctions are concentrated in North American river systems (as indicated in Box 3.7).

A detailed examination of bird extinctions since 1500 AD indicates that the geographical distribution of extinctions may be changing over time. Although more than 80% of birds are found on continents, all extinctions prior to 1800 occurred on islands. This pattern has started to change in recent years with more extinctions occurring on continents (Figure 3.2).

Photo: © Zoological Society of London.

Photo 3.10
The last confirmed report of the Thylacine *Thylacinus cynocephalus* (Extinct) in Tasmania was in 1930, and the last captive animal died in 1936. The Thylacine was driven to extinction primarily by direct persecution, but habitat loss, competition with domestic dogs and disease all played a role.

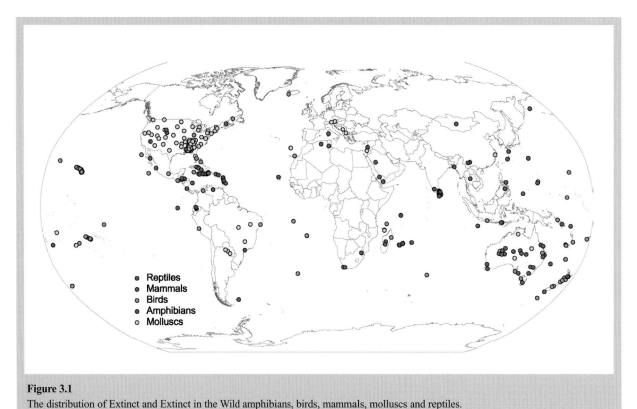

- Reptiles
- Mammals
- Birds
- Amphibians
- Molluscs

Figure 3.1
The distribution of Extinct and Extinct in the Wild amphibians, birds, mammals, molluscs and reptiles.

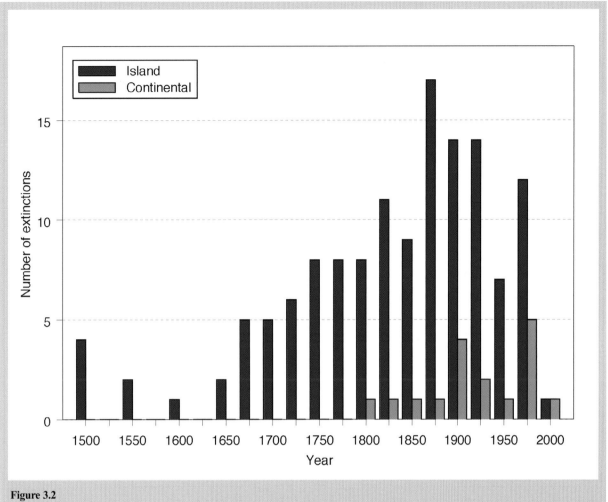

Figure 3.2
The number of bird extinctions that have occurred on islands and continents since 1500 AD.

While there is no doubt that island species have been particularly prone to extinction, it is important to note that significant numbers of extinctions might have taken place in certain continental tropical regions where there has been very limited survey effort. Such a bias in sampling possibly explains the concentration of mollusc extinctions in North America. Thus Figure 3.1 highlights regions where large numbers of extinctions are known to have taken place, but it does not provide much insight into regions where even basic knowledge of the recent history of extinctions is lacking.

3.7 What are the Causes of Extinction?

Humans have played a significant role in the extinction of species prior to historic times (see Box 3.9) but the true extent of such anthropogenic impacts during the Holocene (the last 11,000 years) remains unclear. However, after 1500 AD it is clear that humans are responsible for most recorded extinctions.

Box 3.9

Prehistoric Human-Caused Extinctions

The strong correlation between the arrival of humans and a rapid increase in extinction has been demonstrated in regions such as Australia (Roberts *et al*. 2002), the Americas (Alroy 2001) and Madagascar (Goodman and Patterson 1997), but nowhere is the pattern more evident than in the human colonization of oceanic islands and subsequent extinction of birds (Milberg and Tyrberg 1993; Pimm *et al*. 1994; Steadman 1995; Steadman *et al*. 1999). On the tropical Pacific Islands, Steadman (1995) and Steadman *et al*. (1995) have estimated that more than 2,000 species of birds became extinct during the period of prehistoric human colonization (most of which were flightless rails). If this estimate is correct, then about one-fifth of all birds extant during the early Holocene (about 11,000 years ago) are now extinct (Milberg and Tyrberg 1993).

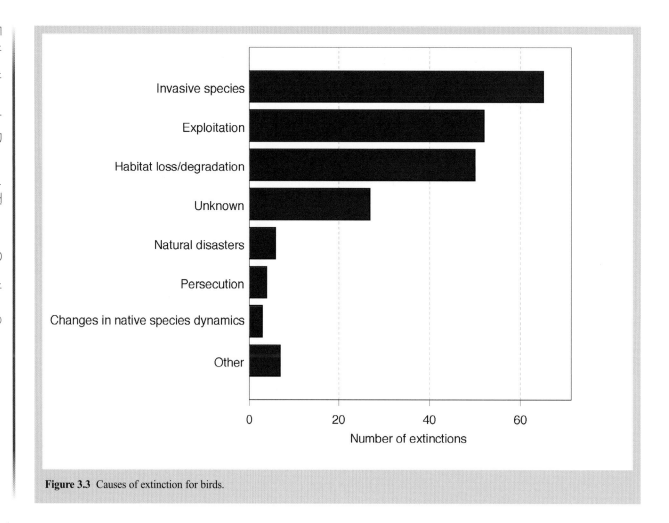

Figure 3.3 Causes of extinction for birds.

The exact causes of most extinctions are poorly documented, but invasive alien species, habitat loss, and over-exploitation have all been major factors (see Section 6). Even when species are relatively well studied it is often difficult to identify the main cause of extinction as most species are threatened by more than one process and these often interact in unpredictable ways. Furthermore, the threat process that causes a species to become susceptible to extinction (such as habitat loss) may be very different to the final process that drives it to extinction (such as a hurricane).

Relatively good data exist for birds indicating that the impacts of invasive alien species, over-exploitation by humans, and habitat destruction and degradation have been the major causes of extinctions (see Figure 3.3), with invasive species being associated with the extinction of at least 65 species. Predation by introduced dogs, pigs and mongooses, and habitat destruction by sheep, rabbits and goats have been implicated in the extinctions of some of these species. However, it is predation by introduced rats and cats, and diseases caused by introduced pathogens that have been the most deadly overall, contributing to the extinction of some 30, 20 and 10 species respectively.

3.8 Documented Extinctions over the Past 20 Years

While little has been documented about most historic extinctions, much more information is available on species that have been lost over the past few decades. This section focuses on extinctions over the past 20 years to provide greater insight into patterns of recent extinction and to highlight those species that have most recently disappeared.

At least 27 species are recorded as having become Extinct or Extinct in the Wild during the last 20 years (1984–2004) (Tables 3.2 and 3.3). Inherent in identifying very recent extinctions is the problem of extinctions not being included because they are not yet confirmed. For example, eight species of birds are thought to have become Extinct or Extinct in the Wild over the past 20 years, but they are not included, as further research is needed prove the last individual has died (Box 3.2).

Table 3.2

Species recorded as having become Extinct over the last 20 years (1984 – 2004)

Key: ■ = habitat loss; ■ = disease; ■ = global warming / pollution; ■ = natural disaster; ■ = exploitation / persecution; ■ = restricted range; ■ = invasive species (not disease); ■ = unknown.

Kingdom	Class	Species	Common Name	Date of EX (or last recorded sighting)	Place of extinction (BioRegion)	Major causes of extinction
ANIMALIA	Amphibia	*Atelopus ignescens*	Jambato Toad	1988 (last record)	Ecuador (Neotropics)	■ ■
	Amphibia	*Atelopus longirostris*		1989 (last record)	Ecuador (Neotropics)	■ ■
	Amphibia	*Bufo periglenes*	Golden Toad	1989 (last record)	Costa Rica (Neotropics)	■ ■ ■
	Amphibia	*Eleutherodactylus chrysozetetes*		1989 (last record)	Honduras (Neotropics)	■ ■
	Amphibia	*Eleutherodactylus milesi*		1983 (last record)	Honduras (Neotropics)	■ ■
	Amphibia	*Rheobatrachus vitellinus*	Northern Gastric Brooding Frog	1985 (last record)	Australia (Australasian / Oceanic)	■ ■
	Amphibia	*Cynops wolterstorffi*	Yunnan Lake Newt	1986 (last record)	China (Palearctic)	■ ■ ■
	Aves	*Moho braccatus*	Kauai 'O'o	1987 (last report of vocalizations)	Hawaiian Islands (Kaua'i) (Australasian / Oceanic)	■ ■ ■
	Aves	*Podilymbus gigas*	Atitlán Grebe	1986	Guatemala (Neotropics)	■
	Aves	*Myadestes myadestinus*	Kama'o	1989 (last sighting)	Hawaiian Islands (Kaua'i) (Australasian / Oceanic)	■ ■ ■
PLANTAE	Magnoliopsida	*Cyanea dolichopoda*	Haha	Post-1990	Hawaiian Islands (Kaua'i) (Australasian / Oceanic)	■
	Magnoliopsida	*Argyroxiphium virescens*	Silversword	1996 (death of hybrid individuals)	Hawaiian Islands (Maui) (Australasian / Oceanic)	■ ■
	Magnoliopsida	*Crudia zeylanica*		1990s	Sri Lanka (Indo-Malayan)	■
	Magnoliopsida	*Nesiota elliptica*	St. Helena Olive	2003	St. Helena (Afrotropic)	■
	Magnoliopsida	*Oldenlandia adscenionis*		1985	Ascension Island (Australasian / Oceanic)	■

Table 3.3

Species recorded as having become Extinct in the Wild in the last 20 years (1984 – 2004)

Key: ■ = habitat loss; ■ = disease; ■ = global warming / pollution; ■ = natural disaster; ■ = exploitation / persecution; ■ = restricted range; ■ = invasive species (not disease); ■ = unknown.

Kingdom	Class	Species	Common Name	Date of EW	Place of EW (BioRegion)	Major causes of extinction in wild	Possibility of re-introduction
ANIMALIA	Amphibia	*Bufo baxteri*	Wyoming Toad	Mid 1990s	United States (Nearctic)	■ ■	Re-introduction programme underway, but no self-sustaining population established in the wild, probably due to chytridiomycosis. Captive breeding programme in place
	Aves	*Corvus hawaiiensis*	Hawaiian Crow	2002 (last sighting in wild)	Hawaiian Islands (Hawaii) (Australasian / Oceanic)	■ ■ ■ ■	Attempt failed because some reintroduced birds died; remainder re-captured and further plans being developed.
	Aves	*Crax mitu*	Alagoas Curassow	Late 1980s (last sighting in wild)	Brazil (Neotropics)	■ ■ ■	Suitable area of habitat remains, but reintroduction appears difficult.
	Aves	*Gallirallus owstoni*	Guam Rail	1987	Guam (Australasia / Oceanic)	■	140 individuals in captivity, re-introduction is underway. Small introduced population on Rota, North Mariana Islands.
	Mammalia	*Oryx dammah*	Scimitar-horned Oryx	1996 (last sighting in wild)	Chad (Afrotropic)	■ ■	3,395 individuals in captivity. Successful reintroduction in Tunisia.
PLANTAE	Magnoliopsida	*Mammillaria glochidiata*		Post-1993	Mexico (Neotropics)	■	Unknown.
	Magnoliopsida	*Mammillaria guillauminiana*		1997	Mexico (Neotropics)	■	Unknown.
	Magnoliopsida	*Clermontia peleana*	'Oha Wai	2000	Hawaiian Islands (Hawaii, Maui) (Australasian / Oceanic)	■ ■	Unknown. Only one individual remains in cultivation.
	Magnoliopsida	*Cyanea pinnatifida*	Haha	2002	Hawaiian Islands (Oahu) (Australasian / Oceanic)	■	Unknown. Specimens held at National Tropical Botanic Garden in USA.
	Magnoliopsida	*Cyanea truncata*	Punaluu Cyanea	1980s	Hawaiian Islands (Oahu and Molokai) (Australasian / Oceanic)	■	Unknown.
	Magnoliopsida	*Commidendrum rotundifolium*	Bastard Gumwood	1986	St. Helena (Afrotropic)	■ ■ ■	Trees have been successfully established; efforts need to be made to propagate through seed.
	Magnoliopsida	*Rhododendron kanehirai*		1984	Taiwan (Indo-Malayan)	■	Unlikely, as native habitat was completely destroyed.

Twelve of the post-1983 extinctions were of flowering plants, six were of birds, eight were of amphibians and one was of a mammal. All of these species were terrestrial, although all of the amphibians were also freshwater-dependant. In total, fourteen recently Extinct species were from islands, while thirteen were continental species. This pattern is very different from that of extinctions over the past 500 years, during which time documented extinctions have always been much greater on islands than on continents. The greatest concentration of very recent documented extinctions has taken place on the Hawaiian archipelago, which has seen the recent demise of five plant species and three bird species. These extinctions, in addition to an extinction in the wild on Guam, result in Oceania having more recorded extinctions over the last 20 years than any other biogeographic realm.

Most of species that have become Extinct or Extinct in the Wild over the last 20 years had restricted ranges. Of the 27 recently Extinct species, approximately 85% had a restricted range in historic times. The Atitlán Grebe *Podilymbus gigas*, for example, was restricted to Lake Atitlán in Guatemala, while the St. Helena Olive *Nesiota elliptica* was found only at high elevations of St. Helena Island's eastern central ridge. However, several somewhat more widespread species have been lost over the last 20 years. The Jambato Toad *Atelopus ignescens*, for example, was originally widespread throughout the humid forests of Ecuador's northern Andes at elevations of 2,800–4,200m. Surveys in the 1960s, 70s and 80s found this species to be abundant, but population sizes began to decline rapidly in approximately 1984 (Ron *et al.* 2003). There have been no records since 1988, and the species is considered to be Extinct, apparently the result of infection with the chytrid fungus, probably linked to extreme droughts.

Several of the recently EX and EW species experienced extremely rapid declines. The Northern Gastric Brooding Frog *Rheobatrachus vitellinus*, for example, underwent a very rapid population reduction in 1984–5, seemingly the result of infection by the chytrid fungus, and perhaps forest fires that spread throughout its habitat. Despite always having had a restricted range (it was found only in undisturbed forest from 400–1,000m above sea level in the Eungella National Park), this species was considered common across its range until January 1985 (McDonald *et al.* 2001), but there have been no records since May of that year. The Guam Rail *Gallirallus owstoni* experienced a similarly dramatic decline following the accidental introduction of the Brown Tree Snake *Boiga irrelgularis* in the 1940s (Haig *et al.* 1990, Wiles *et al.* 2003). Previously widespread, this species became Extinct in the Wild in 1987 following a collapse in its population size from 2,000 individuals in 1981 to 100 in 1983 (BirdLife International 2004a).

The most commonly recorded threat to the species that have been lost over the last 20 years is habitat loss, which had a severe impact on thirteen of these species. In addition, other major threats have included the introduction and invasion of non-native species (impacting nine species), and disease (in particular the fungal amphibian disease chytridiomycosis (see Box 3.4) which impacted seven species, and avian pathogens, spread by introduced mosquitoes, which impacted three species) (see Tables 3.2 and 3.3). It is noteworthy that over-exploitation has not played a significant role in these recent extinctions, and also that diseases have had a relatively larger impact than they did over the last 500 years.

Photo 3.11
The Atitlàn Grebe *Podilymbus gigas* (Extinct) was endemic to Lake Atitlán, Guatemala. The extinction of this species in 1986 was the result of a number of independent factors that combined, drastically reduced the population to levels where it was no longer viable.

Key Findings

- The number of documented extinctions (844 species since 1500 AD) grossly under-represents the number of extinctions that have taken place in historic times, due to very incomplete and uneven sampling, both geographically and taxonomically.

- An additional 208 species could already be Extinct, but further information is required to confirm this.

- Data from the *IUCN Red List* indicate a current extinction rate that is at least two, and probably three, orders of magnitude higher than the background rate typical over the planet's geological history.

- Very little is known about marine and freshwater extinctions, but preliminary evidence from North America indicates a very high level of extinctions in freshwater habitats.

- Although information is still very limited, there is growing evidence that marine species are less resilient to extinction in the face of threats than was once thought.

- Although the island species have experienced the greatest number of extinctions in historic times, continental extinctions are becoming more frequent, and account for almost 50% of the extinctions confirmed over the last 20 years.

- Humans have been the main cause of extinction since 1500 AD with invasive alien species, habitat loss, and over-exploitation being the main causal factors.

- While habitat loss and invasive alien species have been major drivers of extinction over the last 20 years, over-exploitation appears to have had little impact in causing non-marine extinctions over this time period, but disease appears to be a growing threat.

Photo: © Wendy A. Strahm.

Photo 3.12
The Bottle Palm *Hyophorbe lagenicaulis* (Critically Endangered) endemic to Round Island, Mauritius, almost went extinct. Numbers declined to just seven individuals because of the lack of regeneration due to the impacts of introduced goats and rabbits. An effective eradication programme resulted in the removal of all the goats and rabbits by the late 1980s. An active seed-planting programme is now helping the recovery of this species, and it is widely cultivated worldwide.

Trends in the Status of Threatened Species

Photo 4.1
The striking Rufous-collared Kingfisher *Actenoides concretus* (Near Threatened) is confined to the Sundaic lowlands. Forest destruction in the Sundaic lowlands of Indonesia has been so extensive that all primary formations are expected to disappear by 2010, and the situation is little different in Thailand and Malaysia.

4.1 Introduction

The world's biodiversity is being destroyed rapidly (Balmford *et al.* 2003; Jenkins *et al.* 2003). It is important to quantify this by measuring trends in the status of biodiversity in order to gain a better understanding of the impact that humans are having, and to determine how successful we are at addressing biodiversity loss. In particular we need indicators for measuring progress towards achieving the target set by the nations of the world for significantly reducing the rate of loss of biological diversity by 2010. We do not yet have an adequate way of monitoring progress towards achieving this target. However, the Convention on Biological Diversity (CBD) has recommended developing a number of indicators, including one based on changes in status of threatened species.

Here we present "Red List Indices" (RLIs) which show how the overall threat status (projected extinction risk) of particular sets of species changes over time. These are based on the number of species in each Red List Category and the number changing between categories as a consequence of genuine improvement or deterioration in status (see Appendix 2d for further details). The Red List Programme developed the RLI because changes in the total number of species on the *IUCN Red List* (or in different categories) over time cannot simply be used to examine trends in the threat status of sets of species, for several reasons. For example,

many category changes result from improved knowledge or taxonomic revisions, but such revisions are not indicative of changes in overall status. Furthermore, in many taxonomic groups the subset of species that have been assessed for the *IUCN Red List* may be biased towards rare, well known, or high profile species or those from particular regions or families. Using data on the world's birds and amphibians, these problems have been overcome to produce RLIs that are robust, temporally sensitive, representative and comprehensive. They provide unique baseline data against which progress towards meeting the CBD 2010 target can be judged, and they allow finer-scale resolution of trends in particular biogeographic realms, ecosystems and habitats.

4.2 Red List Indices for Birds 1988–2004

4.2.1 The Red List Index for All Birds

The Red List Index (RLI) for birds shows that there has been a steady and continuing deterioration in the threat status (projected extinction risk) of the world's birds between 1988 and 2004, with an overall change in the index value of -6.90% over this period (Figure 4.1). No change would indicate that the average status of all bird species was the same as in 1988. To put this into context, if 10% of species in categories Near Threatened (NT) to Critically Endangered (CR) had deteriorated in status sufficiently to be uplisted one

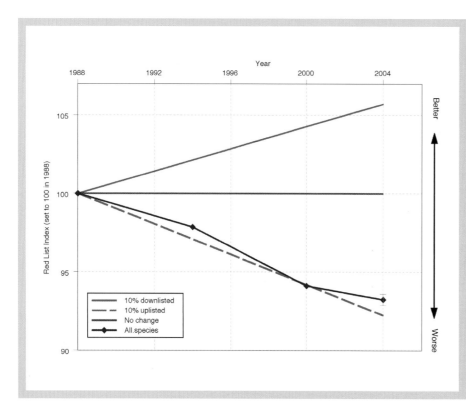

Figure 4.1
The Red List Index (RLI) for all bird species for 1988–2004 (250 genuine status changes out of 2,469 species in categories Extinct in the Wild (EW) to Near Threatened (NT) in at least one assessment), with hypothetical indices showing trends if no species had changed category, and if 10% of species in the categories from NT to Critically Endangered (CR) had been uplisted to a higher category of threat or downlisted to a lower category of threat over the period. Error bars for 2004 RLI value are based on estimated number of genuine status changes for 2000–2004 not yet detected owing to information time-lags (see Appendix 2d for further details of methods).

Box 4.1

Most Threatened Birds are Deteriorating in Status

The Red List Index measures movement between categories of the *IUCN Red List*. However, these categories are relatively broad; species often have to undergo considerable changes in population size, population trend or range size in order to cross the thresholds between categories. To determine qualitative trends between 2000 and 2004 in the status of all threatened bird species, not just those moving between Red List Categories, a worldwide network of over 100 experts was consulted. They were asked to judge from their detailed knowledge whether the status of each species had improved, stayed the same, or deteriorated during the period. Assessments were obtained for 72% of

threatened birds (859 species). Of these, only 11% were judged to have improved in status, 43% had remained the same and 45% had deteriorated in status since 2000 (see Figure below). Similar proportions were found for the subset of Critically Endangered species: 14% were judged to have improved in status, 40% had stayed the same, and 46% had deteriorated in status. Of the species for which the experts scored 'unknown' status changes or for which no assessment could be obtained, many were also likely to be declining. In combination with declining trends shown by the Red List Index, this snapshot survey indicated that threatened birds are in serious trouble, and that the problem is getting worse.

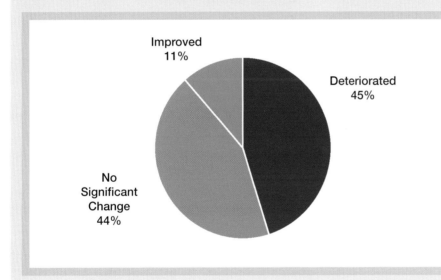

Figure Box 4.1
Changes in the status of the world's threatened birds 2000–2004 according to 'expert' assessment.

Taken from BirdLife International (2004b).

category (i.e., to a category of higher threat) between 1988 and 2004, the index would have changed by -7.8% (Figure 4.1). It is worth noting that species often have to undergo considerable changes in population size, population trend or range size in order to cross thresholds between categories and hence contribute to trends in the RLI. However, almost half of all threatened bird species are estimated to have declined in status during 2000–2004 regardless of whether or not they were uplisted to higher categories of threat (see Box 4.1).

4.2.2 The Red List Index for Birds by Realm and Ecosystem

Disaggregating the RLI shows that the threat status of birds has deteriorated worldwide at a more-or-less similar rate and proportional extent in the Nearctic, Neotropical, Palearctic,

Afrotropical and Australasian/Oceanic realms. The Indomalayan realm shows a steeper rate of deterioration during the 1990s (see Figure 4.2). This was a result of the intensifying destruction of forests in the Sundaic lowlands of Indonesia, which escalated particularly in the late 1990s and led to predictions of almost total loss of lowland forest in Sumatra by 2005 and in Kalimantan by 2010 (Holmes 2000; Collar *et al.* 2001). As a consequence of these increasing rates of habitat loss, many species were uplisted to higher categories of threat under criterion A (rapid population declines). However, it is notable that there has been a substantial deterioration in the threat status of birds of shrubland/grassland habitats as well as forest, and in the two other major ecosystems (freshwater and marine), indicating that birds in a broad spectrum of environments are deteriorating in status (Figure 4.3).

Photo 4.2
Rhinoceros Hornbill *Buceros rhinoceros* (Near Threatened) from the Sundaic lowlands of Indonesia, Malaysia and Thailand. Threatened by forest destruction and in parts of its range by hunting for food and hat feathers.

Photo 4.3
The wide ranging Black-browed Albatross *Thalassarche melanophrys* (Endangered) was uplisted from Vulnerable in 2003. All 21 species of albatross are now listed as globally under threat (compared to just three in 1996 and 16 in 2000). All are undergoing long-term declines, with significant numbers drowning after being caught accidentally on baited hooks set by longline fisheries.

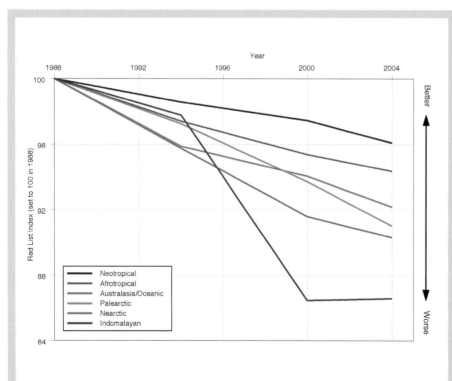

Figure 4.2
Red List Indices (RLIs) for birds in different biogeographic realms for 1988–2004. Sample sizes: Afrotropical = 41 genuine status changes out of 394 species in categories Extinct in the Wild (EW) to Near Threatened (NT) in at least one assessment; Indomalayan = 100 out of 585 species; Nearctic = 9 out of 92 species; Neotropical = 49 out of 834 species; Australasian/Oceanic = 53 out of 614 species; Palearctic = 34 out of 238 species.

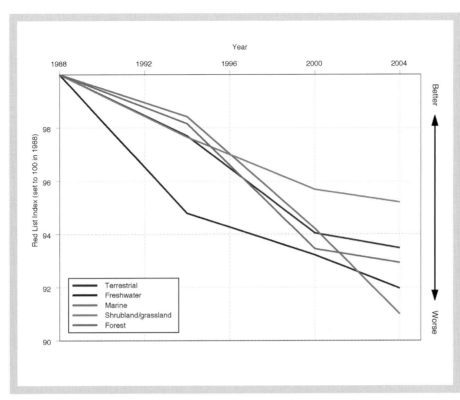

Figure 4.3
Red List Indices (RLIs) for birds in the marine, freshwater and terrestrial ecosystems, and for birds in forest and shrubland/grassland habitats, for 1988–2004. Sample sizes: Marine = 12 genuine status changes out of 133 species in categories Extinct in the Wild (EW) to Near Threatened (NT) in at least one assessment; Freshwater = 31 out of 226 species; Terrestrial = 206 out of 2329 species; forest = 169 out of 1,513 species; shrubland/grassland = 45 out of 481 species.

4.2.3 The Red List Index for Birds by Family

Breaking down the RLI for birds by particular families or species-groups shows that the threat status of albatrosses and petrels has deteriorated particularly severely in recent years (Figure 4.4). This is closely linked to the expansion of commercial longline fisheries (both legal and illegal), which cause incidental mortality of albatrosses and other seabirds when they are caught on baited hooks and drown (Tuck *et al.* 2001, 2003; BirdLife International 2004b).

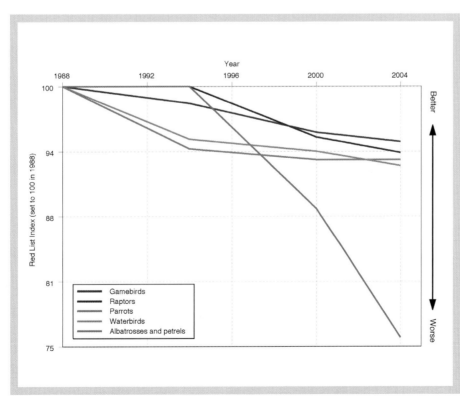

Figure 4.4
Red List Indices (RLIs) for five bird families and species-groups for 1988–2004. Sample sizes: Waterbirds = 36 genuine status changes out of 238 species in categories Extinct in the Wild (EW) to Near Threatened (NT) in at least one assessment; Raptors = 10 out of 93; Gamebirds = 15 out of 123; Parrots = 19 out of 148; Albatrosses and petrels = 6 out of 28.

4.3 Preliminary Red List Indices for Amphibians 1980–2004 (Retrospectively Assessed)

4.3.1 Preliminary Red List Index for All Amphibians

The RLI for amphibians, based on assessments in 2004, and retrospective classifications for 1980 (see Appendix 2d for methods), shows that the threat status of the world's amphibians has deteriorated substantially (Figure 4.5). The index value changed by -13.7% over this period. The net decline is equivalent to c. 30% of species in each 1980 category from Near Threatened (NT) to Critically Endangered (CR) being uplisted by one category (i.e., to a category of higher threat; Figure 4.5). Furthermore, the rate of deterioration is likely to have been underestimated: a conservative approach was adopted in identifying genuine deteriorations between 1980 and 2004. In addition, 23% of amphibians are listed as Data Deficient (and hence are excluded from the RLI), and with better information many of these may well prove to be threatened and to have undergone serious declines through this period.

It is also worth noting that, out of the 4,048 amphibian species (70.9%) for which trends have been recorded, 61.0% (2,468 species) are estimated to be declining, 38.3% (1,552 species) are stable, and just 0.69% (28 species) are increasing.

Photo: © Michael and Patricia Fogden.

Photo 4.4
Darwin's Frog *Rhinoderma darwini* (Vulnerable) from central Chile and nearby Argentina is one of only two members of the family Rhinodermatidae. The females deposit eggs in the leaf litter. When the larvae inside the eggs begin to move, the adult males ingest the eggs and incubate them in their vocal sacs. The larvae develop inside the male and emerge after metamorphosis, as shown in this photo. This species appears to be in decline, even in well protected habitats, for unclear reasons. The only other member of the family, *Rhinoderma rufum* from Chile, disappeared around 1978, and it is Possibly Extinct.

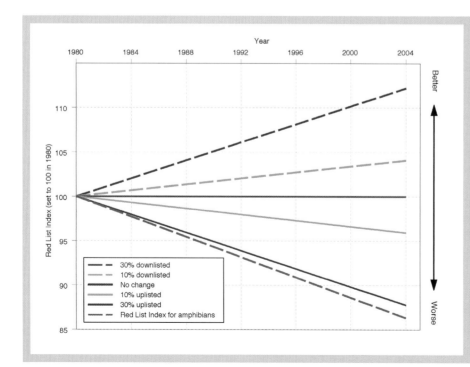

Figure 4.5
A preliminary Red List Index (RLI) for all amphibian species for 1980–2004 (retrospective assessment; 496 genuine status changes out of 2,225 species in categories Extinct in the Wild (EW) to Near Threatened (NT) in at least one assessment), with hypothetical indices showing trends if no species had changed category, and if 10% or 30% of species in the categories from NT to Critically Endangered (CR) had been uplisted to a higher category of threat or downlisted to a lower category of threat over the period.

4.3.2 Preliminary Red List Index for Amphibians by Realm and Ecosystem

The RLI for amphibians in different realms shows that species in the Australasian/Oceanic realm have shown the steepest deterioration in status, followed by those in the Palearctic and Neotropical realms (Figure 4.6). However, the steep rate of deterioration in the Australasian/Oceanic realm is probably biased by the fact that a large proportion of species are listed as Data Deficient in this region (31.6% compared to a mean of 21.6% in all other realms). Many of these are in the family Microhylidae (narrow-mouthed toads - 61.6% compared to 3.9% in all other realms), which is one of the groups least affected by the fungal disease chytridiomycosis (believed to be one of the major threats to amphibians: see section 6). This family is especially diverse in the remote, poorly surveyed regions of New Guinea, where it is the dominant component in the frog fauna. Data Deficient species are excluded when calculating the index value, giving any genuine status changes a greater proportional significance. Further information is likely to show that the majority of these Australasian/Oceanic Data Deficient species have not undergone substantial status changes over the period, giving a RLI for this realm that shows a smaller rate of decline. The severity of the declines in the Palearctic realm is largely driven by the increasing levels of exploitation of amphibians in China over the period, while the steep decline in the RLI for amphibians in the Neotropical realm largely reflects the severe impacts that chytridiomycosis appears to have had on these species.

Photo: © Harold Cogger.

Photo: © Michael and Patricia Fogden.

Photo: © Michael and Patricia Fogden.

Photo 4.5
The spectacular Corroboree Frog *Pseudophryne corroboree* (Critically Endangered) has declined dramatically in distribution and abundance, and is now restricted to a few fragmented populations in subalpine and montane areas of New South Wales, Australia. Fewer than 250 mature individuals are thought to survive.

Photo 4.6
The Green-eyed Frog *Rana vibicaria* (Critically Endangered) was once abundant in Costa Rica and western Panama. Its populations crashed in the late 1980s, and there were no records in Costa Rica after 1990, until 2002 when a small population was rediscovered. There have been no recent records from Panama.

Photo 4.7
This species of harlequin toad, *Atelopus varius* (Critically Endangered), was once abundant in Costa Rica and western Panama. Over 100 separate populations were once known from Costa Rica. Declines began at Monteverde in 1988, and by 1996 it was believed to be extinct in Costa Rica. Serious population crashes have also taken place in Panama, though it was recorded as recently at 2002. A small population was rediscovered in Costa Rica in 2003.

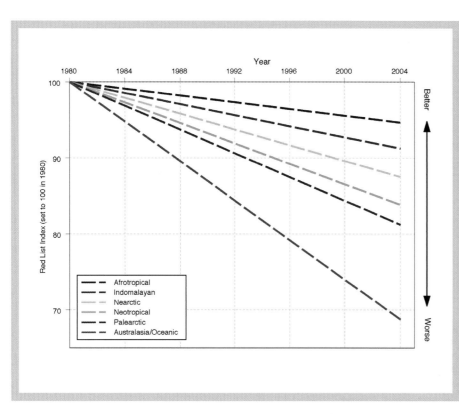

Figure 4.6
Preliminary Red List Indices (RLIs) for amphibians in different biogeographic realms for 1980–2004 (retrospective assessment). Sample sizes: Afrotropical = 29 genuine status changes out of 287 species in categories Extinct in the Wild (EW) to Near Threatened (NT) in at least one assessment; Indomalayan = 60 out of 399 species; Nearctic = 29 out of 118 species; Neotropical = 332 out of 1,260 species; Australasian/Oceanic = 38 out of 88 species; Palearctic = 36 out of 148 species.

The threat status of amphibians in the freshwater and terrestrial ecosystems has deteriorated at broadly similar rates (Figure 4.7). This is to be expected, because 64.0% of species are common to both ecosystems. Nevertheless, declines have been more severe for freshwater amphibians. This is likely to be because chytridiomycosis appears to have a greater impact on freshwater species (Berger *et al.* 1998; Lips *et al.* 2003), and because such species are often sensitive to changes in water quality such as those brought about by logging (Inger 1966; Amiet 1989). Although terrestrial species often have tiny ranges, this does not seem to be sufficient to compensate for the greater susceptibility of freshwater-dependent species.

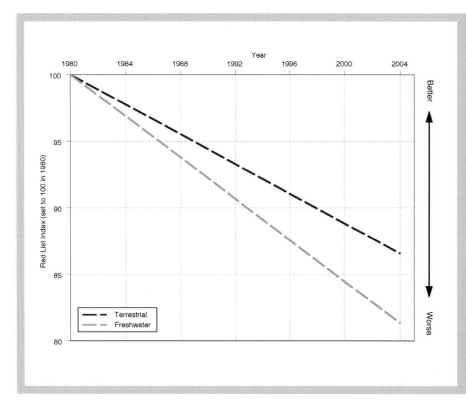

Figure 4.7
Preliminary Red List Indices (RLIs) for amphibians in freshwater and terrestrial ecosystems for 1980–2004 (retrospective assessment). Sample sizes: freshwater = 381 genuine status changes out of 1,369 species in categories Extinct in the Wild (EW) to Near Threatened (NT) in at least one assessment; terrestrial = 473 out of 2,151 species.

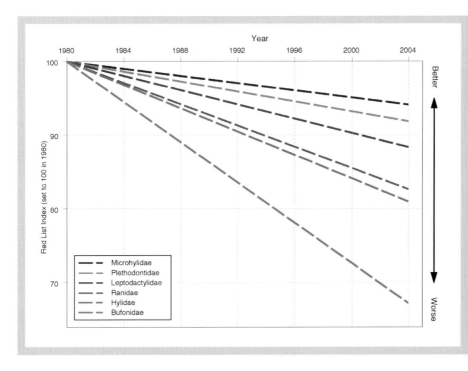

Figure 4.8
Preliminary Red List Indices (RLIs) for selected amphibian families for 1980–2004 (retrospective assessment). Sample sizes: Bufonidae: 106 genuine status changes out of 233 species in categories Extinct in the Wild (EW) to Near Threatened (NT) in at least one assessment; Leptodactylidae: 121 out of 584 species; Hylidae: 68 out of 241 species; Ranidae: 56 out of 222 species; Microhylidae: 10 out of 89 species; Plethodontidae: 34 out of 204 species.

4.3.3 Preliminary Red List Index for Amphibian Families

Some families of amphibians have undergone more serious declines than others (Figure 4.8). Of the larger amphibian families, toads (Bufonidae) have shown the steepest rate of deterioration in threat status, and this is probably a reflection of the high level of susceptibility of the genus *Atelopus* to chytridiomycosis (Lötters *et al.* 2003).

4.4 Comparison of Red List Indices for Birds and Amphibians

The Red List Indices for birds (1988–2004) and amphibians (1980–2004) show remarkably similar slopes (changing by -0.422% per year for birds and -0.571% per year for amphibians; Figure 4.9). For birds there were 250 genuine category changes over 16 years (1988–2004). This represents 15.8% of species in categories Near Threatened (NT) to Critically Endangered (CR) in 1988 moving to higher or lower categories by an average of 1.21 categories, which equates to *c*. 10% of species in each category from NT to CR deteriorating by one category (Figure 4.1). For amphibians, 496 species underwent genuine category changes over 24 years (1980–2004). This represents 24% of species in categories NT to CR in 1980 changing on average 1.46 categories (nearly all deteriorating), equating to *c*. 30% of species in categories NT to CR deteriorating by one category (Figure 4.5). In other words, a higher proportion of

amphibians deteriorated in threat status, and they did so by a greater degree, but when this is considered over the longer time-frame compared to birds (24 years vs. 16 years), the rate of decline of RLI is similar. This is presumably because many bird and amphibian species that underwent status changes during these time periods will have been impacted in a similar way by the same habitat loss. However, amphibians have also been severely impacted by chytridiomycosis. It is presumably a coincidence that the proportion of amphibians that have changed status as a result of this threat more-or-less balances the proportion of birds impacted by, for example, exploitation or invasive species (a particularly significant threat on oceanic islands, where there are few amphibians).

4.4.1 Trends in the Status of the Most Threatened Birds and Amphibians

To examine trends in the status of the most threatened species, we can examine RLIs with each category weighted by its relative extinction risk (see Appendix 2d for details). Movements of species in and out of the highest threat categories largely drive trends in such indices. The preliminary RLI weighted by extinction risk for amphibians shows a much steeper decline than the equivalent bird index (Figure 4.10). This is because a much higher proportion of amphibians than birds moved into the Critically Endangered (CR) and Critically Endangered (Possibly Extinct) (CR(PE)) categories over the period (see Appendix 2c for a definition of Possibly Extinct). The allocation to CR(PE) was less strictly applied to amphibians compared to birds (see

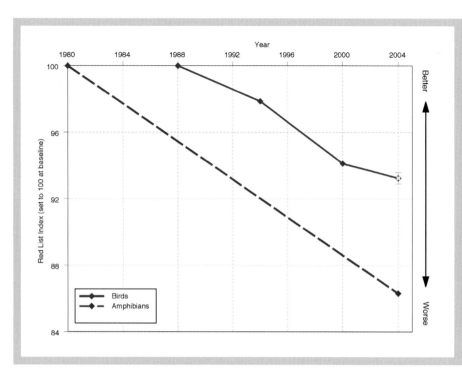

Figure 4.9
The Red List Index (RLI) for all bird species for 1988–2004 and a preliminary RLI for all amphibians for 1980–2004 (retrospective assessment). Sample sizes: birds: 250 genuine status changes out of 2,469 species in categories Extinct in the Wild (EW) to Near Threatened (NT) in at least one assessment; amphibians: 496 out of 2,225 species. Error bars for 2004 RLI value for birds based on estimated number of genuine status changes for 2000–2004 not yet detected owing to information time-lags (see Appendix 2d for further details of methods).

Appendix 2c). However, when the index value was recalculated setting all CR(PE) species to CR, the index still shows a rapid decline, indicating a genuine deterioration in the status of amphibians in the highest categories of threat.

The RLI weighted by extinction risk for birds shows that the rate of deterioration appeared to almost level out during 2000–2004 (although the error bars indicate that in the next few years the belated discovery of genuine status changes for this period could reduce this apparent levelling out; Figure 4.10). This is because for the species closest to extinction, the number that deteriorated in status was almost balanced by the number improving in status owing to conservation action. However, it should be emphasised that one Critically Endangered species went Extinct in the Wild during the period (Hawaiian Crow *Corvus hawaiiensis*), and another is highly likely to have done so (Spix's Macaw *Cyanopsitta spixii*).

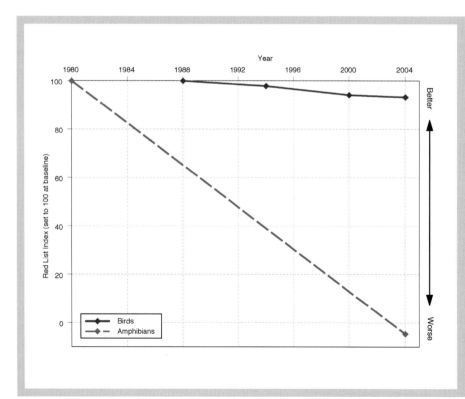

Figure 4.10
The Red List Indices (RLIs) weighted by extinction risk for all bird species for 1988–2004 and for all amphibian species for 1980–2004 (retrospective assessment). Sample sizes: birds: 250 genuine status changes out of 2,469 species in categories Extinct in the Wild (EW) to Near Threatened (NT) in at least one assessment; amphibians: 496 out of 2,225 species. Error bars for 2004 RLI value for birds based on estimated number of genuine status changes for 2000–2004 not yet detected owing to information time-lags (see Appendix 2d for further details).

4.5 Trends for Other Taxonomic Groups

Appendix 3a gives the total number of threatened species for each major taxonomic group on the *IUCN Red List* from 1996 to 2004. In many groups, the numbers of threatened species have increased in recent years. However, as discussed earlier, the total numbers cannot be used to interpret trends in the status of species, because many category changes result from improved knowledge or taxonomic revisions. Only for birds and amphibians have these different reasons for change been analysed. Among the other groups, future analysis is likely to identify significant numbers of species that underwent genuine deteriorations in status during 2000–2004 among primates (owing to increasing levels of habitat loss and hunting) and tortoises and freshwater turtles (owing to unsustainable levels of exploitation in Southeast Asia).

Currently, Red List data on population trends are generally inadequate for analysis for most groups other than birds and amphibians. There are some notable exceptions: for example, population trends are available for 260 species of cycads (Cycadopsida, 288 species in total). Of these, 79.6% (207 species) are declining, 20.4% (53 species) are stable and none are considered to be increasing. Trend information can also be inferred for many marine fishes from fisheries data, despite the lack of Red List assessments, indicating major declines (see Box 4.2).

Photo: © John S. Donaldson.

Photo 4.8
Cycas tansachana (Critically Endangered) a treelike cycad known only from limestone outcrops near Saraburi, Thailand. The plant is restricted in occurrence and under severe pressure from plant collectors and limestone mining operations in the area.

Box 4.2

Fisheries have Collapsed on a Global Scale

Marine fishes are among the poorest represented groups on the *IUCN Red List*, as only 487 of a potential 15,000 species have been assessed. Although Red List data are not complete enough to infer trends in the status of threatened marine fishes over time, data from marine fish groups that are well assessed (chondrichthyan fishes (sharks, rays and chimaeras), syngnathids (seahorses and relatives) and groupers and wrasses) do indicate clearly that exploitation is an important and significant threat to marine species. Despite the lack of Red List assessments, there is plenty of evidence from fisheries data to suggest that the conservation status of exploited marine species is deteriorating.

Fisheries data collected by the Food and Agriculture Organization (FAO) of the United Nations illustrate the rapidly worsening status of exploited marine fishes. FAO has analysed landings records for 200 major fishery resources that account for 77% of world marine fish production. The fisheries have been classified according to four stages of a generalized fishery development model. In the first 'Undeveloped' stage, catches are low and steady, in the second 'Developing' stage catches are rising rapidly, in the third 'Mature' phase, catches reach a peak and start to fall, and in the final 'Senescent' stage, catches are dropping rapidly and the fishery is over-exploited. Their analysis shows a striking shift from undeveloped to senescent fisheries over the last fifty years. Specifically, 60% of the world's major fish resources are mature or senescent and therefore in need of urgent management and conservation attention (FAO 1997a).

continued overleaf...

Box 4.2 *continued*

Fisheries have Collapsed on a Global Scale

These severe fishery declines are of great importance when considering the extinction risk of an exploited species, even though the concept of collapsed fisheries being threatened with extinction is only recently becoming more acceptable. A lack of recovery from low numbers, and low potential recovery rates from low numbers are both logical, defensible metrics of extinction risk. It is often assumed that fishing mortality is the primary factor inhibiting population recovery but this is not the case, as illustrated by the failure by Atlantic Cod *Gadus morhua*, as well as many other commercially exploited species, to recover following its collapse (Hutchings 2001).

Photo: © John E. Randall.

Photo 4.9
The Humphead Wrasse *Cheilinus undulatus* (Endangered) is widely distributed but is nowhere common. Wherever it is fished, even if only moderately, density quickly declines and it appears to be extirpated from several edge of range locations. It is particularly heavily exploited at the centre of its range in southeastern Asia for the live reef fish trade. Fishery-dependent and trade-related data suggest declines over the last 10–15 years in exploited areas.

Photo: © Wolcott Henry.

Photo 4.10
Catches of the Whale Shark *Rhincodon typus* (Vulnerable) have declined with populations apparently depleted by harpoon fisheries in several countries targeting localized concentrations of this huge, slow-moving and behaviourally-vulnerable species, and there is incidental capture in other fisheries.

Based on information provided by Elodie Hudson

Key Findings

• The *IUCN Red List* is a valuable source of data for examining trends in the state of biodiversity.

• Red List Indices provide a robust way of illustrating the net changes to the threat status of particular groups over time.

• Red List Indices show that birds and amphibians are slipping towards extinction at an increasing rate.

• Underlying data draw attention especially to threats from forest loss and long-line fisheries (birds) and disease, habitat loss and exploitation (amphibians).

• The limited information on overall trends for other taxonomic groups suggests that declines are occurring in these groups too.

• The IUCN Red List Programme is improving the taxonomic coverage of the Red List Indices.

Geography of the Red List

Photo: © Peter Paul van Dijk.

Photo 5.1
The Keeled Box Turtle *Pyxidea mouhotii* (Endangered) inhabits the forest floor leaf litter of localized areas of evergreen forests from northeastern India through Myanmar, Lao PDR and Viet Nam to southern China. The species has been harvested in large numbers for the Asian turtle consumption trade, as well as for the international pet trade. Populations have disappeared and remaining populations, including those in formally designated protected areas, appear to be declining.

5.1 Introduction

The geographic range of a species can be assessed using a variety of techniques (Gaston 1994). First, and at the coarsest resolution, species distributions have traditionally been mapped through known occurrence in predefined geographic units, such as countries (Mittermeier 1988) or geopolitical units (Brummitt 2001), and ecological systems and biomes (Olson *et al.* 2001). Second, are polygon range maps ("Extent of Occurrence" (EOO) defined in IUCN (2001) and Appendix 2e), based on a combination of known records and specialist knowledge, although these greatly overestimate occupancy within the range (Corsi *et al.* 2000). Third, the finest resolution approach is to compile point data – known point occurrences (often supported by museum or herbarium specimens) of a given species in a given place at a given time – but uneven sampling is a serious problem for the assessment of point data (Peterson *et al.* 1998; Peterson and Watson 1998). These sampling problems can be reduced by development of inductive range models (Peterson *et al.* 2002) or the establishment of grid based sampling systems to produce atlas data (Udvardy 1981). Data limitations mean that it has not yet been possible to use these latter two approaches across entire taxonomic groups, worldwide.

This section presents a geographic analysis of the *IUCN Red List* data through these three approaches. The first – counting species occurrences in predetermined geographic units (Section 5.2) – has been used in previous analyses of the Red List (Baillie and Groombridge 1996; Hilton-Taylor 2000). The second – analysis of EOO range maps (Section 5.3) for individual species – has previously been possible only for threatened birds (BirdLife International 2000), and so the incorporation of EOO data in the documentation required when submitting a species assessment for inclusion on the *IUCN Red List* allows us remarkable new insights. The third – mapping known point occurrences – is still in its infancy, despite its importance to conservation on the ground (Collar 1993–94, 1996), but here we are able to illustrate the potential provided by mapping selected species at the site scale.

5.2 Mapping Species to Predetermined Geographic Units

The distribution of threatened species is summarized here following five predetermined geographic classifications. One of these is political (countries), the other four ecological (ecological systems, biogeographic realms, biomes, and habitats). The occurrence of threatened species in all of these (with the exception of biomes) is evaluated by using the relevant required documentation for including species on the *IUCN Red List* (see IUCN 2001, pp. 27–29).

5.2.1 Countries

The richness of threatened species per country is useful to give context as a coarse measure of threats to biodiversity, but is heavily conflated by area (Balmford and Long 1995) and driven by the occurrence of widespread species (Lennon *et al.* 2004). Dividing threatened species richness by total numbers of species per country does give a useful measure of relative threat to a nation's biodiversity. The presentation of threatened species occurrences by country is also useful in providing a crosscheck to national Red Lists, and *vice versa* (Hilton-Taylor *et al.* 2000; Rodriguez *et al.* 2000), given the important implications of these for national conservation policy (see Section 8). Particularly informative are the numbers of threatened species endemic (see Appendix 2e for a definition of this term) to each country, because they can guide a "doctrine of ultimate responsibility" for each nation's contribution to global biological heritage (Mittermeier *et al.* 1998).

In Appendix 3j, using the country occurrence documentation data from the 2004 *IUCN Red List*, we list the numbers of threatened species and threatened national endemic species per country for the six taxonomic groups for which the coverage of species in the Red List is most complete: mammals, birds, amphibians, turtles, conifers and cycads; a seventh group, the chondrichthyan fishes (sharks, rays and chimaeras), are also included because although only a third of species have been assessed, it is the largest marine group currently on the Red List. Comparative geographic analyses are impossible for groups that have not been comprehensively assessed. For example, endemic vascular plants have been comprehensively assessed in Ecuador (Valencia *et al.* 2000) and a handful of other countries, but not globally, and so any analysis of threatened plant distributions would be greatly biased towards such countries. We, therefore, restrict data assessment and presentation to those taxonomic groups within which data from all species can be analysed.

Photo © Suzanna León-Yánez.

Photo 5.2
Siphocampylus ecuadoriensis (Endangered) is a shrub endemic to the Ecuadorian Andes. The species is threatened by the ongoing conversion of native vegetation to pasture and ongoing deforestation within protected areas where it occurs.

Several overall patterns stand out from Appendix 3j. First, there is a rather high level of correspondence between the numbers and, especially, proportions of threatened species per country, for each of the seven taxonomic groups. The main exceptions to this pattern appear to be driven by ecological constraints. For example, amphibians have very poor dispersal abilities over saltwater, and so do not occur naturally in many oceanic island nations important for threatened birds such as Mauritius or Vanuatu. Second, while those countries with the largest numbers of threatened and threatened endemic species lie in the continental tropics, those with the highest proportions of threatened endemics are generally tropical island nations (such as Cuba, with >50% of threatened species endemic for five of the seven taxa considered here). This is a combined result of the low species richness of islands and the ecological naïveté of those species that do occur on islands (Diamond 1991). The exception to this pattern is amphibians, for which threatened species have such tiny ranges that nearly all are national endemics.

Considering Appendix 3j country-by-country, the exceptional importance of five countries, Australia, Brazil, China, Indonesia, and Mexico, stands out. Other countries or territories holding particularly large numbers of threatened species include Colombia, India, New Caledonia, Peru, South Africa, and Viet Nam (all of these are among the top three countries for at least one taxonomic group) while Colombia, India, Malaysia, Myanmar, New Caledonia, Papua New Guinea, the Philippines, South Africa, and the United States are all among the top three countries for numbers of threatened endemics for at least one taxonomic group. Additional countries characterized by particularly high proportionate threat in multiple taxa include Madagascar, São Tomé and Principe, and the Seychelles.

Photo: © Juan Pratginestós/WWF-Brazil.

Photo 5.3
Although Brazil currently has 22% of its 95 primate species listed as threatened, one of these, the Golden Lion Tamarin *Leontopithecus rosalia* (Endangered), is showing signs of recovery after nearly 30 years of conservation efforts.

Photo: © Anna Nekaris.

Photo 5.4
In Sri Lanka, the loss of forest cover has impacted many species including the Slender Loris *Loris tardigradus* (Endangered).

5.2.2 Ecological Systems

The most straightforward framework for assessing the ecological distributions of threatened species is to divide the planet's surface into three systems: terrestrial, freshwater, and marine. This classification is complicated by those species that live in the interface between systems (e.g., shorebirds) and those that live in multiple systems (e.g., many amphibians). These are a small proportion of species overall, however – most species occur only in one of the three ecological systems.

The numbers and proportions of total and threatened mammals, birds, amphibians, turtles, chondrichthyan fishes (sharks, rays and chimaeras), conifers and cycads occurring in each of the three ecological systems (as coded on the *IUCN Red List*) are shown in Table 5.1. The absolute number of threatened species known from marine systems is low, primarily a reflection of the recording biases towards terrestrial and freshwater taxa. Even including those taxonomic groups for which comprehensive assessments have yet to be conducted yields only 187 threatened marine species, as opposed to 4,427 that live on land. Assessments in freshwater systems are rather further ahead than marine systems: 1,388 freshwater species (including taxa not yet comprehensively assessed) are listed as threatened. This is wholly an artefact of the fact that major aquatic groups (above all, fish) have yet to be comprehensively assessed for the Red List.

Considering the proportions of threatened species per system gives a rather different picture, without any clear patterns. Among mammals, a considerably higher proportion of freshwater species is threatened than of marine or terrestrial species. Among birds, turtles and chondrichthyan fishes, on the other hand, a considerably higher proportion of marine species is threatened than of freshwater or terrestrial species. A slightly higher proportion of terrestrial amphibians are threatened than of freshwater species. Across all seven taxa, the proportion of threatened freshwater species is slightly higher (25%) than that for marine and terrestrial systems (22 and 21% respectively), as expected from the intensity of threat to freshwater (McAllister *et al.* 1997).

5.2.3 Biogeographic Realms

Biogeographic realms are the eight continent-scale terrestrial and freshwater regions distinguished by characteristic biota that reflect shared evolutionary histories (Udvardy 1975). In Table 5.2 the numbers and proportions of threatened mammals, birds, and amphibians occurring in and endemic to each of the eight biogeographic realms are summarized.

Much the greatest numbers of threatened species, for all taxa, occur in the tropical continents: the Neotropical, Afrotropical, and Indomalayan realms. The Australasia and Palearctic realms have many less threatened species, the Nearctic less still (although it has more threatened amphibians than Australasia), and the Antarctic realm has almost no threatened species. Oceania, while having a low richness of threatened species, has a remarkably high proportionate threat, reflecting again the vulnerability of oceanic island biodiversity. Proportionate threat is remarkably similar between biogeographic realms and taxa, although rather low for Nearctic mammals and Australasian amphibians, and high for Indomalayan and Neotropical amphibians.

Table 5.1

Total numbers of species and numbers of threatened species from well-assessed taxonomic groups occurring in marine, freshwater and terrestrial ecological systems (with proportions indicated in parentheses). Some species occur in more than one system, and so are counted multiple times in the table.

	Marine	Freshwater	Terrestrial
Mammals			
Total	130	130	4,765
Threatened	27 (21%)	42 (32%)	1,081 (23%)
Birds			
Total	351	1,350	9,761
Threatened	96 (27%)	132 (10%)	1,137 (12%)
Turtles			
Total	7	159	185
Threatened	6 (86%)	96 (60%)	115 (62%)
Amphibians			
Total	0	3,908	5,436
Threatened	0 (0%)	1,100 (28%)	1,790 (33%)
Chondrichthyan Fishes			
Total	355	26	0
Threatened	58 (16%)	18 (69%)	0 (0%)
Conifers			
Total	0	1	618
Threatened	0 (0%)	0 (0%)	153 (25%)
Cycads			
Total	0	0	288
Threatened	0 (0%)	0 (0%)	151 (52%)
Combined			
Total	843	5,574	21,053
Threatened	187 (22%)	1,388 (25%)	4,427 (21%)

Table 5.2

Total numbers of species, and numbers and percentages of threatened species, from well-mapped taxonomic groups (mammals, birds, amphibians) occurring in and (in parentheses) endemic to each of the eight terrestrial biogeographic realms. Marine mammals are excluded.

Realm	Species			Threatened species			Percentage species threatened		
	Mammals n = 4,853	Birds n = 9,917	Amphibians n = 5,708	Mammals n = 1,101	Birds n = 1,213	Amphibians n =1,856	Mammals	Birds	Amphibians
Antarctica	0	36	0	0	9	0	0%	25%	0%
12,315,000 km²	(0)	(4)	(0)	(0)	(1)	(0)	(0%)	(25%)	(0%)
Afrotropical	1,167	2,228	930	239	229	235	20%	10%	25%
21,739,000 km²	(1,037)	(1,746)	(913)	(227)	(199)	(229)	(22%)	(11%)	(25%)
Indomalayan	956	2,000	882	234	227	295	24%	11%	33%
8,524,000 km²	(515)	(758)	(722)	(183)	(165)	(257)	(36%)	(22%)	(36%)
Australasia	693	1,669	545	171	190	70	25%	11%	13%
9,248,000 km²	(614)	(1,330)	(515)	(169)	(128)	(64)	(28%)	(10%)	(12%)
Nearctic	512	696	298	39	54	73	8%	8%	24%
22,609,000 km²	(233)	(58)	(235)	(27)	(18)	(56)	(12%)	(31%)	(24%)
Neotropical	1,304	3,808	2,732	214	430	1,118	16%	11%	41%
19,372,000 km²	(1,040)	(3,217)	(2,660)	(203)	(377)	(1,100)	(20%)	(12%)	(41%)
Oceania	15	272	3	8	94	1	53%	35%	33%
47,000 km²	(10)	(157)	(3)	(7)	(84)	(1)	(70%)	(54%)	(33%)
Palearctic	967	1,528	395	171	122	100	18%	8%	25%
53,372,000 km²	(454)	(188)	(255)	(112)	(49)	(76)	(25%)	(26%)	(30%)

The Food and Agricultural Organization (FAO) of the United Nations, which has defined 19 marine regions (Fishing Areas) worldwide, provide a marine analogue of the biogeographic realms. Coding against these marine regions is required documentation when submitting assessments of marine species for inclusion on the *IUCN Red List* (IUCN 2001), and so for those few marine megafaunal groups that have been comprehensively assessed, it is therefore now possible to begin to unveil geographic patterns in the geography of threat in the marine system. Table 5.3 summarizes the numbers of threatened marine mammals, seabirds, chondrichthyan fishes, and seahorses in each FAO Fishing Area (we cannot assess relative threat because the latter two groups have not yet been comprehensively assessed, but sufficient species have been assessed for comparative purposes).

Relative to the other three groups, marine mammals appear to be an outlier with much the largest numbers of threatened species occurring in the northern Pacific Ocean regions. By contrast, the regions holding the greatest numbers of threatened seabirds, chondrichthyan fishes and seahorses are concentrated in the 'coral triangle' region of the eastern Indian Ocean and southwest and western central Pacific. The Arctic and Antarctic Oceans hold the fewest threatened species across all taxa (with the exception of threatened seabirds, a number of species of which occur in Antarctica). The results for the chondrichthyan fishes need to be treated as preliminary as the concentrations of threatened species may simply be a reflection of where assessment workshops have been held to date (see Box 2.3).

Table 5.3

Numbers of threatened marine mammals (cetaceans, seals and sirenians), seabirds, chondrichthyan fishes (sharks, rays and chimaeras), and seahorses in each FAO Fishing Area. Note: only marine mammals and seabirds have been comprehensively assessed.

FAO Area	Marine mammals (n = 30)	Seabirds (n = 80)	Chondrichthyan fishes (n = 58)	Seahorses (n = 16)
Arctic Sea	5	0	0	0
Atlantic - Antarctic	5	14	0	0
Atlantic - eastern central	8	3	10	0
Atlantic - northeast	7	1	9	0
Atlantic - northwest	9	2	4	1
Atlantic - southeast	6	20	8	1
Atlantic - southwest	6	16	18	0
Atlantic - western central	7	2	7	1
Indian Ocean - Antarctic	5	15	0	0
Indian Ocean - eastern	6	25	26	7
Indian Ocean - western	6	19	23	3
Mediterranean and Black Sea	6	1	9	0
Pacific - Antarctic	5	11	0	0
Pacific - eastern central	12	24	6	2
Pacific - northeast	10	10	3	0
Pacific - northwest	12	9	14	5
Pacific - southeast	7	31	6	1
Pacific - southwest	7	41	13	3
Pacific - western central	6	21	31	8

Photo 5.5
The Northwest Pacific (Asia) Grey Whale Stock *Eschrichtius robustus* (Critically Endangered) is geographically distinct, and is thought to have less than 50 reproductive individuals. This subpopulation was hunted to near extinction and remains severely depleted.

Photo 5.6
The Wandering Albatross *Diomedea exulans* (Vulnerable) is a wide-ranging pelagic species of the southern oceans, but most of its breeding colonies are on Subantarctic islands. The main cause of decline is the impact of longline fisheries.

5.2.4 Biomes

At a finer scale, it is possible to assess the distributions of threatened species across biomes. Biomes represent global-scale variation in the structure, dynamics and complexity of terrestrial and freshwater communities and ecosystems that are driven by key global-scale patterns such as temperature and precipitation. Olson *et al.* (2001) identified 14 biomes worldwide, a classification followed here in the interest of standardization. In Figures 5.1 and 5.2 we graph the numbers and proportions of threatened mammals, birds and amphibians occurring in and endemic to each biome.

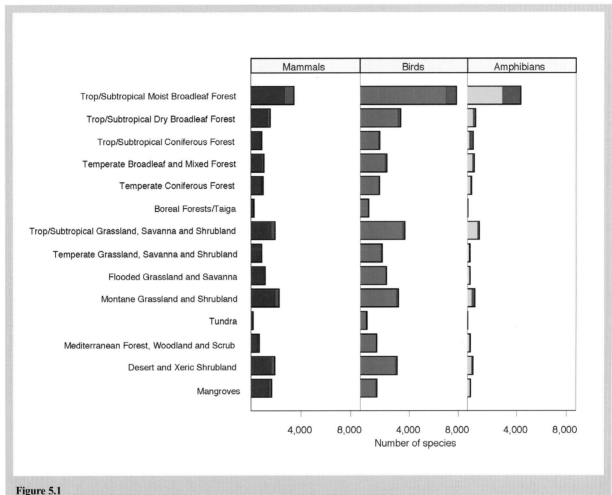

Figure 5.1

Numbers of threatened mammals, birds and amphibians occurring in each biome (proportion of threatened species indicated in red).

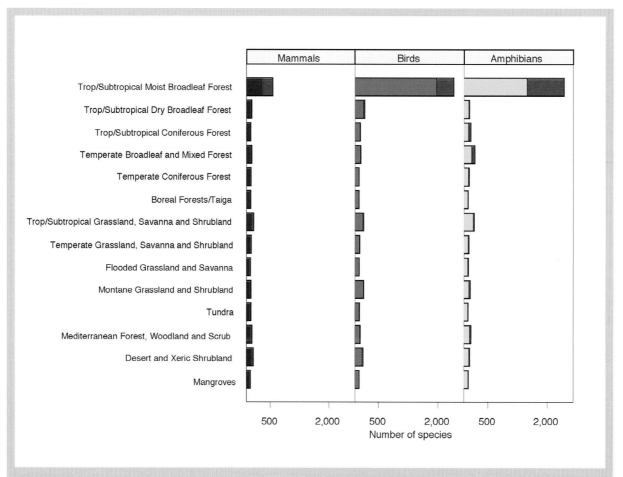

Figure 5.2

Numbers of threatened mammals, birds and amphibians endemic to each biome (proportion of threatened species indicated in red).

The results of this analysis are stark: Tropical/Subtropical Moist Broadleaf Forest is far and away the richest biome in terms of numbers of species and of threatened species for all three taxa, and is to a first approximation the only biome holding significant numbers of endemics or of threatened endemics for any of the three taxa. Tropical/Subtropical Dry Broadleaf Forest, Tropical/Subtropical Grassland, Savanna and Shrubland, Montane Grassland and Shrubland, and Desert and Xeric Shrubland all hold moderately large numbers of species and of threatened species for all three taxa (with the exception of the latter, which holds only a handful of threatened amphibians). The high-latitude biomes of Boreal Forests/Taiga and Tundra hold very few species, and even the Mediterranean Forest, Woodland and Scrub are remarkably depauperate (though this will probably not be the case once comprehensive plant data are included).

Photo: © Asad Rahmani.

Photo 5.7

The Lesser Florican *Sypheotides indica* (Endangered) is a dry grassland species from India, Nepal and Pakistan. It has a very small, declining population, primarily a result of loss and degradation of its habitat.

5.2.5 Habitats

The finest ecological scale at which one can assess the distribution of threatened species is the scale of habitats, and, indeed, coding species up to their habitat preferences is part of the required documentation in the Red List assessment process (IUCN 2001). The importance of each major habitat for threatened and non-threatened birds and amphibians is illustrated in Figure 5.3 (these data have yet to be comprehensively compiled for any other taxa). Not surprisingly, given the results above for biomes, forest habitats are clearly the most important across both taxa. Grassland and shrubland habitats also hold high numbers of species. For amphibians, inland wetland habitats are exceptionally important, particularly for those species that have a larval stage. Another interesting pattern to emerge is the tendency of both bird and amphibian species to use artificial habitats (both terrestrial and aquatic), although

analyses of the relative importance of each habitat type for birds reveals that these are nonetheless of minor importance (BirdLife International 2004b). Not surprisingly, considering the bias here towards terrestrial vertebrates, marine habitats come out as having few species (with the exception of marine representatives of the birds), as do desert habitats (which would likely come out stronger were data on reptiles and plant groups such as cacti included). When one considers the proportion of threatened species in a habitat as a percentage of the total occurring, marine emerges as particularly important for birds, almost certainly a result of the threatened status of, in particular, species in the order Procellariiformes (albatrosses, petrels and shearwaters). For amphibians, forest habitats clearly emerge as holding the largest numbers of threatened species, although at least 28% of amphibians in freshwater habitats are considered threatened.

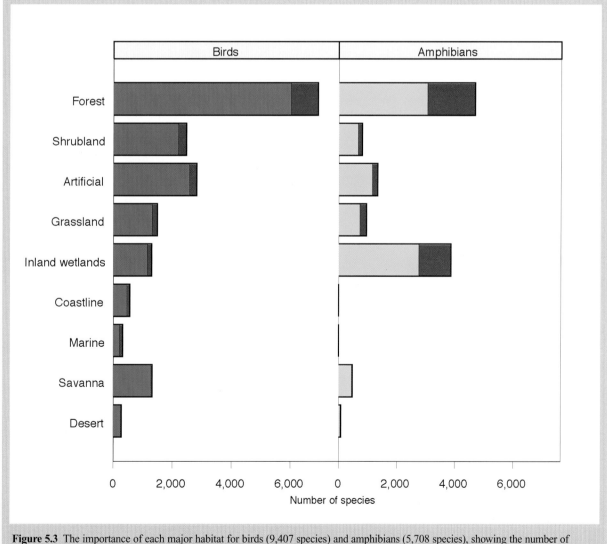

Figure 5.3 The importance of each major habitat for birds (9,407 species) and amphibians (5,708 species), showing the number of threatened species (in red) relative to the totals. Extinct species are excluded.

5.3 Mapping Species' Extent of Occurrences

Analysis of Extent of Occurrence (EOO) data has never before covered more than a single continent, for example, Africa (mammals, birds, snakes and amphibians; Brooks *et al.* 2001). However, such data are now available worldwide for all mammal, turtle and amphibian species (as part of the documentation required for assessing the status of species for the *IUCN Red List*). Data for non-threatened, Old World birds are not yet available, but all threatened (BirdLife International 2000, updated 2004a) and Western Hemisphere (Ridgely *et al.* 2003) species now have EOO data compiled.

5.3.1 Species Richness

In Figure 5.4, the species richness of all species of mammals, Western Hemisphere birds, freshwater turtles, and amphibians is mapped. Species richness patterns are primarily driven by the distributions of common, widespread species (Lennon *et al.* 2004), but they nonetheless provide context for threatened species distributions (Section 5.3.3).

The most obvious pattern from these data is that for all taxa the tropics hold much higher species richness than do the temperate, boreal and polar regions. Figure 5.5 demonstrates this by plotting the number of species in each 5-degree latitudinal band for all mammals, threatened birds, and amphibians. As expected from the relationship between the number of species in an area and the size of that area (Rosenzweig 1992), some of this pattern is explained by variation in landmass across latitudinal bands. However, species richness is much higher in the tropics than would be expected based on area alone, peaking around the equator for all taxa.

The other pattern obvious from Figure 5.4 is one of covariance between taxa. Thus, for example, species richness per grid cell is tightly correlated between mammals, freshwater turtles, and amphibians. Considering the Western Hemisphere only yields similarly high correlation coefficients for each of these three taxa compared to birds. Obviously, there are taxon specific differences driven by particular biological traits. Birds, for example, have the ability to disperse over water more than most of the taxa mapped here, and so occur in larger numbers on islands,

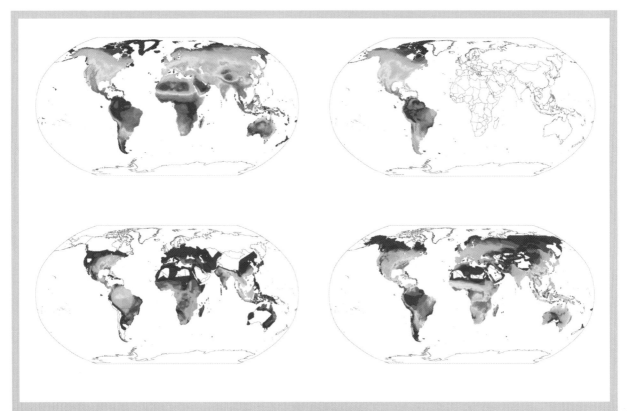

Figure 5.4 Species richness maps for four taxonomic groups: clockwise from top left: mammals (marine species excluded); Western Hemisphere birds; amphibians; and turtles (at a half-degree resolution). Dark red colours correspond to higher richness, dark blue to lowest. Colour scale based on 20 equal-area classes. Maximum richness equals 258 for mammals, 877 species for Western Hemisphere birds, 21 species for turtles, and 142 amphibians.

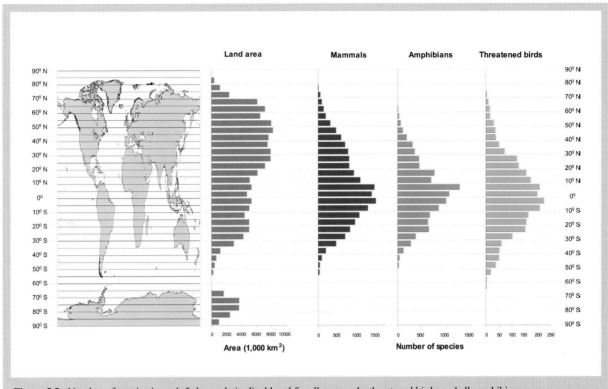

Figure 5.5   Number of species in each 5-degree latitudinal band for all mammals, threatened birds, and all amphibians.

while ectothermic (cold-blooded) reptiles flourish in desert regions generally depauperate in other animal taxa. Other differences are less easily explained, such as the high richness of mammal species in East Africa, and of turtles and amphibians in the southeastern USA. In general, these differences will increase with increasing evolutionary (and hence often corresponding ecological) difference between taxa (Reid 1998); one expects less correlation between mammal and plant distributions, for instance, than one would between mammal and bird distributions.

5.3.2 Restricted-Range Species

There is a widespread correlation between species' range size and extinction risk (Purvis *et al.* 2000b), and, indeed, geographic range is inherent in the Red List Criteria (see Appendix 2a). It is well known that the frequency distribution of species' range sizes has a strong right skew; most species have small range sizes (Gaston 1996). Absolute values vary within this general pattern. More mobile species, such as birds, tend to have large distributions, while those of very sedentary species, such as amphibians, are generally much smaller (Figure 5.6). Nevertheless, the shape of frequency distributions of species' range sizes appears to be similar across all taxa examined to date (with the median range size consistently an order of magnitude smaller than the mean), probably

because consistent processes are shaping these distributions (Gaston 1998).

Not only do most species have small ranges, but also these narrowly distributed species tend to co-occur in 'centres of endemism' (Anderson 1994). In Figure 5.7 a threshold approach is applied to map the centres of endemism inhabited, respectively, by more than two overlapping mammal, bird and amphibian species (freshwater turtles are also included, for comparison) with global distributions of less than 50,000 sq. km. The most consistent pattern emerging is that almost all centres of endemism lie in isolated or topographically varied regions. This is true for both geographical isolates such as mountains, peninsulas and islands. Perhaps as a consequence of this, they also tend to be near the coast. Another consistent pattern revealed by Figure 5.7 is the extreme concentration of centres of endemism in the tropics. This is the geographical manifestation of 'Rapoport's rule' (Rapoport 1982), which states that the mean latitude of a species' range correlates with the species' range size, although the generality of this 'rule' has been questioned (Gaston 1999) and it may be explicable by chance alone rather than by any underlying biological cause (Colwell and Hurtt 1994). The degree of overlap between centres of endemism across birds, mammals and amphibians is remarkable (Figure 5.8).

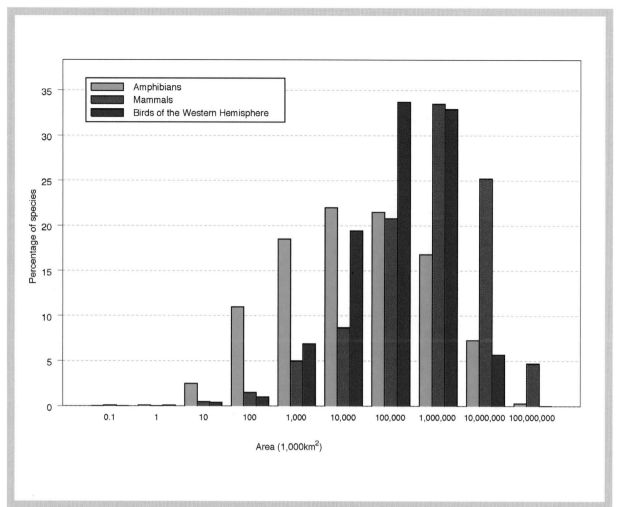

Figure 5.6
Frequency distribution of $\log_{10}$ transformed range sizes for mammals (marine species excluded; 4,734 species, mean = 1.7×10^6 km²; median = 2.5×10^5 km²), birds (species endemic to the Western Hemisphere only; 3,980 species, mean = 2.1×10^6 km²; median = 4.0×10^5 km²), and amphibians (4,409 species, mean = 4.0×105 km²; median = 1.8×104 km²). Data Deficient species are excluded. The $\log_{10}$ transformation makes the distribution look slightly left-skewed, but in fact the untransformed distribution is strongly right-skewed, that is, most species have very small range sizes.

5.3.3 Threatened Species Richness

Just as species are not evenly distributed across the planet, so threats to species are not evenly distributed (Sanderson *et al.* 2002). The species richness of threatened mammals, birds, freshwater turtles, and amphibians is illustrated in Figure 5.9. The maps show interesting similarities and differences between the groups. All four taxa show marked concentrations of threatened species in southern Brazil, Madagascar, the Western Ghats of India, the eastern Himalayas, central China, mainland Southeast Asia, Sumatra, Borneo, and the Philippines; threatened mammals, birds and amphibians are also concentrated in the Andes, West Africa, Cameroon, the Albertine Rift of Central Africa, the Eastern Arc Mountains of Tanzania, and Sri Lanka. Somewhat not surprisingly then, these same regions have all been identified as "biodiversity hotspots" (Myers *et al.* 2000; Mittermeier *et al.* 2004). All of these patterns are heavily driven by the maps of restricted-range species (Figure 5.7).

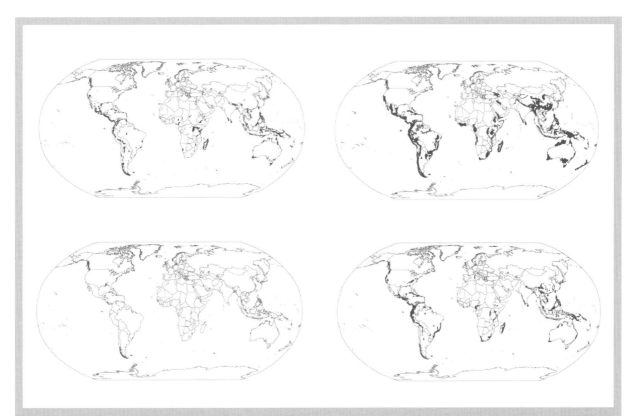

Figure 5.7 Centres of endemism inhabited, respectively, by more than two overlapping species with global distributions of less than 50,000 sq. km (mapped at a quarter-degree cell). Clockwise from top left: mammals; birds; amphibians; and turtles.

Birds
Mammals
Amphibians
Birds and Mammals
Birds and Amphibians
Mammals and Amphibians
Birds, Mammals and Amphibians

Figure 5.8 Overlap of centres of endemism inhabited, respectively, by more than two overlapping mammal, bird, and amphibian species with global distributions of less than 50,000 sq. km (mapped at a quarter-degree cell). This map excludes freshwater turtles (shown above), which have not yet been comprehensively assessed.

Photo: © de Saix.

Photo 5.8
Hyperolius rubrovermiculatus (Endangered), one of the African reed frogs, is only known from the Shimba Hills in coastal Kenya, where it is intrinsically at risk because of its small range.

Photo: © Roland Seitre.

Photo 5.9
Although the Grey-necked Picathartes *Picathartes oreas* (Vulnerable) has a relatively wide range, its population throughout west-central Africa is highly fragmented, and considered small and possibly in overall decline.

Photo: © Tasso Leventis.

Photo 5.10
Pygmy Hog *Sus salvanius* (Critically Endangered) found in the tall grasslands of the northern Indian subcontinent. Numbers remaining in the wild are very low and all hopes rest on a successful breeding and reintroduction programme. This juvenile animal was photographed at the Pygmy Hog Research and Breeding Centre in Basistha (near Guwahati, Assam, India).

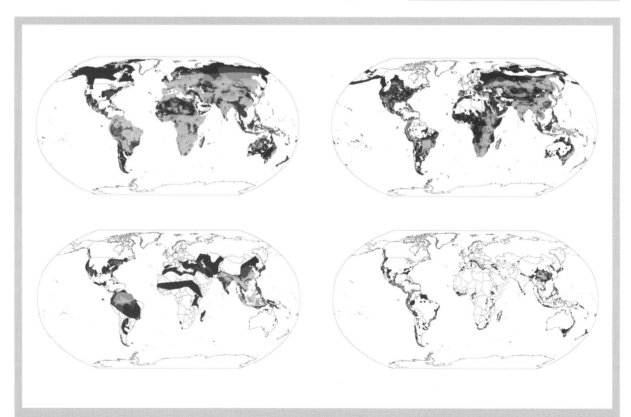

Figure 5.9   Threatened species richness maps for four taxonomic groups clockwise from top left: mammals (marine species excluded); birds; amphibians; and turtles (at a half-degree resolution). Dark red colours correspond to higher richness, dark blue to lowest. Colour scale based on 10 equal-area classes. Maximum richness equals 25 species for mammals, 25 species for birds, 16 species for turtles, and 44 species for amphibians.

The mammal map (Figure 5.9) is noteworthy in that there is at least one threatened mammal species in most parts of the world. This is probably a reflection of the propensity for large-bodied, widely distributed mammals to become globally threatened. In addition to the geographic regions listed above, important concentrations of threatened mammals also occur in the eastern Amazon basin, southern Europe, Kenya, Sumatra, Java, the Philippines, New Guinea and Australia. Interestingly, Mesoamerica and the Caribbean islands are relatively unimportant for threatened mammals (in the case of the Caribbean, this is probably due to past extinctions (see Section 3)), but, on the other hand, clearly stand out for amphibians.

The bird map differs from the others in that the importance of oceanic islands is emphasized. Other areas that are of great importance for threatened birds, but which are not listed above, include the Caribbean islands, the Cerrado woodlands of Brazil, the highlands of South Africa, the plains of northern India and Pakistan, Sumatra, the Philippines, the steppes of central Asia, eastern Russia, Japan, southeastern China, and New Zealand. As for mammals, Mesoamerica and Australia are relatively less important. However, in contrast to mammals, the Amazon basin, Europe, Java and New Guinea are of relatively lower importance for threatened birds.

Threatened freshwater turtles exhibit rather different species richness patterns than the other taxa. In addition to the fact that their species richness is very low in the Atlantic Forest, Cerrado, Tropical Andes, Guinean Forests of West Africa, Eastern Arc Mountains and Coastal Forests and other hotspots holding so many threatened mammals, birds, and amphibians, they also concentrate in some surprising areas. These include the Amazon (due to the presence of the large, wide ranging, and heavily persecuted river turtles of the genus *Podocnemis*), the eastern and southwestern United States, and Asia Minor.

The most noteworthy aspect of the amphibian map, is that most of the world is devoid of threatened amphibian species (the opposite situation to that of mammals). However, threatened amphibians occur more densely in smaller areas than either mammals or birds (up to 44 species per half degree grid square, compared with 24 for both mammals and birds). The fact that concentrations of threatened amphibians are often in tiny areas of the montane tropics makes it hard to see all them clearly on a global map. The majority of the world's known threatened amphibians occur from Mexico south to northern Peru, and on the Caribbean islands. Most of the other important concentrations of globally threatened amphibians mirror the pattern for the other three groups, although eastern Australia and the southwestern Cape region of South Africa are also centres of amphibian threat. It should be emphasized that the paucity of data from certain parts of the world is probably severely underestimating concentrations of threatened amphibians, especially in the Albertine Rift, Eastern Himalayas, much of mainland Southeast Asia, Sumatra, Sulawesi, the Philippines, and Peru.

Photo 5.11
Gastrotheca ovifera (Endangered) is a species of marsupial frog. The eggs are carried on the female's back, which hatch into froglets. This species is restricted to the Venezuelan coastal range, where some populations appear to be in decline.

Photo: © Michael and Patricia Fogden.

An alternative perspective on the geography of threatened species is to measure numbers of threatened species relative to the overall numbers of a particular taxonomic group present. This is shown here for mammals, Western Hemisphere birds, freshwater turtles, and amphibians in Figure 5.10. The results are highly sensitive to change in areas with low overall species richness (e.g., the movement of a single species in the depauperate polar regions from one category of threat to another could make a large difference to the overall map), but nevertheless reveal some interesting additional patterns. For all four groups the proportion of fauna in danger of global extinction is high in island ecosystems such as the Caribbean, Madagascar, Sundaland, the Philippines, and New Zealand. For amphibians the map of relative threatened species richness largely parallels that for all species, whereas the relative distribution of threatened mammals and turtles is much more expansive. This covers threatened but species-poor areas of the temperate zone, such as California, the fringes of the Sahara, and central China; for amphibians the Argentinean Pampas and Asia Minor also stand out, as does northeast Canada for mammals.

Lack of comprehensive geographic and threat assessment for other species groups precludes the presentation of maps for these taxa. However, the availability of such data is likely to reveal many broad similarities with the patterns presented above for mammals, birds and amphibians, as well as some differences. For example, distribution patterns of threatened reptiles (in particular lizards) are likely to highlight the importance of some arid ecosystems. It is already known that some distribution patterns of threatened plants do not match those of most animal groups, some notable examples being the Cape Floral Region and Succulent Karoo of South Africa, and the deserts of the southwestern United States and northern Mexico. There are also very different patterns of threat among some freshwater groups. For example, the Mississippi drainage system is probably the global centre for threatened freshwater mussels. Patterns of threat in marine ecosystems will, of course, be completely different, and data on these patterns are still largely unavailable. However, the importance of the southern oceans in general, and the Tasman Sea and the southwestern Pacific around New Zealand for globally threatened seabirds can be seen in Box 5.1.

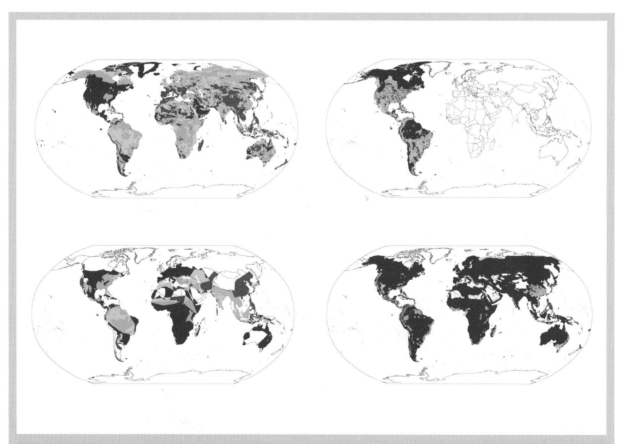

Figure 5.10 Threatened species richness relative to the overall number of species present in four taxonomic groups: clockwise from top left: mammals (marine species excluded); Western Hemisphere birds; amphibians; and turtles (at a half-degree resolution). Dark red colours correspond to higher richness, dark blue to lowest. Colour scale based on five equal-area classes.

Photo: © Janice Golding.

Photo 5.12
Bastard Quiver Tree *Aloe pillansii* (Critically Endangered) is an example of one of the many threatened succulent plants found in the Succulent Karoo region of South Africa.

Photo: © Craig Hilton-Taylor.

Photo 5.13
The Mulanje Cedar *Widdringtonia whytei* (Endangered) is confined to the Mulanje massif in southern Malawi. This is an Alliance for Zero Extinction (AZE) locality.

Box 5.1

The Open Oceans are Important for Threatened Birds

The ranges of globally threatened seabirds cover marine areas in the Economic Exclusion Zones of many countries, but also encompass large parts of the open oceans outside national sovereignty. For example, the highest densities of threatened birds at sea are found in international waters in southern oceans, with a particular concentration in the Tasman Sea and the southwestern Pacific around New Zealand. International cooperation is therefore required to conserve such species, many of which are threatened through incidental capture by commercial longline fisheries.

Taken from BirdLife International (2004b)

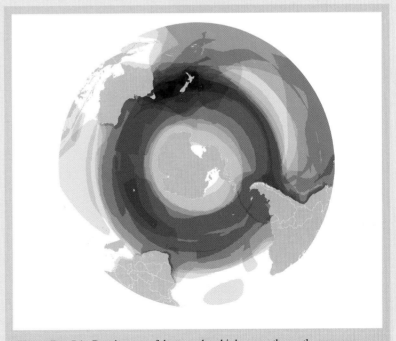

Figure Box 5.1 Density map of threatened seabirds across the southern oceans

5.4 Mapping Species to the Locality Scale

As the spatial resolution of data on the geographic distributions of threatened species increases, so does the utility of these data for conservation (Collar 1993–4, 1996), but, unfortunately, the effort required to compile the data does as well. Nevertheless, the world's museums and herbaria represent a vast storehouse of such fine-scale geographic biodiversity data, and a number of initiatives are underway that suggest that these data will become increasingly available in the future (Bisby *et al.* 2000).

This said, synthesis of the numerous point data already available not only provides much finer resolution insight into the distribution of threatened species, but also provides a basis for establishing targets for site-scale conservation actions on the ground (see Section 8). The effort necessary to compile such data means that we are a long way from being able to show localities globally for all threatened species across multiple taxa. It is possible, however, to show important cross-sections of the data by trading these dimensions off against each other. Thus to allow mapping globally we have to compromise depth of coverage within

taxa on the Red List. It is now possible to map localities (defined in Appendix 2e) for all threatened species within an individual taxon continentally (for birds, at least), and at a finer, regional scale, to map localities for all threatened species in the region of interest.

One important dataset concerns the distribution of Critically Endangered (CR) and Endangered (EN) species restricted to a single locality (www.zeroextinction.org). Figure 5.11 maps all sites known to hold the last remaining populations of a CR or EN mammal, bird, amphibian, or conifer species (as well as those reptiles assessed globally to date; cycads are pending). Broadly, most of these sites lie in the tropics, as one would expect, especially on islands. Interestingly, the map shows much stronger pattern in Latin America (Baja California, Caribbean, Tropical Andes, Atlantic Forest) and Africa (Cameroon Highlands, East African Highlands, Madagascar) than it does in Southeast Asia, where sites are scattered liberally across the continent.

A much broader approach is to compile data on all localities for all threatened species within given taxonomic groups. This clearly requires much greater investment in data collection and compilation, and so to date can only be presented as examples for specific geographic regions. One

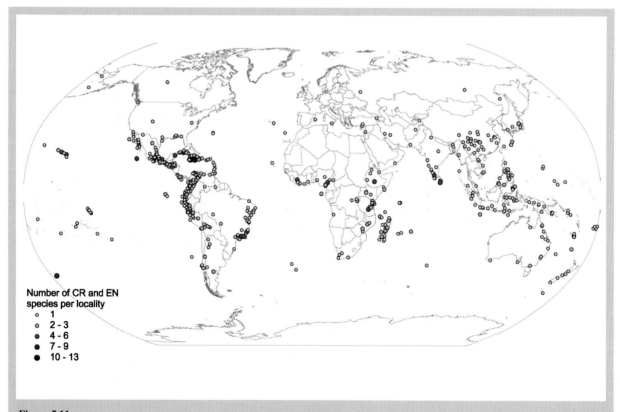

Number of CR and EN
species per locality
○ 1
◦ 2 - 3
● 4 - 6
● 7 - 9
● 10 - 13

Figure 5.11

Map of localities (n=595) holding endemic, Critically Endangered (CR) or Endangered (EN) mammal, bird, turtle, crocodile, iguana, amphibian, and conifer species (source: the Alliance for Zero Extinction).

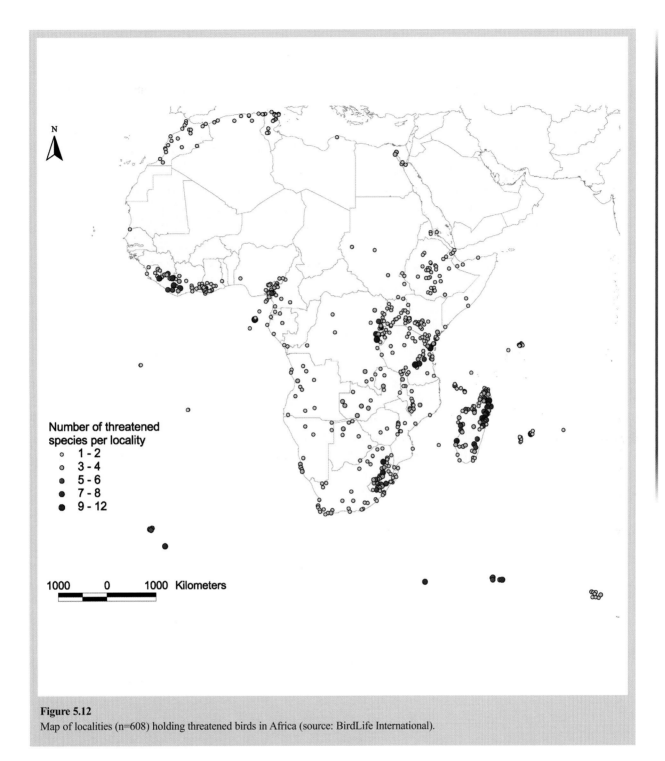

Figure 5.12
Map of localities (n=608) holding threatened birds in Africa (source: BirdLife International).

of the best examples comes from Africa, where the occurrence of all threatened bird species (Vulnerable (VU) species must exceed 10 pairs or 30 individuals at a single locality to be included in this dataset) has been mapped at the locality scale using the Important Bird Areas approach of BirdLife International (Collar and Stuart 1988; Fishpool and Evans 2001; Figure 5.12). Similar work has been completed in the Middle East, Europe, Asia, Canada, Mexico and the Andes, and is on-going in the Pacific, the rest of the Americas, Antarctica and marine areas. To date, some 4,032

sites holding threatened birds have been identified worldwide. Localities holding threatened bird species are highly clustered: in Africa, regions like the Mediterranean coast, Upper Guinea, the Cameroon highlands, the East and South African montane highlands, Madagascar, and the Indian Ocean Islands have particular concentrations of sites holding threatened birds. The Miombo-Mopane woodlands of South-central Africa hold a number of sites, albeit spread fairly far apart, and the Sahara-Sahel, Congo Forests, and Kalahari have very few localities hosting threatened species.

Expansion of the identification of individual localities holding threatened species beyond birds to cover all species on the Red List hits the most serious data limitations. However, new data from Madagascar, incorporating numbers of threatened mammals, birds, reptiles, amphibians, freshwater fish, and plants, demonstrates that this approach is possible for a wide range of taxa. Figure 5.13 represents a map of those 141 localities across Madagascar holding populations of these species. The map emphasizes the pattern of clustering seen for birds at the pan-African scale. Thus, a large number of localities holding threatened species are located in the country's eastern rain forest, western dry forest, and southwestern spiny forest, while the long-deforested central plateau holds very few (although the latter is also a region where many species extinctions have probably gone unrecorded).

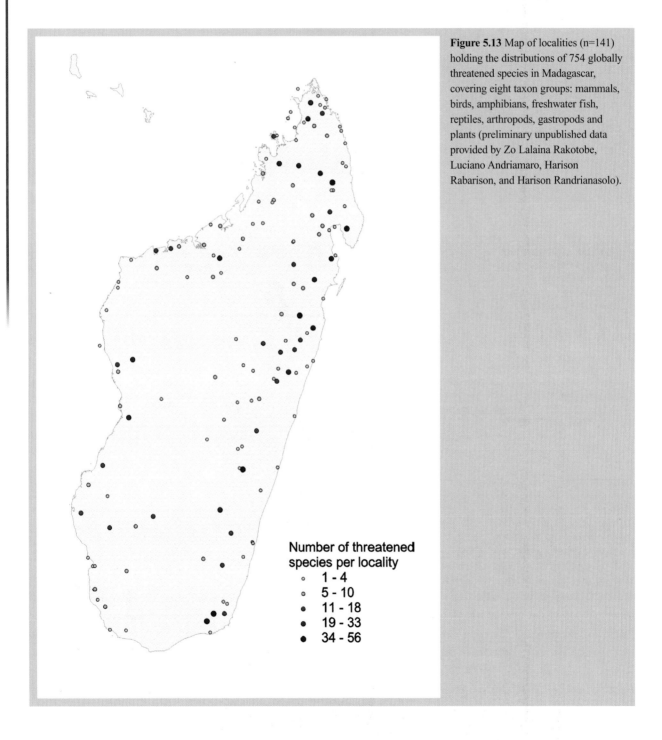

Figure 5.13 Map of localities (n=141) holding the distributions of 754 globally threatened species in Madagascar, covering eight taxon groups: mammals, birds, amphibians, freshwater fish, reptiles, arthropods, gastropods and plants (preliminary unpublished data provided by Zo Lalaina Rakotobe, Luciano Andriamaro, Harison Rabarison, and Harison Randrianasolo).

Number of threatened
species per locality
   ∘   1 - 4
   ∘   5 - 10
   •   11 - 18
   •   19 - 33
   •   34 - 56

Photo: © P.J. Stephenson.

Photo 5.14
The Aquatic Tenrec *Limnogale mergulus* (Endangered) requires clean and fast flowing water and is therefore threatened by the increasing siltation of the rivers, due to soil erosion following deforestation in Madagascar.

Photo: © Frank Todd.

Photo 5.15
Madagascar Teal *Anas bernieri* (Endangered) has a very small population that is declining rapidly due to habitat loss and hunting.

Photo: © Paul Loiselle.

Photo 5.16
Pachypanchax sakaramyi (Critically Endangered) is an endemic Madagascan killifish known only for certain from a few small puddles fed by a leaking water tap, following the diversion of the headwaters of the Sakaramy River for domestic use by local people.

Key Findings

- The overall message from this section is that threatened species are distributed highly unevenly around the surface of the planet.

Within this, five other key conclusions emerge:

- Patterns of threatened species distributions are remarkably congruent between taxa analysed. Differences are driven by underlying range-size distributions among taxonomic groups (e.g., birds tend to have larger range sizes than amphibians), and by ecological limitations of specific taxa (e.g., birds are better able to disperse over saltwater than amphibians).

- Most threatened species occur in the tropics, especially on mountains and islands. In the marine realm, the 'coral triangle' of the western Pacific and eastern Indian Ocean holds the most threatened species in most taxa.

- The uneven distribution of threatened species means that most known threatened species occur in a few countries. Australia, Brazil, China, Indonesia, and Mexico hold particularly large numbers of threatened species and endemics.

- Most threatened species assessed to date are terrestrial. The smaller numbers of threatened species in marine and freshwater systems are artefacts of lack of assessment, and preliminary indications suggest that freshwater species, in particular, may actually be proportionately more seriously threatened than terrestrial species.

- Decisions regarding resolution of mapping involve trade-offs regarding the geographic extent of mapping, the breadth of taxonomic coverage, and the depth of coverage through the Red List Categories.

Photo: © Dave Currie.

Photo 5.17
The Seychelles Scops-owl *Otus insularis* (Endangered) is endemic to Mahé in the Seychelles. Previously Critically Endangered, this owl's status has recently improved as its favoured upland forest habitat has increased in extent over the last 40 years. However, the population is still extremely small and the species is susceptible to introduced predators such as Black Rat *Rattus rattus* and Barn Owl *Tyto alba*.

The Many Causes of Threat

Photo: © Michael and Patricia Fogden.

Photo 6.1
The Golden-eyed Leaf Frog *Agalychnis annae* (Endangered) was once a common species in the mountains of Costa Rica. In the late 1980s, its populations crashed and it disappeared from almost all of its range, and now it survives only in heavily disturbed and polluted habitats in the suburbs of San José.

6.1 Introduction

The influence of human activities on wild species has grown at an unprecedented rate. Although some species respond positively to anthropogenic pressures, the great majority show only limited tolerance of increasingly widespread and rapid changes to ecosystems worldwide. The major human-induced impacts on biodiversity are: habitat destruction and fragmentation; invasive alien species; over-utilization; disease; pollution and contaminants; incidental mortality; and climate change.

In the *2004 IUCN Red List of Threatened Species™*, data on threats to species have been collated comprehensively for all amphibians and all threatened birds, and also for 78% of threatened mammals, and so the analyses presented here are restricted to these three groups. However, because birds, mammals and amphibians are not fully representative of species as a whole, some case studies to illustrate important threats in some other taxonomic groups are also included.

Analyses of the data on threats to bird, mammal and amphibian species evaluated for the 2004 *IUCN Red List* (for methods, see Appendix 2f) show that the most pervasive threat that they face is habitat destruction and degradation (see Figure 6.1) driven by agricultural and forestry activities. Over-exploitation, invasive alien species, pollution and disease are other important threats, but birds, mammals and amphibians differ in terms of the relative importance of these. Incidental mortality, human disturbance and persecution have so far had less impact in terms of the total numbers of species affected, but they can be serious for some susceptible groups. Climate change as a result of human activity is a major, and relatively recent threat, but its impacts on species are difficult to detect, especially since it probably operates to some extent by increasing the impact of other factors (for example disease in amphibians). In addition, the impacts and expected consequences of climate change are uncertain and often fall outside the time window used for Red List assessments. Recent work examining the potential consequences of climate change across a range of global habitats suggests that

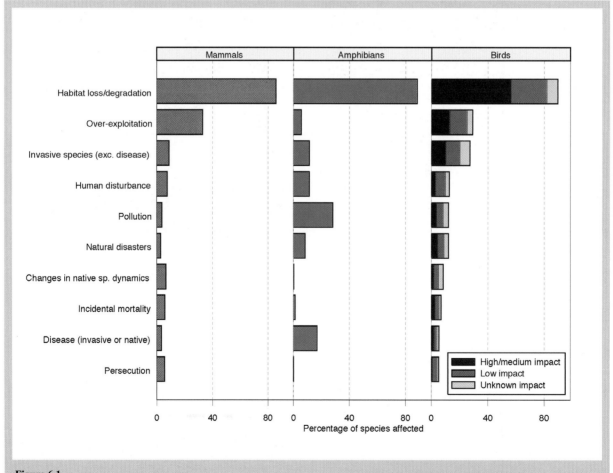

Figure 6.1
The major threats to globally threatened mammal, amphibian and bird species (definitions of high, medium and low impact for birds are given in Appendix 2f).

it could ultimately lead to the extinction of 15 - 37% of the species in their sample (Thomas *et al.* 2004). The impact of climate change is not included in the following analyses but IUCN is actively examining ways to integrate climate change impacts into the Red List assessments.

6.2 Habitat Destruction and Degradation

It is estimated that since historical times the world has lost *c.* 40% of its original 60 million km² of forest cover through human activity (FAO 1997b). This loss continues today with *c.* 14.6 million hectares of forests destroyed each year, totalling a 4.2% loss of natural forest cover during the 1990s, with the rates of loss being highest in Africa and South America (FAO 2000). It is no surprise therefore, that habitat destruction is a major threat to the world's biodiversity. For many species the habitat degradation that accompanies selective resource exploitation, or that occurs in habitats next to cleared areas, can have serious negative consequences too.

Many tropical forest species, for instance, rely on pristine or near-pristine primary forest, and show low tolerance to selective logging. The problem is made worse by the fragmentation of natural habitats which results in smaller, more isolated sub-populations, with reduced possibilities for dispersal and increased risks of local and ultimately global extinction.

Photo: © Jean-Christophe Vié.

Photo 6.2
Deforestation in the Amazonian forests.

Photo: © Sue A. Mainka.

Photo 6.3
Selective logging in southeast Asia.

Photo: © Craig Hilton-Taylor.

Photo 6.4
Wheat fields in southern Africa.

Photo: © Craig Hilton-Taylor.

Photo 6.5
Dam construction in Africa.

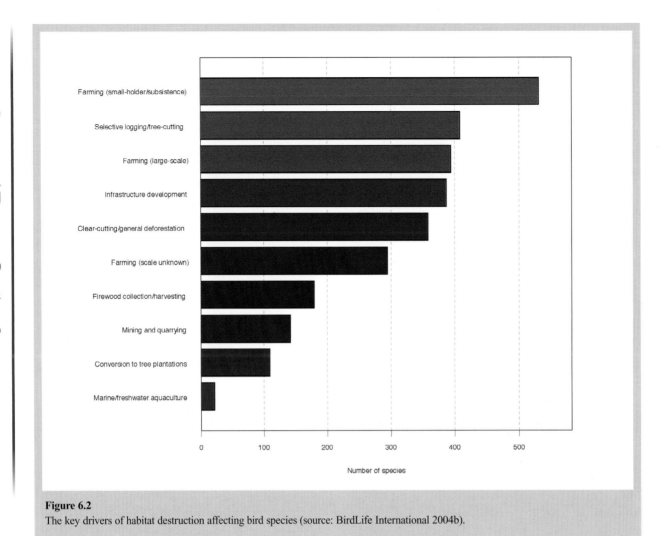

Figure 6.2
The key drivers of habitat destruction affecting bird species (source: BirdLife International 2004b).

Habitat destruction and degradation is the major threat faced by globally threatened birds and amphibians affecting 86% and 88% of threatened species (1,045 and 1641 species respectively; see Figure 6.1), and 86% (652 species) of the 760 threatened mammals for which data are available (Figure 6.1). This is because the majority of these species occur in tropical forests, where the most serious habitat loss is taking place (Figures 5.1, 5.2 and 5.3).

It has been possible to examine some of the key drivers of habitat destruction using the bird data (see Figure 6.2). Of the 1,045 globally threatened birds affected by habitat destruction, large-scale agricultural activities (including crop farming, livestock ranching, and perennial crops such as coffee and oil palm) impact nearly half. A similar proportion is affected by smallholder or subsistence farming. Selective logging or tree-cutting and general deforestation affect some 30%, firewood collection and the harvesting of non-woody vegetation affect c. 15% and conversion to tree plantations some 10%. Overall, over 70% and 60% of globally threatened birds are impacted by agricultural and forestry activities respectively. Infrastructure development (including human settlement and industrial development) is a threat to over 30% of globally threatened birds.

Habitat loss is not restricted to deforestation, and it is noteworthy that preliminary evidence suggests that this is the most serious threat to freshwater fish, and also affects over 40% of marine species in the North American assessment (see Box 6.1). In freshwater, habitat loss includes factors such as dam construction, dredging, and canalization.

Box 6.1

Threats to Fishes

Over-exploitation has been implicated as the leading threat to the world's marine fishes (Reynolds *et al.* 2002; Dulvy *et al.* 2003; Hutchings and Reynolds 2004). The *IUCN Red List's* coverage is too sparse and patchy to provide a comprehensive survey of threats. However, a fairly complete assessment of the status of North American marine fishes carried out by the American Fisheries Society (Musick *et al.* 2000b) suggests that 55% of the 82 fishes considered to be threatened with extinction have suffered from over-exploitation (see Figure Box 6.1.1 below). These species were assessed using different criteria from those used by the IUCN, but this is unlikely to affect the conclusion that over-exploitation is the main problem. Those species that are most susceptible often suffer from a combination of high value and catchability (e.g., forming spawning aggregations), as well as low intrinsic rates of population turnover associated with late maturity (Reynolds *et al.* 2002; Dulvy *et al.* 2003). Thus, large groupers, croakers, sharks, and skates are of particular concern. It remains to be seen whether habitat destruction could eventually supplant over-exploitation as the main threat globally, given the recent widespread degradation of coral reefs, exacerbated by climate change, and development pressures on coastal habitats.

For freshwater fishes, there is strong evidence that habitat loss is more important than over-exploitation as a cause of threat (see Figure below). In this respect, freshwater fishes are similar to birds and mammals. These data are based on very conservative estimates of the number of species that are extinct, or probably extinct, globally (Harrison and Stiassny 1999). As with marine species, IUCN assessments of freshwater fishes are too sparse for confident predictions about true percentages that are under threat. However, preliminary analyses suggest that for the 20 countries for which assessments are most complete in the Red List, 17% of freshwater fish species are threatened. This estimate is comparable to the 20% figure suggested by Leidy and Moyle (1998). Unlike the case for marine fishes, freshwater species are also facing additional growing threats from introductions of alien species. Anadromous fishes, which migrate between marine and freshwaters, feature especially prominently on threatened lists, especially those that are large-bodied and late-maturing. They are usually valuable to fisheries and susceptible when passing through bottlenecks (which are often blocked by dams). The world's sturgeon species combine the worst of all of these features, and most are Endangered or Critically Endangered.

Photo: © Jeremy Stafford-Deitsch.

Photo 6.6
The Shark Ray or Bowmouth Guitarfish *Rhina ancylostoma* (Vulnerable) is a widely distributed Indo-west Pacific inshore species taken by multiple artisanal and commercial fisheries throughout its range both as a target species and as bycatch. Flesh is sold for human consumption in Asia and the fins from large animals fetch exceptionally high prices.

continued overleaf...

Box 6.1 *continued*

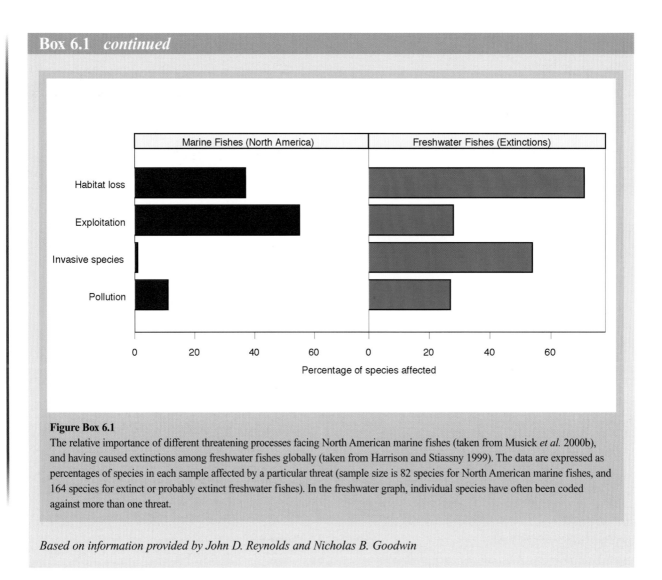

Figure Box 6.1
The relative importance of different threatening processes facing North American marine fishes (taken from Musick *et al.* 2000b), and having caused extinctions among freshwater fishes globally (taken from Harrison and Stiassny 1999). The data are expressed as percentages of species in each sample affected by a particular threat (sample size is 82 species for North American marine fishes, and 164 species for extinct or probably extinct freshwater fishes). In the freshwater graph, individual species have often been coded against more than one threat.

Based on information provided by John D. Reynolds and Nicholas B. Goodwin

6.3 Over-exploitation

Humans have harvested and traded species since time immemorial: for food, medicine, fuel, material use (especially timber), and for cultural, scientific and leisure (i.e., sport) activities. This use of nature is fundamental to the economies and cultures of many nations (e.g., Mainka and Trivedi 2002). For example, wild meat is not only a vital source of protein, but also generates valuable income for rural populations. However, expanding markets and increasing demand, combined with improved access and techniques for capture, and increased ease of transportation and techniques of preservation, are causing the exploitation of many species beyond sustainable levels.

Over-exploitation has been identified as a major threat faced by globally threatened birds and amphibians affecting 30% and 6% of threatened species respectively (see Figure 6.1) and 33% of the 760 threatened mammals for which data are available (Figure 6.1).

Threatened mammal species appear to be more impacted by over-exploitation than either birds or amphibians, and it is likely that when the mammals are fully coded for their threats, over-exploitation will prove to affect an even higher percentage of species than is indicated on Figure 6.1. Data in the 2004 Red List indicate that 250 species of threatened mammals are subject to over-exploitation, and larger mammals, especially ungulates and carnivores, are particularly targeted. Mammals are used extensively in the wild meat trade, notably in tropical Africa and in southeast Asia (Bakarr *et al.* 2001; Robinson and Bennett 2000). Some mammal species are also harvested for medicinal use, especially in eastern Asia.

In all, 345 globally threatened birds are threatened by over-exploitation for human use, primarily through hunting for food (262 species) and trapping for the cage-bird trade (117 species). The species that are targeted are often large and conspicuous, such as cranes and storks. Some families are particularly affected, with more than 10% of their species threatened by over-exploitation. Many species are at risk in some cases, including 52 species of parrots and 44 species each of pigeons and pheasants. Other families, notably waterfowl, birds of prey and rails, are also heavily hunted, although smaller proportions are affected overall. Nearly all countries and territories of the world (212, 89%) harbour bird species that are threatened by over-exploitation, but this threat appears to be particularly prevalent in Asia.

There are 133 threatened amphibian species known to be utilized by humans, mainly for the pet trade (84 species), food (79 species) and medicine (31 species). Although utilization of a species is not necessarily a major threat to the species' survival, for 104 amphibians it is. Most amphibians threatened by exploitation for food and medicine are found in Asia, and many of the species in the pet trade are found in South America and Madagascar. In Asia, exploitation for food is mainly directed towards the larger-bodied species of the family Ranidae, as well as, for example, the Chinese Giant Salamander *Andrias davidianus* that is listed as Critically Endangered. The species in the pet trade are usually salamanders and the colourful small frogs, in particular of the genera *Dendrobates, Epipedobates* and *Mantella.*

For some groups of species, and in some ecosystems, over-exploitation is a particularly serious threat. Examples include the turtles and tortoises in eastern and southeastern Asia, where almost all species are in serious decline as a result of harvesting for human consumption and medicine, mainly in China (see Box 2.2). Many of these species have deteriorated in Red List status over the last decade. Since 1996, the number of Critically Endangered turtle species has increased from 10 to 25, and the number of Endangered turtle species from 28 to 47. This near doubling of the number of seriously threatened turtle species in less than ten years is almost entirely due to over-utilization.

The evidence so far available suggests that over-exploitation is the most serious threat to marine fish species (see Box 6.1). Extensive over-utilization of other marine species has been well documented for groups such as marine turtles, whales and marine invertebrates.

Photo: © Sue A. Mainka.

Photo 6.7
There is still an active and lucrative market for animal furs and skins in some Asian countries.

Photo: © Jean-Christophe Vié.

Photo 6.8
Parrots and a cracid trapped and killed in South America for the wild meat trade.

Photo: © Henk Wallays.

Photo 6.9
This species of crocodile newt, *Tylototriton shanjing* (Near Threatened) is known from central, western and southern Yunnan, China. Although still very common in parts of its range, over-harvesting for use in traditional Chinese medicine is becoming a serious threat. It is also becoming popular in the international pet trade.

Photos 6.10 and 6.11 (top to bottom)
Turtle shells and dried seahorses are both used extensively in traditional medicine and large quantities are offered for sale in Asian markets.

Photo 6.12
The invasive alien Black Rat *Rattus rattus* (Least Concern) has a marked impact on the native faunas of island states. The rat here is taking a New Zealand Fantail *Rhipidura fulginosa* (Least Concern) chick. Although the Fantail is very widespread, the rat could have a marked impact if introduced to all islands within the bird's range.

6.4 Invasive Alien Species

Humans have been transporting animals and plants from one part of the world to another for thousands of years, sometimes deliberately (e.g., livestock released by sailors onto islands as a source of food) and sometimes accidentally (e.g., rats escaping from boats). In most cases, such introductions are unsuccessful, but when they do become established as an invasive alien species (defined by IUCN (2000) as "an alien species which becomes established in natural or semi-natural ecosystems or habitat, is an agent of change, and threatens native biological diversity"), the consequences can be catastrophic. Invasives can affect native species directly by eating them, competing with them, and introducing pathogens or parasites that sicken or kill them or, indirectly, by destroying or degrading their habitat. Invasives have been identified as a major threat faced by globally threatened birds and amphibians affecting 30% and 11% of threatened species (326 and 212 species respectively; see Figure 6.1) and 8% of the 760 threatened mammals for which data are available (Figure 6.1).

Island species are particularly susceptible to invasives because of their isolated evolutionary history, with 67% of oceanic-island globally threatened birds affected directly or indirectly by invasive species, compared to 17% on continental islands and just 8% on continents (see Figure 6.3). This susceptibility is spectacularly illustrated by the demise of Polynesian Partulid snails (see Box 6.2). The much lower percentages of threatened mammals and amphibians affected by invasives than birds are probably a reflection of the limited abilities of these groups to colonize oceanic islands.

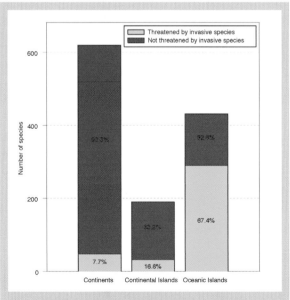

Figure 6.3 The percentage of globally threatened birds affected by invasives, comparing islands and continents.

Box 6.2

The Demise of Polynesian Partulid Snail

Since the 1970s, French Polynesia has seen one of the most dramatic examples of extinction caused by an invasive species. Seventy-two percent of the *Partula* snail species native to the Society Islands have gone extinct as a result of the introduction of the predatory Wolf Snail *Euglandina rosea* (T. Coote pers. comm.). The Wolf Snail was originally introduced to Tahiti in 1975 as a biological control agent with the aim of halting the spread of the Giant African Snail *Achatina fulica*. However, *E. rosea* instead developed a taste for the smaller partulid snails (genera *Partula* and *Samoana*) and their rapid decline began. The invasive Wolf Snail was not confined to Tahiti. It spread rapidly, at a rate of approximately 1.5 km^2 per year (T. Coote pers. comm.). By 1977 it had reached Moorea and by 1992 it was present on all six Society Islands.

The greatest loss of Partulid diversity occurred on the island of Raiatea. In a twelve-year period following the introduction of *E. rosea* in 1986, all 33 native *Partula* species disappeared in the wild (T. Coote pers. comm.). Just four of Raiatea's *Partula* species remain alive in captivity. It is possible that the only species in the genus *Samoana* (*S. attenuata*) has also disappeared.

The success of *ex situ* conservation efforts is vital if the last surviving individuals of species that are Extinct in the Wild are to be maintained. Fifteen *Partula* and possibly one *Samoana* species are currently Extinct in the Wild. The International Partulid Conservation Programme (IPCP) was established in 1994, and today 22 Partulid taxa (19 species and three subspecies) are maintained and bred in fifteen collaborating zoos worldwide. In addition the IPCP and their local collaborators perform and support studies on the population dynamics of native and alien species in the wild, and investigate methods for the *in situ* conservation of partulid snails.

The *in situ* conservation effort has enabled the development of predator proof Partulid reserves (initially on Moorea and most recently on Tahiti) aimed at protecting surviving wild Partulid populations and providing a mechanism by which the Extinct in the Wild species might be reintroduced (Coote *et al.* 2004). These reserves have informed the development of similar reserves on Hawaii to protect threatened Achatinelline tree snail species from the same invasive predator threat. The IPCP is currently assisting the French Polynesian Government develop a conservation strategy for the region's endemic molluscs and their associated habitats (P. Pearce-Kelly pers. comm.).

Unfortunately there is no immediate possibility of completely eradicating *E. rosea* from the many Polynesian islands it has now invaded, but the above conservation effort, together with possible future developments of species-specific control methods provide hope that the remaining Partulid species might yet have a viable future.

Based on information provided by Trevor Coote, Paul Pearce-Kelly and Mary Seddon, IUCN/SSC Mollusc Specialist Group

Photo: © Dave Clarke.

Photos 6.13 and 6.14
The Partulid reserve on the island of Moorea, Tahiti. Inset is *Partula saturalis strigosa* (Extinct in the Wild), which can possibly be reintroduced into such a reserve in the future.

6.5 Disease

Diseases can cause chronic population declines, dramatic die-offs or reductions in the reproductive success and survival of individual species. Some diseases now appear to be spreading to populations previously unaffected, including to species already seriously threatened by other factors. Invasive diseases have already been implicated in the extinction of some species. Overall, diseases (both native and invasive) affect some 5% of globally threatened birds (67 species). For threatened mammals, only 26 species (3% of the 760 species for which data are available) are impacted by disease (Figure 6.1). However, it is the amphibians that are particularly affected by disease with some 17% of threatened species potentially impacted (317 species; see Figure 6.1).

Amphibian species have been recorded as declining since the early 1970s but initially conservationists assumed that factors such as habitat loss were to blame. By 1988 these declines had become much more serious: for example, at one site in Costa Rica, 40% of the amphibian fauna disappeared over a short period in the late 1980s (Pounds *et al.* 1997). Reports of declines and extinctions accelerated during the 1990s but it wasn't until 1996 that the cause was linked to an emerging, highly pathogenic disease, following a study that looked at the pattern of disappearances of 14 species of frogs endemic to Australia's east coast (Laurance *et al.* 1996). In 1998 a previously unknown chytrid fungus, named *Batrachochytrium dendrobatidis*, was identified as the agent (Berger *et al.* 1998; Longcore *et al.* 1999), and this has now been implicated in many reported amphibian declines.

Three aspects of the biology of *B. dendrobatidis* help to explain the observed patterns of amphibian decline. First, this chytrid will grow in culture only in cool temperatures. This may explain why montane species are more likely to decline than lowland species and why the disease expresses itself in the winter in Arizona, United States (Bradley *et al.* 2002). Second, *B. dendrobatidis* appears to occur only in aquatic habitats, which would explain why amphibians that spend at least part of their life cycle near streams are more likely to decline. Third, chytrids attack the keratinized beak of tadpoles, explaining why tadpoles in affected areas can be missing their beaks. Examination of museum specimens of frogs shows that chytrids were present in the United States as early as 1974 and in Australia as early as 1978 (Carey *et al.* 1999; Pounds and Puschendorf 2004), dates that are close to the times that declines were first noted. More recently, studies in Africa have shown the presence of chytrids dating

Photo: © Robert Puschendorf.

Photo 6.15
The decline of the harlequin toad, *Atelopus varius* (Critically Endangered), in Costa Rica and Panama has been dramatic. It has disappeared from suitable habitats, and the cause of its decline might be the fungal disease, chytridiomycosis, the incidence of which might be related to extreme climatic events, in particular drought.

Photo: © Ross Alford.

Photo 6.16
Torrent Tree Frog *Litoria nannotis* (Endangered) endemic to the wet tropics of north Queensland, Australia is undergoing rapid decline, even in protected areas, possibly due to the incidence of the fungal disease chytridiomycosis.

as far back as the 1930s, suggesting an African origin of *B. dendrobatidis* (Weldon *et al.* in press).

Although amphibians have been far more heavily impacted by disease than any group so far studied, it can also be important in other groups of species. Diseases such as canine distemper and rabies can have a major impact on large carnivores. For example, approximately 80% of the Web Valley population of the Endangered Ethiopian Wolf *Canis simensis* died in a rabies outbreak in 2003 (S. Williams *in litt.*), and the African Lion *Panthera leo* population in the Serengeti National Park was heavily impacted by canine distemper in 1994 (Roelke-Parker *et al.* 1996). Disease has also been a factor in the extinction of three bird and one plant species over the last 20 years (see Tables 3.2 and 3.3). There is concern that, as a result of increasingly widespread and serious environmental changes, newly emerging diseases will become a much more serious threat to species (Daszak *et al.* 2001).

Photo: © Jack Jeffrey Photography.

Photo 6.17
The accidental introduction of mosquitoes *Culex quinqufasciatus*, bringing with them avian malaria *Plasmodium relictum* and avian pox *Poxvirus avium*, has had devastating consequences on Hawaiian birds. An Apapane *Himatione sanguinea* (Least Concern) and mosquito are shown here.

Photo: © Troy Inman.

Photo 6.18
Canine distemper impacted the African Lion *Panthera leo* (Vulnerable) population in the Serengeti National Park, Tanzania.

Photo: © Guy Shorrock / RSPB Images.

Photo 6.19
The once abundant White-rumped Vulture *Gyps bengalensis* (Critically Endangered) has declined dramatically in South Asia due to the toxic effects of a veterinary drug, Diclofenac.

6.6 Pollution and Contaminants

Pollution directly affects species through mortality and sub-lethal effects such as reduced fertility. Pollution can also have strong indirect effects by degrading habitats or reducing food supplies. Overall, pollution affects some 12% and 29% of globally threatened bird and amphibian species (187 and 529 species respectively; see Figure 6.1) and 4% (28 species) of the 760 threatened mammals for which data are available (Figure 6.1). The much higher percentage of threatened amphibians impacted by pollution than birds or mammals is probably a reflection of the larger number of species that are dependent on aquatic ecosystems.

Perhaps the most dramatic recent example of the potentially devastating effects of pollution on wild species relates to vultures (Oaks *et al.* 2004; Schultz *et al.* 2004). In South Asia, vultures in the genus *Gyps* have declined by more than 95% in recent years owing to the toxic effects of a veterinary drug, Diclofenac, which is consumed when the birds feed on carcasses of animals treated with the drug.

Diclofenac is widely used in human medicine globally, but was introduced to the veterinary market on the Indian subcontinent during the early 1990s. Vultures have traditionally disposed of carcasses in cities, villages and the countryside, reducing the risk of disease and helping with sanitation. With the vultures gone, carcasses are likely to take much longer to be stripped, increasing the risk to human health. Feral dogs are filling the scavenging void, and their growing numbers also increase health and safety risks, as they are carriers of rabies. There is now an urgent need to control the veterinary use of the drug, and to establish captive breeding populations of the three vulture species concerned.

6.7 Incidental Mortality

For a few threatened species, incidental mortality can be the greatest threat. For example, the growth of longline fishing around the world is an increasing threat to many marine species. Albatrosses, for example, are coming into increasing contact with commercial fishing fleets, leading to the death through bycatch of thousands of individuals. All 21 species

Photo: © Fabio Olmos.

Photo 6.20
Black-browed Albatross *Thalassarche melanophrys* (Endangered) caught on a baited longline.

are now evaluated as globally threatened or Near Threatened, largely because of interactions with fisheries. It will take many years for these long-lived, slow-breeding species to recover from serious declines; assuming that such declines can actually be halted. Other groups of seabirds, such as penguins and petrels, are also heavily impacted by this threat. Overall, 83 species of threatened birds (7%) and 44 species of threatened mammals (6% of the species for which data are available) are affected by incidental mortality. For amphibians, this is a minor threat.

Incidental mortality has also caused major declines in other marine species, examples include six species of sawfish (*Pristis* spp. – four species Endangered and two Critically Endangered), the Leatherback Turtle (*Dermochelys coriacea* – Critically Endangered), the Vaquita (*Phocoena sinus* – Critically Endangered), and Hector's Dolphin (*Cephalorhynchus hectori* – Endangered).

6.8 Climate Change

The Earth is undergoing profound changes to its climate. There is now little doubt that this results from human activities, mainly the burning of fossil fuels. Climatic changes have occurred throughout Earth's history. However, these recent changes are different because they are taking place faster and are unlikely to be reversed by natural processes. As yet few species have been identified as being threatened on the *IUCN Red List* specifically owing to climate change. However, there are many examples of the effects of climate change on species from around the world, which taken together, provide compelling evidence that climate change will be catastrophic for many species. Climate change may alter species' distribution, abundance, phenology (the timing of events such as migration or breeding), morphology (size and shape), and genetic composition.

Modelling studies show that the ranges occupied by many species will become unsuitable for them as the climate changes. The climate space that is suitable for particular species may shift in latitude or altitude, contract or even disappear. Many species will probably not be able to keep up with their changing climate space. As species move at different rates, the community structure of ecosystems will also become disrupted. Both local and global extinctions are likely. One recent global study estimated that 15–37% of regionally endemic species could be committed to extinction by 2050 (Thomas *et al.* 2004), while another study in Queensland, northern Australia, shows that the

number of extinctions will increase rapidly if temperatures rise by more than *c.* 2°C (Williams *et al.* 2003). Some groups of species will be particularly hard hit, for example the Proteaceae, a plant family with many endemic species in South Africa (see Box 6.3).

Extreme weather events, most likely a result of climate change, have been shown to correlate with amphibian declines in a few areas. In three tropical regions (highland Costa Rica, Andean Ecuador, and montane Puerto Rico), the requisite combination of amphibian population and climate data are available for analysis. In the highland Costa Rica site, 20 species of frogs and toads, including the Golden Toad *Bufo periglenes*, declined or disappeared abruptly in 1988, with subsequent abrupt declines of survivors in 1994 and 1998. Each of these decline events occurred during unusually dry periods when typical periods of cloud-borne mist failed to occur (Pounds *et al.* 1999). Andean Ecuador was home to the spectacular Jambato Toad *Atelopus ignescens*, which abruptly disappeared from 47 sites from where it was known in the 1980s, just after the two driest years recorded during the period 1962–1998 (Ron *et al.* 2003). Similarly, dry weather is correlated with the disappearance of three species and the decline of six species of frogs from the genus *Eleutherodactylus* in Puerto Rico (Burrowes *et al.* 2004). It is now considered likely that there is an interaction between the chytrid fungus linked to amphibian declines (see Disease in 6.5 above) and extreme climatic events (droughts) (Ron *et al.* 2003; Burrowes *et al.* 2004).

The timescale over which climate change is likely to lead to extinctions of some species is probably longer than the 100-year period that is most commonly used in the *IUCN Red List*. IUCN is working on developing new methods to identify species and habitats that are susceptible to climate change through a recently constituted task force.

6.9 Other Threats

The remaining threats, such as human disturbance, natural disasters, changes in native species dynamics, and persecution generally affect relatively small numbers of threatened birds, mammals and amphibians (Figure 6.1). However, some of these can have important impacts on particular groups of species. A notable example among mammals, are large carnivores, for which persecution is often the most serious threat.

Box 6.3

Extinction Risk from Future Land-Use and Climate Change – the Proteaceae in the Cape Floristic Region of South Africa

In South Africa's Cape Floristic Region, agriculture, invasive alien plants and urbanization have severely impacted many endemic plants and animals. This is reflected in some 1,400 plant species listed in the national Red List at present (Hilton-Taylor 1996). In the future, climate change is expected to be an additional major threat to biodiversity in this unique region at the southern tip of Africa (Midgley *et al.* 2002, 2003). The Proteaceae are one of the three characteristic plant families in the fynbos (the major vegetation type in the Cape Floristic Region), and they have been extensively mapped and studied through the Protea Atlas Project at South Africa's National Botanical Institute (now the South African National Biodiversity Institute).

Using spatially explicit predictions of future threats to biodiversity, Bomhard (2004) has investigated the potential impacts of future land-use and climate change on the extinction risk of the Proteaceae. He calculated a future Red List status for 229 Proteaceae species endemic to the Cape Floristic Region for the year 2020, and compared it to their currently proposed Red List status. For this study, different land-use and climate change scenarios were developed for 2020. Two of these scenarios

considered only the impacts of future habitat transformation (i.e., the spread of agriculture, invasive alien plants and urbanization), providing a worst-case and best-case scenario of future land-use conditions in the region. Two other scenarios, identical in their consideration of land-use change, included the impacts of rapid anthropogenic climate change.

From the present to 2020, up to 54 of the 229 Proteaceae species could be uplisted by up to three threat categories, and the proportion of threatened species could rise by up to 6% under the overall worst-case scenario (see Figures Box 6.3.1 and Box 6.3.2 below). With increasing threat levels, the number of Least Concern species decreases from 75 at present to 53 under the overall worst-case scenario, whereas the number of Critically Endangered and Extinct species increases, particularly under the climate change scenarios. For example, the number of Critically Endangered species increases from three at present to six with high habitat transformation and 12 with climate change and high habitat transformation. There are no extinctions predicted due to land-use change according to these simulations, but four of the study species could become extinct due to climate change.

Photo: © Nick Helme.

Photo 6.21 Redelinghuys Pincushion.

Photos 6.21 and 6.22

The Redelinghuys Pincushion *Leucospermum arenarium* (Endangered) and the Malmesbury Conebush *Leucadendron thymifolium* (Endangered) are both examples of the protea family that are likely to be impacted by climate change in the future.

Photo by: © Nigel Forshaw.

Photo 6.22 Malmesbury Conebush.

continued on next page...

Box 6.3 *continued*

The Many Causes of Threat – Section 6

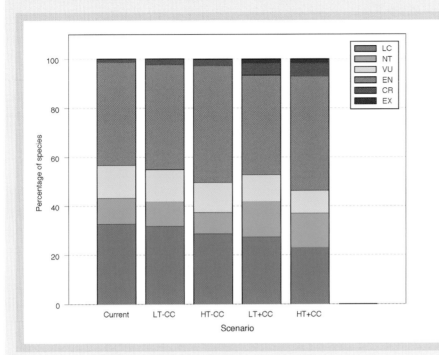

Figure Box 6.3.1
Red List status of all study species under current conditions; low and high future habitat transformation excluding climate change (LT - CC, HT - CC); and low and high future habitat transformation including climate change (LT + CC, HT + CC).

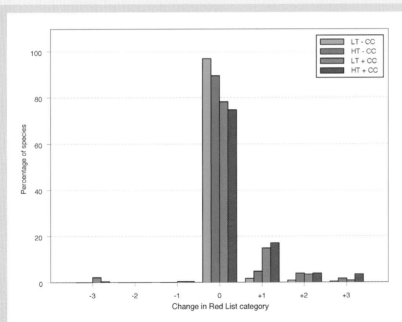

Figure Box 6.3.2
Change in Red List status (number of categories downlisted or uplisted) of all study species for the future compared to current conditions. Future scenarios are low and high habitat transformation excluding climate change (LT - CC, HT - CC), and low and high habitat transformation including climate change (LT + CC, HT + CC).

With changing climates, some currently suitable habitats will become unsuitable, and if species cannot move to areas where future climates are suitable for them, they are eventually committed to extinction. It is predicted that the worst affected areas will be the low-lying areas on the West Coast and Southwest of the Cape Floristic Region. Such species and regions of concern can now be prioritized for monitoring and planning; eventually leading to appropriate conservation action guided by the principles of climate change integrated conservation strategies (Hannah *et al.* 2002a and b).

Based on information provided by Bastian Bomhard

6.10 Threatening Processes and Patterns of Extinction

The threats described so far are proximate external threats or pressures. Their impact is affected by various other factors (described below) and, as a result, substantial differences in the patterns of threat and extinction are observed both between different groups of species (e.g., birds versus amphibians) and within similar groups of species (e.g., a family or genus of birds or amphibians).

6.10.1 Spatial Variation in Threats

Human populations are growing and influencing the environment differently in different parts of the world (see Section 7). In general, species face the highest threats when people arrive or rapidly expand their activities in a particular region, and many recent extinctions have followed patterns of human exploration and settlement, especially on islands (MacPhee and Flemming 1999). For example, the earliest Pacific island migrations led to the extinction of probably thousands of species (Olson *et al.* 1982; Steadman 1995), and the rapid expansion of intensive agriculture in northwestern Europe led to declines in farmland bird species (Robinson and Sutherland 2002).

Current examples can be seen in the Red List information. For example, of the 435 amphibian species that qualify for a more threatened IUCN category than they did in 1980, species fall into three groupings: those experiencing heavy exploitation (55 species mainly in East and Southeast Asia); those experiencing significant habitat loss (198 species, especially in Southeast Asia, West Africa, and the Caribbean); and those experiencing declines, even where suitable habitat remains, for reasons that are not fully understood, although disease interacting with climate change is emerging as the most likely cause (189 species, mainly in South America, Mesoamerica, the Caribbean, the United States and Australia). Seven species are experiencing heavy exploitation and experiencing decline even in suitable habitat. The most important threats to amphibians therefore show significant variation geographically.

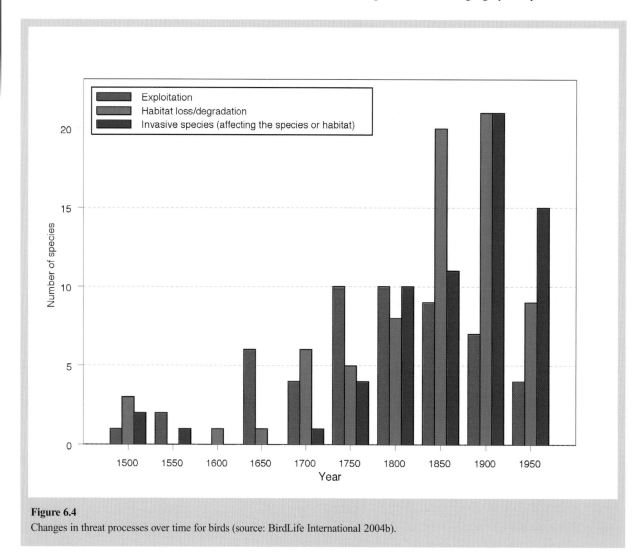

Figure 6.4
Changes in threat processes over time for birds (source: BirdLife International 2004b).

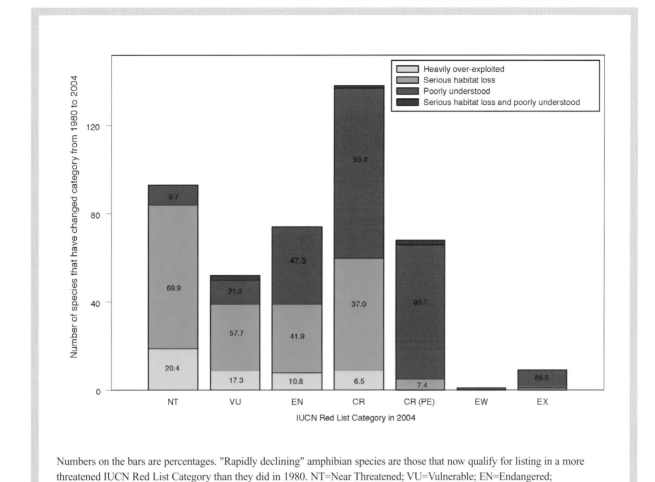

Numbers on the bars are percentages. "Rapidly declining" amphibian species are those that now qualify for listing in a more threatened IUCN Red List Category than they did in 1980. NT=Near Threatened; VU=Vulnerable; EN=Endangered; CR=Critically Endangered; CR(PE)=Critically Endangered (Possibly Extinct); EW=Extinct in the Wild; EX=Extinct.

Figure 6.5
The number of "rapidly declining" amphibian species in the IUCN Red List Categories, broken into the major types of threat they are facing, with the threat level increasing from left to right.

6.10.2 Temporal Variation in Threats

Human activities and their effects on the environment have changed over hundreds of years. This results in a temporal variation in threats. For example, at a global level over-exploitation and invasive alien species were the predominant causes of extinction in historical times in birds. Over time, extinctions caused by over-exploitation have declined, and habitat loss and invasives have become the dominant causes (Figure 6.4). For amphibians, the data have been analysed in a different way by examining how the major threats that have caused 435 species to deteriorate in Red List status since 1980 (see 6.10.1 above) vary between the IUCN Red List Categories (see Figure 6.5). The percentage of species experiencing poorly understood population declines, even in suitable habitat, increases with increasing extinction risk, indicating that the factors that cause these declines (probably

disease interacting with climate change) are driving species towards extinction very rapidly, compared to habitat loss and over-exploitation.

6.10.3 Intrinsic Vulnerability

Studies on a range of taxa have identified correlations between susceptibility to extinction and intrinsic biological traits (see reviews by Purvis *et al.* 2000b and Fisher and Owens 2004; Box 6.4). Vulnerability to local extinctions is associated with low abundance and high habitat specificity. Among larger bodied groups, such as birds and mammals, small geographic range size is also important and, when tested alongside island living, has been found to explain most of the apparent high risk faced by island endemics (Manne *et al.* 1999; Purvis *et al.* 2000b). In other taxa, especially fish and invertebrates, small ranges appear less important, perhaps because their local densities are much

101

higher, or because the threats they face are less related to small range areas. Among the vertebrates, large body size and slow reproductive rates are closely related to one another, and a number of studies have shown one or both to significantly increase extinction risk (Gaston and Blackburn 1995; Bennett and Owens 1997). This is as predicted; slow reproductive turnover will limit the recovery of species from declines caused by any threatening process, and species with larger body sizes are favoured for exploitation by humans. In the cases where both body size and life history have been studied, life history has been shown to be more important in carnivores (Purvis *et al.* 2000a; Cardillo *et al.* 2004) and, interestingly in the extinctions of large mammals in the Late Quaternary (Cardillo and Lister 2002; Johnson 2002). In marine fishes, large body size and slow population growth rates contribute to species declines (Dulvy *et al.* 2003), and the most significant impact of recent fisheries activities has been to deplete the upper trophic levels of fish – the top carnivores (Pauly *et al.* 1998). Top predators also appear to be especially threatened in mammals (Purvis *et al.* 2000a; Cardillo *et al.* 2004).

Many of these studies take quite a broad approach to examining correlations, and unsurprisingly, more detailed examinations reveal more complex patterns. For example, habitat loss might be expected to most affect those species that are ecologically specialized, whereas processes such as human persecution and introduced predators may have more of an impact on species with long generation times. This expectation is borne out for birds (Owens and Bennett 2000). In the mammalian carnivores, slow reproductive rates and low population density are more strongly correlated with

high threat in species that inhabit areas of human population density (Cardillo *et al.* 2004).

6.10.4 Extinction Filters

The impact of threats on certain species can also be influenced by whether or not the threats are new (resulting in so-called extinction filters). There is much evidence for the existence of extinction filters, whereby prior exposure to a threat selectively removes those populations most vulnerable to it, leaving behind a community which is more resilient to similar threats in future, even if depauperate (Balmford 1996). This important concept explains much of the variation in past extinction rates and can be used to inform future predictions. For example, the impact of introduced rats on island-nesting seabirds appears less marked on islands with native rats or land crabs, as these seabirds have evolved in the presence of predators. In a similar fashion corals may be less likely to bleach in response to rising sea temperatures in areas where they have been repeatedly exposed to temperature stresses in the past (Brown *et al.* 2000; Podestá and Glynn 2001; West and Salm 2003).

6.10.5 Extinction Lags

The time period from the introduction of a threat to the extinction of a species can be highly variable, resulting in so-called extinction lags. The nature of the threat is obviously one important factor: some processes that increase mortality (disease, pollution) may lead to almost immediate consequences on the population, whereas the effects of over-exploitation can be delayed by long generation times of the target species, and by a focus on older age classes. It is with habitat loss that the lag times will often be the longest.

Box 6.4

What is Most Important in Determining Extinction Risk?

The degree to which extinctions are due to external threats versus intrinsic characteristics has recently been investigated for some higher taxa. Among mammals about 50% of the variation in extinction risk is explained by variation in species' biological traits (Purvis *et al.* 2000b and c), with the remainder being attributable to human pressures and the interactions between human pressures and biological traits. Evidence that threat level is most highly correlated with human population density (Harcourt and Parks 2003) may not imply causality since human density and species richness correlate positively at continental scales (Balmford *et al.* 1996). However, in one study of mammalian carnivores where both human

pressures and biological traits are taken into consideration it transpires that variation in human pressure does not on its own account for much variation in extinction risk. Extinction risk in the mammal order Carnivora is predicted more strongly by biology than exposure to human populations. However, biology interacts strongly with human population density to determine risk; biological traits explain 80% of variation in risk for species with high levels of exposure to human populations, compared to 45.1% for carnivores generally (Cardillo *et al.* 2004).

Photo 6.23
Nectophrynoides viviparus (Vulnerable) occurs in the Uluguru and Udzungwa Mountains and in the Southern Highlands of eastern and southern Tanzania. It is threatened by ongoing forest loss. It is one of very few species of frogs that gives birth to live young.

Photo: © David Moyer – Wildlife Conservation Society.

Recent evidence indicates that for vertebrates facing habitat loss and fragmentation, it may be decades to hundreds of years before species finally become extinct. Theoretically, the time from habitat loss to local extinction will be determined by the degree of fragmentation, the time since the threat took place, the spatial configuration of the fragments, as well as the biology of the species involved (Hanski and Ovaskainen 2002). In practice, estimates of the time from fragmentation to species extinction have been estimated for tropical forest bird species. Data on birds in Kenyan tropical forest fragments suggests that species loss approximates an exponential decay with a half-life of approximately 50 years for fragments of roughly 1,000 hectares. (Brooks *et al.* 1999). In Amazonian forest fragments less than 100 hectares in area, one half of the bird species were lost in less than 15 years, whereas fragments over 100 hectares lost species over timescales of a few decades to perhaps a century (Ferraz *et al.* 2003).

These time lags are important. On the one hand they mean that our estimates of current extinction may be serious underestimates of the ultimate legacy of habitat loss. For example, for African primate populations Cowlishaw (1999) estimated that over 30% of all those species that will ultimately be lost as a result of historical deforestation have still to go extinct locally. On the other hand, the lag times offer time for reversal of the trend so long as the period to habitat recovery is not longer than the time to extinction.

Key Findings

- Habitat destruction and associated degradation and fragmentation is the biggest threat faced by birds, mammals and amphibians, these being the only groups that have been extensively assessed so far.

- Agricultural and forestry activities are the key drivers of habitat loss affecting birds.

- The interaction between a spreading disease and extreme climatic events (drought) is the leading hypothesis for widespread amphibian declines.

- Invasive alien species are a particular threat to birds on islands.

- Unsustainable harvesting for food, medicine and the pet trade are additional major threats to birds, mammals and amphibians as well as other species groups, with mammals, turtles and marine species being particularly affected.

- Incidental mortality as a result of fisheries is an increasing threat, especially for seabirds, marine mammals, and other marine species.

- Intrinsic biological factors play a major role in determining how threatened species are, and larger bodied, slow breeding species tend to be more at risk.

Photo: © Jean-Christophe Vié.

Photo 6.24
The Nubian Ibex *Capra nubiana* (Endangered) occurs in rocky desert areas in northeast Africa and parts of western Asia. The species faces numerous threats including direct competition with livestock for food and water, hunting, and habitat degradation.

The Social and Economic Context of the Red List

Photo: © Jeremy Stafford-Deitsch.

Photo 7.1
The Great White Shark *Carcharodon carcharius* (Vulnerable) is a widely but sparsely distributed top predator with a very low reproductive potential and high vulnerability to target and bycatch fisheries (commercial and recreational). The notoriety of this shark as an ultimate Hollywood monster encourages inflated values for Great White products, and encourages illicit trade in shark parts that is difficult to assess and control. Where detailed population data are available, these indicate that the abundance and average size of white sharks have declined.

7.1 Introduction

For conservation action to be effective, it is important to understand not just the needs of individual species, but also the context in which conservation efforts will need to take place. A better understanding of human demand and impact on natural resources can help inform decisions and guide conservation efforts so that conflicts in interests between humans and biodiversity can be minimized. Here we compare current distribution patterns of threatened species with recent and future human demographic variables, and with gross national income at the national level. The analysis focuses on threatened mammals, birds and amphibians, as these are the only groups that have been completely assessed for threatened status, and for which distribution maps are available for almost all threatened species. This analysis is not focused on determining causal relationships between social and economic factors and the status of threatened species, but rather on illustrating patterns of association that illuminate some of the challenges faced when trying to conserve biodiversity in an increasingly human-dominated world.

7.2 Human population

7.2.1 Current Population Density

In order to highlight those regions where human demands on resources and biodiversity conservation are most likely to be in conflict, the current human population density and distribution of threatened species were compared (Figure 7.1; for methodology used, see Appendix 2g).

The regions of the world that have few threatened species and low human population density are at high latitudes, in arid regions, or in wilderness areas (an example of each being northern Canada, the Sahara Desert, and the Amazon basin). Such regions can be considered good opportunities for preventive conservation measures since there is little human demand at present for resources and species are currently relatively unthreatened. Regions that have a large number of threatened species but a relatively low human population density, for example Bolivia and the Russian Far East, are uncommon.

Figure 7.1
The total number of threatened species of mammals, birds and amphibians compared to human population density. Each grid cell is coded according to the combined value of the two variables.

Photos 7.2 and 7.3 (top to bottom)
Many parts of the world are impacted by high population densities of people (**Photo 7.2**), however, there are still a number of unpopulated wilderness areas like the Sahara Desert (**Photo 7.3**) that have few threatened species.

In some regions, such as Europe and eastern North America, high population densities coincide with low numbers of threatened species. This is partly due to decreasing numbers of species with increasing latitude (Figure 5.5), but perhaps also a reflection of species susceptible to habitat loss in these regions having declined a long time ago (see Section 6.10.4 on extinction filters). In general, these regions are less of a concern for the conservation of globally threatened species than most other parts of the world.

The regions where high human population density and high numbers of threatened species overlap are mostly in Asia (in particular southeast China, the Western Ghats of India, the Himalayas, Sri Lanka, Java (Indonesia), the Philippines, and parts of Japan) as well as the Albertine Rift in Central Africa and the Ethiopian Highlands. These regions present the greatest conservation challenges, as the needs of billions of humans must be met while also working to prevent the extinction of large numbers of species.

7.2.2 Population growth

To gain some understanding of how the human context changes with time, the annual human population growth for 2002 for each country (World Bank 2004) was compared to the number of threatened species (Figure 7.2; for methodology used, see Appendix 2g).

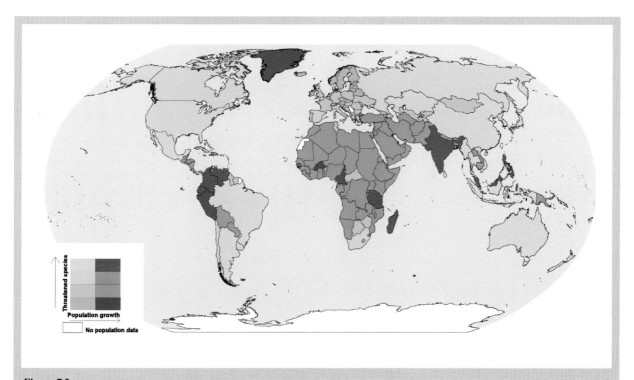

Figure 7.2
Country-level map of the total number of threatened species of mammals, birds and amphibians compared to human population growth in 2002. Each country is coded according to the combined value of the two variables.

Photo 7.4
New York City – high population densities in eastern North America coincide with low numbers of threatened species.

Photo 7.5
Most African countries, despite very high population growth rates, have a relatively low population density, and a subsistence lifestyle is still commonplace.

Photo 7.6
Many developing nations are experiencing high population growth and face conflicting needs between the developed and undeveloped sectors of the population.

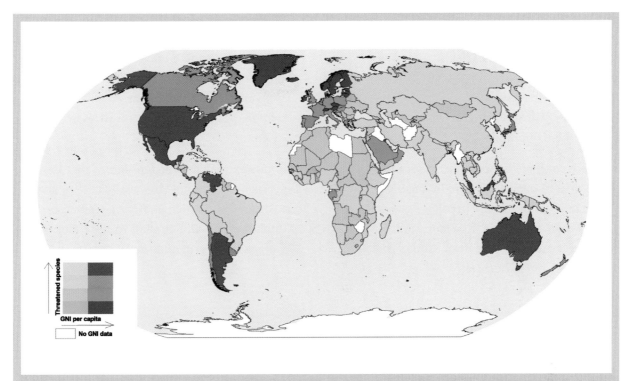

Figure 7.3
Country level map of the total number of threatened species of mammals, birds and amphibians compared to Gross National Income (GNI) per capita in 2003. Each country is coded according to the combined value of the two variables.

The countries that are most densely populated at present are not necessarily those that are currently experiencing a high human population growth rate. In general the highest human population densities are found in Asia whereas the highest population growth rates are in Africa. Most African countries, however, currently have a relatively low level of population density so the impact of population growth might be more easily absorbed. With the annual rate of population growth declining in almost all countries, it is debatable whether these African countries will ever reach the high population density levels of some Asian countries today. Countries with high population growth rates and high numbers of threatened species such as Cameroon, Colombia, Ecuador, India, Madagascar, Malaysia, Peru, Philippines, Tanzania, and Venezuela are areas where conflicts between the needs of threatened species and increasing human populations are anticipated to rapidly intensify. Countries that currently have a low human population density but a high rate of population growth could be opportunistic places for pre-emptive conservation initiatives, for example Bolivia, Papua New Guinea, Namibia, Angola, and the countries of northern Africa. The Amazonian slopes of the Andes is also a region of relatively low human population density at present, and all of the Andean countries have relatively high population growth rates, as well as being extremely important for threatened species.

7.3 Economic factors

Conserving biodiversity requires significant financial resources. By comparing a country's economic strength (measured as Gross National Income (GNI) per capita) to the number of threatened species, an indication of both the need for conservation and the availability of financial resources can be determined (Figure 7.3; for methodology used, see Appendix 2g).

Countries with relatively strong economies but a large number of threatened species include Argentina, Australia, Malaysia, Mexico, United States, and Venezuela. However not all of these countries have significant funds available for threatened species conservation. Those countries that have a large number of threatened species but a relatively low GNI per capita include Brazil, Cameroon, China, Colombia, Ecuador, India, Indonesia, Madagascar, Peru, and the Philippines. These countries share a large responsibility towards conserving globally threatened species but are less likely to have financial resources available for conservation purposes. Other countries, particularly those in Europe, have significant financial resources but generally very few globally threatened species.

Key Findings

- People and threatened species are often concentrated in the same areas. At present these areas are mostly in Asia as well as the Albertine Rift in Central Africa and the Ethiopian Highlands.

- Future conflicts between the needs of threatened species and rapidly increasing human populations are predicted to occur in Cameroon, Colombia, Ecuador, India, Madagascar, Malaysia, Peru, Philippines, Tanzania, and Venezuela.

- Countries that currently have a low human population density but a high rate of population growth could be opportunistic places for pre-emptive conservation initiatives. For example, Bolivia, Papua New Guinea, Namibia, Angola, and the countries of North Africa.

- Countries with a large number of threatened species are often not financially able to invest in conservation, such as Brazil, Cameroon, China, Colombia, Ecuador, India, Indonesia, Madagascar, Peru, and the Philippines.

Photo: © John E. Randall.

Photo 7.7
The Queen Triggerfish *Balistes vetula* (Vulnerable) is considered to be an excellent food fish but may be poisonous to some people. The species is a popular gamefish and is captured for the aquarium trade. It is a widespread species in the Atlantic, occurring in the east from the Azores south to Angola and in the west from Massachusetts in the US south to Brazil.

Conservation Responses

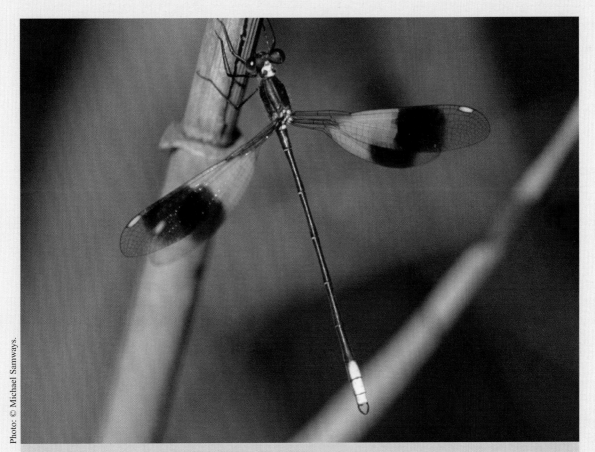

Photo: © Michael Samways.

Photo 8.1
Basking Malachite Damselfly *Chlorolestes apricans* (Endangered) a localized endemic from the Eastern Cape, South Africa, was on the verge of extinction, but raising its profile is now leading to conservation action.

8.1 Introduction

Most threats to biodiversity are the result of human actions, and human actions alone can prevent many species from becoming extinct. This section provides an overview of the main types of responses that can be applied to the conservation of the world's species, with a focus on those at greatest risk of extinction. It is mostly based on information on conservation measures required or in place for each species, collected through the Red List assessment process. Here, five broad groups of conservation responses are considered:

• **Research action**, which provides the knowledge on which other conservation responses are based;

• **Communication and education**, which creates the public awareness needed to support most conservation practice, and the human capacity required for implementing it;

• **Policy-based actions**, fundamental to provide the institutional support, human and financial resources, and legal framework required for effective species conservation;

• **Habitat and site-based actions**, which protect species in their natural habitats; and

• **Species-based actions**, addressing species-specific threats and conservation needs required for ensuring the species' long-term persistence.

This section discusses conservation responses in relation to the *IUCN Red List,* and does not attempt to be a comprehensive analysis of each of these types of responses. Only preliminary data are available on the extent of conservation responses required by species, and even less exists on which conservation responses are already in place. Such data, and consequently the information provided in this section, are highly biased towards the better-assessed groups (birds and amphibians).

The Red List Programme does not endorse any particular conservation responses discussed in this section, as these need to be decided on a case-by-case basis. In practice, most species require not one but a combination of several responses that adequately address the species' particular ecological requirements and the specific threats affecting it. Naturally, not all conservation responses are equally effective to all species, and some take longer to produce effects than others. Understanding which responses work best with particular species and threats is thus critical to informing conservation decisions in the face of scarce conservation resources, but the effectiveness of conservation

responses has thus far been poorly documented. A notable exception is a 2004 review of 5,500 key actions proposed for 1,186 threatened birds in 2000 (BirdLife International 2000; Figure 8.1). This revealed that 67% of these species have had at least some of these actions implemented (as determined from a review by a worldwide network of over 100 experts), even though the full set of proposed actions has been undertaken for only 5% of the species, and for at least 17% of the species no action has been carried out. However, not all of the actions implemented have already benefited species directly: for only 24% of globally threatened bird species this has been the case, by mitigating threats or through inferred or measured effects on population size, trends and productivity. For 26% of the species, the action has had no direct benefit yet, and for the remaining 17% of species where one or more actions have been implemented, the effects are unknown. Actions that have not directly benefited species have not necessarily been ineffective, as some involve essential research (which paves the way for effective conservation management) and some take time to produce noticeable effects.

8.2 Research Action

Conservation action frequently needs to be tailored to the specific circumstances affecting particular species. It is thus more effective if supported by adequate knowledge on the species (taxonomy, biology and ecology, population numbers and trends, range, and habitat status), on the threats affecting the species, and the most effective measures for addressing those threats. Although the *IUCN Red List* is biased towards the better-studied groups and regions, many species already assessed by the Red List still require substantial improvement in the knowledge base to support effective conservation action.

The Red List Category Data Deficient (DD) is assigned to a species when there is inadequate information to make a direct, or indirect, assessment of its risk of extinction based on its distribution and/or population status (IUCN 2001). There are currently 3,580 species listed on the *IUCN Red List* as DD (see Tables 2.2 and 2.3), including 2,882 animals and 698 plants. These figures demonstrate that even for the best-known taxonomic groups there are still substantial numbers of species lacking even the basic information needed to determine their threat status. Data Deficient species are mainly concentrated in regions with high biodiversity that have been poorly studied (as is the example with amphibians in Figure 8.2). Similarly, 23% (18 out of 78) of DD birds are found in the very poorly studied New

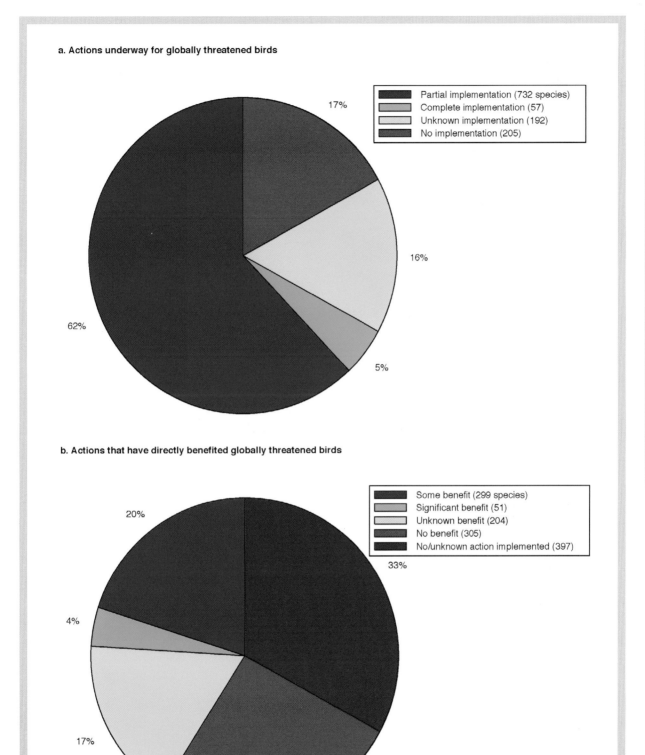

a. Actions underway for globally threatened birds

Partial implementation (732 species)
Complete implementation (57)
Unknown implementation (192)
No implementation (205)

17%

16%

5%

62%

b. Actions that have directly benefited globally threatened birds

Some benefit (299 species)
Significant benefit (51)
Unknown benefit (204)
No benefit (305)
No/unknown action implemented (397)

20%

4%

17%

26%

33%

Figure 8.1
The extent and effectiveness of conservation actions underway for globally threatened birds (source: BirdLife International 2004b).
(a) Level of implementation of the 5,500 key actions proposed for 1,186 globally threatened birds in 2000 (BirdLife International 2000).
(b) Effect of the actions implemented in benefiting the species' conservation status.

Guinea region. Our understanding of the distribution of many Data Deficient species is tempered by records of specimens collected only once (e.g., many species of gerbil *Gerbillus* in North Africa), some of which might not be valid species. However, many DD species might well be threatened, and therefore in need of conservation attention.

Consequently, DD species, and the regions where they occur, are priorities for research action (though not necessarily for immediate conservation action). Having said this, a map of DD species does not necessarily highlight the areas that are the least known (especially in very poorly known groups and regions), as it does not account for undescribed species.

Photo 8.2
The Indian Ocean Bottlenose Dolphin *Tursiops aduncus* (pictured here) was only recently recognized as being distinct from the Bottlenose Dolphin *T. truncatus*. But due to the muddled taxonomy, widespread distribution ranges and considerable overlap in occurrence, both species are listed as Data Deficient until greater clarity is obtained.

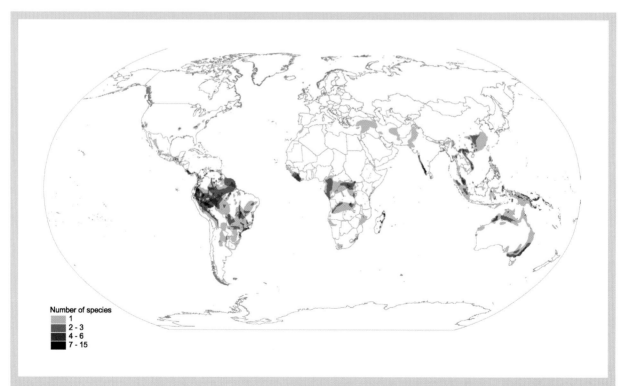

Number of species
1
2 - 3
4 - 6
7 - 15

Figure 8.2
Global distribution map of Data Deficient amphibian species, mapped as the number of species per square degree cell. Note: this map is only an approximation, as for most DD species extent of occurrence is poorly known; this map does not include the 90 DD species whose range is unknown.

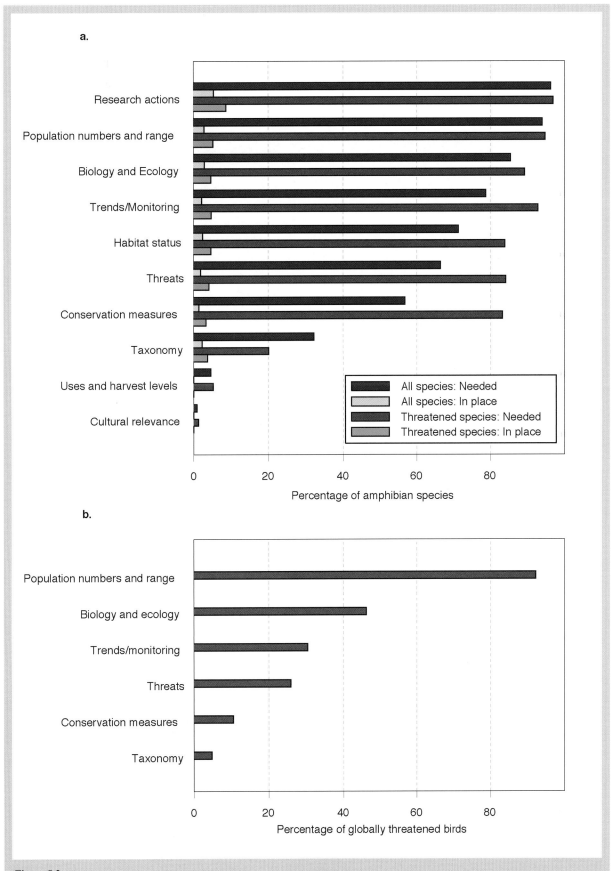

Figure 8.3
Research actions: (a) needed and in place for all species and for all threatened species of amphibians; and (b) needed for globally threatened birds.

For the other non DD species on the *IUCN Red List*, there are at least some data on which the status assessment was based. In many cases, however, this information is very limited, and further research is urgently needed to guide conservation actions aimed at improving species' conservation status. For amphibians, for example, 97% of all threatened species need research action, but for only 9% of the species is some action already in place (though the reliability of these numbers is low). For birds, research action is needed for 92% of all globally threatened species (Figure 8.3). Most species in need of research action require baseline information on their population numbers and range (fundamental to guiding *in situ* conservation action, establishing baselines for monitoring), and knowledge of the species' population and range trends (critical for the application of the IUCN Red List Criteria). Monitoring of range and population trends is frequently needed, and this will contribute directly to the development of biodiversity indicators (see Section 4; Butchart *et al.* in press a and b). Many species lack basic data on biology and ecology needed to understand habitat requirements, capacity for population recovery, dispersal ability, and vulnerability to environmental change. In some cases, further research is needed to clarify the taxonomic status of species, which may reveal currently unknown species that face high extinction risk (Figure 8.3). Better data are frequently needed on the threats affecting species' populations and on the effectiveness of conservation measures (e.g., the threats responsible for drastic declines in amphibian species in many parts of the world, and adequate conservation responses; Collins and Storfer 2003; Kiesecker *et al.* 2003).

8.3 Communication and Education

Increased stewardship of natural resources is urgently needed, not only in the communities in direct contact with particular threatened species, or inhabitants of cities in those countries holding these species, but worldwide. Indeed, most of the ultimate causes of species' declines lie in patterns of consumption of people living in distant parts of the world. Communication and education actions (e.g., Box 8.1) are fundamental to promoting responsible decisions. These include: recognizing and being willing to pay higher prices for products (such as wood) and services (such as tourism) obtained in ways that promote habitat protection; reducing patterns of over-consumption; providing public support for policies that promote conservation; and providing private support to conservation action. Zoos, aquariums and botanical gardens play an important role in raising the public awareness and understanding of the threats and conservation needs of threatened species (Miller *et al.* 2004). Effective conservation action requires adequate technical capacity, which is frequently lacking in those parts of the world that need it the most. Local technical capacity is fundamental to: the collection and interpretation of data on the conservation status of, and threats to, species; supporting decisions on effective conservation responses; and guiding the implementation of conservation programmes. Capacity development also includes institutional strengthening, the development of legal and policy frameworks, and ensuring that a variety of stakeholders have an active role in decision-making on protected areas and their management (Carabias and Rao 2003).

Photo 8.3
Botanical gardens play a major role in educating the public about threatened plants and the need to conserve them.

The *IUCN Red List* plays an important role in many of these communication and education processes. As a reliable standard for the identification of globally threatened species, it is an invaluable tool for efforts aimed at raising awareness for the need to conserve species and their habitats. The more than 120 Specialist Groups and Task Forces of the IUCN Species Survival Commission (IUCN/SSC), which provide the bulk of the Red List data, contribute directly to local capacity building and raising awareness. The IUCN/SSC Action Plans synthesize the available information on species threat status and provide guidance for future conservation action.

Box 8.1

The Yellow-eared Parrot and the Wax Palm

A good example of community education and awareness playing an important role is in the conservation of the Critically Endangered Yellow-eared Parrot *Ognorhynchus icterotis* and the Vulnerable Wax Palm *Ceroxylon quindiuense* on which the Parrot depends for nesting and roosting. Wax palms are traditionally cut down to adorn processions and churches throughout the Colombian Andes each Palm Sunday (one week before Easter Sunday). Fundación ProAves, a Colombian Non-Governmental Organization, has successfully been working with the Roman Catholic Church to support alternatives to cutting down wax palms for adorning traditional processions, in addition to an intensive environmental awareness campaign nationwide. ProAves also helped to establish an ecological group, "Friends of Nature", which distributed palm and parrot posters, held musical concerts and theatre productions, and worked on capacity-building of the local police.

Based on information provided by Paul Salaman

Photos: © Fundacion ProAves - www.proaves.org.

Photos 8.4, 8.5 and 8.6
Conservation action is addressing some of the key issues but the future of the yellow-eared Parrot *Ognorhynchus icterotis* (Critically Endangered) remains extremely uncertain.

8.4 Policy-Based Actions

Policy-based actions are essential for providing the institutional support, human and financial resources, and legal framework required to ensure effective species conservation. Frequently, such actions occur through the development and implementation of legislation at the national or sub-national levels, or through international agreements (Table 8.1; Figure 8.4). Legislation is sometimes directed at the protection of particular species, such as by regulating the harvesting of individuals (e.g., Convention for the Regulation of Whaling; Table 8.1 and Box 8.2), their trade (e.g., CITES; Figure 8.5), or alterations in their habitat (e.g., Ramsar Convention; Table 8.1). Legislation can also promote habitat protection, most noticeably through the creation of protected areas: 241 countries or territories are recognized by the *2004 World Database on Protected Areas* as having officially designated protected areas of some type (WDPA Consortium 2004). Legislation may also protect habitat by regulating land use patterns at a broader scale (e.g., Brazil's Forest Code; Table 8.1), or through the regulation of anthropogenic activities that are frequently the least direct but most pervasive causes of species declines (e.g., pollution generated by industry, transport leading to the introduction of invasive species, consumption of fossil fuels leading to climate change; Table 8.1).

The role of multilateral environmental agreements (Table 8.1; Figure 8.4) has grown during the last decade, as human impacts intensify and span across national boundaries more often. There are now more than 500 international treaties that concern the environment, and most countries have ratified key international treaties (although significant gaps remain). These agreements are a means to adopt harmonized approaches and resolve trans-boundary problems with neighbouring states. They increasingly offer access to worldwide knowledge, tools and financial resources, and they can give conservation agencies a stronger mandate domestically (Steiner *et al.* 2003). Nevertheless, most conservation action takes place at the national level, and the national legal framework remains crucial in the effective implementation of the vast majority of conservation programmes (Table 8.1). Naturally, legislation is only useful if adequately implemented, and such implementation is lacking in many cases.

Policy-based actions are frequently implemented as a top-down approach, but their effectiveness is in many cases hindered by a lack of involvement with the local communities that are the direct users of biodiversity

resources, and by inadequate financial resources for their implementation. Community management promotes a stewardship of the natural resources, particularly when complemented by the development of adequate livelihood alternatives. Outstanding examples of community management can be found in the web site of the Equator Initiative (http://www.undp.org/equatorinitiative/index.htm), a United Nations Development Programme initiative designed to reduce poverty through the conservation and sustainable use of biodiversity in the equatorial belt by fostering, supporting and strengthening community partnerships. One of those examples is Torra Conservancy, a community-based conservancy covering 352,000 hectares of land in the Kunene region of northwestern Namibia, which has established sustainable hunting and eco-tourism activities that have earned significant profits for the entire community.

Photo: © John S. Donaldson.

Photo 8.7
All cycads are listed on Appendices I or II of CITES. The endemic Chinese cycad *Cycas panzhihuanensis* (Near Threatened), although still abundant, is rapidly declining due to habitat loss and collection for the horticultural trade.

Table 8.1

Examples of national legislation and international agreements for the conservation of particular species, for the protection of sites or habitats, and for the regulation of activities that can pose threats to biodiversity. Dates correspond to the date when the agreement entered into force. For international agreements, there is an indication of whether their scope is universal (any country can ratify it) or regional. Note: many of these laws/agreements could be listed under two or more categories (e.g., the European Union Habitats Directive simultaneously provides for the protection of species and sites/habitats, and for the regulation of activities).

	National legislation	International agreements
Species	*United States Endangered Species Act* (1973): the species listed are protected from exploitation and disturbance, and their habitats are subject to legal protection. *Philippines Fisheries Code* (1998): prohibits the gathering, possession, and exportation of scleractinian corals.	*Convention for the Regulation of Whaling* (1935; universal): initially prohibited the taking or killing of right whales (including North-Cape Whales, Greenland Whales, Southern Right Whales, Pacific Right Whales and Southern Pygmy Right Whales), and now regulates all whaling. *Convention on International Trade in Endangered Species of Wild Fauna and Flora* (*CITES*; 1975; universal): regulates international trade of the species listed. *Convention on the Conservation of Migratory Species of Wild Animals* (*CMS or Bonn Convention*; 1983; universal): protects listed species of wild animals that migrate across or outside national boundaries, and provides for the development of agreements to conserve particular species. *North Pacific Anadromous Fish Commission Convention* (1993; regional): prohibits all salmon fishing in the northern Pacific Ocean and its adjacent seas beyond the 200-mile exclusive economic zones.
Sites and habitats	*Brazil's Forestry Law* (1965): establishes that each rural property in the Amazonian basin must preserve at least 80% of its forest cover. *Thailand's Wild Animals Reservation and Protection Act* (1960) and *National Park Act* (1961): legal basis for the creation of conservation areas or protected areas, including national parks (144 sites), wildlife sanctuaries (53 sites), forest parks (42 sites), wildlife non–hunting areas (52 sites), biosphere reserves (1 sites), World Heritage Natural sites (1 site), watershed class 1 and conservation mangroves.	*Convention on Biological Diversity* (1992; universal): the programmes of work developed under the CBD encourage Parties to take a wide range of actions to biodiversity conservation and sustainable use. *European Union Habitats Directive* (1992; regional): the natural habitat listed must be maintained at a favourable status, particularly through the creation of a network of protected sites (Natura 2000 network). *Convention on Wetlands of International Importance Especially as Waterfowl Habitat* (*Ramsar Convention*; 1975; universal): provides the framework for national action and international cooperation for the conservation and wise use of wetlands and their resources, in particular through the designation of sites under the Ramsar List of Wetlands of International Importance. *Convention concerning the Protection of the World Cultural and Natural Heritage* (*World Heritage Convention*; 1972; universal): provides for the identification, protection and preservation of cultural and natural heritage (including habitats of threatened species) around the world considered to be of outstanding value to humanity. Countries submit places for designation under the World Heritage List.
Activities	*China's Law on Environmental Impact Assessment* (2003): requires that governmental and non-governmental planning involving land utilization, urban engineering, communication, and natural resource exploration goes through the process of an environmental impact assessment. *Australian Quarantine Act* (1908): strict control measures aimed at preventing the introduction of pests and diseases (mainly established to protect the agricultural sector, but also human health and the native flora and fauna).	*United Nations' Moratorium on High Seas Drift Net Fishing* (1992; universal): in force in all the world's oceans, enclosed seas, and semi-enclosed seas (international waters only). *OSPAR Convention for the Protection of the Marine Environment of the North-East Atlantic* (1992; regional): guides international cooperation on the protection of the marine environment by the prevention and elimination of pollution from land-based sources, dumping or incineration, and offshore sources. *United Nations Framework Convention on Climate Change* (1994; universal) and *Kyoto Protocol* (adopted in 1997, not yet into force; universal): caps greenhouse gas emissions in participating industrialized nations from 2008 to 2012 and establishes an international market in emissions credits that will allow these nations to seek out the most cost-effective means to reduce atmospheric concentrations of greenhouse gases. *United Nations' International Conference on Ballast Water Management for Ships* (adopted in 2004, not yet into force; universal): makes provisions to control and manage ships' ballast water and thus prevent, minimize and ultimately eliminate the transfer of harmful aquatic organisms and pathogens across the seas and oceans of the world.

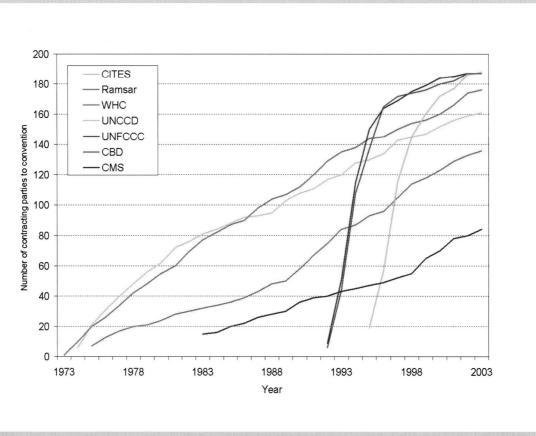

Figure 8.4
Rate of ratification of the main international treaties that concern biodiversity conservation (source: BirdLife International 2004b): Convention on International Trade in Endangered Species of Wild Fauna and Flora (CITES); Convention on Wetlands of International Importance (Ramsar Convention); World Heritage Convention (WHC); UN Convention to Combat Desertification (UNCCD); United Nations Framework Convention on Climate Change (UNFCCC); Convention on Biological Diversity (CBD); and Convention on the Conservation of Migratory Species of Wild Animals (CMS).

Box 8.2

Southern Right Whales

Exploitation of Southern Right Whales *Eubalaena australis* is traditionally supposed to have begun in the 1770s, when first American, and then British and French whalers moved into the South Atlantic. By 1850 they had removed an estimated 125,000–150,000 right whales in the Southern Hemisphere, and the population had declined to less than one-tenth of its original size. Despite this reduction, right whales only received protection in 1935, when a League of Nations agreement came into effect, by which time there may have been as few as 300 individuals left in the Southern Hemisphere. For decades a sighting of a Southern Right Whale was a rare event, but since the 1970s there have been encouraging signs of a recovery in a number of localities. Regular aerial

surveys off Argentina, Australia and South Africa have recorded rates of increase of 7–8% a year, close to the maximum possible biologically (Best *et al.* 2001). In other localities, notably Namibia, New Zealand and Mozambique, signs of recovery have been slower in coming. Nevertheless, by 1997 there were an estimated 7,000 right whales in the Southern Hemisphere, or about one-eighth to one-tenth of original numbers. This is more southern right whales than at any time in the last 150 years.

Based on information provided by Peter Best, IUCN/SSC Cetacean Specialist Group

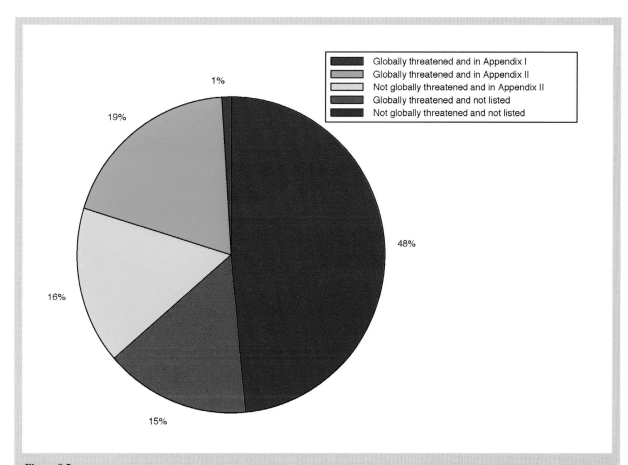

■	Globally threatened and in Appendix I
■	Globally threatened and in Appendix II
■	Not globally threatened and in Appendix II
■	Globally threatened and not listed
■	Not globally threatened and not listed

Figure 8.5
Current coverage of those amphibian species threatened by over-exploitation for international trade in Appendices I and II of the Convention on International Trade in Endangered Species of Wild Fauna and Flora (CITES). Appendix I of CITES includes species threatened with extinction (trade permitted only when the purpose of the import is not commercial); Appendix II includes species not necessarily threatened with extinction, but for which trade must be controlled in order to avoid utilization incompatible with their survival. The Global Amphibian Assessment revealed 99 amphibian species that are adversely impacted by exploitation for the international trade, including 35 species that are globally threatened. Currently, only 36 of these species (16 of the globally threatened species) are listed on Appendices I or II of CITES.

8.5 Habitat and Site-Based Actions

Retaining viable populations in their native habitats is an essential conservation response for ensuring the long-term persistence of species (although such actions are frequently not sufficient on their own; e.g., Newmark 1996). Habitat and site-based conservation actions are needed for 73% of all amphibian species, 88% of the threatened amphibians, and 76% of the threatened birds. On the positive side, the Global Amphibian Assessment reported that some action is already in place for 65% of the threatened amphibians (Figure 8.6).

Photo: © Malcolm Largen.

Photo 8.8
Leptopelis susanae (Endangered) is a treefrog that occurs only in the Gughe Mountains of southern Ethiopia, where it is threatened by forest clearance. It does not occur in any protected areas.

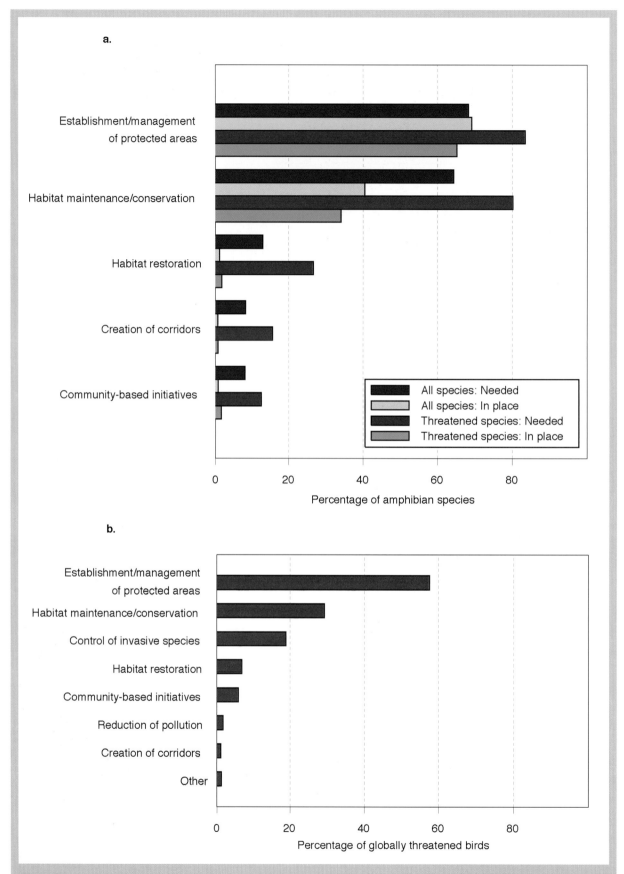

Figure 8.6
Habitat and site-based conservation responses: (a) needed and in place for all species and for threatened species of amphibians; and (b) needed for globally threatened birds.

Habitat and site-based action frequently takes place by maintaining or conserving existing habitat, with the aim of preventing future habitat loss and degradation (the main threat to biodiversity; see section 6.2). In some cases, however, maintaining the quality of current habitat might not be sufficient, and habitat management is required to increase carrying capacity (e.g., control of brood parasites, for Kirtland's Warbler *Dendroica kirtlandii*, Box 8.3), or habitat restoration may be needed to recreate the conditions in which species can persist (e.g., eradication of invasive predators of the Rarotonga Monarch *Pomarea dimidiata*, Box 8.4).

Box 8.3

Kirtland's Warbler

The recent recovery of Kirtland's Warbler *Dendroica kirtlandii* illustrates the potential of active habitat management in securing populations of threatened species (Probst *et al.* 2003). The warbler's exacting requirements for breeding habitat – stands of young (5–23 years old) Jack Pine *Pinus banksiana* growing on well-drained soils – mean that its breeding range is confined to a small area in Michigan's Lower Peninsula, United States. Counts of singing males in 1951 and 1961 totalled 432 and 502 respectively, but this declined to 201 in 1971. A suite of measures was then put in place to stabilize the population.

These measures included the control of Brown-headed Cowbird *Molothrus ater* (a brood parasite of the warbler), annual population censuses, and active management of the species' Jack Pine habitats. The population remained relatively stable between 1971–1987, with suitable habitat regenerating after wildfires or management action apparently offset by 'losses' due to the increasing over-maturity of many older pine stands. However, following further management action and two large wildfires, the amount of suitably aged habitat doubled between 1987 and 1990, and the warbler population more than tripled between 1990 and 2000 in response. By 2000, the population had reached the maximum projected carrying capacity within its core breeding range (in Michigan's Lower Peninsula), with the number of peripheral breeding records (in Wisconsin and Michigan's Upper Peninsula) increasing over the same period.

Photo: © Dave Currie

Photo 8.9
Kirtland's Warbler *Dendroica kirtlandii* (Vulnerable).

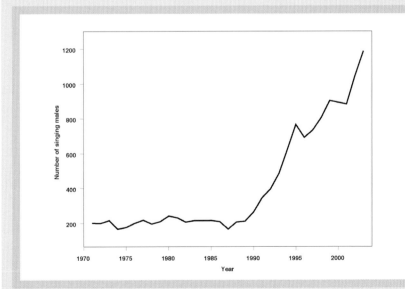

Figure Box 8.3
As a result of intensive habitat management, the breeding population of Kirtland's Warbler more than tripled between 1990 and 2000.

Taken from BirdLife International (2004b)

Box 8.4

Rarotonga Monarch

The Rarotonga Monarch (or Kakerori) *Pomarea dimidiata* is endemic to the Pacific island of Rarotonga (in the Cook Islands). Although common in the mid-1800s, the species subsequently declined rapidly, and following the collection of a few specimens in the early 1900s, was not recorded again until 1973. In 1983, 21 birds were discovered, and a survey in 1987 estimated the population to number 38 individuals, but declining (Robertson *et al.* 1994). A recovery plan was prepared in 1988, and implementation began later the same year.

Intensive control of predators (particularly black rats *Rattus rattus*) reduced adult mortality from 24% to 9%, with nesting success increasing from 15% to 63% (Robertson *et al.* 1994). By 2000, the population had reached 221 individuals (see figure below), and in 2001–2003 30 young birds were transferred to the rat-free island of Atiu (200km northeast of Rarotonga) in an apparently successful attempt to establish a second 'insurance' population (H. Robertson and E. Saul *in litt.* 2004).

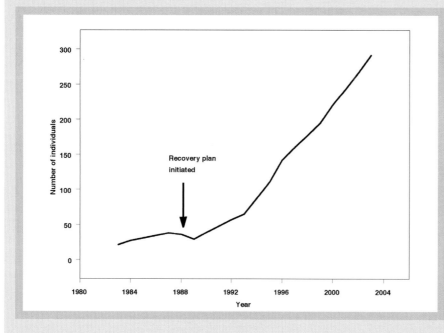

Figure Box 8.4
Intensive management has led to the recovery of Rarotonga Monarch (Endangered).

Taken from BirdLife International (2004b), and based on information provided by Hilary Aikman, Rod Hitchmough, Don Merton and Hugh Robertson (New Zealand Department of Conservation) and Ed Saul (Takitumu Conservation Area, Cook Islands)

Protected areas are areas of land and/or sea especially dedicated to the protection and maintenance of biological diversity, and of natural and associated cultural resources, and managed through legal or other effective means (IUCN 1994b). They are a major tool for habitat protection, and to create the conditions for effective habitat management and restoration. Most countries of the world have established networks of protected areas, with 11.5% of the global land area, but less than 0.5% of the world's oceans, under some type of formal protection (Chape *et al.* 2003). Existing protected areas make a valuable contribution to species conservation worldwide (Bruner *et al.* 2001), with many species now restricted to protected areas, having lost their habitat elsewhere (e.g., the Critically Endangered Pygmy

Hog *Sus salvanius*, which had a previously extensive range in the Himalayan foothills and is now restricted to the Manas Sanctuary in India; Oliver and Roy 1993; see also Box 8.5 on the Southern White Rhinoceros *Ceratotherium simum simum*). In practice, however, protected areas have a wide diversity of legal status and management types (Brandon *et al.* 1998), and quite variable effectiveness in retaining their biodiversity values (Harcourt *et al.* 2001).

Moreover, there are many species not yet covered by any protected area: a global gap analysis revealed 1,486 species, including 846 threatened species, of mammals, birds, amphibians and freshwater turtles and tortoises not covered by protected areas in any part of their ranges (Table 8.2). These "gap species", identified by overlaying the

Box 8.5

Southern White Rhinoceros

The Southern White Rhinoceros *Ceratotherium simum simum*, which had been fairly widespread throughout Namibia, Botswana, Zimbabwe, Mozambique and South Africa early in the nineteenth century, had by the turn of the twentieth century been reduced to two relict populations on the Zimbabwe-Mozambique border and in Umfolozi Game Reserve in KwaZulu-Natal, South Africa. The former became extinct, leaving the small population of 20-50 rhinos in Umfolozi Game Reserve, which was proclaimed in 1897, as the only ones left in the world. Afforded protection, numbers increased, and the population expanded into the adjoining Hluhluwe Game Reserve, and by 1960 there were at least 700 animals, possibly more as game counts in those days normally underestimated numbers. Within a year it had become both possible and necessary to capture animals for translocation to other reserves within their former range,

and hence the Natal Parks Board's "Operation Rhino" was launched. Over the next 30 or so years, more than 4,500 white rhinos were moved out of the Hluhluwe-Umfolozi Park and other reserves in KwaZulu-Natal. Many have been donated to conservation authorities in especially Namibia, South Africa, Zimbabwe, Botswana and Mozambique, and since 1986 more than 1,000 have been sold, mainly by auction to the private sector. By 2002, the numbers of free-ranging southern white rhinos in Africa had increased to over 11,500 distributed between 250 populations in seven countries, of which about 11,000 were in South Africa. The Southern White Rhino is now listed as Near Threatened on the *IUCN Red List*. A quarter of Africa's Southern White Rhino population is privately owned, and it is an important contributor to the economic viability of the wildlife industry.

Photo: © Craig Hilton-Taylor.

Photo 8.10
Southern White Rhinoceros *Ceratotherium simum simum* (Near Threatened).

Based on information provided by Martin Brooks, IUCN/SSC African Rhino Specialist Group

distribution maps of species with the *2004 World Database on Protected Areas*, correspond to 13% of all species and 19.9% of all threatened species analysed. The number of gap species doubles if only protected areas of reasonable size (>1,000 ha) and of stricter conservation classifications (IUCN Protected Area Categories I-IV; IUCN 1994b) are considered (Table 8.2). It is noteworthy that the information on whether or not each amphibian species occurs in a protected area, provided by the Global Amphibian Assessment experts, indicates that a higher fraction of

amphibians (33% of all species, 39% of all threatened species) are identified as gap species than by the methodology outlined by Rodrigues *et al.* (2004) (see Table 8.2 and Appendix 2h). Irrespective of the exact numbers, these results demonstrate that the global network of protected areas is still far from completed in terms of coverage of species, and even less so for the coverage of threatened species. The gap species are mainly concentrated in regions of high endemism in the world's tropical forests, particularly in montane regions and islands (Figure 8.7).

Table 8.2

Numbers of species of mammals, turtles, amphibians and threatened birds whose ranges do not overlap any protected area, or which do not overlap any protected area larger than 1,000ha classified under IUCN Protected Area Categories I-IV ("gap species"). Values in parenthesis are the percentage of gap species analysed within a given taxonomic group. Values in italics are the estimates of the number of amphibian gap species obtained from the Global Amphibian Assessment database. For methods, see Appendix 2h and Rodrigues *et al.* 2004.

Taxon	Number of species analysed	Numbers of gap species	
		Current network (all protected areas)	Current network (protected areas >1,000ha and IUCN I-IV)
Threatened mammals	1,063	149 (14.0%)	338 (31.8%)
Threatened birds	1,208	243 (20.1%)	472 (39.1%)
Threatened turtles	119	12 (10.1%)	33 (27.7%)
Threatened amphibians	1,856	442 (23.8%)	877 (47.3%)
		728 (39.2%)	
All threatened species	4,245	846 (19.9%)	1,720 (40.5%)
All mammals	4,735	258 (5.5%)	644 (13.5%)
All turtles	273	21 (7.7%)	48 (17.6%)
All amphibians	5,619	964 (17.2%)	1,922 (34.2%)
		1,851 (32.9%)	
All species analysed (mammals, amphibians, turtles and threatened birds)	11,834	1,486 (12.6%)	3,085 (26.1%)

Number of gap species
- 1
- 2 - 6
- 7 - 15
- 16 - 28

Figure 8.7

Density map of gap species of mammals, amphibians, freshwater turtles and tortoises, and threatened birds per half-degree cell, created by overlaying the ranges of all threatened species not covered by any protected area.

A finer-scale approach for investigating species coverage in protected areas is by mapping sites known to be essential for the persistence of each species and investigating their level of formal protection. As an example of the uses of the Red List, BirdLife International has been collecting this information through their Important Bird Area (IBA) programme. This programme seeks to locate, document and protect networks of sites (areas that can be delimited and, potentially, managed for conservation) critical for the conservation of the world's birds (e.g., Fishpool and Evans 2001). Of the 608 IBAs identified for the presence of globally threatened birds in Africa, 219 (36%) are not protected, highlighting 44 species (20% of the total number on Africa) not covered by protected areas (Figure 8.8a). Key Biodiversity Areas (KBAs) expand the IBA approach to other taxa (Eken et al. in press). A preliminary analysis of KBAs for eight taxa (mammals, birds, amphibians, freshwater fish, reptiles, arthropods, gastropods, and plants) in Madagascar revealed 91 unprotected sites, corresponding to 65% of the 141 sites identified thus far, and translating into 78 gap species (Figure 8.8b). The Alliance for Zero Extinction (AZE) (www.zeroextinction.org) has been mapping site occurrences of a particular subset of globally threatened species: those Critically Endangered (CR) or Endangered (EN) species that are restricted to single localities. Of the 595 AZE sites identified so far for mammal, bird, turtle, crocodile, iguana, amphibian, and conifer species, at least 257 (43%) are not protected, corresponding to 299 gap species (Figure 8.8c). Again, these numbers confirm that large fractions of the world's threatened species are lacking coverage in protected areas.

Investigating species coverage in protected areas is just a first step for assessing their effectiveness as conservation tools. Except for particular species/regions (e.g., Caro 2000; Sinclair et al. 2002), little information exists on the extent to which protected areas are affecting the overall conservation status of species. However, some insights can be obtained by comparing the coverage in protected areas for species with different population trends. We found a statistically significant association between species of amphibians that are gaps and species that are decreasing, while non-gap species are more likely to be stable or increasing than

Table 8.3

Comparison of percentages of species with decreasing and stable/increasing populations for gap and non-gap species of amphibians and threatened birds. Amphibian gap species were identified through two methods (see Table 8.2): overlap between maps of species distributions and of protected areas (global gap analysis; Rodrigues et al. 2004) and through information from specialists (Global Amphibian Assessment). More gap species tend to be decreasing than would be expected by chance, while the tendency is for non-gap species to have higher percentages of stable or increasing species. For methods, see Appendix 2h.

			Decreasing	Stable or increasing	Total species of known trend
Amphibians	Global gap analysis	Gap species	387 (83.6%)	76 (16.4%)	463
		Non-gaps	2,081 (58.0%)	1,504 (42.0%)	3,585
	Global Amphibian Assessment	Gap species	731 (71.1%)	297 (28.9%)	1,028
		Non-gaps	1,737 (57.5%)	1,283 (42.5%)	3,020
	All species (gaps and non-gaps)		2,468 (61.0%)	1,580 (39.0%)	4,048
Threatened birds	Gap species		135 (70%)	58 (30%)	193
	Non-gaps		837 (90%)	94 (10%)	931
	All species (gaps and non-gaps)		972 (86%)	152 (14.0%)	1,124

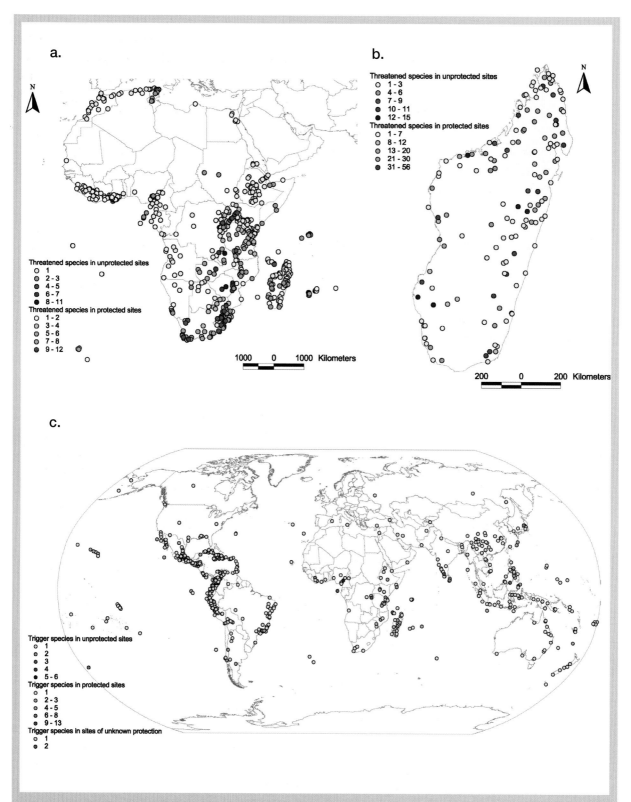

Figure 8.8

Maps of the coverage of threatened species in protected areas and gaps in protection at the site scale; three examples: (a) African Important Bird Areas triggered by the presence of globally threatened bird species (Fishpool and Evans 2001; BirdLife International 2004b). (b) Key Biodiversity Areas of Madagascar triggered by the presence of globally threatened species of mammals, birds, amphibians, freshwater fish, reptiles, arthropods, gastropods and plants (preliminary unpublished data provided by Zo Lalaina Rakotobe, Luciano Andriamaro, Harison Rabarison, and Harison Randrianasolo). (c) Sites identified that are triggered by the occurrence of Critically Endangered or Endangered species that are restricted to a single site (www.zeroextinction.org; for 47 sites, protected status is unknown). In all cases, sites with partial protection are coded as "protected".

expected, but an opposite tendency for threatened birds (Table 8.3). These mixed results do not clarify whether protected areas are contributing to preventing species declines overall.

Photo 8.11
The African Wild Dog *Lycaon pictus* (Endangered) has disappeared from much of its former range due to ongoing conflict with humans, infectious disease, and habitat fragmentation.

For many species, habitat protection requires conservation action at a scale larger than that of single protected areas. This is the case for species with very large spatial requirements (e.g., the Endangered African Wild Dog *Lycaon pictus*, whose home ranges can extend beyond 2,000km², larger than 95% of protected areas in Africa; Woodroffe *et al.* in press), migratory species (e.g., the Critically Endangered Atlantic Sturgeon *Acipenser sturio*; Beamesderfer and Farr 1997), and species predicted to suffer substantial range shifts due to climate change (e.g., several threatened species of Proteaceae in South Africa; Midgley *et al.* 2003; see Box 6.3). For these species, *in situ* conservation requires the establishment of networks of protected areas, adequately connected though a matrix of favourable habitat that allows for species movement through, and persistence in, the broader landscape.

8.6 Species-Based Actions

In many cases, habitat protection on its own is not sufficient, and direct intervention is required to mitigate or eliminate specific threats to species. *Ex situ* conservation (through captive breeding/artificial propagation) can offer insurance against extinctions by providing a source population for future re-introductions or reinforcement of wild populations. Currently, there are 36 species of animals and 25 species of plants classified as Extinct in the Wild (e.g., Box 8.6), and for which any chance of recovery requires a combination of *ex situ* conservation, recovery of the conditions required for species' persistence in natural habitats, and successful re-introductions (provided suitable habitat exists and/or threats have ceased). Captive breeding combined with re-introductions or population reinforcement have already prevented many species from becoming extinct (e.g., the Mallorcan Midwife Toad *Alytes muletensis*, Box 8.7; and the Black-footed Ferret *Mustela nigripes*, Box 8.8), and might be particularly pertinent for the conservation of several species of Asian freshwater turtles and tortoises, currently over-exploited as local food sources and for the international trade (van Dijk *et al.* 2000). *Ex situ* conservation might also be the only measure currently available for preventing the extinction of many amphibian species that are suffering drastic declines (Young *et al.* 2001; see section 6.5). The Global Amphibian Assessment identified this as a required measure for 201 (11%) of the globally threatened species.

Translocation is another species-based action that has been crucial in rescuing species from extinction. These can be either re-introductions into previous habitat from where the species has been lost (e.g., Southern White Rhinoceros; Box 8.5) or benign introductions into areas of suitable habitat that have not been previously colonized by the species (e.g., translocation of Rarotonga Monarch and Black Robin individuals to predator-free islands; Boxes 8.4 and 8.9).

Species threatened by over-exploitation typically require conservation measures that either prevent or discourage harvesting (e.g., trade control through CITES; Table 8.1), or promote sustainable use. The latter may involve harvest management (e.g., Whiskery Shark; Box 8.10) or commercialization of farmed individuals (e.g., crocodile farming in Papua New Guinea and Cuba; Ross 1998) to reduce pressure on wild populations. The capture, shearing and release of wild Vicuñas *Vicugna vicugna* in the Southern Andes is an example of an ancient method of sustainable use (Torres 1992). Many species may benefit from well-managed programmes of non-consumptive uses, particularly tourism (e.g., marine turtles, Tisdell and Wilson 2002; and gorillas, McNeilage *et al.* 2001).

Box 8.6

St. Helena Redwood

Formerly common growing below St. Helena's central ridge at 500–750m, the endemic Redwood *Trochetiopsis erythroxylon* grew with a tall straight trunk to a height of 6 metres, with a hard reddish-brown wood and large white pendant, campanulate flowers flushing pink when fading. It was the tree preferred by early settlers of the island for building and was also used extensively for tanning. Early in the 18th century within 60 years of the island being settled, it had become extremely rare. By 1875, the Redwood was reduced to just 17 or 18 trees, two in the wild and the rest cultivated in gardens. It finally became Extinct in the Wild around 1960 when the last tree at High Peak died.

The story for the past 40 years is no less harrowing. The Redwoods derived from this single tree were frail and prone to die-back, with older trees not attaining a height of more than 2.5m. Eight trees were planted around the island in private gardens, which prevented cross-pollination and further eroded the gene pool when individuals died without propagation. Recent glass house experiments provided direct proof that the Redwood is suffering from inbreeding depression, which has a severe effect on fitness (Rowe 1995). In 2003, over 300 Redwoods (the largest number of Redwoods the island has known for over three centuries), were established in a small plot of private land below the central ridge. There is considerable difference in the growth and vigour of the individuals, which indicates that fitness can to a certain extent (to what extent is not known at this stage) be rescued by crossing. A further obstacle to the survival of this species comes in the form of a tiny, probably endemic, Tineid moth whose larvae bore into living wood. How severe an effect it will have on future re-introduction efforts is yet to be seen. For now the goal must be to maximize out-breeding to try to recover the vigour indicated by historic descriptions. With continuity of effort we might be successful in keeping Redwoods alive within their historic range but the successful re-introduction of the St. Helena Redwood can only be judged by generations to come when it is reinstated in stature and successfully regenerating.

Based on information provided by Rebecca Cairns-Wicks, IUCN/SSC South Atlantic Islands Plant Specialist Group

Photo: © Rebecca Cairns-Wicks.

Photo 8.12
St. Helena Redwood *Trochetiopsis erythroxylon* (Critically Endangered).

Box 8.7

Mallorcan Midwife Toad

The Mallorcan Midwife Toad *Alytes muletensis* was originally described in 1977 from fossil remains found on the island of Mallorca, in the Balearic Islands of Spain. In 1979, living tadpoles and small toads of this species were first discovered in the remote, narrow limestone gorges of the Sierra de Tramuntana mountains in the north of the island.

In all, a total of 13 separate breeding populations were discovered; combined, these contained an estimated world population of 1,000 to 3,000 animals.

Both fossil and subfossil remains of this species suggest that it was widespread over much of Mallorca until about 2,000 years ago. The species then greatly declined following the introduction to the island of the predatory Viperine Snake *Natrix maura* and the competitive Green Frog *Rana perezi*. More recently, the species has suffered from habitat loss through the over-extraction of water from the streams in which it breeds. In view of the severe population fragmentation and continuing decline of the already small global population of this species, it was listed as Critically Endangered in the *1996 IUCN Red List of Threatened Animals*.

During 1985, a captive-breeding programme was initiated for the toad; this had the specific aim of providing animals for re-introduction at suitable release sites. The first re-introductions took place in 1989, and following these initial releases the species was re-introduced into several more sites. In addition to the re-introduction process, conservation measures were undertaken to assist in the recovery of the existing wild populations (Burley and Garcia 1997).

The re-introductions and associated habitat creation and management programmes have been very successful. Both the range and number of populations of the Mallorcan Midwife Toad have moderately, but constantly, increased. While the current, successful recovery programme will probably need to be continued indefinitely, the conservation status of the species is considered to have improved so much that it has been listed as Vulnerable on the 2004 *IUCN Red List*.

Based on information provided by Joan Mayol Serra, Richard Griffiths and Neil Cox

Photo 8.14
The Bwindi population of the Mountain Gorilla *Gorilla beringei* in Uganda (this population is Critically Endangered while the species as a whole is Endangered) benefits from tourism.

Box 8.8

Black-footed Ferret

The Black-footed Ferret *Mustela nigripes*, one of North America's rarest mammals, depends on an endangered ecosystem for survival. Prairie dogs *Cynomys* spp., keystone species of this ecosystem and the ferrets' main prey, have been seriously decimated over the last century. Black-footed ferrets were considered to be Extinct in the Wild in 1985, when the last known free-ranging population collapsed due to an epizootic of canine distemper, combined with a widespread epidemic of sylvatic plague. In an effort to save the species, all free-ranging ferrets remaining in the wild (18 animals), were brought into captivity. As a result of effective captive breeding and re-introduction programmes, and a certain amount of good fortune, black-footed ferrets are making a come-back from the brink of extinction. Since 1987, almost 5,000 kits have been born in captivity and more than 1,800 ferrets have been released in the wild steppes of North America. Re-introduction efforts began in 1991 and, to date, black-footed ferrets have been released into prairie dog complexes of Wyoming, South Dakota, Montana, Arizona, Colorado, Utah, and Mexico.

Adaptation of significant research findings into management techniques has notably enhanced recovery efforts. Since 1998, and for the first time since the initiation of the Black-footed Ferret recovery programme, there were more black-footed ferrets in the wild (approximately 400 adults and juveniles) than there were in captivity. The current programme direction focuses on identifying and developing more effective and cost-efficient breeding and re-introduction techniques, and on preserving and managing habitat that can support large, widely distributed prairie dog complexes of all prairie dog species. The successful re-establishment of black-footed ferrets will help increase awareness of prairie dog conservation needs and, consequently, all other species that depend on this ecosystem will benefit from efforts to recover this very seriously threatened carnivore.

Based on information provided by Astrid Vargas

Photo 8.13
Black-footed Ferret
Mustela nigripes
(currently listed as
Extinct in the Wild,
but is pending
reassessment).

Box 8.9

Black Robin

The Black Robin *Petroica traversi* is endemic to the Chatham Islands (New Zealand). The spectacular rescue of this species from its tiny refuge on Little Mangere Island is one of the most remarkable successes in species conservation (Butler and Merton 1992; Aikman *et al.* 2001). Following human settlement of the islands, black robins declined rapidly as their forest habitat was lost and degraded, and due to predation by introduced rats and cats. In 1976, when the population had declined to just seven birds, the remaining individuals were relocated to nearby Mangere Island, where 120,000 trees had been planted to provide suitable habitat. Nevertheless, by 1980, numbers

had fallen to five (four males and a single female) – the smallest population of any bird species for which precise figures were known at the time. Nest protection, supplementary feeding, and a cross-fostering programme (with the congeneric Tomtit *P. macrocephala*) were then established, and the population began to recover steadily. Individuals were later introduced to South East Island, and by 1989 the population had topped 100 individuals (Butler and Merton 1992), at which point management ceased. The population continued to rise until carrying capacity was reached in the late 1990s, since when it has been stable at around 250 birds (D. Merton *in litt.* 2004).

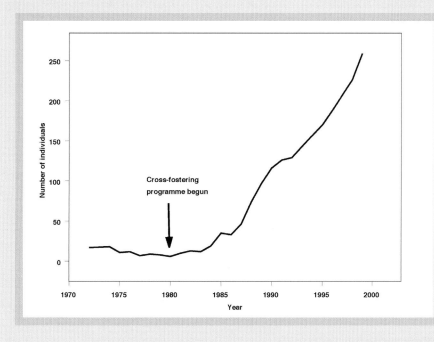

Figure Box 8.9
Intensive management has led to the recovery of the Black Robin (Endangered).

Taken from BirdLife International (2004b), and based on information provided by Don Merton

Responses preventing the spread of infectious agents or parasites (e.g., quarantine regulations and the control of ships' ballast water; Table 8.1) are fundamental in reducing such threats. However, responses that address the disease agents/parasites directly are becoming more pertinent as increasing numbers of globally threatened species are being affected by disease (see Sections 3.8 and 6.5). Such responses include vaccination (e.g., against the morbillivirus that affected the Critically Endangered Mediterranean Monk

Seal *Monachus monachus*, Osterhaus *et al.* 1998; against rabies for the Endangered African Wild Dog *Lycaon pictus*, Woodroffe 2001), but also the removal of the affected individuals, removal of other disease hosts/reservoirs, reduction of connectivity between affected and healthy populations, provision of medicine, and translocation of healthy individuals to captivity or to places non-affected by the disease.

Whiskery Shark

Whiskery sharks *Furgaleus macki*, have been caught in commercial fisheries in Western Australia since the 1940s. In the early years, longline fisheries captured small numbers, but introduction of multifilament gillnets in the 1960s increased catches. Concerns about mercury levels in sharks in the mid-1970s saw a reduction in catches for a few years. However, once these concerns were addressed and dedicated well-equipped shark fishing vessels entered the fishery, levels of fishing effort and catches rose dramatically. The late 1970s and early 1980s saw the Whiskery Shark population reduced to approximately 30% of pre-harvest levels. In the mid-1980s Western Australia introduced management to the gillnet fishery, restricting levels of fishing effort, and taking other management measures (Simpfendorfer and Donohue 1998). Since then Whiskery Shark abundance has remained relatively stable at 30–40% of pre-harvest over a period of 12 years (approximately two generations) (Simpfendorfer *et al.* 2000). The final phase of management measures was implemented in 2000/01 and early indications are that there have been significant and steady increases in the species' abundance in the centre of its range for the last 4–5 years, that the size of mature females has begun to increase, and that a 'pulse' of young adult whiskery sharks is currently recruiting into the fishery. To ensure the continued recovery of this stock, two-month closures of significant portions of the species range within the target fishery are being considered to further reduce adult mortality and boost recruitment. Continued management of the fishery has maintained Whiskery Shark abundance at this lower level and should lead to a gradual recovery of the stock in the short to medium term.

Based on information provided by Colin Simpfendorfer and Rory McAuley, IUCN/SSC Shark Specialist Group

Key Findings

• **Globally threatened species frequently require a combination of conservation responses to ensure their continued survival, encompassing research, species-specific actions, site and habitat based actions, policy responses, and communication and education.**

• **While many species already receive some conservation attention, many others do not, and the majority require substantially greater action to improve their status.**

• **Species can be, and many already have been, saved from extinction. However, this requires a combination of sound research, careful co-ordination of efforts, and, in some cases, intensive management.**

• **Improving the effectiveness of conservation action requires a better understanding of the needs for such action across species, the extent to which it is being applied, and the effects it has had in preventing species extinctions.**

• **The *IUCN Red List* information can be used in many different ways as a conservation tool. The Red List can be used to: provide information on the conservation status of individual species; guide the listing of individual species in national or international legislation; aid in conservation planning and priority setting; help to identify priority species for conservation action and recovery planning; and support educational programmes.**

Conclusions

Photo: © Paul Loiselle.

Photo 9.1
Paretroplus menarambo (Extinct in the Wild) a freshwater fish endemic to Madagascar epitomizes captive breeding efforts to save threatened Malagasy fish. This species is now solidly established in captivity thanks to animals collected in 1993 and shipped back to Old World Exotic Fish in Homestead, Florida, USA.

9.1 The *IUCN Red List* and the 2010 Target

The global community has recognized that biodiversity loss must be stemmed. In 2002, the World Summit on Sustainable Development re-affirmed the commitment of Parties to the Convention on Biological Diversity (CBD) to reduce the rate of biodiversity loss by 2010. Achieving this goal (itself only the first step towards halting, and eventually reversing, biodiversity loss) will require concerted and well-focused action, not just by Governments but also by a very wide range of organizations and individuals.

The *IUCN Red List of Threatened Species*™ provides a key tool in helping to achieve this goal. The 2004 *IUCN Red List* provides objective information on the threat status of an unprecedented number of species. This assessment presents analyses at a range of geographical scales and from ecological and geopolitical perspectives, examines the nature and impact of threats, and outlines current and potential conservation measures. It should help to inform several crucial questions:

- How much progress are we making in achieving the 2010 target?

- What are the most urgent conservation needs – which taxa are in trouble, where and why?

- What are the most pressing research needs – where are the most significant gaps in our knowledge?

- What responses are in place, and which ones might still be needed?

The *IUCN Red List* is intended to be policy-relevant and useful for conservation planning and priority setting. However, it is not intended to be prescriptive. Biodiversity conservation is far too complex for the *IUCN Red List* to be taken as the last word on what and where to conserve. Rather, the *IUCN Red List* provides information that can assist real-world decision-making when set in the wider context of society, economics and ecology.

With this in mind, what is the 2004 *Global Species Assessment* telling us?

9.2. How is the State of Biodiversity Changing?

To measure whether or not we are succeeding in reducing the rate of biodiversity loss a series of indicators are needed that are representative across the full spectrum of biodiversity, easy to interpret by decision makers, and realistic to produce over time. Within this context, IUCN has developed a Red List Index that charts the net changes to the threat status of particular groups over time.

For the first time, this report presents Red List Indices for two completely assessed groups, birds and amphibians. For birds, the Red List Index shows that their overall threat status (projected extinction risk) has deteriorated steadily between 1988 and 2004. A preliminary Red List Index for amphibians shows a similar rate of decline, from 1980 to 2004, although with a steeper rate of deterioration in the status of the species at highest extinction risk. Underlying data draw attention especially to threats from forest loss and longline fisheries (birds) and disease, climate change and exploitation (amphibians).

For most other groups, it is not yet possible to assess trends in status as data are lacking. An exception is the Cycads (Cycadopsida, 288 species in total). Within this group, population trends show that 79.6% (207 species) are declining, 20.4% (53 species) are stable and none are considered to be increasing. There is a growing body of evidence pointing to a serious deterioration in the conservation status of both freshwater and marine species, but species from these systems are still poorly assessed in the *IUCN Red List*.

In February 2004, the Parties to the Convention on Biological Diversity agreed to test and develop a specific set of indicators for assessing progress towards the 2010 biodiversity target. 'Change in status of threatened species' is one of these indicators. The Red List Index presented here measures this change and is being considered now for adoption by the Convention. An increasing projected risk of extinction implies an increase in the rate of biodiversity loss. The data from birds, amphibians and cycads suggest that we are not yet on track to meet the 2010 target of reducing the rate of loss.

9.3 Which Species are in Trouble?

For only four major taxonomic groups have we assessed the status of at least 90% of the species. The *IUCN Red List* shows that that 12% of birds, 23% of mammals, 32% of amphibians and 34% of gymnosperms are globally threatened. Threatened species in these groups total 4,475 (29%) of the 15,589 threatened species on the *IUCN Red List*. Percentages of threat for most other taxonomic groups cannot be stated because too few species in each have been evaluated against the Red List Criteria. (The initial focus of assessment effort is often on species suspected to be threatened, thus creating a bias.)

Among **mammals**, the percentage of threatened species has decreased since the 2000 *IUCN Red List* analysis. However, this is due to changes in taxonomy and knowledge, not improvements in conservation status. There are significantly more threatened species than expected among the orders Artiodactyla (deer, antelopes, cattle, sheep, goats, etc.), Carnivora (cats, dogs, weasels, bears, etc.), Primates, Perissodactyla (equids, rhinos and tapirs), and Sirenia (dugongs and manatees). The last two of these taxa have few species, so extinctions could cause a disproportionate loss of evolutionary novelty.

The fourth assessment of the status of all the world's **birds** reveals substantial deterioration of status among Indomalayan forest species and seabirds. Particularly high proportions of threatened species are found among albatrosses, petrels, shearwaters, penguins, cranes, rails, parrots, pheasants, and pigeons.

This report outlines the very serious situation facing **amphibians** globally, which may be indicative of the state of freshwater species as a whole. The situation may be even graver than the numbers suggest, since too little is known about 23% of amphibian species to make a threat assessment. Several families of amphibians appear to be disproportionately threatened, in particular the Hynobiidae (Asian salamanders), Plethodontidae (lungless salamanders), Astylosternidae (Cameroonian stream frogs), Bufonidae (true toads), Rhacophoridae (Asian tree frogs), Leptodactylidae (typical Neotropical frogs), Leiopelmatidae (New Zealand frogs), Nasikabatrachidae (Indian burrowing frog), Rhinodermatidae (Darwin's frogs), and Sooglossidae (Seychelles frogs). Both members of the Rheobatrachidae (gastric-brooding frogs) are now Extinct, representing the loss of an entire vertebrate family.

Although **reptiles** have not been a major focus of Red List assessment activity to date, the rapidly deteriorating status of tortoises and freshwater turtles in Southeast Asia has resulted in many important changes in the listings of these species.

Fishes also have not yet been a major focus of Red List assessments. However, regional assessments show high threat levels among freshwater fish; 27% of 1,085 species assessed in East Africa and 20% of 801 species assessed in North America are threatened. There are few assessments for marine fish but preliminary analysis of the chondrichthyan fishes (sharks, rays and chimaeras) shows that 18% of the 373 species so far assessed (about a third of the total) are threatened.

No **invertebrate** groups have yet been comprehensively assessed, and only a tiny proportion (below 0.3%) of the total species have been evaluated. Regional analyses show levels of threat varying widely, from 7% of 294 East African dragonflies to 54% of 1,975 North American snails.

Although 8,321 threatened species of **plants** appear on the 2004 *IUCN Red List*, the number evaluated against the Red List Criteria represents only about 4% of the total number of species. Full evaluations have been done for conifers, with 25% of 618 species threatened, and cycads, with a very high 52% of 288 species threatened. The overall proportion of threatened species for plants as a whole remains unknown, but regional assessments and sampling analyses suggest a figure of approximately 20%.

We have already lost many species. On the 2004 *IUCN Red List*, 844 species are listed as Extinct or Extinct in the Wild. A further 122 amphibians and 18 birds are considered Critically Endangered (Possibly Extinct). Historically, most recorded extinctions have occurred on islands, especially within Oceania, but mainland species represent 48% of the 27 extinctions documented within the last 20 years. For most groups, the number of extinctions is likely to be seriously under-recorded.

9.4 Where is the Threat of Extinction Greatest?

9.4.1 Geopolitical Units

Countries with the most threatened and threatened endemic species lie mainly in the continental tropics, while those with the highest proportion of threatened endemics are mainly tropical island nations. Nearly all countries have at least some national responsibility for threatened species, but some particularly stand out. Australia, Brazil, China, Indonesia, and Mexico have particularly large numbers of threatened species. Colombia, India, Malaysia, Myanmar, New Caledonia, Papua New Guinea, the Philippines, South Africa, and the United States have high numbers of threatened endemics for at least one taxonomic group. Madagascar, São Tomé and Principe, and the Seychelles have particularly high proportions of threatened species across multiple taxa.

The distribution of threatened species shows a complex relationship with human population density, population growth, and economic wealth. Areas with high human population densities and few threatened species are mainly in the higher latitudes. There are few areas that have low human population densities and high numbers of threatened species. Countries with relatively low population densities, but high rates of population growth and many threatened species (mainly in Africa) represent opportunities to plan for conservation as part of sustainable development. Many of the countries with the most threatened species have relatively low Gross National Incomes per capita, highlighting the need to view biodiversity conservation as a global responsibility.

9.4.2 Ecological Systems

The seven taxa for which we have relatively complete datasets include many more terrestrial than freshwater or (especially) marine species, and so probably do not provide a clear picture of the relative degree of threat across ecological systems. Among mammals, freshwater species are more threatened than marine or terrestrial ones. Among amphibians, species associated with flowing water are significantly more threatened than those living in still water. Among birds, turtles and chondrichthyan fishes (sharks, rays and chimaeras) the marine species are the most threatened.

9.4.3 Areas of Species Richness

The greatest numbers of threatened species, for mammals, birds and amphibians, occur in the tropical continents: the Neotropical, Afrotropical, and Indomalayan realms. This is related in part to the enormous importance of tropical and subtropical moist broadleaf forest — for all three taxa this is by far the richest biome for numbers of threatened species and threatened endemic species.

Oceania, while having low richness of threatened species, has remarkably high proportionate threat, evidence of the vulnerability of oceanic island biodiversity. Threatened marine mammals concentrate in the northern Pacific Ocean and threatened seabirds, chondrichthyan fishes and seahorses (the latter two not comprehensively assessed) in the eastern Indian Ocean and southwest and west-central Pacific.

Although forests are the most important habitat type for both threatened birds and amphibians, grassland and shrubland habitats also hold high numbers of threatened species. For amphibians, inland wetland habitats are exceptionally important. The importance of artificial habitats for both birds and amphibians is also evident.

Mammals, birds, turtles and amphibians all show concentrations of threatened species in centres of endemism in southern Brazil, Madagascar, the Western Ghats of India, the eastern Himalayas, central China, mainland Southeast Asia, Sumatra, Borneo, and the Philippines. Threatened mammals, birds and amphibians are also concentrated in the Andes, West Africa, Cameroon, the Albertine Rift of Central Africa, the Eastern Arc Mountains of Tanzania, and Sri Lanka. For birds, the map shows the importance of oceanic islands, while turtles concentrate in the Amazon, the eastern and southwestern United States, and Asia Minor. While threatened mammals are relatively widespread, threatened amphibians are geographically highly restricted, clustering strongly in particular areas, and are particularly concentrated in the area from southern Mexico southwards to northern Peru, and on the Caribbean islands.

9.5 What are the Main Pressures?

Habitat destruction and degradation is by far the most important immediate threat to birds, mammals and amphibians, impacting between 85 and 90% of threatened species in all three groups. Other significant threats to birds include over-exploitation (30% of threatened species) and invasive alien species (30%, overall, but affecting 67% of threatened bird species on oceanic islands). Mammals are more susceptible to over-exploitation than either birds or amphibians, with at least 33% of species affected. Amphibians are impacted by a broad array of significant threats, notably pollution (including climate change, 29% of threatened species), disease (17%), invasive alien species (11%), human disturbance (mainly fire, 11%), natural disasters (8%), and over-exploitation (6%).

Incidental mortality through longline fishing is now a major cause of increased mortality for albatrosses and other seabirds. As a result, all 21 species of albatrosses are now listed as globally threatened or Near Threatened. This is a side effect of the increased pressure of fisheries in general, a very significant cause of threat for many marine species (although many are yet to be evaluated). Though comprehensive data are lacking, over-exploitation for wild meat appears to be an increasing source of threat for many vertebrate species, especially mammals.

Very often, threats act together in a synergistic way and therefore need to be dealt with collectively. For example, climate change is likely to have many direct effects on species, some of which are already detectable. However, it is also hastening the spread of invasive alien species, including new diseases, and in many places is likely to exacerbate human pressures on natural habitats.

It is also difficult to address these immediate threats without tackling their underlying causes — which include some of the world's most intractable social and economic problems.

9.6 What are the Most Pressing Research Needs?

The 2004 *Global Species Assessment* demonstrates how little we still know about the world's biodiversity. Regarding Red List assessments, there are major gaps in the marine and freshwater systems, among plants, and even among terrestrial vertebrates such as reptiles.

Efforts to fill these gaps are already under way. A Global Reptile Assessment is beginning this year. The IUCN Freshwater Biodiversity Assessment is continuing its work and will be coordinating evaluations in new regions. A number of initiatives are underway for fish and invertebrates, often involving IUCN/SSC Specialist Groups. Further concentrated efforts are needed. The world's botanists face a particular challenge in achieving Target 2 of the Global Strategy for Plant Conservation, "A preliminary assessment of the conservation status of all known plant species" by 2010.

Even within groups that have been comprehensively assessed, many species remain Data Deficient — including 1,294 amphibians, 380 mammals, and even 78 birds. These species are important targets for further research. Among species known to be threatened, nearly all amphibians and birds (95% and 92%) still require baseline information on their population numbers and range.

However, the fact that we have many gaps in our knowledge should not be an excuse for inaction. The 2004 *IUCN Red List* already provides much clear information to help guide conservation planning and priority setting. And the 15,589 threatened species on the list require urgent conservation attention if they are not to slip further towards extinction.

9.7 What Responses are in Place?

Conservation measures are being taken for many species all over the world, ranging from species-specific actions to broad changes in national, regional or global policy. We are only just beginning to measure these responses in relation to individual threatened species. Information on birds suggests that, encouragingly, at least some action is underway for 67% of threatened species, but that, less encouragingly, these actions have only benefited 24% of species so far.

Many case studies show that well-focused species-centred actions can succeed in reducing threat and improving status. There are also many examples of constructive policy responses, some of which begin to address the underlying causes of threat. The *IUCN Red List* can be used to provide guidance to many of these, including international agreements such as the Convention on International Trade in Endangered Species of Wild Fauna and Flora (CITES) and the Convention on the Conservation of Migratory Species of Wild Animals (CMS).

The *IUCN Red List* can also be used to identify gaps in responses at the site scale, for example through the key biodiversity areas process and the Alliance for Zero Extinction. These analyses can in turn be used to target effort and investment on the ground.

Conservation action works. The 2004 *Global Species Assessment* shows that we need much more of it, and need to focus it better using the constantly improving information at our disposal. That means more resources, and resources better applied.

Photo: © Zhigang Jiang.

Photo 9.2
Przewalski's Gazelle *Procapra przewalskii* (Critically Endangered) is endemic to China. Threats include habitat loss, competition with livestock for food, and blocked migration routes. Fewer than 250 of these timid antelopes remain and the species' future is uncertain as continuing habitat degradation, wolf predation and inbreeding are causing further declines.

References

Photo: © Cristian Echeverria.

Photo 10.1
The Alerce *Fitzroya cupressoides* (Endangered), confined to southern Chile and adjacent Argentina, is one of the largest trees in temperate South America and as a result has been heavily logged since the end of the 16th century. The species has been eliminated from nearly all the lowland sites, and at higher altitudes the trees are often burnt and illegally logged. Present estimates of the area occupied by the remaining stands is 20,000 ha, 15% of their original extent when Europeans arrived.

Aikman, H., Davis, A., Miskelly, C.M. and O'Connor, S. 2001. *Chatham Islands Threatened Birds*. Department of Conservation, Wellington, New Zealand.

Alford, R.A., Dixon, P.M. and Pechmann, J.H.K. 2001. Global amphibian population declines. *Nature* 412(6846): 499–500.

Alroy, J. 2001. A multi-species overkill simulation of the end-Pleistocene megafaunal mass extinction. *Science* 292: 1893–1986.

Amiet, J.-L. 1989. Quelques aspects de la biologie des Amphibiens Anoures du Cameroun. *Année Biologique* 28(2): 73–136.

AmphibiaWeb. 2004. Information on amphibian biology and conservation. [web application]. Berkeley, CA: AmphibiaWeb. Available at: http://www.amphibiaweb.org/. (Accessed: 31 August 2004).

Anderson, S. 1994. Area and endemism. *Quarterly Review of Biology* 69: 451–471.

Atkinson, I.A.E. 1985. The spread of commensal species of *Rattus* to oceanic islands and their effect on island avifaunas. In: P.J. Moors (ed.), *Conservation of Island Birds*, pp. 35–81. ICBP Technical Publication number 3. International Council for Bird Preservation, Cambridge, UK.

Baillie, J. and Groombridge, B. (compilers and editors) 1996. *1996 IUCN Red List of Threatened Animals*. IUCN, Gland, Switzerland and Cambridge, UK.

Bakarr, M.I., Fonseca, G.A.B., Mittermeier, R.A., Rylands, A.B. and Walker Painemilla, K. (eds) 2001. *Bushmeat Utilization in the African Rain Forests – Perspectives Toward a Blueprint for Conservation Action*. Advances in Applied Biodiversity Science no. 2. Center for Applied Biodiversity Science, Conservation International, Washington, DC, USA.

Balmford, A. 1996. Extinction filters and current resilience: the significance of past selection pressures for conservation biology. *Trends in Ecology and Evolution* 11: 193–196.

Balmford, A., Green, R.E. and Jenkins, M. 2003. Measuring the changing state of nature. *Trends in Ecology and Evolution* 18: 326–330.

Balmford, A., Green, M.J.B. and Murray, M.G. 1996. Using higer-taxon richness as a surrogate for species richness: I. Regional tests. *Proceedings of the Royal Society of London Series B – Biological Sciences* 263: 1267–1274.

Balmford, A. and Long, A. 1995. Across-country analyses of biodiversity congruence and current conservation effort in the tropics. *Conservation Biology* 9: 1539–1547.

Baum, J.K., Myers, R.A., Kehler, D.G., Worm, B., Harley, S.J. and Doherty, P.A. 2003. Collapse and conservation of shark populations in the Northwest Atlantic. *Science* 299: 389–392.

Beamesderfer, R.C.P. and Farr, R.A. 1997. Alternatives for the protection and restoration of sturgeons and their habitat. *Environmental Biology of Fishes* 48: 407–417.

Bell, B.D., Carver, S., Mitchell, N.J. and Pledger, S. 2004. The recent decline of a New Zealand endemic: how and why did populations of Archey's frog *Leiopelma archeyi* crash over 1996–2001. *Biological Conservation* 120: 193–203.

Bennett, P.M. and Owens, I.P.F. 1997. Variation in extinction risk among birds: Chance or evolutionary predisposition? *Proceedings of the Royal Society of London Series B – Biological Sciences* 264(1380): 401–408.

Berger, L., Speare, R., Daszak, P., Green, D.E., Cunningham, A.A., Slocombe, R., Goggin, C.L., Hyatt, D., MacDonald, K.R., Hines, H.B., Lips, K.R., Marantelli, G. and Parkes, H.H. 1998. Chytridiomycosis causes amphibian mortality associated with population declines in the rainforests of Australia and Central America. *Proceedings of the National Academy of Sciences of the United States of America* 95: 9031–9036.

Best, P.B., Bannister, J.L., Brownell, R.L. and Donovan, G.P. 2001. Right whales: worldwide status. *Journal of Cetacean Research and Management* Special Issue 2: i–ix + 309.

Biju, S.D. and Bossuyt, F. 2003. New frog family from India reveals an ancient biogeographical link with the Seychelles. *Nature* 425: 711-714.

BirdLife International. 2000. *Threatened Birds of the World*. Lynx Edicions and BirdLife International, Barcelona, Spain and Cambridge, UK.

BirdLife International. 2004a. *Threatened Birds of the World 2004*. CD-ROM. BirdLife International, Cambridge, UK.

BirdLife International. 2004b. *State of the World's Birds 2004 – Indicators for our changing world*. BirdLife International, Cambridge, UK.

Bisby, F.A., Shimura, J., Ruggiero, M., Edwards, J. and Haeuser, C. 2002. Taxonomy, at the click of a mouse. *Nature* 418: 367.

Bomhard, B. 2004. Potential impacts of future land use and climate change on the Red Data Book status of the Proteaceae in the Cape Floristic Region. MSc Thesis, University of Cape Town.

Bosch, J., Martínez-Solano, I. and García-París, M. 2001. Evidence of a chytrid fungus infection involved in the decline of the common midwife toad (*Alytes obstetricans*) in protected areas of central Spain. *Biological Conservation* 97: 331–337.

Bradley G.A., Rosen, P.C., Sredl, M.J., Jones, T.R. and Longcore J.E. 2002. Chytridiomycosis in native Arizona frogs. *Journal of Wildlife Diseases* 38: 206–212.

Bramwell, D. 2002. How many plant species are there? *Plant Talk* 28: 32–34.

Bramwell, D. 2003. On the size of the world's threatened flora. *Plant Talk* 32: 4–5.

Brandon, K., Redford, K.H. and Sanderson, S.E. (eds) 1998. *Parks in Peril – People, Politics and Protected Areas*. Island Press for The Nature Conservancy, Washington, DC, USA.

Brooks, T., Balmford, A., Burgess, N., Fjeldså, J., Hansen, L.A., Moore, J., Rahbek, C. and Williams, P. 2001. Toward a blueprint for conservation in Africa. *BioScience* 51: 613–624.

Brooks, T.M., Pimm, S.L. and Oyugi, J.O. 1999. Time lag between deforestation and bird extinction in tropical forest fragments. *Conservation Biology* 13: 1140–1150.

Brown, B.E., Dunne, R.P., Warner, M.E, Ambarsari, I., Fitt, W.K., Gibb, S.W. and Cummings, D.G. 2000. Damage and recovery of Photosystem II during a manipulative field experiment on solar bleaching in the coral *Goniastrea aspera*. *Marine Ecology Progress Series* 195: 117–124.

Brummitt, R.K. (ed.) 2001. *World Geographical Scheme for Recording Plant Distributions*. Edition 2. Plant Taxonomic Database Standards No. 2. Edition 2, August 2001. Published for the International Working Group on Taxonomic Databases for Plant Sciences (TDWG). Hunt Institute for Botanical Documentation, Carnegie Mellon University, Pittsburgh, USA.

Bruner, A.G., Gullison, R.E., Rice, R.E. and Fonseca. G.A.B. 2001. Effectiveness of Parks in Protecting Tropical Biodiversity. *Science* 291(5501): 125–128.

Burley, K.R. and Garcia, G. 1997. The recovery programme for the Mallorcan Midwife Toad *Alytes muletensis*: an update. *Dodo, Journal of the Wildlife Preservation Trusts* 33: 80–90.

Burrowes, P.A., Joglar, R.L. and Green, D.E. 2004. Potential causes for amphibian declines in Puerto Rico. *Herpetologica* 60: 141–154.

Burton, J.A. 2003. The context of Red Data Books, with a complete bibliography of the IUCN publications. In: H.H. de Iongh, O.S. Bánki, W. Bergmans and M.J. van der Werff ten Bosch (eds), *The Harmonization of Red Lists for Threatened Species in Europe*, pp. 291–300. Proceedings of an International Seminar 27 and 28 November 2002. The Netherlands Commission for International Protection, Mededelingen No. 38, Leiden.

Butchart, S.H.M., Stattersfield, A.J., Bennun, L.A., Shutes, S.M., Akçakaya, H.R., Baillie, J.E.M., Stuart, S.N., Hilton-Taylor, C. and Mace, G.M. In press a. Measuring global trends in the status of biodiversity: Red List Indices for birds. *Public Library of Science, Biology*.

Butchart, S.H.M., Stattersfield, A.J., Bennun, L.A., Shutes, S.M., Akçakaya, H.R., Baillie, J.E.M., Stuart, S.N., Hilton-Taylor, C. and Mace, G.M. In press b. Using IUCN Red List Indices to measure progress towards the 2010 target and beyond. *Philosophical Transactions of the Royal Society*.

Butler, D. and Merton, D. 1992. *The Black Robin: Saving the World's Most Endangered Bird*. Oxford University Press, Auckland, New Zealand.

Camhi, M., Fowler, S., Musick, J.A., Bräutigam, A. and Fordham, S.V. 1998. *Sharks and their relatives: ecology and conservation*. Occasional Paper of the IUCN Species Survival Commission No. 20. IUCN/SSC Shark Specialist Group. IUCN, Gland, Switzerland and Cambridge, UK.

Carabias, J. and Rao, K. (eds) 2003. *Capacity Needs to Manage Protected Areas – Asia*. The Nature Conservancy, Mexico City, Mexico.

Cardillo, M. and Lister, A. 2002. Evolutionary biology: death in the slow lane. *Nature* 419: 440–441.

Cardillo, M., Purvis, A., Sechrest, W., Gittleman, J.L., Bielby, J. and Mace, G.M. 2004. Human population density and extinction risk in the world's carnivores. *Public Library of Science, Biology* 2(7): 909–914.

Carey, C., Cohen, N. and Rollins-Smith, L.A. 1999. Amphibian declines: an immunological perspective. *Developmental and Comparative Immunology* 23: 459–472.

Carlton, J.T., Geller, J.B., Reaka-Kudla, M.L. and Norse, E.A. 1999. Historical extinctions in the sea. *Annual Review of Ecology and Systematics* 30: 525–538.

Caro, T.M., Rejmánek, M. and Peleky, N. 2000. Which mammals benefit from protection in East Africa. In: A. Entwistle and N. Dunstone (eds), *Priorities for the Conservation of Mammalian Diversity – Has the Panda had its day?*, pp. 221–238. Cambridge University Press, Cambridge, UK.

Casey, J.M. and Myers, R.A. 1998. Near extinction of a large, widely distributed fish. *Science* 281: 690–692.

Cavanagh, R.D., Kyne, P.M., Fowler, S.L., Musick, J.A. and Bennett, M.B. (eds) 2003. Conservation Status of Australian Chondrichthyans: Report of the IUCN Shark Specialist Group Australia and Oceania Regional Red List Workshop. University of Queensland, School of Biomedical Sciences, Brisbane, Australia.

CBD Secretariat. 2002. *Global Strategy for Plant Conservation.* Publication of Decision VI/9, Sixth meeting of the Conference of the Parties to the Convention on Biological Diversity 2002.

Chape, S., Blyth, S., Fish, L., Fox, P., and Spalding, M. (compilers) 2003. *2003 United Nations List of Protected Areas.* IUCN, Gland, Switzerland and Cambridge, UK, and UNEP World Conservation Monitoring Centre, Cambridge, UK.

Chaplin, S.J., Gerrard, R.A., Watson, H.M., Master, L.L. and Flack, S.R. 2000. The geography of imperilment: Targeting conservation towards critical biodiversity areas. In: B.A. Stein, L.S. Kutner and J.S. Adams (eds), *Precious Heritage: The Status of Biodiversity in the United States,* pp. 159–199. Oxford University Press, New York, USA.

Coleman, F., Koenig, C.C., Eklund, A.-M. and Grimes, C.B. 1999. Management and conservation of temperate reef fishes in the grouper-snapper complex of the southeastern United States. In: J.A. Musick (ed.), *Life in the Slow Lane: Ecology and Conservation of Long-lived Marine Animals,* pp. 233–242. American Fisheries Society Symposium 23. Bethesda, MD, USA.

Collar, N.J. 1993–94. Red Data Books, action plans, and the need for site-specific synthesis. *Species* 21–22: 132–133.

Collar, N.J. 1996. The reasons for Red Data Books. *Oryx* 30: 121–130.

Collar, N.J., Andreev, A.V., Chan, S., Crosby, M.J., Subramanya, S. and Tobias, J.A. (eds) 2001. *Threatened Birds of Asia: the BirdLife International Red Data Book.* BirdLife International, Cambridge, UK.

Collar, N.J. and Andrew, P. 1988. *Birds to Watch: the ICBP World Checklist of Threatened Birds.* ICBP and IUCN, Cambridge, UK.

Collar, N.J., Crosby, M.J. and Stattersfield, A.J. 1994. *Birds to Watch 2: the World List of Threatened Birds.* BirdLife International, Cambridge, UK.

Collar, N.J. and Stuart, S.N. 1988. *Key Forests for Threatened Birds in Africa.* International Council for Bird Preservation, Cambridge, UK.

Collen, B., Purvis, A. and Gittleman, J.L. 2004. Biological correlates of description date in carnivores and primates. *Global Ecology and Biogeography* 13: 459–467.

Collins, J.P. and Storfer, A. 2003. Global amphibian declines: sorting the hypotheses. *Diversity and Distributions* 9: 89–98.

Conservation Breeding Specialist Group (SSC/IUCN). 2002. *Evaluation et Plans de Gestion pour la Conservation (CAMP) de la Faune de Madagascar: Lémuriens, Autres Mammifères, Reptiles et Amphibiens, Poissons d'eau douce et Evaluation de la Viabilité des Populations et des Habitats de* Hypogeomys antimena *(Vositse).* CBSG, Apple Valley, Minnesota, USA.

Colwell, R.K. and Hurtt, G.C. 1994. Nonbiological gradients in species richness and a spurious Rapoport effect. *American Naturalist* 144: 570–595.

Coote, T., Clarke, D., Hickman, C., Murray, J. and Pearce-Kelly, P. 2004. Experimental release of endemic *Partula* species, extinct in the wild, into a protected area of Natural Habitat on Moorea. *Pacific Science* 58(3): 429–434.

Corsi, F., de Leeuw, J. and Skidmore, A.K. 2000. Modeling species distribution with GIS. In: L.F. Boitani and T. Fuller (eds), *Research Techniques in Animal Ecology: Controversies and Consequences,* pp. 389–434. Columbia University Press, New York, USA.

Cowlishaw, G. 1999. Predicting the pattern of decline of African primate diversity: an extinction debt from historical deforestation. *Conservation Biology* 13: 1183–1193.

Daszak, P., Cunningham, A.A. and Hyatt, A.D. 2001. Anthropogenic environmental change and the emergence of infectious diseases in wildlife. *Acta Tropica* 78: 103–116.

Davis, G.E., Haaker, P.L. and Richards, D.V. 1998. The perilous condition of white abalone *Haliotis sorenseni,* Bartsch, 1940. *Journal of Shellfish Research* 17: 371–875.

Dayton, P.K., Thrush, S.F., Agardy, M.T. and Hofman, R.J. 1995. Environmental effects of marine fishing. *Aquatic Conservation – Marine and Freshwater Ecosystems* 5: 205–232.

De Iongh, H.H., Bánki, O.S., Bergmans, W. and van der Werff ten Bosch, M.J. (eds). 2003. *The Harmonization of Red Lists for Threatened Species in Europe.* Proceedings of an International Seminar 27 and 28 November 2002. The Netherlands Commission for International Protection, Mededelingen No. 38, Leiden.

Denney, N.H., Jennings, S. and Reynolds, J.D. 2002. Life history correlates of maximum populations growth rates in marine fishes. *Proceedings of the Royal Society of London Series B – Biological Sciences* 269(506): 2229–2237.

Diamond, J.M. 1972. Biogeographic kinetics: estimation of relaxation times for avifaunas of Southwest Pacific Islands. *Proceedings of the National Academy of Sciences of the United States of America* 69: 3199–3203.

Diamond, J.M. 1991. A new species of rail from the Solomon Islands and convergent evolution of insular flightlessness. *Auk* 108: 461–470.

Donaldson, J. (ed.) 2003. *Cycads. Status Survey and Conservation Action Plan.* IUCN/SSC Cycad Specialist Group. IUCN, Gland, Switzerland and Cambridge, UK.

Dulvy, N.K. and Reynolds, J.D. 2002. Predicting extinction vulnerability in skates. *Conservation Biology* 16: 440–450.

Dulvy, N.K., Sadovy, Y. and Reynolds, J.D. 2003. Extinction vulnerability in marine populations. *Fish and Fisheries* 4: 25–64.

Eken, G., Bennun, L.A., Brooks, T.M., Darwall, W., Fishpool, L.D.C., Foster, M., Knox, D., Langhammer, P., Matiku, P., Radford, L., Salaman, P., Sechrest, W., Smith, M.L., Spector, S. and Tordoff, A. In press. Key Biodiversity Areas as site conservation targets. *BioScience*.

Erwin, T.L. 1982. Tropical forests: their richness in Coleoptera and other Arthropod species. *The Coleopterist's Bulletin* 36: 74–75.

FAO. 1997a. *Review of the State of World Fishery Resources: Marine Fisheries.* Food and Agriculture Organization, Rome.

FAO. 1997b. *The State of the World's Forests 1997.* Food and Agriculture Organization, Rome.

FAO. 2000. *Global Forest Resource Assessment 2000.* Food and Agriculture Organization, Rome.

Farjon, A. 2001. *World Checklist and Bibliography of Conifers.* 2nd edition. World Checklists and Bibliographies, 3. Royal Botanic Gardens, Kew.

Ferraz, G., Russell, G.J., Stouffer, P.C., Bierregaard, R.O., Pimm, S.L. and Lovejoy, T.E. 2003. Rates of species loss from Amazonian forest fragments. *Proceedings of the National Academy of Sciences of the United States of America* 100: 14069–14073.

Fisher, D.O. and Owens, I.P.F. 2004. The comparative method in conservation biology. *Trends in Ecology and Evolution* 19: 391–398.

Fishpool, L.D.C. and Evans, M.I. (eds) 2001. *Important Bird Areas in Africa and Associated Islands: Priority Sites for Conservation.* BirdLife Conservation Series No. 11. Newbury and Cambridge, Pisces Publications and BirdLife International.

Fowler, S.L., Cavanagh, R.D., Camhi, M., Burgess, G.H., Cailliet, G.M., Fordham, S.V., Simpfendorfer, C.A. and Musick, J.A. (eds) In press. *Sharks, Rays and Chimaeras: the Status of the Chondrichthyan Fishes.* IUCN SSC Shark Specialist Group. IUCN, Gland, Switzerland and Cambridge, UK.

Froese, R. and Pauly, D. (eds) 2004. FishBase. [web application]. Available at: http://www.fishbase.org/. (Accessed: 31 August 2004).

Frost, D.R. 2004. Amphibian Species of the World: an Online Reference. Version 3.0 (22 August, 2004). Electronic Database accessible at http://research.amnh.org/herpetology/amphibia/index.html. American Museum of Natural History, New York, USA.

Gärdenfors, U. 1996. Application of IUCN Red List Categories on a regional scale. In: J. Baillie and B. Groombridge (compilers and editors), *1996 IUCN Red List of Threatened Animals*, pp. Intro 63–66. IUCN, Gland, Switzerland and Cambridge, UK.

Gaston, K.J. 1994. Measuring geographic range sizes. *Ecography* 17: 198–205.

Gaston, K.J. 1996. Species-range-size distributions: patterns, mechanisms and implications. *Trends in Ecology and Evolution* 11: 197–201.

Gaston, K.J. 1998. Species-range size distributions: products of speciation, extinction and transformation. *Philosophical Transactions of the Royal Society of London Series B – Biological Sciences* 353: 219–230.

Gaston, K.J. 1999. Why Rapoport's Rule does not generalise. *Oikos* 84: 309–312.

Gaston, K.J. and. Blackburn, T.M. 1995. Birds, body size and the threat of extinction. *Philosophical Transactions of the Royal Society of London Series B – Biological Sciences* 347(1320): 205–212.

Gaston, K.J. and Blackburn, T.M. 1997. Evolutionary age and risk of extinction in the global avifauna. *Evolutionary Ecology* 11: 557–565.

Goodman, S.M. and Patterson, B.D. (eds) 1997. *Natural Change and Human Impact in Madagascar.* Smithsonian Institution, Washington, DC, USA.

Govaerts, R. 2001. How many species of seed plants are there? *Taxon* 50: 1085–1090.

Govaerts, R. 2003. How many species of seed plants are there? – a response. *Taxon* 52: 583–584.

Graham, K.J., Andrew, N.L. and Hodgson, K.E. 2001. Changes in relative abundances of sharks and rays on Australian south east fishery trawl grounds after twenty years of fishing. *Marine and Freshwater Research* 52: 549–561.

Grimes, C.B. and Turner, S.C. 1999. The complex life history of tilefish *Lopholatilus chamaeleonticeps* and vulnerability to exploitation. In: J.A. Musick (ed.), *Life in the Slow Lane: Ecology and Conservation of Long-lived Marine Animals*, pp. 17–26. American Fisheries Society Symposium 23. Bethesda, MD, USA.

Groombridge, B. (ed.) 1993. *1994 IUCN Red List of Threatened Animals*. IUCN, Gland, Switzerland and Cambridge, UK.

Groombridge, B. and Jenkins, M.D. 2002. *World Atlas of Biodiversity*. Prepared by the UNEP World Conservation Monitoring Centre. University of California Press, Berkeley, USA.

Haig, S.M., Ballou, J.D. and Derrickson, S.R. 1990. Management options for preserving genetic diversity: reintroduction of the Guam Rail to the wild. *Conservation Biology* 4: 290–300.

Hall, B.L. and Moreau, R.E. 1962. A study of the rare birds of Africa. *Bulletin of the British Museum (Natural History) Zoology* 8: 313–378.

Hallingbäck, T. and Hodgetts, N. (compilers) 2000. *Mosses, Liverworts and Hornworts. Status Survey and Conservation Action Plan for Bryophytes*. IUCN/SSC Bryophyte Specialist Group. IUCN, Gland, Switzerland and Cambridge, UK.

Hammond, P.M. 1992. Species inventory. In: B. Groombridge (ed.), *Global Biodiversity: status of the Earth's living resources*, pp. 17–39. Chapman and Hall, London, UK.

Hammond, P.M. 1995. The current magnitude of biodiversity. In: V.H. Heywood (ed.), *Global Biodiversity Assessment*, pp. 113–138. Cambridge University Press, Cambridge.

Hannah, L., Midgley, G.F., Lovejoy, T., Bond, W.J., Bush, M., Lovett, J.C., Scott, D. and Woodward, F.I. 2002a. Conservation of biodiversity in a changing climate. *Conservation Biology* 16: 264–268.

Hannah, L., Midgley, G.F. and Millar, D. 2002b. Climate change-integrated conservation strategies. *Global Ecology and Biogeography* 11: 485–495.

Hanski, I. and Ovaskainen, O. 2002. Extinction debt at extinction threshold. *Conservation Biology* 16: 666–673.

Harcourt, A.H. and Parks, S.A. 2003. Threatened primates experience high human densities: adding an index of threat to the IUCN Red List Criteria. *Biological Conservation* 109: 137–149.

Harcourt, A.H., Parks, S.A. and Woodroffe, R. 2001. Human density as an influence on species/area relationships: double jeopardy for small African reserves? *Biodiversity and Conservation* 10: 1011–1026.

Harrisson, I.J. and Stiassny, M.L.J. 1999. The quiet crisis: a preliminary listing of the freshwater fishes of the world that are extinct or "missing in action". In: R.D.E. MacPhee (ed.), *Extinctions in Near Time: Causes, Contexts and Consequences*, pp. 271–331. Kluwer Academic/Plenum Publishers. New York, USA.

Hawkins, J.P., Roberts, C.M. and Clark, V. 2000. The threatened status of restricted-range coral reef fish species. *Animal Conservation* 3: 81–88.

Hilton-Taylor, C. 1996. Red Data List of southern African Plants. *Strelitzia* 4: iii, 1–117.

Hilton-Taylor, C. (compiler). 2000. *2000 IUCN Red List of Threatened Species*. IUCN, Gland, Switzerland and Cambridge, UK.

Hilton-Taylor, C., Mace, G.M., Capper, D.R., Collar, N.J., Stuart, S.N., Bibby, C.J., Pollock, C. and Thomsen, J.B. 2000. Assessment mismatches must be sorted out: they leave species at risk. *Nature* 404: 541.

Hodkinson, I.D. and Casson, D. 1991. A lesser predilection for bugs: Hemiptera (Insecta) diversity in tropical rain forests. *Biological Journal of the Linnean Society* 43: 101–109.

Hoenig, J.M. and Gruber, S.H. 1990. Life-history patterns in the elasmobranches: implications for fisheries management. In: H.L. Pratt Jr., S.H. Gruber and T. Taniuchi (eds), *Elasmobranchs as Living Resources: Advances in the Biology, Ecology, Systematics, and the Status of Fisheries*, pp. 1–16. US Department of Commerce National Oceanic and Atmospheric Administration (NOAA). Technical Report NMFS 90.

Holmes, D.A. 2000. *Deforestation in Indonesia: a view of the situation in 1999*. World Bank, Jakarta.

Houlahan, J.E., Findlay, C.S., Schmidt, B.R., Meyer, A.H. and Kuzmin, S.L. 2000. Quantitative evidence for global amphibian population declines. *Nature* 404: 752–755.

Huntsman, G.R., Potts, J., Mays, R.W. and Vaughan, D. 1999. Groupers (Serranidae, Epinephelinae): endangered apex predators of reef communities. In: J.A. Musick (ed.), *Life in the Slow Lane: Ecology and Conservation of Long-lived Marine Animals*, pp. 217–231. American Fisheries Society Symposium 23. Bethesda, MD, USA.

Hutchings, J.A. 2000. Collapse and recovery of marine fishes. *Nature* 406: 882–885.

Hutchings, J.A. 2001. Conservation biology of marine fishes: perceptions and caveats regarding assignment of extinction risk. *Canadian Journal of Fisheries and Aquatic Sciences* 58: 108–121.

Hutchings, J.A. and Myers, R.A. 1994. What can be learned from the collapse of a renewable resource? Atlantic cod, *Gadus morhua*, of Newfoundland and Labrador. *Canadian Journal of Fisheries and Aquatic Sciences* 51: 2126–2146.

Hutchings, J.A. and Reynolds, J.D. 2004. Marine fish population collapses: consequences for recovery and extinction risk. *BioScience* 54: 297–309.

Inger, R.F. 1966. The amphibians of Borneo. *Fieldiana: Zoology* 52: 1–402.

Isaac, N.J.B., Mallet, J. and Mace, G.M. 2004. Taxonomic inflation: its influence on macroecology and conservation. *Trends in Ecology and Evolution* 19(9): 464–469.

IUCN. 1994a. *IUCN Red List Categories*. Prepared by the IUCN Species Survival Commission. IUCN, Gland, Switzerland.

IUCN. 1994b. *Guidelines for Protected Area Management Categories*. IUCN World Commission on Protected Areas and World Conservation Monitoring Centre, Gland, Switzerland and Cambridge, UK.

IUCN. 1995. *IUCN Guidelines for Re-introductions*. IUCN, Gland, Switzerland.

IUCN. 2000. IUCN *Guidelines for the Prevention of Biodiversity Loss Caused by Alien Invasive Species*. IUCN, Gland, Switzerland.

IUCN. 2001. *IUCN Red List Categories and Criteria: Version 3.1*. IUCN Species Survival Commission. IUCN, Gland, Switzerland and Cambridge, UK.

IUCN 2004. *2004 IUCN Red List of Threatened Species*. [web application]. Available at: http://www.iucnredlist.org.

IUCN Species Survival Commission, Conservation International Center for Applied Biodiversity Science and NatureServe. 2004. IUCN Global Amphibian Assessment. [web application]. Available at: http://www.globalamphibians.org/.

Iverson, J.B, Kiester, A.R., Hughes, L.E. and Kimerling, A.J. 2003. The EMYSystem – World Turtle Database 2003. [web application]. Available at: http://emys.geo.orst.edu/. (Accessed: 31 August 2004).

Jablonski, D. 1986. Background and mass extinctions: the alternation of macroevolutionary regimes. *Science* 231: 129–133.

Jackson, J.B.C., Kirby, M.X., Berger, W.H., Bjorndal, K.A., Botsford, L.W., Bourque, B.J., Bradbury, R.H., Cooke, R., Erlandson, J., Estes, J.A., Hughes, T.P., Kidwell, S., Lange, C.B., Lenihan, H.S., Pandolfi, J.M., Peterson, C.H., Steneck, R.S., Tegner, M.J. and Warner, R.R. 2001. Historical overfishing and the recent collapse of coastal ecosystems. *Science* 293: 629–637.

Jenkins, M., Green, R.E. and Madden, J. 2003. The challenge of measuring global change in wild nature: are things getting better or worse? *Conservation Biology* 17: 20–23.

Johnson, C.N. 2002. Determinants of loss of mammal species during the Late Quaternary 'megafauna' extinctions: life history and ecology, but not body size. *Proceedings of the Royal Society of London Series B – Biological Sciences* 269: 2221–2227.

Kiesecker, J.M., Blaustein, A.R. and Belden, L.K. 2001. Complex causes of amphibian population declines. *Nature* 410(6829): 681–684.

Laurance, W.F., McDonald, K.R. and Speare, R. 1996. Epidemic disease and the catastrophic decline of Australian rain forest frogs. *Conservation Biology* 10: 406–413.

Leidy, R.A. and Moyle, P.B. 1998. Conservation status of the world's freshwater fish fauna: an overview. In: P.L. Fieldler and P.M. Kareiva (eds), *Conservation for the Coming Decade*. Second edition, pp. 187–227. Chapman and Hall, New York, USA.

Lennon, J.J., Koleff, P., Greenwood, J.J.D. and Gaston, K.J. 2004. Contribution of rarity and commonness to patterns of species richness. *Ecology Letters* 7: 81–87.

Lips, K.R., Reeve, J.D. and Witters, L.R. 2003. Ecological traits predicting amphibian population declines in Central America. *Conservation Biology* 17: 1078–1088.

Longcore, J.E., Pessier, A.P. and Nichols, D.K. 1999. *Batrachochytrium dendrobatidis* gen. and sp. nov., a chytrid pathogenic to amphibians. *Mycologia* 91: 219–227.

Lötters, S., La Marca, E. and Vences, M. 2003. Redescriptions of two toad species from the genus *Atelopus* from coastal Venezuela. *Copeia* 2004: 221–233.

Lu, S.Y. and Pan, F.J. 1997. *Rhododendron kanehirai*. In: IUCN. 2003. *2003 IUCN Red List of Threatened Species*. [web application]. Available at www.iucnredlist.org. (Accessed: 27 September 2004).

Mabberley, D.J. 1997. *The Plant-Book. A portable dictionary of the higher plants*. Second edition. Cambridge University Press, Cambridge, UK.

Mace, G.M. and Balmford, A. 2000. Patterns and proceses in contemporary mammalian extinction. In: A. Entwistle and N. Dunstone (eds), *Priorities for the Conservation of Mammalian Diversity. Has the Panda Had its Day?*, pp. 28–52. Cambridge University Press, Cambridge, UK.

MacPhee, R.D.E. and Flemming, C. 1999. *Requiem Æternam*: the last five hundred years of mammalian species extinctions. In: R.D.E. MacPhee (ed.), *Extinctions in Near Time: Causes, Contexts and Consequences*, pp. 333–371. Kluwer Academic/Plenum Publishers, New York, USA.

Magin, C. 2003. Dominica's frogs are croaking. *Oryx* 37: 406.

Mainka, S.A. and Trivedi, M. (eds) 2002. *Links between Biodiversity Conservation, Livelihoods and Food Security: The Sustainable use of Wild species for Meat.* Occasional Paper of the IUCN Species Survival Commission No. 24. IUCN, Gland, Switzerland and Cambridge, UK.

Mallon, D. and Kingswood, S. 1999. *Oryx dammah*. In: IUCN. 2003. *2003 IUCN Red List of Threatened Species.* [web application]. Available at www.iucnredlist.org. (Accessed: 27 September 2004).

Manne, L.L., Brooks, T.M. and Pimm, S.L. 1999. Relative risk of extinction of passerine birds on continents and islands. *Nature* 399: 258–261.

Manzanilla, J. and La Marca, E. 2004. Museum records and field samplings as source of data pointing to population crashes for *Atelopus cruciger*, a proposed critically endangered species from the Venezuelan coastal range. *Memoria de la Fundación La Salle de Ciencias Naturales* 62(157): 5–29.

Master, L.L., Flack, S.R. and Stein, B.A. 1998. *Rivers of Life: Critical Watersheds for Protecting Freshwater Biodiversity.* The Nature Conservancy, Arlington, Virginia, USA.

Master, L.L., Stein, B.A., Kutner, L.S. and Hammerson, G.A. 2000. Vanishing assets: Conservation status of U.S. species. In: B.A. Stein, L.S. Kutner and J.S. Adams (eds), *Precious Heritage: The Status of Biodiversity in the United States*, pp. 93–118. Oxford University Press, New York, USA.

May, R.M., Lawton, R.H. and Stork, N.E. 1995. Assessing extinction rates. In: J.H. Lawton and R.M. May (eds), *Extinction Rates,* pp. 1-24. Oxford University Press, Oxford, UK.

McAllister, D.E., Hamilton, A.L. and Harvey, B. 1997. Global freshwater biodiversity: striving for the integrity of freshwater ecosystems. *Sea Wind* 11(2): 1–106.

McDonald, K.R., Alford, R.A. and Cunningham, M. 2001. *Rheobatrachus vitellinus*. In: IUCN. 2003. *2003 IUCN Red List of Threatened Species.* [web application]. Available at www.iucnredlist.org. (Accessed: 27 September 2004).

McNeilage, A., Plumptre, A.J., Brock-Doyle, A. and Vedder, A. 2001. Bwindi Impenetrable National Park, Uganda: gorilla census 1997. *Oryx* 35(1): 39–47.

Midgley, G.F., Hannah, L., Millar, D., Rutherford, M.C. and Powrie, L.W. 2002. Assessing the vulnerability of species richness to anthropogenic climate change in a biodiversity hotspot. *Global Ecology and Biogeography* 11: 445–451.

Midgley, G.F., Hannah, L., Millar, D., Thuiller, W. and Booth, A. 2003. Developing regional and species-level assessments of climate change impacts on biodiversity in the Cape Floristic Region. *Biological Conservation* 112: 87–97.

Milberg, P. and Tyrberg, T. 1993. Naive birds and noble savages: a review of man-caused prehistoric extinctions of island birds. *Ecography* 16(3): 229–250.

Miller, A.G. and Guarino, L. 1994. Somali-Masai Regional Centre of Endemism: CPD Site SWA4. Socotra, Yemen. In: S.D. Davis, V.H. Heywood and A.C. Hamilton (eds), *Centres of Plant Diversity. A guide and strategy for their conservation.* Volume 1: 312–316. IUCN Publications Unit, Cambridge, UK.

Miller, B., Conway, W., Reading, R.P., Wemmer, C., Wildt, D., Kleiman, D., Monfort, S., Rabinowitz, A., Armstrong, B. and Hutchins, M. 2004. Evaluating the Conservation Mission of Zoos, Aquariums, Botanical Gardens, and Natural History Museums. *Conservation Biology* 18(1): 86–93.

Mittermeier, R.A. 1988. Primate diversity and the tropical forest. In: E.O. Wilson (ed.), *Biodiversity*, pp. 145–154. National Academy Press, Washington D.C., USA.

Mittermeier, R.A., Robles-Gil, P., Hoffmann, M., Pilgrim, J.D., Brooks, T.B., Mittermeier, C.G., Lamoreux, J.L. and Fonseca, G.A.B. 2004. *Hotspots Revisited: Earth's Biologically Richest and Most Endangered Ecoregions.* CEMEX, Mexico City, Mexico.

Mittermeier, R.A., Robles Gil, P. and Mittermeier, C.G. 1998. *Megadiversity*. Cemex, Mexico City, Mexico.

Musick, J.A., Burgess, G., Caillet, G., Camhi, M. and Fordhman, S. 2000. AFS Policy Statement: Management of sharks and their relatives (Elasmobranchii). *Fisheries* 25(3): 9–13.

Musick, J.A., Harbin, M.M., Berkeley, S.A., Burgess, G.H., Eklund, A.M., Findley, L., Gilmore, R.G., Golden, J.T., Ha, D.S., Huntsman, G.R., McGovern, J.C., Parker, S.J., Poss, S.G., Sala, E., Schmidt, T.W., Sedberry, G.R., Weeks, H. and Wright, S.G. 2000. Marine, estuarine and diadromous fish stocks at risk of extinction in North America (exclusive of Pacific salmonids). *Fisheries* 25: 6–30.

Myers, N., Mittermeier, R.A., Mittermeier, C.G., Fonseca, G.A.B. and Kent, J. 2000. Biodiversity hotspots for conservation priorities. *Nature* 403: 853–858.

Myers, R. and Worm, B. 2003. Rapid depletion of predatory fish communities. *Nature* 423: 280–283.

Newmark, W.D. 1996. Insularization of Tanzanian parks and the local extinction of large mammals. *Conservation Biology* 10(6): 1549–1556.

Novotny, V., Basset, Y., Miller, S.E., Weiblen, G.D., Bremer, B., Cizek, L. and Drozd, P. 2002. Low host specificity of herbivorous insects in a tropical forest. *Nature* 416: 841–844.

Oaks, J.L., Gilbert, M., Virani, M.Z., Watson, R.T., Meteyer, C.U., Rideout, B.A., Shivaprasad, H.L., Ahmed, S., Chaudhry, M.J.I., Arshad, M., Mahmood, S., Ali, A. and Khan, A.A. 2004. Diclofenac residues as the cause of vulture population decline in Pakistan. *Nature* 427: 630–633.

Oldfield, S., Lusty, C. and MacKinven, A. (compilers) 1998. *The World List of Threatened Trees*. World Conservation Press, Cambridge, UK.

Oliver, W.L.R. and Deb Roy, S. 1993. The Pygmy Hog (*Sus salvanius*). In: W.L.R. Oliver (ed.), *Pigs, Peccaries and Hippos Status Survey and Action Plan*, pp. 121–129. IUCN, Gland, Switzerland.

Olson, D.M., Dinerstein, E., Wikramanayake, E.D., Burgess, N.D., Powell, G.V.N., Underwood, E.C., D'Amico, J.A., Itoua, I., Strand, H.E., Morrison, J.C., Loucks, C.J., Allnutt, T.F., Ricketts, T.H., Kura, Y., Lamoreux, J.F., Wettengel, W.W., Hedao, P. and Kassem, K.R. 2001. Terrestrial ecoregions of the world: a new map of life on Earth. *BioScience* 51: 933–938.

Olson, S.L., and James, H.F. 1982. Fossil birds from the Hawaiian Islands – evidence for wholesale extinction by man before Western contact. *Science* 217: 633–635.

Osterhaus, A., van de Bildt, M., Vedder, L., Martina, B., Niesters, H., Vos, J., van Egmond, H., Liem, D., Baumann, R., Androukaki, E., Kotomatas, S., Komnenou, A., Abou Sidi, B., Jiddou, A.B. and Barham, M.E.O. 1998. Monk seal mortality: virus or toxin? *Vaccine* 16(9–10): 979–981.

Owens, I.P.F. and Bennett, P.M. 2000. Ecological basis of extinction risk in birds: habitat loss versus human persecution and introduced predators. *Proceedings of the National Academy of Sciences of the United States of America* 97: 12144–12148.

Parker, S.J., Berkeley, S.A., Golden, J.T., Gunderson, D.R., Heifetz, J., Hixon, M.A., Larson, R., Leaman, B.M., Love, M.S., Musick, J.A., O'Connell, V.M., Ralston, S., Weeks, H.J. and Yoklavich, M.M. 2000. AFS Policy Statement: Management of Pacific rockfish. *Fisheries* 25(3): 22–29.

Pauly, D., Christensen, V., Dalsgaard, J., Froese, R. and Torres, F. 1998. Fishing down marine food webs. *Science* 279: 860–863.

Peterson, A.T., Ball, L.G. and Cohoon, K.P. 2002. Predicting distributions of Mexican birds using ecological niche modelling methods. *Ibis* 144: 27–32.

Peterson, A.T., Navarro-Sigüenza, A.G. and Benítez-Díaz, H. 1998. The need for continued scientific collecting: a geographic analysis of Mexican bird specimens. *Ibis* 140: 288–294.

Peterson, A.T. and Watson, D.M. 1998. Problems with areal definitions of endemism: the effects of spatial scaling. *Diversity and Distributions* 4: 189–194.

Pimm, S.L. and Brooks, T.M. 1997. The sixth extinction: how large, how soon, and where? In: P.H. Raven (ed.), *Nature and Human Society: the Quest for a Sustainable World*, pp. 46–62. National Academy Press, Washington, DC, USA.

Pimm, S.L., Moulton, M.P. and Justice, L.J. 1994. Bird extinctions in the central Pacific. *Proceedings of the Royal Society of London Series B – Biological Sciences* 344: 27–33.

Pimm, S.L., Russell, G.L., Gittleman, J.L. and Brooks, T.M. 1995. The future of biodiversity. *Science* 269: 347–350.

Pitman, N.C.A. and Jørgensen, P.M. 2002. Estimating the size of the world's threatened flora. *Science* 298(1): 989.

Podestá, G.P. and Glynn, P.G. 2001. The 1997–1998 El Niño event in Panama and Galapagos: an update of thermal stress indices relative to coral bleaching. *Bulletin of Marine Science* 69: 43–59.

Pounds, J.A., Fogden, M.P.L. and Campbell, J.H. 1999. Biological response to climate change on a tropical mountain. *Nature* 398: 611–615.

Pounds, J.A., Fogden, M.P.L., Savage, J.M. and Gorman, G.C. 1997. Test of null models for amphibian declines on a tropical mountain. *Conservation Biology* 11: 1307–1322.

Pounds, J.A. and Puschendorf. R. 2004. Clouded futures. *Nature* 427: 107–108.

Probst, J.R., Donner, D.M., Bocetti, C.I. and Sjogren, S. 2003. Population increase in Kirtland's Warbler and summer range expansion to Wisconsin and Michigan's Upper Peninsula, USA. *Oryx* 37(3): 365–373.

Purvis, A., Agapow, P.-M., Gittleman, J.L. and Mace, G.M. 2000a. Nonrandom extinction and the loss of evolutionary history. *Science* 288: 328–330.

Purvis, A., Gittleman, J.L., Cowlishaw, G. and Mace, G.M. 2000b. Predicting extinction risk in declining species. *Proceedings of the Royal Society of London Series B – Biological Sciences* 267: 1947–1952.

Purvis, A., Jones, K.E. and Mace, G.M. 2000c. Extinction. *BioEssays* 22: 1123–1133.

Rapoport, E.H. 1982. *Areography: Geographical Strategies of Species*. Pergamon Press, New York, USA.

Raup, D.M. 1986. Biological extinction in Earth history. *Science* 231: 1528–1533.

Reid, W.V. 1998. Biodiversity hotspots. *Trends in Ecology and Evolution* 13: 275–280.

Reynolds, J.D., Dulvy, N.K. and Roberts, C.R. 2002. Exploitation and other threats to fish conservation. In: P.J.B. Hart and J.D. Reynolds (eds), *Handbook of Fish Biology and Fisheries*. Volume 2, Fisheries, pp. 319–341. Blackwell Publishing, Oxford, UK.

Reynolds, J.D., Jennings, S. and Dulvy, N.K. 2001. Life histories of fishes and population responses to exploitation. In: J.D. Reynolds, G.M. Mace, K.H. Redford and J.G. Robinson (eds), *Conservation of Exploited Species*, pp. 147–168. Cambridge University Press, Cambridge, UK.

Richter, B.D., Braun, D.P., Mendelson, M.A. and Master, L.L. 1997. Threats to imperiled freshwater fauna. *Conservation Biology* 11: 1081–1093.

Ridgely, R.S., Allnutt, T.F., Brooks, T., McNicol, D.K., Mehlman, D.W., Young, B.E. and Zook, J.R. 2003. *Digital Distribution Maps of the Birds of the Western Hemisphere*. Version 1.0. CD-ROM. NatureServe, Arlington, USA.

Roberts, C.M., McClean, C.J., Veron, J.E.N., Hawkins, J.P., Allen, G.R., McAllister, D.E., Mittermeier, C.G., Schueller, F.W., Spalding, M., Wells, F., Vynne, C. and Werner, T.B. 2002. Marine biodiversity hotspots and conservation priorities for tropical reefs. *Science* 295: 1280–1284.

Robertson, H.A., Hay, J.R., Saul, E.K. and McCormack, G.V. 1994. Recovery of the Kakerori: an endangered forest bird of the Cook Islands. *Conservation Biology* 8(4): 1078–1086.

Robinson, J.G. and Bennett, E.L. (eds). 2000. *Hunting for Sustainability in Tropical Forests*. Columbia University Press, New York, USA.

Robinson, R.A. and Sutherland, W.J. 2002. Post-war changes in arable farming and biodiversity in Great Britain. *Journal of Applied Ecology* 39: 157–176.

Rodrigues, A.S.L., Andelman, S.J., Bakarr, M.I., Boitani, L., Brooks, T.M., Cowling, R.M., Fishpool, L.D.C., Fonseca, G.A.B., Gaston, K.J., Hoffmann, M., Long, J.S., Marquet, P.A., Pilgrim, J.D., Pressey, R.L., Schipper, J., Sechrest, W., Stuart, S.N., Underhill, L.G., Waller, R.W., Watts, M.E.J. and Yan, X. 2004. Effectiveness of the global protected area network in representing species diversity. *Nature* 428: 640–643.

Rodríguez, J.P., Ashenfelter, G., Rojas-Suárez, F., Garcia Fernandez, J.J., Suárez, L. and Dobson, A.P. 2000. Local data are vital to conservation worldwide. *Nature* 403: 241.

Roelke-Parker, M.E., Munson, L., Packer, C., Kock, R., Cleaveland, S., Carpenter, M., O'Brien, S.J., Pospischil, A., Hofmann-Lehmann, R., Lutz, H., Mwamengele, G.L.M., Mgasa, M.N., Machange, G.A., Summers, B.A. and Appel, M.J.G. 1996. A canine distemper virus epidemic in Serengeti lions (*Panthera leo*). *Nature* 379: 441–445.

Ron, S.R., Duellman, W.E., Coloma, L.A. and Bustamante, M.R. 2003. Population decline of the Jambato Toad *Atelopus ignescens* (Anura: Bufonidae) in the Andes of Ecuador. *Journal of Herpetology* 37: 116–126.

Rosenzweig, M.L. 1992. Species diversity gradients: we know more and less than we thought. *Journal of Mammalogy* 73: 715–730.

Ross, J.P. (ed.) 1998. *Crocodiles: Status Survey and Conservation Action Plan*. Second edition. IUCN/SSC Crocodile Specialist Group. IUCN, Gland, Switzerland and Cambridge, UK.

Ross, P. 2001. Chinese alligator: back from the brink? *World Conservation* 32(3): 21

Rowe, R. 1995. The population biology of *Trochetiopsis*: a genus endemic to St. Helena. DPhil Thesis, University of Oxford.

Russell, G.J., Brooks, T.J., McKinney, M.M. and Anderson, C.G. 1998. Present and future taxonomic selectivity in bird and mammal extinctions. *Conservation Biology* 12: 1365–1376.

Sadovy, Y. 2001. The threat of fishing to highly fecund fishes. *Journal of Fish Biology* 59 (Supplement A): 90–108.

Sadovy, Y. and Cheung, W.L. 2003. Near extinction of a highly fecund fish: the one that nearly got away. *Fish and Fisheries* 4: 86–99.

Sadovy, Y., Kulbicki, M., Labrosse, P., Letourneur, Y., Lokani, P. and Donaldson, T.J. 2003. The humphead wrasse, *Cheilinus undulatus*: synopsis of a threatened and poorly known giant coral reef fish. *Reviews in Fish Biology and Fisheries* 13(3): 327–364.

Sanderson, E.W., Jaiteh, M., Levy, M.A., Redford, K.H., Wannebo, A.V. and Woolmer, G. 2002. The human footprint and the last of the wild. *BioScience* 52: 891–904.

Schmid, R. 1998. Statistics for numbers of extant taxa of major groups in Mabberley. *Taxon* 47: 245.

Scotland, R.W. and Wortley, A.H. 2003. How many species of seed plants are there? *Taxon* 52: 101–104.

Scott, P., Burton, J.A. and Fitter, R. 1987. Red Data Books: the historical background. In: R. Fitter and M. Fitter (eds), *The Road to Extinction*, pp. 1–5. IUCN, Gland, Switzerland.

Shultz, S., Sagar Baral, H., Charman, S., Cunningham, A.A., Das, D., Ghalsasi, G.R., Goudar, M.S., Green, R.E., Jones, A., Nighot, P., Pain, D.J. and Prakash, V. In press. Diclofenac poisoning is widespread in declining vulture populations across the Indian subcontinent. *Proceedings of the Royal Society of London B – Biological Sciences Supplement.*

Simon, N. 1966. Red Data Book. *Volume 1. Mammalia: a compilation.* IUCN, Morges, Switzerland.

Simpfendorfer, C. and Donohue, K. 1998. Keeping the fish in fish'n'chips: research and management of the Western Australian shark fishery. *Marine and Freshwater Research* 49: 593–600.

Simpfendorfer, C.A., Donohue, K. and Hall, N.G. 2000. Stock assessment and risk analysis for the whiskery shark (*Furgaleus macki* (Whitley)) in south-western Australia. *Fisheries Research* 47(1): 1–17.

Sinclair, A.R.E., Mduma, S.A.R. and Arcese, P. 2002. Protected areas as biodiversity benchmarks for human impact: agriculture and the Serengeti avifauna. *Proceedings of the Royal Society of London Series B – Biological Sciences* 269(1508): 2401–2405.

Smith, M.L., Carpenter, K.E. and Waller, R.W. 2002. Introduction to the oceanography, geology, biogeography, and fisheries of the tropical and subtropical Western Central Atlantic. In: K.E. Carpenter (ed.), *The Living Marine Resources of the Western Central Atlantic. Volume 1. Introduction, molluscs, crustaceans, hagfishes, sharks, batoid fishes and chimaeras*, pp. 1–23. Food and Agriculture Organization, Rome.

Stattersfield, A.J., Crosby, M.J., Long, A.J. and Wege, D.C. 1998. *Endemic Bird Areas of the World: Priorities for Biodiversity Conservation.* BirdLife International, Cambridge, UK.

Steadman, D.W. 1995. Prehistoric extinctions of Pacific island birds: biodiversity meets zooarcheology. *Science* 267: 1123–1131.

Steadman, D.W., White, J.P. and Allen, J. 1999. Prehistoric birds from New Ireland, Papua New Guinea: Extinctions on a large Melanesian island. *Proceedings of the National Academy of Sciences of the United States of America* 96: 2563–2568.

Stein, B.A., Adams, J.S., Master, L.L., Morse, L.E. and Hammerson, G.A. 2000. A remarkable array. Species diversity in the United States. In: B.A. Stein, L.S. Kutner and J.S. Adams (eds), *Precious Heritage. The status of biodiversity in the United States*, pp. 55–92. Oxford University Press, New York, USA.

Steiner, A., Kimball, L.A. and Scanlon, J. 2003. Global governance for the environment and the role of Multilateral Environmental Agreements in conservation. *Oryx* 37(2): 227–237.

Stine, B. and Wagner, W. In press. Plant extinctions: chiaroscuro in shades of green. In: G.A. Krupnick and W.J. Kress (eds), *Plant Conservation: A Natural History Approach.* University of Chicago Press, Chicago, USA.

Tan, B., Geissler, P., Hallingbäck, T. and Söderström, L. 2000. The 2000 IUCN World Red List of Bryophytes. In: T. Hallingbäck and N. Hodgetts (compilers), *Mosses, Liverworts and Hornworts. Status Survey and Conservation Action Plan for Bryophytes*, pp. 77–90. IUCN/SSC Bryophyte Specialist Group. IUCN, Gland, Switzerland and Cambridge, UK.

Thomas, C.D., Cameron, A., Green, R.E., Bakkenes, M., Beaumont, L.J., Collingham, Y.C., Erasmus, B.F.N., Ferreira de Siqueira, M.F., Grainger, A., Hannah, L., Hughes, L., Huntley, B., van Jaarsveld, A.S., Midgley, G.F., Miles, L., Ortega-Huerta, Peterson, A.T., Phillips, O.L. and Williams, S.E. 2004. Extinction risk from climate change. *Nature* 427: 145–148.

Thorne, R.F. 2002. How many species of seed plants are there? *Taxon* 51: 511–512.

Tisdell, C. and Wilson, C. 2002. Ecotourism for the survival of sea turtles and other wildlife. *Biodiversity and Conservation* 11(9): 1521–1538.

Torres, H. (compiler and editor) 1992. *South American Camelids. An Action Plan for their Conservation.* IUCN/SSC South American Camelid Specialist Group. IUCN, Gland, Switzerland.

Tuck, G.N., Polacheck, T. and Bulman, C.M. 2003. Spatio-temporal trends of longline fishing effort in the Southern Ocean and implications for seabird bycatch. *Biological Conservation* 114: 1–27.

Tuck, G.N., Polacheck, T., Croxall, J.P. and Weimerskirch, H. 2001. Modelling the impact of fishery by-catches on albatross populations. *Journal of Animal Ecology* 38: 1182–1196.

Udvardy, M.D.F. 1975. *A Classification of the Biogeographical Provinces of the World.* Occasional Paper of the IUCN Species Survival Commission No. 18. IUCN, Morges, Switzerland.

Udvardy, M.D.F. 1981. An overview of grid-based atlas works in ornithology. *Studies in Avian Biology* 6: 103–109.

Uetz, P. (compiler). 2004. EMBL Reptile Database. [web application]. Available at: http://www.embl-heidelberg.de/~uetz/LivingReptiles.html. (Accessed: 31 August 2004).

Valencia, R., Pitman, N., León-Yánez, S. and Jørgensen, P.M. 2000. *Libro Rojo de las Plantas Endémicas del Ecuador 2000.* Publicaciones del Herbario QCA, Pontificia Universidad Católica del Ecuador, Quito, Ecuador.

van Dijk, P.P., Stuart, B.L. and Rhodin, A.G.J. (eds). 2000. Asian Turtle Trade: Proceedings of a Workshop on Conservation and Trade of Freshwater Turtles and Tortoises in Asia. *Chelonian Research Monographs* 2: 1-164.

Wagner, W.L., Bruegmann, M.M., Herbst, D.R. and Lau, J.Q.C. 1999. *Hawaiian Vascular Plants at Risk.* Bishop Museum Press Honolulu. Honolulu, USA.

Walter, K.S. and Gillett, H. (eds) 1998. *1997 IUCN Red List of Threatened Plants.* Compiled by the World Conservation Monitoring Centre. IUCN, Gland, Switzerland and Cambridge, UK.

WDPA Consortium. 2004. *2004 World Database on Protected Areas.* IUCN-WCPA and UNEP-WCMC, Gland, Switzerland, Washington, DC, USA and Cambridge, UK.

Weldon, C., du Preez, L.H., Hyatt, A.D., Muller, R. and Speare, R. In press. Out of Africa: evidence for the origin of the amphibian chytrid fungus. *Emerging Infectious Diseases.*

West, J.M. and Salm, R.V. 2003. Resistance and Resilience to Coral Bleaching: Implications for Coral Reef Management and Conservation. *Conservation Biology* 17(4): 956–967.

Wiles, G.J., Bart, J., Beck, R.E. Jr. and Aguon, C.F. 2003. Impacts of the Brown Tree Snake: Patterns of Decline and Species Persistence in Guam's Avifauna. *Conservation Biology* 17(5): 1350–1360.

Williams, P.H. 1998. Key sites for conservation area-selection methods for biodiversity. In: G.M. Mace, A. Balmford and J.R. Ginsberg (eds), *Conservation in a Changing World,* pp. 211–250. Cambridge University Press, Cambridge, UK.

Williams S.E., Bolitho, E.E. and Fox, S. 2003. Climate change in Australian tropical rainforests: an impending environmental catastrophe. *Proceedings of the Royal Society, London Series B – Biological Sciences* 270: 1887–1892.

Willis, F., Moat, J. and Paton, A. 2003. Defining a role for herbarium data in Red List assessments: a case study of *Plectranthus* from eastern and southern tropical Africa. *Biodiversity and Conservation* 12(7): 1537–1552.

Wilson, D.E. and Reeder, D.M. (eds) 1993. *Mammal Species of the World: a Taxonomic and Geographic Reference.* Second edition. Smithsonian Institution Press, Washington, DC, USA and London, UK.

Wilson, D.E., and Reeder, D.M. (eds) In press. *Mammal Species of the World. A Taxonomic and Geographic Reference.* Third edition. Smithsonian Institution Press. Washington DC, USA.

Woodroffe, R. 2001. Assessing the risks of intervention: immobilization, radio-collaring and vaccination of African wild dogs. *Oryx* 35(3): 234–244.

Woodroffe, R., McNutt, J.W. and Mills, M.G.L. In press. *Lycaon pictus.* In: C. Sillero-Zubiri, M. Hoffmann and D.W. Macdonald (eds), *Canids: Foxes, Wolves, Jackals and Dogs. Status Survey and Conservation Action Plan.* IUCN/SSC Canid Specialist Group. IUCN, Gland, Switzerland and Cambridge, UK.

World Bank. 2004. *World Development Indicators 2004.* World Bank, Washington DC, USA.

Young, B.E., Lips, K.R., Reaser, J.K., Ibanez, R., Salas, A.W., Cedeno, J.R., Coloma, L.A., Ron, S., La Marca, E., Meyer, J.R., Muñoz, A., Bolanos, F., Chaves, G. and Romo, D. 2001. Population declines and priorities for amphibian conservation in Latin America. *Conservation Biology* 15(5): 1213–1223.

Appendices

Photo: © Tony Comacho.

Photo 11.1
The Riverine Rabbit *Bunolagus monticularis* (Critically Endangered) is found only in the central Karoo region of South Africa and the current population is estimated to be fewer than 250 mature individuals. With ongoing habitat loss and fragmentation, and direct threats from trapping, feral cats and dogs, and hunting pressure, the population decline is not expected to stop in the near future.

Appendix 1. The IUCN Red List Programme

1.1 Global Assessments: Introduction

The mandate of the *IUCN Red List* has expanded to identify large-scale patterns and trends in the status of species. Identifying taxonomic groups or regions that tend to have species that are facing a high or low probability of extinction can be accomplished by conducting multi-species analyses. The traditional approach for obtaining Red List assessments is through the SSC Specialist Groups. However, new approaches are now being developed in order to rapidly increase the taxonomic coverage and the frequency and rigour of such assessments.

In 2001, the Species Survival Commission (SSC) of the World Conservation Union (IUCN) and the Center for Applied Biodiversity Science (CABS) at Conservation International (CI) began the Biodiversity Assessment Initiative, an exciting and ambitious project of establishing biodiversity monitoring baselines for over 100,000 of the world's species.

The Global Amphibian Assessment was the first phase of the Biodiversity Assessment Initiative, in collaboration with NatureServe. IUCN/SSC and CI/CABS are also collaborating with other partners to complete a global assessment of all mammals (scheduled for completion in 2006), and also an assessment of all reptiles. The primary focus of the Initiative will turn to reptiles, also in collaboration with NatureServe, with completion scheduled for 2007. The goals for each species group assessment are the same: to map the distribution and assess the conservation status of each species in order to establish global baselines for biodiversity monitoring and conservation planning. Some of the new approaches being adopted are outlined below.

1.1.1 The Global Amphibian Assessment (GAA)

The Global Amphibian Assessment (GAA) greatly enhances our current knowledge of amphibians. Importantly, for the first time all amphibians have been assessed against the IUCN Red List Categories and Criteria (IUCN 2001). The assessment includes all 5,743 currently described species of amphibian, although new species are still being discovered at a rapid rate and these will be incorporated in future updates of the assessment. Prior to the GAA, fewer than 1,000 species had been assessed, mainly in Australia, North America and Europe. The assessment began in April of 2001

and took over three years to complete. Full details about the GAA can be seen at http://www.globalamphibians.org/, but a summary of the process is provided here.

Objectives:

• To determine the scale (both the magnitude of threat and the geographic focus) of the current extinction crisis in amphibians.

• To identify the most important geographic areas and habitats which need to be conserved to avoid species extinctions.

• To identify the major threats and to propose mitigating measures and prioritized conservation actions to address them.

• To establish a network focused on amphibians so that the Global Amphibian Assessment can be kept current, and expertise can be targeted to address the highest conservation priorities.

Coordination:

The central coordination of the project was done by the IUCN/SSC - CI/CABS Biodiversity Assessment Unit based at the Center for Applied Biodiversity Science at Conservation International (CI/CABS). The small coordinating team was dependent on the expertise of the world's amphibian experts for the success of the Global Amphibian Assessment. A full listing of all the participants in the assessment can be found in the Acknowledgements.

The GAA was implemented in five main stages: data collection, data review, data consolidation, data analysis, and the determination of future steps.

Data collection:

For every amphibian species currently known, the following data were collected:

• Species systematics

• Geographic range (including a distribution map)

• Red List assessment

• Population information

• Habitat preferences

• Major threats

• Conservation measures

• Species utilization

• Other general information

• Important literature references

The task of collecting the initial data was divided into 33 geographic regions that were defined to cover the global distribution of all amphibians. Regional coordinators were appointed and given the responsibility of collecting data on all the amphibians in their region.

Data Review:

All the data collected in the initial stage of the assessment were subject to peer review. For most regions this was done through expert workshops, and in a small number of regions it was completed through individual review of the data by leading herpetologists in the region. There were 14 workshops held in various countries to review the data. At each workshop amphibian experts for the region were invited to participate and contribute their knowledge as well as review the data already compiled by the regional coordinators.

Data Consolidation:

As the review of data was completed, region-by-region, the information was consolidated by the coordinating team at the Biodiversity Assessment Unit. Specific tasks that needed to be addressed included:

• ensuring consistency in the application of the Red List Categories and Criteria between regions and taxonomic groups;

• proofreading and correcting the text accounts for all species;

• final editing of maps to ensure that small islands near the coast are not incorrectly included in species distributions;

• final resolution of remaining outstanding issues, mainly to do with taxonomic problems; and

• inclusion of newly described species, and other taxonomic changes.

Data Analysis:

Some of the findings from the GAA are presented in this publication, while the data themselves are available on http://www.globalamphibians.org and http://www.iucnredlist.org. A book containing the data on CD as well as an in depth analysis of the data will also be made available in 2005 or 2006.

Future Steps:

A framework is being established that will enable an ongoing process of maintaining and updating the GAA database to be implemented. In particular, a new IUCN/SSC Global Amphibian Specialist Group (GASG) is being formed consisting of regional sections. It is hoped that the GAA will generate widespread interest among herpetologists to take part in the group. In addition to catalysing conservation actions on behalf of amphibians, the GASG members will have the responsibility of keeping the GAA results updated. The intention is for the GAA to not be a one-off project, but rather the start of an ongoing process to implement global long-term monitoring of amphibians.

1.1.2 The Global Mammal Assessment (GMA)

All mammal species were assessed for the first time in 1996 (Baillie and Groombridge 1996). However, although a great deal is known about mammalian biology, systematics, distribution patterns and conservation status, this knowledge is neither uniform nor complete. Moreover, of the more than 5,000 mammal species known worldwide, the threat status of more than 2,500 is insufficiently known or inadequately documented.

A number of mammal data initiatives have emerged in recent years among various organizations and a partial overlap across some of these initiatives calls for interaction between them. In light of this, a meeting of representatives of the major initiatives was held in February 2002 at the National Center for Ecological Analysis and Synthesis in Santa Barbara, California. The meeting resulted in the creation of the 'Global Mammal Partnership' comprising IUCN/SSC, the University of Virginia, Institute of Applied Ecology/University of Rome-Italy, NatureServe, CI/CABS, WWF, Institute of Zoology-ZSL/Imperial College-UK, Smithsonian Institution and Bat Conservation International.

Within the context of this partnership, IUCN/SSC together with CI/CABS, the Institute of Zoology, the Institute of Applied Ecology, and the University of Virginia, have initiated the Global Mammal Assessment (GMA) with the goal of consolidating all the available information on the systematics, distribution, ecology, and conservation status of mammals. The GMA will review the status of all mammal species (*c.* 5,416 described species), map the geographic distributions, assess the degree of threat, and record essential habitats, important threats, conservation measures in place and needed, and utilization details for each species.

The GMA will follow a similar strategy to the groundbreaking work of the Global Amphibian Assessment (GAA) described above. However a key difference between the GAA and GMA is that the SSC already has an established, comprehensive network of mammal Specialist Groups. This network comprises approximately 2,000 members arranged within 34 Specialist Groups (for further details see http://www.iucn.org/themes/ssc/sgs/sgs.htm). As a result, the data gathering and assessment process will be done either through the existing Specialist Group structures or in certain cases will be workshop-based.

The existing SSC mammal Specialist Group structure is very strong for certain groups of mammals (e.g., Antelope, Canid, Cat, Small Carnivore, and Lagomorph) and all of these groups have produced at least one IUCN/SSC Action Plan in the last decade. Consequently, species falling within the jurisdiction of these well-supported and well-coordinated groups can be adequately assessed by the members of these groups. Funding to support the activities of these groups will be raised wherever possible.

In contrast, the SSC mammal network is somewhat less developed for small mammals (e.g., bats, insectivores, rodents, etc.), and for these taxa the data collection and assessment process is largely being carried out by means of regional workshops involving all the relevant experts. Workshops proved to be the most important tool for the GAA, providing a platform for discussion, interaction, and group peer-review of species relationships, life-history data and distribution maps. Such workshops have proved to be most productive in terms of collating the greatest amount of species-based information within a relatively short time period. The workshops for these taxa will be divided according to geographic region, particularly focusing on regions where information is the poorest: e.g., Africa, Madagascar, south and southeast Asia, Central America (Mesoamerica), and South America.

The GMA process is now well underway, and some results are already evident in this publication and in the 2004 *IUCN Red List* with the inclusion of 854 new assessments for mammals. These included, for example, all Canid species reassessed by the Canid Specialist Group, and the results from the GMA workshop on African small mammals (788 species of bats, insectivores and rodents). These new assessments are provisional, as they still need to be fully reviewed by the GMA coordinating team to ensure global consistency. The final results of the GMA are expected to appear in the *2006 IUCN Red List of Threatened Species™*.

1.1.3 The Global Reptile Assessment (GRA)

The Global Reptile Assessment was launched in July 2004, focusing on assessments of the world's *c.* 8,000 species of reptiles. A similar model to that used for the GAA will be used for the GRA. Two workshops for the GRA are already planned; a workshop to assess the status of Mediterranean reptiles will be held in Spain in December 2004 under the auspices of the IUCN Regional Office for the Mediterranean, while a second workshop to assess reptiles in Mexico is being planned by NatureServe, to be held in early 2005.

1.1.4 Freshwater Biodiversity Assessment Programme

The Species Programme of IUCN initiated a Freshwater Biodiversity Assessment Programme in 2003 to put in place a factual underpinning to support efforts to conserve and manage freshwater biodiversity. The specific objectives of this programme are to:

- build expertise and capacity on freshwater biodiversity through establishment of regional networks;

- establish a freshwater biodiversity information system within the SSC Species Information Service (SIS);

- carry out threatened status (IUCN Red List) assessments for key groups of freshwater species;

- identify critical sites for the conservation of these species groups;

- determine key threatening processes and priority conservation actions in each region;

- assess the priority requirements for freshwater biodiversity conservation; and

- communicate the results of the project to governments, donors and NGO's in order to raise awareness and include freshwater biodiversity conservation in their priorities for action.

The main activities of the programme so far have focussed on regional assessments. The first regional freshwater biodiversity assessment was completed for eastern Africa in December 2003. This assessment provides the most comprehensive baseline dataset for freshwater taxa in eastern Africa and the results will be made widely available throughout the region. Approximately 1,700 taxa were assessed, including >1,000 freshwater fishes, 215 molluscs, 304 dragonflies and damselflies, 38 crabs, and 91 aquatic plants. All the assessments of threatened status are still to be evaluated but some were processed for inclusion in the 2004 *IUCN Red List* (see also Box 2.4 for the provisional results).

The Freshwater Biodiversity Assessment Programme is establishing a Global Freshwater Fish Specialist Group in collaboration with Wetlands International. The group is to have a regional structure of sub-groups with their own vice-chairs who will form a steering committee under the leadership of a Global Chair. However, until this Specialist Group is fully functional the Freshwater Biodiversity Assessment Programme assists the Red List Programme in evaluating all freshwater species assessments submitted for inclusion in the Red List. For example, the Conservation

Breeding Specialist Group facilitated a Conservation Assessment and Management Plan (CAMP) Workshop in May 2001 which assessed the status of approximately 95 freshwater fish taxa endemic to Madagascar (Conservation Breeding Specialist Group 2002). The process to peer review and update these assessments was coordinated by the Freshwater Biodiversity Assessment Programme and the results are included in the 2004 *IUCN Red List.*

The current focus of the programme is on raising funds to expand the assessments to other regions and continents, with the goal of achieving global coverage as rapidly as possible. A funding proposal has been submitted to extend the eastern Africa assessment to the rest of Africa. If successful this project will include a number of case studies to demonstrate best practices for integrating the biodiversity datasets into the development planning process. Regional assessments are also planned for the La Plata River basin in South America, Europe, and the Mekong River Basin in southeast Asia.

Funding opportunities for single taxon global assessments are also being investigated. But under the auspices of the Odonata Specialist Group, a Global Dragonfly Assessment (covering more than 5,000 species of dragonflies and damselflies) is already well underway.

1.1.5 The Global Marine Species Assessment

The collaboration between IUCN/SSC and CI/CABS is now in the process of expanding to include marine species. Funds are currently being sought to implement an assessment of all species of marine fishes (more than 15,000 species) in three years, from 2005 to 2007. This Global Marine Species Assessment (GMSA) will be implemented in a similar manner to the GAA, and will probably include at least 20 expert data review workshops. The GMSA will also work closely with existing SSC Specialist Groups working on marine species, such as the Shark Specialist Group, Grouper and Wrasse Specialist Group, Coral Reef Fish Specialist Group, and Cetacean Specialist Group. Prior to the launch of the GMSA, IUCN/SSC and CI/CABS will hold expert consultations to agree protocols for the mapping of marine species, and to enhance the IUCN Habitat Authority File to provide better coverage of marine and coastal habitats. The GMSA will hugely improve the still very poor coverage of marine species in the *IUCN Red List.*

1.1.6 The Global Plant Assessment

A complete assessment of the world's plants is a daunting task given that the estimated number of species ranges from 223,000 to 422,000 species. However, a number of initiatives are underway to address this situation, especially since the Parties to the Convention on Biological Diversity (CBD) adopted the Global Strategy for Plant Conservation (GSPC) in April 2002 (CBD Secretariat 2002). Target 2 of the GSPC is a "preliminary assessment of the conservation status of all known plant species, at national, regional and international levels" by 2010.

IUCN, through the SSC plant Specialist Groups, is encouraging all of its members to complete plant species assessments for the Red List. However, to date only two Specialist Groups have been able to assess all the species under their jurisdiction, namely the Conifer Specialist Group (618 species) and the Cycad Specialist Group (288 species). The Carnivorous Plant Specialist Group has completed assessments for two genera: *Nepenthes* and *Sarracenia* (91 species; generally referred to as pitcher plants). Plans are also well-advanced to start a Global Palm Assessment under the auspices of Fairchild Tropical Garden in Miami, Florida and the SSC Palm Specialist Group, which will assess the status of all of the world's palms (*c.* 2,200 species). However, all these taxonomic groups are relatively small and certainly not representative of overall plant diversity. In order to increase the number of assessments to reach anything like the 34,000 listed in the *1997 IUCN Red List of Threatened Plants* (Walter and Gillett 1998) requires major initiatives involving multiple organizations and multiple approaches to fast-track the process:

1. A joint project proposal is being developed by IUCN and Plantlife International to undertake plant and important site assessments in ten plant-rich countries around the world (as a pilot phase project). In turn, this work will help countries meet the target adopted at the 2002 World Summit on Sustainable Development to "significantly reduce the rate of biodiversity loss by 2010". The project will provide both tools and capacity building so that countries can identify their most threatened plant species as well as their most important areas for plant biodiversity. Once this information is known, plant conservation action plans at both species and site level will be developed. While identification of threatened species and important plant areas alone will not conserve the plants, this information is essential in developing adequate conservation strategies. It is also fundamental to implementing several targets of the Global Strategy for Plant Conservation. The ten pilot countries will act as models in their region for other countries that are also committed to achieving the plant conservation targets adopted in the Global Strategy for Plant Conservation. By training trainers in these conservation techniques, this pilot phase will achieve a multiplier effect as well as develop

models and protocols that may be used elsewhere. This project will provide technical and logistical support to these pilot countries to enable them to undertake this fundamental work on which all plant conservation activities need to be based.

2. The IUCN Species Programme has developed a framework for regional and national Red List priorities, and is seeking close collaboration with a number of plant-rich countries where plant assessment work is well advanced. For example, Spain has compiled a national Red List and these assessments need to be incorporated into the *IUCN Red List* as has been done for Ecuadorian endemics (see Box 2.6). The 1997 Plant Red List incorporated large numbers of assessments from Australia, South Africa and the US. These are once again clearly target countries for inclusion, as the information is available in each country but, due to different methods of assessment, has not yet been included in the *IUCN Red List*. Specific projects aimed at assessing plants in "hot spots" such as the Caucasus, China and eastern Africa are under development.

3. Target 1 of the GSPC is "a widely accessible working list of plant species, as a step towards a complete world flora" (CBD Secretariat 2002). Several leading botanical organizations are involved in tackling this target, and the IUCN Species Programme is collaborating with some of these (in particular the Royal Botanic Gardens (RBG), Kew and Missouri Botanical Garden) to seek ways in which their work on target one can be linked to target two. Methodologies are being developed by RBG Kew and Missouri to enable herbarium data to be used to obtain, relatively quickly, preliminary Red List assessments for large numbers of species that can then be examined and assessed more carefully by the relevant expert networks for the *IUCN Red List* (see Willis *et al.* 2003).

4. There are some taxonomic groups that stand out in terms of their overall contribution to plant diversity worldwide (species richness and occurrence in a wide variety of ecosystems), particularly legumes, orchids, grasses, ferns, bryophytes, lichens, and some families of bulbs and trees. These are all poorly represented on the *IUCN Red List* at present and should be the focus of specific species assessment programmes. Several Specialist Groups have suggested focussing their attention onto discrete, relatively taxonomically stable groups, which could then be included in global analyses. For example the Orchid Specialist Group (SG) has recommended selecting a few tribes (e.g., the Cypripedioideae, Cymbideae, Orchidae, etc.); the Bulb SG two families (Amaryllidaceae and Iridaceae); the Global Tree SG several families or genera (e.g., *Rhododendron*,

Aceraceae, Fagaceae, Magnoliaceae, Dipterocarpaceae, etc. – this work is already well-underway with institutional support provided to the SG by Fauna and Flora International); and the Pteridophyte SG selected eight families (Lycopodiaceae, Ophioglossaceae, Aspleniaceae, etc.) for which global assessments could take place. The SSC has also recognized the need to form a Legume Specialist Group that works in close collaboration with the International Legume Database & Information Service (see http://www.ildis.org), and it has been suggested that the subfamily Papilionoideae is a group that could be totally assessed. Other groups, although not represented globally, could also be completely assessed. These include some families of succulent plants (e.g., Cactaceae, Crassulaceae, Aizoaceae, etc.).

For non-vascular plants, the Bryophyte SG has suggested evaluating the genus *Macromitrium*, which has about 700 species, which occur in Asia, Africa, South and North America, and Australia. And although technically not plants, the Lichen SG has proposed the family Lobariaceae, which consists of three larger genera (*Lobaria*, *Sticta*, *Pseudocyphellaria*), which have a wide distribution in all continents except Antarctica (382 species). Note that the majority of these species are probably threatened (although not yet formally listed on the *IUCN Red List*).

1.1.7 State of the World's Birds

Better information is available for birds than for any other comparable group of organisms. Although many gaps remain, a great deal is known about their taxonomy, distribution, habitat preferences, movements, numbers, population trends, ecology, and behaviour. Compared to other groups, birds are easy to observe. They are relatively big, attractive and conspicuous; most are active by day; they can be identified in the field, from a distance; and although they are diverse, the number of species (*c.* 10,000) is manageable. For all these reasons, people enjoy watching birds and are able to provide useful data (BirdLife International 2004b).

This huge array of information is brought together in a meaningful way for conservation. Since 1980, BirdLife International (and its precursor the International Council for Bird Preservation) has published Red Data Books, presenting information on globally threatened birds. BirdLife International have, since 1988, published four complete assessments of the status of all the world's bird species (Collar and Andrew 1988; Collar *et al.* 1994; BirdLife International 2000, 2004a). A new approach was adopted by BirdLife to solicit up-to-date information for the

2004 edition of *State of the World's Birds*. This was the development of internet-based discussion forums on specific species, groups of species or particular areas. The discussion forums are open to anyone who wishes to register, and each of the discussion groups is moderated. This approach has helped improve the flow of information and made the assessment process more participatory and transparent.

The 2004 *IUCN Red List* now includes assessments for all the world's bird species (including Least Concern species) as provided by BirdLife International. But for full details on the supporting documentation for each species, users are referred to the searchable World Bird Database on the web at http://www.birdlife.net/datazone/search/species_search.html or the CD-ROM version (BirdLife International 2004a).

1.2 Regional Red Lists

A large number of regional (i.e., sub-national, national and regional) Red Data Books and Red Data Lists have been published around the world (e.g., for an account of Red List activities in European countries see the papers in de Iongh *et al.* 2003). In some of these publications, the Red List assessments are based on classification systems of threat (e.g., the Heritage conservation status ranks used in the United States and elsewhere (Master *et al.* 2000)) developed and adopted within the country concerned; many of the older publications are based on the pre-1994 system of qualitative IUCN Red List Categories (as used for example in Groombridge 1993 and Walter and Gillett 1998); but an ever increasing number of regional Red List assessments are based on the IUCN Red List Categories and Criteria (IUCN 1994a, 2001). The IUCN Red List Categories and Criteria, however, were developed primarily for application at the global level. Hence assessments of non-endemic species at national levels based on these criteria could result in incorrect and even misleading (especially when linked to conservation priority setting schemes) listings (see Gärdenfors 1996). As a result, IUCN through the Red List Programme has formulated regional guidelines to guide the assessment of endemic and non-endemic species (IUCN 2003; a downloadable PDF version is available at http://www.iucn.org/themes/ssc/redlists/regionalguidelines.htm).

The regional application guidelines are not a fixed set of rules that must be followed but a set of best-practice guidelines that indicate the preferred approaches to be followed and the issues that need to be addressed. Adoption of the regional guidelines is encouraged as they help make regional Red Lists more comparable, they promote the sharing of species information between neighbouring countries, and they promote better flow of information between the regional and global levels.

A National Red List Advisory Group (NRLAG) has been established by the IUCN/SSC Red List Committee to actively promote the use of the guidelines, and to act as an advisory group on best practice. The NRLAG intends developing three inter-related projects: (1) a survey of the Convention on Biological Diversity focal points to evaluate their approach to national threatened species lists; (2) an evaluation and analysis of several countries which have or are planning to apply the IUCN Red List Criteria at a national level; and (3) to hold a workshop involving the selected test countries where the different experiences and problems can be shared and solutions developed. The NRLAG is particularly interested in the linkages between Red Lists and conservation policy and priority setting for conservation actions.

Compilers of regional Red Lists are encouraged to submit assessments of all endemic species for possible inclusion in the *IUCN Red List*. All submissions must include the necessary supporting documentation (IUCN 2001; see http://www.iucnredlist.org/info/organization.html) and are subject to peer review by the relevant Red List Authorities.

Although we encourage the development of regional or even taxonomic Red Data Books and Lists, and promote the use of the regional application guidelines and the IUCN Red List Categories and Criteria, the Red List Consortium cannot guarantee the quality of the assessments in all these publications as they are often produced completely independently of IUCN.

1.3 Red List Programme Future Goals

The future goals of the Red List Programme are to continue development and support of the Specialist Group network with emphasis on taxa that are currently poorly represented on the *IUCN Red List*. There will also be an emphasis on the complete assessment and reassessment of selected groups of taxa. Such assessments of complete taxonomic groups help avoid the current situation where Least Concern species are not reported, making analysis of the Red List results difficult. This will include groups that have already been completely assessed such as birds, mammals, amphibians, cycads, and conifers as well as target groups that will be assessed for the first time using a similar approach to the GAA or GMA (as described above). These large-scale assessments include reptiles (*c.* 8,000 species, assessment initiated in 2004 as described above), freshwater fishes (*c.* 10,000 species, initiated in 2003 as described above), sharks, rays and chimeras (*c.* 1,000 species, to be completed in 2006), and freshwater molluscs (*c.* 5,000 species, initiated in 2004). Furthermore, a preliminary assessment of all plant species is also planned for 2010 as part of the Global Strategy for Plant Conservation (see above). These complete assessments will allow the identification of global patterns such as centres of threatened species, non-threatened species, species richness, and endemism. Re-assessments will enable the identification of trends in the status of species over time.

Red List Indices (as described in Section 4) will continue to be calculated for birds and amphibians and will soon include mammals and other groups where possible. However, this becomes impractical when considering regular and complete assessments of some of the large and less well-studied groups such as fungi (*c.* 70,000 species), plants (*c.* 280,000 species) and insects (*c.* 950,000 species). One way of addressing this problem is to use a random or representative sample of species from all major taxonomic groups. A working group under the IUCN/SSC Red List Committee is currently developing such a sampled approach (the 'Global Sentinel' project). This project will repeatedly assess the status of a sample of species from all major taxonomic groups. The Red List Index generated will provide information on changes in extinction risk of all species, major taxonomic groups, biogeographic regions, and systems (marine, freshwater and terrestrial). This will provide the general public and decision makers with a global index of extinction risk which will be much more representative of all biodiversity.

Finally, the Red List Consortium aims to continue the development of Red List web sites to ensure that the information on the status of species is readily available in a suitable form such that all those involved in conservation planning can use it. Each annual update of the *IUCN Red List* web site includes the addition of new features to make the system more user-friendly and the data more accessible. A fundamental aspect to the data collection process and to making the information available to all potential users is the ongoing development of the underlying Species Information Service (SIS; for further details see http://www.iucn.org/themes/ssc/programs/sisindex.htm). The ultimate aim is to provide a web-enabled user-friendly and interactive platform where the latest information on the status of the world's species, including geo-spatial information, can easily be accessed and analysed.

Appendix 2. Methodology

Appendix 2a. General

Throughout this publication reference is made to the IUCN Red List Categories and Criteria (IUCN 1994a, 2001). These are intended to be an easily and widely understood system for identifying and classifying species at high risk of global extinction. The general aim of the system is to provide an explicit, objective framework for the classification of the broadest range of species according to their extinction risk. It is important to note that although the Red List system may focus attention on those taxa at highest risk, it is not intended to be the sole means of identifying and setting priorities for conservation action.

Summaries of the Red List Categories (Table A2a.1) and Criteria (Table A2a.2) are presented below. However, readers are referred to the full version of the system available at http://www.iucnredlist.org/info/categories_criteria2001.html. PDF versions in English, French and Spanish can also be downloaded from http://www.iucn.org/themes/ssc/redlists/RLcats2001booklet.html.

During the development of the Red List Categories and Criteria and the subsequent Criteria Review process, a number of difficult issues were encountered that were not fully resolved. As solutions arise, rather than constantly modifying the Red List Criteria, a set of 'User Guidelines' have been developed that provide advice on how to deal with some of these issues, and how to apply the criteria under particular circumstances (in other words, they are best practice guidelines). These 'User Guidelines' are in effect a living document that is periodically updated; the latest PDF version of which can be downloaded from http://www.iucn.org/themes/ssc/redlists/RedListGuidelines.pdf.

Table A2a.1

IUCN Red List Categories (IUCN 2001)

Threatened species are listed on one of the three categories printed in RED.

Category	Abbreviation	Definition
Extinct	EX	Species for which extensive surveys show there is no reasonable doubt that the last individual has died.
Extinct in the Wild	EW	Species that survive only in cultivation, in captivity or as a naturalized population (or populations) well outside the past range.
Critically Endangered	CR	Species that are facing an extremely high risk of extinction in the wild (i.e., when the best available evidence indicates that they meet any of the criteria A to E for Critically Endangered in Table A2a.2).
Endangered	EN	Species that are facing a very high risk of extinction in the wild (i.e., when the best available evidence indicates that they meet any of the criteria A to E for Endangered in Table A2a.2).
Vulnerable	VU	Species that are facing a high risk of extinction in the wild (i.e., when the best available evidence indicates that they meet any of the criteria A to E for Vulnerable in Table A2a.2).
Near Threatened	NT	Species that do not qualify for Critically Endangered, Endangered or Vulnerable now, but are close to qualifying for or are likely to qualify for a threatened category in the near future.
Least Concern	LC	Species that do not qualify for Critically Endangered, Endangered, Vulnerable or Near Threatened. Widespread and abundant species are included in this category.
Data Deficient	DD	Species for which there is inadequate information to make a direct, or indirect, assessment of extinction risk based on distribution and/or population status. A species in this category may be well studied, and its biology well known, but appropriate data on abundance and/or distribution are lacking. Data Deficient is therefore not a category of threat.
Not Evaluated	NE	A species is Not Evaluated when it has not yet been evaluated against the criteria (see Table A2a.2). NE species are not shown on the *IUCN Red List*.

The 1994 version included an additional category which is used for some species, but once they are all reassessed it will no longer be used (IUCN 1994a):

Category	Abbreviation	Definition
Lower Risk/ conservation dependent	LR/cd	Species that are the focus of a continuing species-specific or habitat-specific conservation programme targeted towards the species in question, the cessation of which would result in the species qualifying for one of the threatened categories within five years.

Table A2a.2

Summary of the five criteria (A-E) used to evaluate if a species belongs in a threatened category (Critically Endangered, Endangered or Vulnerable)

Use any of the criteria A-E	Critically Endangered	Endangered	Vulnerable
A. Population reduction (declines measured over the longer of 10 years or 3 generations)			
A1	≥ 90%	≥ 70%	≥ 50%
A2, A3 & A4	≥ 80%	≥ 50%	≥ 30%

A1. Population reduction observed, estimated, inferred, or suspected in the past where the causes of the reduction are clearly reversible AND understood AND have ceased, based on and specifying any of the following:
- (a) direct observation
- (b) an index of abundance appropriate to the taxon
- (c) a decline in AOO, EOO and/or habitat quality
- (d) actual or potential levels of exploitation
- (e) effects of introduced taxa, hybridization, pathogens, pollutants, competitors or parasites.

A2. Population reduction observed, estimated, inferred, or suspected in the past where the causes of reduction may not have ceased OR may not be understood OR may not be reversible, based on (a) to (e) under A1.

A3. Population reduction projected or suspected to be met in the future (up to a maximum of 100 years) based on (b) to (e) under A1.

A4. An observed, estimated, inferred, projected or suspected population reduction (up to a maximum of 100 years) where the time period must include both the past and the future, and where the causes of reduction may not have ceased OR may not be understood OR may not be reversible, based on (a) to (e) under A1.

	Critically Endangered	Endangered	Vulnerable
B. Geographic range in the form of either B1 (extent or occurrence) AND/OR B2 (area or occupancy)			
B1. Extent of occurrence	< 100 km^2	< 5,000 km^2	< 20,000 km^2
B2. Area of occupancy	< 10 km^2	< 500 km^2	< 2,000 km^2
AND at least 2 of the following:			
(a) Severely fragmented or # locations	= 1	≤ 5	≤ 10
(b) Continuing decline in any of: (i) extent of occurrence; (ii) area of occupancy; (iii) area, extent and/or quality of habitat; (iv) number of locations or subpopulations; (v) number of mature individuals			
(c) Extreme fluctuations in any of: (i) extent of occurrence; (ii) area of occupancy; (iii) number of locations or subpopulations; (iv) number of mature individuals			

	Critically Endangered	Endangered	Vulnerable
C. Small population size and decline			
Number of mature individuals	< 250	< 2,500	< 10,000
AND C1 and/or C2:			
C1. An estimated continuing decline of at least: (up to a maximum of 100 years)	25% in 3 years or 1 generation	20% in 5 years or 2 generations	10% in 10 years or 3 generations
C2. A continuing decline **AND** (a) and/or (b):			
a (i) # mature individuals in each subpopulation:	≤ 50	≤ 250	≤ 1,000
a (ii) or % individuals in one subpopulation at least	90%	95%	100%
(b) extreme fluctuations in the number of mature individuals			

	Critically Endangered	Endangered	Vulnerable
D. Very small or restricted population Either:			
(1) number of mature individuals	≤ 50	≤ 250	≤ 1,000
AND/OR			
(2) restricted area of occupancy	na	na	AOO < 20 km^2 or # locations ≤ 5

	Critically Endangered	Endangered	Vulnerable
E. Quantitative Analysis			
Indicating the probability of extinction in the wild to be:	≥ 50% in 10 years or 3 generations (100 years max)	≥ 20% in 20 years or 5 generations (100 years max)	≥ 10% in 100 years

Appendix 2b. Globally Threatened Species

Numbers of Described Species

The numbers of described species presented in Table 2.1 are derived from several different sources. There is considerable debate over some of the figures, and those for the invertebrates and the plants have a large degree of uncertainty associated with them (e.g., see Hammond 1992, 1995).

Mammals – From Wilson and Reeder (in press), with deviations based on input from the IUCN/SSC Specialist Groups.

Birds – Provided by BirdLife International from their World Bird Database (see BirdLife International 2004a, 2004b).

Amphibians – Provided by the Global Amphibian Assessment based on *Amphibian Species of the World* (Frost 2004).

Reptiles – Based on EMBL Reptile Database (Uetz 2004).

Fishes – Based on FishBase (Froese and Pauly 2003).

Invertebrates – From Groombridge and Jenkins (2002), but in turn largely based on Hammond (1992, 1995).

Mosses – Based on Hallingbäck and Hodgetts (2000).

Ferns and allies – Based on Groombridge and Jenkins (2002).

Gyymnosperms – Based on Donaldson (2003); Farjon (2001); and Mabberley (1997).

Dicotyledons and Monocotyledons – Based on Thorne (2002), but see Mabberley (1997); Schmid (1998); Govaerts (2001, 2003); Bramwell (2002); and Scotland and Wortley (2003) for alternative views on the numbers of seed plant species.

Numbers Evaluated

The numbers of species evaluated (as shown on Table 2.1) are obtained from the entries in the Red List database (part of the Species Information Service) held at the Red List Office in Cambridge, UK. The origins of this database date back to the production of the *1996 IUCN Red List of Threatened Animals* (Baillie and Groombridge 1996) when most of the animal assessments were incorporated in the database. However, a large number of Least Concern assessments were not captured at the time (for example, most of the Least Concern mammals, turtles, butterflies, etc.). The Red List team have been trying to capture the 'missing' Least Concern assessments, in between processing new assessments for each annual update. But unfortunately, as a complete record of what was assessed was not kept, this is difficult to do in certain cases, as the taxonomy for some groups has changed considerably since 1996. The task has been completed for the mammals, and all amphibians and birds were completely assessed for the 2004 update of the Red List. However, for all the other taxonomic groups, the numbers evaluated are an under-estimate because the Least Concern assessments have not yet been recorded. To exacerbate matters, for some groups, particularly the plants, Least Concern assessments are seldom submitted to the Red List office. This will remain a work in progress until such time as each taxonomic group is completely assessed.

Inclusion of Undescribed Species

The *IUCN Red List* includes assessments for undescribed species under certain special circumstances (namely, that taxonomists are agreed that these are in fact new undescribed species, that their distributions are known, that voucher specimens are deposited in Museums or Herbaria, and most importantly that there is a direct conservation benefit to the listing). There are 143 undescribed species on the 2004 *IUCN Red List* (83 of which are threatened) and these are all effectively treated in this analysis as 'described species'.

Assessing the Significance of Threat Levels per Order and Family of Mammals, Birds and Amphibians

The percentage of threatened species was calculated for each order and family of mammals, birds and amphibians, and compared with the respective average across all species in each of those classes. The significance (or lack thereof) of the difference between the percentage of threat observed in an order or family in relation to the average value in the respective class was assessed using a binomial one-tailed test (p given by the fraction of threatened species in the class). Binomial one-tailed tests were also used to produce the bands of significance level in Figures 2.3 to 2.5.

Appendix 2c. Extinction

IUCN has not yet agreed criteria for determining whether or not Critically Endangered species are 'Possibly Extinct'. The information and analyses in Section 3 for Possibly Extinct birds and amphibians are based on somewhat different approaches.

BirdLife International has developed a framework for classifying Critically Endangered species as 'Possibly Extinct'. This framework has been tested on the 50 or so bird species to which this tag might conceivably apply i.e., those that have not been recorded for a long time, or those whose dwindling populations may have finally disappeared. The framework allows the user to assign such species to one of the following three categories:

CR: species which are likely to be extant, and for which any lack of records probably does not reflect a genuine extinction.

CR(PE): species which are likely to be extinct, but for which there is a small chance that they may still be extant, hence they should not be listed as EX until local or unconfirmed reports have been discounted, and adequate surveys have failed to find the species.

EX: species for which there is no reasonable doubt that the last individual has died (and for which it is not advocated that conservation effort is spent searching for these species).

To determine which category to assign a threatened species, scientists at BirdLife International examined: (1) evidence pertaining to the timing of the last confirmed records; (2) any subsequent unconfirmed records or local reports; (3) the strength of threatening processes currently and historically operating; (4) the adequacy of fieldwork relative to the (presumed) ease of detection of the species; and (5) the extent and quality of remaining suitable habitat (where 'suitable' incorporates the absence of introduced predators, pathogens, etc.).

BirdLife International classified species as Possibly Extinct if, on balance, the evidence that they may be extinct outweighs any evidence that they may be still extant (although the latter remains a slim possibility, so they are not yet classified as Extinct).

Such evidence for extinction may include a combination of the following factors:

a).　There have been no confirmed records for a long time (it is difficult to be more prescriptive: the duration will depend on the intensity of fieldwork and the ease of detection).

b).　For species with recent last records, the decline has been well documented.

c).　There are severe threatening processes operating (e.g., extensive habitat loss, introduction of alien predators, intensive hunting).

d).　The species has attributes known to predispose it to extinction, e.g., it was probably naturally rare and/or had a tiny range (as evidenced by paucity of specimens relative to collecting effort), or flightless, etc. In some cases, allospecies or congeners may have gone extinct through similar threatening processes.

e).　Surveys would have detected it (good/recent surveys have been adequate; species is unlikely to be overlooked).

Evidence that the species may remain extant may include a combination of the following factors:

a).　The lack of records is best explained by inadequate fieldwork (any surveys have been insufficiently intensive/extensive, or inappropriately timed; or the species' range is inaccessible, remote, unsafe or inadequately known).

b).　The lack of records is best explained by the fact that the species is difficult to detect (low density, cryptic, inconspicuous, nocturnal, nomadic, silent or call unknown, identification difficult).

c).　There have been reasonably convincing local reports or unconfirmed sightings.

d).　Suitable habitat (free of introduced predators and pathogens if relevant) remains within the species' known range. In some cases, allospecies or congeners may survive despite similar threatening processes.

The balance of the evidence for and against extinction then allows the species to be placed on a continuum from high to low confidence of extinction, on a spectrum from EX to CR(PE) to CR. The position of a species on this continuum will be influenced by the time since the last confirmed record. For species with recently confirmed records to be placed at the EX end of the spectrum, there needs to be greater confidence in the extinction (i.e., greater confidence in the adequacy of surveys, the absence or inadequacy of local/unconfirmed records, the greater understanding and severity of threatening processes, and the greater documentation of, and confidence in, observed population declines). Deciding the strength of evidence for and against extinction is necessarily subjective. However, this framework helps to make these judgements as objective as possible, by obliging the user to set out the evidence, and to weigh this against the time since the last confirmed record.

This approach to defining 'Possibly Extinct' species identifies those species for which extinction is likely. For amphibians, the phenomenon of rapid population declines is a new one, and the extent to which it tends to result in complete extinction is still not clear. This lack of information makes it difficult to judge the likelihood that extinction has occurred. The Global Amphibian Assessment adopted a more precautionary approach in identifying Possibly Extinct amphibians. The term was applied to all CR species that can no longer be found, and which appear to have declined dramatically, but which do not qualify for EX because of lack of survey effort. Hence the large number of CR(PE) amphibians includes species that are conceivably extinct as well as those that are likely to be extinct.

Appendix 2d. Trends

Methods for calculating Red List Indices

The method for calculating Red List Indices (RLIs) has been developed through the Red List Programme and is published in detail in Butchart *et al.* (in press a and b). RLIs are calculated from the number of species in each IUCN Red List Category in each assessment, and the number of species changing categories as a result of genuine improvement or deterioration in status. Specifically: (1) For species assessed in two consecutive assessments, the total number of species in each Red List Category in the earlier assessment (excluding Data Deficient, Extinct and Possibly Extinct) are multiplied by a category weight (see below), and these are summed to give a total score for the assessment. (2) Over the time period between assessments the net number of genuine changes (losses and gains) in each category is calculated, multiplied by the category weight and summed to give the % change in the total score. (3) The value of the index is set to 100 in the first year of assessment (i.e., 1988 for birds, 1980 for amphibians), and calculated for subsequent assessments by multiplying the previous index value by the % change in the score for the previous time period.

Weighting Categories: 'Equal Steps' Versus 'Extinction Risk' Approaches

There are a number of potential ways to assign weights to IUCN Red List Categories. We examined two: an 'equal steps' approach and an 'extinction risk' approach. In the equal steps approach the weights range from 0 for Least Concern, 1 for Near Threatened, 2 for Vulnerable, etc. to reflect the ordinal ranks of the categories, whereby each step from Least Concern towards Extinct indicates that at least

one measure of extinction risk has become worse. This approach has the advantage of being simple, and the trends in the resulting index are driven by a relatively large number of species (which produces a more robust and representative index). This is because a species moving from Least Concern to Near Threatened contributes just as much to the changing score as a Critically Endangered species going Extinct, and the numbers of species in each category (and moving in and out of each category) increases disproportionately from Critically Endangered to Least Concern. The main disadvantage is that the weights merely reflect the linear hierarchy of categories. However, the steps between lower categories (e.g., Near Threatened to Vulnerable) translate to smaller increases in extinction risk than steps between higher categories (e.g., Endangered to Critically Endangered). In recognition of this, in the extinction risk approach the weights are based on the relative extinction risk associated with each category, ranging from 0.0005 for Near Threatened and 0.005 for Vulnerable to 1.0 for Extinct.

Comparison of the Two Different Approaches

The most important difference between the equal steps versus the extinction risk approaches is the effect of status changes in less threatened or non-threatened species. With the equal steps approach, the index is heavily influenced by movements of species among the lower categories, such as Near Threatened and Vulnerable. With the extinction risk approach, movements of species in and out of Critically Endangered largely influence the RLI. For example, if a Vulnerable species improves in status and becomes Near Threatened, and at the same time, a Critically Endangered species goes extinct, the RLI based on equal steps weights registers no change, but the index based on extinction risk weights shows a substantial decrease. Downlisting of a Vulnerable species to Near Threatened might represent a very substantial population increase, whereas Extinction of a Critically Endangered species might represent the loss of very few individuals. The latter is arguably more significant in terms of genetic diversity, but the former might be more important as an indicator of wider biodiversity trends. Thus, the extinction risk weights emphasize the loss of biodiversity owing to imminent or potential extinctions of species, whereas the equal steps weights allow the index to capture large changes in the populations of less threatened species.

For the RLI for all species in a taxonomic group and for subsets of species (e.g., in particular realms or ecosystems), we used the equal steps approach. This was because for some disaggregated indices, there were few species in the higher threat categories (those effectively driving trends in the index weighted by extinction risk). For birds, for example, only

23% of all genuine status changes (58 species in total) involved moves in or out of the highest threat categories. However, for examining trends in the species closest to extinction, we used the extinction risk approach.

Calculating Error Bars

We calculated, using the following method, the possible range of error associated with the latest (2004) RLI value for birds owing to time-lags before genuine status changes are detected. We estimated how many such undetected category changes there may be for 2000–2004 using the 1994–2000 data (information gathering has improved considerably in recent years, so comparisons with time-lags for the 1988–1994 period are not meaningful). In total, 128 genuine changes for 1994–2000 were identified in 2000, and an additional 17 (13.3%) were identified in the subsequent four years. This suggests that an additional six category changes (13.3% of 45 genuine status changes identified in 2004) may be belatedly detected for 2000–2004. We randomly selected six species from the 9,453 species that did not undergo category changes from 2000 to 2004. We ran 10,000 simulations of six species moving to categories of higher extinction risk, with probabilities for each number of category steps set by the distribution of category changes for 35 species that were uplisted to higher categories of extinction risk in 2004. The maximum value for P (proportional genuine change) from these simulations gave the lower error bar for the 2004 RLI value. Similarly, we ran 10,000 simulations of six species moving to categories of lower extinction risk (with probabilities for each number of category steps set by the distribution of category changes for 10 species downlisted to lower categories in 2004), and took the minimum value for P to give the upper error bar (see Butchart *et al.* in press a for further details).

Data Sources

The data for birds are derived from four assessments (Collar and Andrew 1988, Collar *et al.* 1994, BirdLife International 2000, 2004a; also published in Baillie and Groombridge 1996, Hilton-Taylor 2000 and IUCN 2004). For amphibians, the 2004 data come from the Global Amphibian Assessment (IUCN, Conservation International and NatureServe 2004; IUCN 2004). An IUCN Red List Category for each amphibian species in 1980 was retrospectively assigned by considering the present category and information on the spread of disease, habitat degradation and loss, the introduction of alien species and knowledge of population trends. A conservative approach was adopted, and category changes were only recorded as having taken place when the evidence was considered to be strong. In cases of significant

uncertainty, it was assumed that no change in category had occurred. Given the uncertainty over these retrospectively assigned categories, the RLI for amphibians is represented with a dotted line in Figures 4.6–4.10.

Appendix 2e. Geography of the Red List

Extent of Occurrence

Extent of occurrence is defined as the area contained within the shortest continuous imaginary boundary that can be drawn to encompass all the known, inferred or projected sites of present occurrence of a taxon, excluding cases of vagrancy. This measure may exclude discontinuities or disjunctions within the overall distributions of taxa (e.g., large areas of obviously unsuitable habitat). Extent of occurrence can often be measured by a minimum convex polygon (the smallest polygon in which no internal angle exceeds 180 degrees and which contains all the sites of occurrence) (taken from IUCN 2001, p. 11).

Endemic Species

The term 'endemic species' always requires a qualifier as to where the species is endemic to (e.g., a species endemic to Angola is one that occurs in Angola and nowhere else). As such, endemic species can be very widespread (e.g., a species endemic to the Western Hemisphere may occur from northern Canada to southern Argentina) or very restricted in range (e.g., the range of a terrestrial species endemic to São Tomé and Principe is no larger than 1,200 sq. km).

Species Occurrence in Biogeographic Realms

The occurrence of species in biogeographic realms was determined by overlaying species by species Extent of occurrence (EOO) (see above; IUCN 2001) maps onto the biogeographic realm classification of Olson *et al.* (2001), except for data on total bird species richness, which were provided by J. Lamoreux (unpublished data).

Species Occurrence in Biomes

The occurrence of species in biomes was determined by overlaying species by species EOO polygons onto the biome classification of Olson *et al.* (2001). We considered a species as occurring in a biome if >5% of its EOO overlapped that biome (to minimize commission errors of including species within biomes where they do not occur) or if the species EOO occupied >5% of the biome (whichever is smaller) and considered a species endemic to a biome if >95% of its EOO overlapped that biome (to minimize omission errors in detecting biome-endemic species). Data on Old World bird species richness and endemism were provided by J. Lamoreux (unpublished data).

Species Richness and Threatened Species Richness Maps

In some maps (Figures 5.4, 5.9 and 5.10), the mammal data exclude marine species (pinnipeds, cetaceans, sirenians and a few others). Bird polygons include only breeding ranges of species (but including marine species). Turtles include only freshwater species. Only mammals, birds and amphibians have been globally comprehensively assessed, but turtles are relatively well assessed compared to many other taxonomic groups and are included here for comparative purposes. In all cases, introduced and extinct parts of the range are excluded. Maps are based only on current range, not historical ranges. The richness maps are shown at a half-degree cell, which admittedly does not take into account the species-area relationship.

Centres of Endemism

Standardization is required in order to compare the levels of endemism of different regions. Centres of endemism have traditionally been identified through the overlap of restricted-range species, found using threshold approaches which consider only species with distributions smaller than a given percentile or area (Hall and Moreau 1962). This technique was the first to be applied across an entire higher taxon (Stattersfield *et al.* 1998). While it faces the problem in that the choice of a given threshold is arbitrary (Peterson and Watson 1998), the choice of weighting for alternative methods, such as summing the reciprocals of the range sizes for all species within a given area, is also arbitrary (Williams 1998).

Localities

A locality (Section 5.4) is synonymous with site, and can broadly be defined as having a definable boundary within which the character of habitats, biological communities, and/or management issues have more in common with each other than they do with those in adjacent areas.

Appendix 2f. Threats

Methods for Coding and Analysing the Causes of Threat

In recent years, the threats faced by species that contribute to their IUCN Red List status have been documented by coding the relevant factors according to the IUCN Major Threats Authority File (see http://www.iucnredlist.org/info/major_threats.html, or download the file from http://www.iucn.org/themes/ssc/sis/authority.htm). Threats are coded to provide different levels of details if this information is available: for example, the level 1 coding of

"Habitat destruction and degradation" may be further coded to indicate the driving force leading to such destruction, e.g. "Agriculture", the type of agriculture, e.g. "Crops" and the scale of this threat, e.g. "Agro-industry farming". Thus, the process of coding the threats for each species is complex, and it is far from complete, so constraining the analyses that can be currently performed. In the 2004 *IUCN Red List*, all threatened and Near Threatened bird species and all amphibian species are fully coded for their threats, and most threatened mammal species have also been coded. Thus, in Section 6 "The Many Causes of Threat", it was only possible to perform meaningful threat analyses for threatened birds, mammals and amphibians.

For birds, the timing, scope and severity of the threats is also recorded and these are combined together to provide an indication of the impact of the threat (High, Medium, Low, No/negligible, Past; see below for more details), but this distinction has not yet been made for mammals and amphibians. For comparative purposes, all level 1 threats have been analysed covering all threatened (CR, EN and VU) species and shown according to the % affected. For amphibians, all threats recorded were included, while for birds only those threats identified as having a High, Medium or Low impact were used. Level 1 threats were grouped according to the hierarchy of the Threats Authority File apart from "Disease" which has been shown separately covering both native and alien invasive diseases because of the importance of this threat to amphibian species and because of the difficulty of distinguishing between these two types. In some analyses, all invasive species have also been lumped covering those that affect species directly (e.g., predators which eat the species) and those that affect species indirectly (e.g., herbivores which cause habitat loss).

Threat Impact

For each threat, BirdLife assigns the timing (i.e., past, continuing or future), the scope (i.e., the proportion of the total population affected) and the severity (the overall declines caused by the threat) an "impact score" (0–3). The overall impact of the threat is determined by adding these separate impact scores (see table below).

Thus all threats are recorded without any initial (unrecorded) pre-judgement, but only those with a High/Medium/Low/Unknown impact are included as relevant in relation to the current IUCN Red List status (i.e., excluding those with Negligible impact or Past impact where the threat is unlikely to return).

Table A2f.1

Summary of the BirdLife Method for Scoring Threats

Timing and impact score

DESCRIPTION	IMPACT SCORE
Only in the **past** (and unlikely to return)	special case 1 (see *Calculating Overall Impact*)
Only in the **past** (no direct affect but limiting)	0
Now suspended (could come back in the **long** term)	1
Now suspended (could come back in the **short** term)	2
Continuing	3
Only in the **future** (could happen in the **short** term)	2
Only in the **future** (could happen in the **long** term)	1
Unknown	special case 2 (see *Calculating Overall Impact*)

Scope and impact score

DESCRIPTION	IMPACT SCORE
Affects the **whole** (>90%) population	3
Affects the **majority** (50–90%) of the population	2
Affects the **minority** (<50%) of the population	1
Affects a negligible proportion of the population	0
Unknown	special case 2 (see *Calculating Overall Impact*)

Severity and impact scores

DESCRIPTION	IMPACT SCORE
Causing or likely to cause **very rapid declines** (>30% over 10 years or three generations)	3
Causing or likely to cause **rapid declines** (20-30% over 10 years or three generations)	2
Causing or likely to cause relatively **slow, but significant, declines** (<20% over 10 years or three generations)	1
Causing or likely to cause **fluctuations**	1
Causing or likely to cause negligible declines	0
No decline	0
Unknown	special case 2

Calculating Overall Impact

The overall impact of the threat is calculated by adding the individual scores for **Timing**, **Scope** and **Severity** as follows:

High impact	score	8,9	**Past** impact	special case 1, i.e. if timing = "Only in the **past** (and unlikely to return)" regardless of impact scores for Scope and Severity
Medium impact	score	6,7		
Low impact	score	3,4,5		
No/negligible impact	score	0,1,2	**Unknown**	special case 2, i.e. if "**unknown**" for Timing, Scope or Severity

Appendix 2g. The Social and Economic Context of the Red List

Current Population Density (Section 7.2.1)

LandScan's human population density modelled for 2002 was used as the measure of current human population density. This dataset gives population density modelled at 1km^2 resolution, which was then averaged to give a value within the same quarter-degree grid cell as the species data so that the variables could be compared. The data was also split into three categories (**Low**: 0 to 10 people per 1km^2, **Moderate**: 10 to 100 people per 1km^2, **High**: 100 or more people per 1km^2). The number of threatened species was calculated by totalling the number of threatened mammals, birds and amphibians whose distributions overlap each quarter-degree grid cell across the world. This total was then divided into three categories (**Low**: No threatened species, **Moderate**: 1 to 10 species, **High**: 11 or more species).

Population Growth (Section 7.2.2)

Population growth was divided into two categories (**Low**: less than 1.5% and **High**: greater than 1.5%). The total number of threatened mammals, birds and amphibians was used as the measure of the threatened status of species in each country. This value is obviously biased towards countries with large land areas and high species diversity. A simple correction for land area however, is not appropriate as the number of species per unit area varies with latitude (see Figure 5.2.1 in Section 5). An alternative measure is the number of species that are threatened compared to the overall diversity in a country (see Section 5). This measure enables a comparison between countries, but does not give an indication of the proportion of the global total of threatened species that each country has responsibility for conserving. Hence for this analysis the total number of threatened mammals, birds and amphibians was used to identify those countries which have a greater share of the responsibility for conserving the world's threatened species, regardless of their land area or total species diversity. This total was divided into four categories (**Low**: 0 to 10 species, **Moderately-Low**: 11 to 30 species, **Moderately-High**: 31 to 100 species, **High**: more than 100 species).

Economic Factors (Section 7.3)

In this analysis the Gross National Income (GNI) per capita for each country in 2003 was divided in to two categories (**Low income**: $3,035 or less, and **High income**: $3,036 or more) using pre-defined criteria (following the World Bank Atlas method, World Bank 2004). All those countries for which GNI data were available were used in the analysis. The threatened species data used were the same as for the analysis of population growth shown in Figure 7.2, divided in to the same four categories.

Appendix 2h. Conservation Responses

Protected Area Gap Analysis

For a detailed description of the methods and data in Table 8.2, see Rodrigues *et al.* (2004). Data as in Rodrigues *et al.* (2004) for turtles (Iverson *et al.* 2003) and mammals (compiled by the IUCN/SSC Global Mammal Assessment), but was updated for birds (corresponding now to the *State of the World's Birds 2004* assessment; BirdLife International 2004a) and for amphibians (corresponding to the finalized data obtained from the Global Amphibian Assessment; IUCN, Conservation International and NatureServe 2004). Protected area data was also updated and corresponds now to the *2004 World Database on Protected Areas* (WDPA Consortium 2004).

Relationship between Occurrence in Protected Areas and Population Trends of Amphibians and Threatened Birds

In Table 8.3, species of unknown/unset/fluctuating trends ($n = 1,571$ for amphibians; $n = 84$ for threatened birds) were excluded, while increasing species ($n = 28$ for amphibians, $n = 39$ for threatened birds) were lumped with stable. In all cases, significantly higher percentages of gap species were found to be decreasing than would be expected by chance ($p < 0.001$, obtained through bootstrap, 1,000 replicates), while the tendency is for non-gap species to have higher percentages of stable or increasing species ($p < 0.001$).

Appendix 3. Summary Data

Appendix 3a.

Changes in total numbers of threatened species (CR, EN and VU) by major taxonomic group since 1996 (1998 for plants)

	Number of threatened species		
	1996/98	2000	2004
Vertebrates			
Mammals	1,096	1,130	1,101
Birds	1,107	1,183	1,213
Amphibians	124	146	1,856
Reptiles	253	296	304
Fishes	734	752	800
Subtotal	**3,314**	**3,507**	**5,274**
Invertebrates			
Insects	537	555	559
Molluscs	920	938	974
Crustaceans	407	408	429
Other inverts	27	27	30
Subtotal	**1,891**	**1,928**	**1,992**
Plants			
Mosses	0	80	80
Ferns and allies	0	0	140
Gymnosperms	142	141	305
Dicotyledons	4,929	5,099	7,025
Monocotyledons	257	291	771
Subtotal	**5,328**	**5,611**	**8,321**
Others			
Lichens	0	0	2
Subtotal	**0**	**0**	**2**
Total	**10,533**	**11,046**	**15,587**

Appendix 3b.

Changes in numbers of species in each threatened category (CR, EN and VU) by major taxonomic group since 1996 (1998 for plants)

Taxonomic Group	CR 1996/98	CR 2000	CR 2004	EN 1996/98	EN 2000	EN 2004	VU 1996/98	VU 2000	VU 2004
Vertebrates									
Mammals	169	180	162	315	340	352	612	610	587
Birds	168	182	179	235	321	345	704	680	688
Amphibians	18	25	427	31	38	761	75	83	668
Reptiles	41	56	64	59	74	79	153	161	161
Fishes	157	156	171	134	144	160	443	452	470
Subtotal	**553**	**599**	**1,003**	**774**	**917**	**1,697**	**1,987**	**1,986**	**2,574**
Invertebrates									
Insects	44	45	47	116	118	120	377	392	392
Molluscs	257	222	265	212	237	221	451	479	488
Crustaceans	54	56	56	73	72	79	280	280	294
Other inverts	3	3	5	4	4	3	20	20	22
Subtotal	**358**	**326**	**373**	**405**	**431**	**423**	**1,128**	**1,171**	**1,196**
Plants									
Mosses	0	22	22	0	32	32	0	26	26
Ferns and allies	0	0	32	0	0	38	0	0	70
Gymnosperms	18	17	64	38	41	83	86	83	158
Dicotyledons	823	896	1,228	1,089	1,110	1,825	3,017	3,093	3,972
Monocotyledons	68	79	144	70	83	261	119	129	366
Subtotal	**909**	**1,014**	**1,490**	**1,197**	**1,266**	**2,239**	**3,222**	**3,331**	**4,592**
Total	**1,820**	**1,939**	**2,866**	**2,376**	**2,614**	**4,359**	**6,337**	**6,488**	**8,362**

Appendix 3c.

Mammal orders more or less threatened than expected, relative to the average for mammals as a whole

Order	Number of species	Number threatened species	% threatened species	p-value	p-value class
Artiodactyla	214	81	37.850	0.0000	<0.001
Carnivora	281	84	29.893	0.0183	<0.05
Cetacea	81	14	17.284	0.0871	>0.05
Chiroptera	1,023	259	25.318	0.2281	>0.05
Dasyuromorphia	68	17	25.000	0.4909	>0.05
Dermoptera	2	1	50.000	0.4266	>0.05
Didelphimorphia	66	21	31.818	0.1015	>0.05
Diprotodontia	132	40	30.303	0.0675	>0.05
Hyracoidea	7	3	42.857	0.2287	>0.05
Insectivora	433	129	29.792	0.0051	<0.01
Lagomorpha	82	18	21.951	0.3662	>0.05
Macroscelidea	15	4	26.667	0.5123	>0.05
Microbiotheria	1	1	100.000	0.2427	>0.05
Monotremata	3	1	33.333	0.5657	>0.05
Notoryctemorphia	2	2	100.000	0.0589	>0.05
Paucituberculata	5	1	20.000	0.6481	>0.05
Peramelemorphia	21	7	33.333	0.2312	>0.05
Perissodactyla	17	14	82.353	0.0000	<0.001
Pholidota	7	0	0.000	0.1428	>0.05
Primates	296	114	38.514	0.0000	<0.001
Proboscidea	2	2	100.000	0.0589	>0.05
Rodentia	2,041	346	16.952	0.0000	<0.001
Scandentia	19	6	31.579	0.3051	>0.05
Sirenia	5	5	100.000	0.0008	<0.001
Tubulidentata	1	0	0.000	0.7573	>0.05
Xenarthra	29	8	27.586	0.4071	>0.05

Appendix 3d.

Mammal families more or less threatened than expected, relative to the average for mammals as a whole

Family	Number of species	Number threatened species	% threatened species	p-value	p-value class
Abrocomidae	3	1	33.333	0.5657	>0.05
Acrobatidae	2	0	0.000	0.5734	>0.05
Agoutidae	2	0	0.000	0.5734	>0.05
Ailuridae	1	1	100.000	0.2427	>0.05
Anomaluridae	7	0	0.000	0.1428	>0.05
Antilocapridae	1	0	0.000	0.7573	>0.05
Aotidae	7	2	28.571	0.5368	>0.05
Aplodontidae	1	0	0.000	0.7573	>0.05
Atelidae	20	8	40.000	0.0883	>0.05
Balaenidae	4	2	50.000	0.2495	>0.05
Balaenopteridae	7	4	57.143	0.0640	>0.05
Bathyergidae	15	1	6.667	0.0897	>0.05
Bovidae	135	58	42.963	0.0000	<0.001
Bradypodidae	3	1	33.333	0.5657	>0.05
Burramyidae	5	1	20.000	0.6481	>0.05
Caenolestidae	5	1	20.000	0.6481	>0.05
Callitrichidae	40	10	25.000	0.5180	>0.05
Camelidae	3	1	33.333	0.5657	>0.05
Canidae	36	9	25.000	0.5234	>0.05
Capromyidae	20	16	80.000	0.0000	<0.001
Castoridae	2	0	0.000	0.5734	>0.05
Caviidae	14	0	0.000	0.0204	<0.05
Cebidae	12	4	33.333	0.3288	>0.05
Cercopithecidae	96	44	45.833	0.0000	<0.001
Cervidae	44	12	27.273	0.3762	>0.05
Cheirogaleidae	9	4	44.444	0.1524	>0.05
Chinchillidae	6	2	33.333	0.4487	>0.05
Chrysochloridae	18	11	61.111	0.0010	<0.001
Craseonycteridae	1	1	100.000	0.2427	>0.05
Cryptoproctidae	1	1	100.000	0.2427	>0.05
Ctenodactylidae	5	0	0.000	0.2490	>0.05
Ctenomyidae	38	1	2.632	0.0003	<0.001
Cynocephalidae	2	1	50.000	0.4266	>0.05
Dasypodidae	20	6	30.000	0.3536	>0.05
Dasyproctidae	13	3	23.077	0.6086	>0.05
Dasyuridae	66	15	22.727	0.4503	>0.05
Daubentoniidae	1	1	100.000	0.2427	>0.05

Family	Number of species	Number threatened species	% threatened species	p-value	p-value class
Delphinidae	35	1	2.857	0.0007	<0.001
Didelphidae	66	21	31.818	0.1015	>0.05
Dinomyidae	1	1	100.000	0.2427	>0.05
Dipodidae	51	7	13.725	0.0494	<0.05
Dugongidae	2	2	100.000	0.0589	>0.05
Echimyidae	76	9	11.842	0.0055	<0.01
Elephantidae	2	2	100.000	0.0589	>0.05
Emballonuridae	48	13	27.083	0.3776	>0.05
Equidae	8	6	75.000	0.0036	<0.01
Erethizontidae	12	2	16.667	0.4135	>0.05
Erinaceidae	22	6	27.273	0.4513	>0.05
Eschrichtiidae	1	0	0.000	0.7573	>0.05
Felidae	36	17	47.222	0.0023	<0.01
Furipteridae	2	1	50.000	0.4266	>0.05
Galagonidae	15	1	6.667	0.0897	>0.05
Geomyidae	36	5	13.889	0.0994	>0.05
Giraffidae	2	0	0.000	0.5734	>0.05
Heptaxodontidae	1	1	100.000	0.2427	>0.05
Herpestidae	39	8	20.513	0.3701	>0.05
Heteromyidae	57	6	10.526	0.0077	<0.01
Hippopotamidae	4	3	75.000	0.0468	<0.05
Hipposideridae	77	21	27.273	0.3092	>0.05
Hominidae	4	4	100.000	0.0035	<0.01
Hyaenidae	4	0	0.000	0.3288	>0.05
Hydrochaeridae	1	0	0.000	0.7573	>0.05
Hylobatidae	12	7	58.333	0.0121	<0.05
Hystricidae	11	1	9.091	0.2125	>0.05
Indridae	6	5	83.333	0.0040	<0.01
Iniidae	1	1	100.000	0.2427	>0.05
Kogiidae	2	0	0.000	0.5734	>0.05
Lemuridae	10	8	80.000	0.0003	<0.001
Leporidae	54	12	22.222	0.4341	>0.05
Lipotidae	1	1	100.000	0.2427	>0.05
Loridae	9	2	22.222	0.6210	>0.05
Macropodidae	60	20	33.333	0.0720	>0.05
Macroscelididae	15	4	26.667	0.5123	>0.05
Manidae	7	0	0.000	0.1428	>0.05
Megadermatidae	5	1	20.000	0.6481	>0.05
Megaladapidae	7	2	28.571	0.5368	>0.05
Megalonychidae	2	0	0.000	0.5734	>0.05

Family	Number of species	Number threatened species	% threatened species	p-value	p-value class
Microbiotheriidae	1	1	100.000	0.2427	>0.05
Molossidae	90	17	18.889	0.1417	>0.05
Monodontidae	2	1	50.000	0.4266	>0.05
Mormoopidae	8	1	12.500	0.3854	>0.05
Moschidae	4	1	25.000	0.6712	>0.05
Muridae	1,352	247	18.269	0.0000	<0.001
Mustelidae	66	15	22.727	0.4503	>0.05
Myocastoridae	1	0	0.000	0.7573	>0.05
Myoxidae	29	8	27.586	0.4071	>0.05
Myrmecobiidae	1	1	100.000	0.2427	>0.05
Myrmecophagidae	4	1	25.000	0.6712	>0.05
Mystacinidae	2	2	100.000	0.0589	>0.05
Myzopodidae	1	1	100.000	0.2427	>0.05
Nandiniidae	1	0	0.000	0.7573	>0.05
Natalidae	5	1	20.000	0.6481	>0.05
Nesophontidae	4	4	100.000	0.0035	<0.01
Noctilionidae	2	0	0.000	0.5734	>0.05
Notoryctidae	2	2	100.000	0.0589	>0.05
Nycteridae	16	2	12.500	0.2158	>0.05
Ochotonidae	28	6	21.429	0.4633	>0.05
Octodontidae	10	2	20.000	0.5475	>0.05
Odobenidae	1	0	0.000	0.7573	>0.05
Ornithorhynchidae	1	0	0.000	0.7573	>0.05
Orycteropodidae	1	0	0.000	0.7573	>0.05
Otariidae	16	8	50.000	0.0228	<0.05
Pedetidae	1	0	0.000	0.7573	>0.05
Peramelidae	10	7	70.000	0.0029	<0.01
Peroryctidae	11	0	0.000	0.0470	<0.05
Petauridae	11	5	45.455	0.1033	>0.05
Petromuridae	1	0	0.000	0.7573	>0.05
Phalangeridae	21	4	19.048	0.3969	>0.05
Phascolarctidae	1	0	0.000	0.7573	>0.05
Phocidae	19	4	21.053	0.4951	>0.05
Phocoenidae	6	2	33.333	0.4487	>0.05
Phyllostomidae	149	30	20.134	0.1386	>0.05
Physeteridae	1	1	100.000	0.2427	>0.05
Pitheciidae	39	10	25.641	0.4821	>0.05
Platanistidae	1	1	100.000	0.2427	>0.05
Pongidae	2	2	100.000	0.0589	>0.05
Pontoporiidae	1	0	0.000	0.7573	>0.05

Family	Number of species	Number threatened species	% threatened species	p-value	p-value class
Phyllostomidae	149	30	20.134	0.1386	>0.05
Physeteridae	1	1	100.000	0.2427	>0.05
Pitheciidae	39	10	25.641	0.4821	>0.05
Platanistidae	1	1	100.000	0.2427	>0.05
Pongidae	2	2	100.000	0.0589	>0.05
Pontoporiidae	1	0	0.000	0.7573	>0.05
Potoroidae	11	6	54.545	0.0299	<0.05
Procaviidae	7	3	42.857	0.2287	>0.05
Procyonidae	19	8	42.105	0.0667	>0.05
Pseudocheiridae	17	3	17.647	0.3792	>0.05
Pteropodidae	171	69	40.351	0.0000	<0.001
Rhinocerotidae	5	4	80.000	0.0140	<0.05
Rhinolophidae	72	17	23.611	0.5120	>0.05
Rhinopomatidae	4	1	25.000	0.6712	>0.05
Sciuridae	273	33	12.088	0.0000	<0.001
Solenodontidae	3	3	100.000	0.0143	<0.05
Soricidae	320	85	26.563	0.1861	>0.05
Suidae	14	5	35.714	0.2375	>0.05
Tachyglossidae	2	1	50.000	0.4266	>0.05
Talpidae	42	10	23.810	0.5558	>0.05
Tapiridae	4	4	100.000	0.0035	<0.01
Tarsiidae	7	0	0.000	0.1428	>0.05
Tarsipedidae	1	0	0.000	0.7573	>0.05
Tayassuidae	3	1	33.333	0.5657	>0.05
Tenrecidae	24	10	41.667	0.0456	<0.05
Thryonomyidae	2	0	0.000	0.5734	>0.05
Thylacinidae	1	1	100.000	0.2427	>0.05
Thyropteridae	3	1	33.333	0.5657	>0.05
Tragulidae	4	0	0.000	0.3288	>0.05
Trichechidae	3	3	100.000	0.0143	<0.05
Tupaiidae	19	6	31.579	0.3051	>0.05
Ursidae	8	4	50.000	0.1040	>0.05
Vespertilionidae	367	80	21.798	0.1477	>0.05
Viverridae	34	9	26.471	0.4471	>0.05
Vombatidae	3	1	33.333	0.5657	>0.05
Ziphiidae	19	0	0.000	0.0051	<0.01

Appendix 3e.

Order	Number of species	Number threatened species	% threatened species	*p*-value	*p*-value class
Bird orders more or less threatened than expected, relative to the average for birds as a whole					
Anseriformes	168	32	19.047619	0.0291	< 0.05
Apodiformes	439	36	8.20045558	0.0003	<0.001
Apterygiformes	4	4	100	0.0003	<0.001
Caprimulgiformes	121	8	6.61157025	0.0122	< 0.05
Casuariiformes	361	45	12.465374	0.3002	> 0.05
Ciconiiformes	131	28	21.3740458	0.0093	< 0.01
Coliformes	6	0	0	0.4168	> 0.05
Columbiformes	336	75	22.3214286	0.0000	<0.001
Coraciiformes	221	27	12.2171946	0.3186	> 0.05
Cuculiformes	164	13	7.92682927	0.0178	< 0.05
Falconiformes	312	45	14.4230769	0.3544	> 0.05
Galliformes	287	78	27.1777003	0.0000	<0.001
Gaviiformes	5	0	0	0.4822	> 0.05
Gruiformes	227	76	33.4801762	0.0000	<0.001
Passeriformes	5,829	618	10.6021616	0.0000	<0.001
Pelecaniformes	65	17	26.1538462	0.0051	< 0.01
Piciformes	407	15	3.68550369	0.0000	<0.001
Podicipediformes	22	7	31.8181818	0.0225	< 0.05
Procellariiformes	131	62	47.3282443	0.0000	<0.001
Psittaciformes	374	109	29.144385	0.0000	<0.001
Rheiformes	2	0	0	0.7470	> 0.05
Sphenisciformes	17	10	58.8235294	0.0000	<0.001
Strigiformes	198	32	16.1616162	0.1679	> 0.05
Struthioniformes	1	0	0	0.8643	> 0.05
Tinamiformes	49	8	16.3265306	0.3452	> 0.05
Trogoniformes	40	1	2.5	0.0213	< 0.05

Appendix 3f.

Bird families more or less threatened than expected, relative to the average for birds as a whole

Family	Number of species	Number threatened species	% threatened species	p-value	p-value class
Acanthisittidae	4	2	50	0.0915	> 0.05
Accipitridae	240	37	15.41666667	0.2265	> 0.05
Aegithalidae	8	0	0	0.3113	> 0.05
Aegothelidae	9	1	11.11111111	0.6494	> 0.05
Alaudidae	91	8	8.791208791	0.1154	> 0.05
Alcedinidae	95	12	12.63157895	0.4675	> 0.05
Alcidae	24	6	25	0.0967	> 0.05
Anatidae	165	32	19.39393939	0.0231	< 0.05
Anhimidae	3	0	0	0.6456	> 0.05
Anhingidae	4	0	0	0.5580	> 0.05
Apodidae	102	6	5.882352941	0.0109	< 0.05
Apterygidae	4	4	100	0.0003	<0.001
Aramidae	1	0	0	0.8643	> 0.05
Ardeidae	67	12	17.91044776	0.1919	> 0.05
Artamidae	11	0	0	0.2010	> 0.05
Atrichornithidae	2	1	50	0.2530	> 0.05
Balaenicipitidae	1	1	100	0.1357	> 0.05
Bombycillidae	8	0	0	0.3113	> 0.05
Bucconidae	33	0	0	0.0081	< 0.01
Bucerotidae	56	9	16.07142857	0.3475	> 0.05
Burhinidae	9	0	0	0.2691	> 0.05
Callaeidae	3	2	66.66666667	0.0503	> 0.05
Campephagidae	85	5	5.882352941	0.0200	< 0.05
Capitonidae	84	2	2.380952381	0.0005	<0.001
Caprimulgidae	90	7	7.777777778	0.0661	> 0.05
Cariamidae	2	0	0	0.7470	> 0.05
Casuariidae	3	2	66.66666667	0.0503	> 0.05
Cathartidae	7	1	14.28571429	0.6398	> 0.05
Certhiidae	8	1	12.5	0.7024	> 0.05
Charadriidae	67	9	13.43283582	0.5744	> 0.05
Chionididae	2	0	0	0.7470	> 0.05
Ciconiidae	19	5	26.31578947	0.1045	> 0.05
Cinclidae	5	1	20	0.5178	> 0.05
Climacteridae	7	0	0	0.3602	> 0.05
Cochleariidae	1	0	0	0.8643	> 0.05
Coliidae	6	0	0	0.4168	> 0.05
Columbidae	318	73	22.95597484	0.0000	<0.001
Conopophagidae	10	0	0	0.2325	> 0.05

Family	Number of species	Number threatened species	% threatened species	p-value	p-value class
Coraciidae	17	4	23.52941176	0.1910	> 0.05
Corvidae	119	14	11.76470588	0.3391	> 0.05
Cotingidae	87	17	19.54022989	0.0758	> 0.05
Cracidae	51	16	31.37254902	0.0008	<0.001
Cracticidae	10	0	0	0.2325	> 0.05
Cuculidae	141	11	7.80141844	0.0242	< 0.05
Dendrocolaptidae	52	1	1.923076923	0.0047	< 0.01
Dicaeidae	57	4	7.01754386	0.0987	> 0.05
Dicruridae	24	2	8.333333333	0.3493	> 0.05
Diomedeidae	21	19	90.47619048	0.0000	<0.001
Drepanididae	34	31	91.17647059	0.0000	<0.001
Dromadidae	1	0	0	0.8643	> 0.05
Dromaiidae	3	2	66.66666667	0.0503	> 0.05
Dulidae	1	0	0	0.8643	> 0.05
Emberizidae	614	57	9.283387622	0.0007	<0.001
Estrildidae	138	10	7.246376812	0.0150	< 0.05
Eurylaimidae	15	3	20	0.3333	> 0.05
Eurypygidae	1	0	0	0.8643	> 0.05
Falconidae	64	7	10.9375	0.3463	> 0.05
Formicariidae	233	33	14.16309013	0.4246	> 0.05
Fregatidae	5	2	40	0.1391	> 0.05
Fringillidae	144	12	8.333333333	0.0371	< 0.05
Furnariidae	276	32	11.5942029	0.1930	> 0.05
Galbulidae	18	2	11.11111111	0.5502	> 0.05
Gaviidae	5	0	0	0.4822	> 0.05
Glareolidae	17	2	11.76470588	0.5884	> 0.05
Grallinidae	4	0	0	0.5580	> 0.05
Gruidae	15	9	60	0.0000	<0.001
Haematopodidae	12	2	16.66666667	0.4989	> 0.05
Heliornithidae	3	1	33.33333333	0.3544	> 0.05
Hemiprocnidae	4	0	0	0.5580	> 0.05
Hirundinidae	81	5	6.172839506	0.0287	< 0.05
Hydrobatidae	22	4	18.18181818	0.3490	> 0.05
Icteridae	102	12	11.76470588	0.3602	> 0.05
Indicatoridae	16	0	0	0.0969	> 0.05
Irenidae	14	1	7.142857143	0.4150	> 0.05
Jacanidae	8	0	0	0.3113	> 0.05
Laniidae	86	9	10.46511628	0.2537	> 0.05
Laridae	95	8	8.421052632	0.0884	> 0.05
Leptosomatidae	1	0	0	0.8643	> 0.05

Family	Number of species	Number threatened species	% threatened species	*p*-value	*p*-value class
Megapodiidae	20	9	45	0.0006	<0.001
Meleagrididae	2	0	0	0.7470	> 0.05
Meliphagidae	183	15	8.196721311	0.0172	< 0.05
Menuridae	2	1	50	0.2530	> 0.05
Meropidae	26	0	0	0.0225	< 0.05
Mesitornithidae	3	3	100	0.0025	< 0.01
Mimidae	35	6	17.14285714	0.3367	> 0.05
Momotidae	10	1	10	0.5977	> 0.05
Motacillidae	62	5	8.064516129	0.1372	> 0.05
Muscicapidae	1,551	168	10.83172147	0.0007	<0.001
Musophagidae	23	2	8.695652174	0.3788	> 0.05
Nectariniidae	122	6	4.918032787	0.0016	< 0.01
Numididae	6	1	16.66666667	0.5832	> 0.05
Nyctibiidae	7	0	0	0.3602	> 0.05
Opisthocomidae	1	0	0	0.8643	> 0.05
Oriolidae	30	3	10	0.4045	> 0.05
Otididae	25	5	20	0.2457	> 0.05
Oxyruncidae	1	0	0	0.8643	> 0.05
Paradisaeidae	44	4	9.090909091	0.2694	> 0.05
Paridae	52	1	1.923076923	0.0047	< 0.01
Parulidae	130	17	13.07692308	0.4977	> 0.05
Pedionomidae	1	1	100	0.1357	> 0.05
Pelecanidae	8	2	25	0.2976	> 0.05
Pelecanoididae	4	1	25	0.4420	> 0.05
Phaethontidae	3	0	0	0.6456	> 0.05
Phalacrocoracidae	35	11	31.42857143	0.0052	< 0.01
Phalaropodidae	3	0	0	0.6456	> 0.05
Phasianidae	189	49	25.92592593	0.0000	<0.001
Philepittidae	4	1	25	0.4420	> 0.05
Phoenicopteridae	6	1	16.66666667	0.5832	> 0.05
Phoeniculidae	8	0	0	0.3113	> 0.05
Phytotomidae	3	1	33.33333333	0.3544	> 0.05
Picidae	215	10	4.651162791	0.0000	<0.001
Pipridae	59	4	6.779661017	0.0833	> 0.05
Pittidae	31	9	29.03225806	0.0189	< 0.05
Ploceidae	168	14	8.333333333	0.0253	< 0.05
Podargidae	14	0	0	0.1298	> 0.05
Podicipedidae	22	7	31.81818182	0.0225	< 0.05
Procellariidae	84	38	45.23809524	0.0000	<0.001
Prunellidae	13	0	0	0.1501	> 0.05

Family	Number of species	Number threatened species	% threatened species	p-value	p-value class
Psittacidae	374	109	29.14438503	0.0000	<0.001
Psophiidae	3	0	0	0.6456	> 0.05
Pteroclididae	16	0	0	0.0969	> 0.05
Ptilonorhynchidae	19	1	5.263157895	0.2493	> 0.05
Pycnonotidae	132	13	9.848484848	0.1286	> 0.05
Rallidae	156	53	33.97435897	0.0000	<0.001
Ramphastidae	41	1	2.43902439	0.0188	< 0.05
Raphidae	2	2	100	0.0184	< 0.05
Recurvirostridae	11	1	9.090909091	0.5482	> 0.05
Remizidae	11	0	0	0.2010	> 0.05
Rhabdornithidae	3	0	0	0.6456	> 0.05
Rheidae	2	0	0	0.7470	> 0.05
Rhinocryptidae	47	4	8.510638298	0.2173	> 0.05
Rhynchopidae	3	1	33.33333333	0.3544	> 0.05
Rhynochetidae	1	1	100	0.1357	> 0.05
Rostratulidae	2	0	0	0.7470	> 0.05
Sagittariidae	1	0	0	0.8643	> 0.05
Scolopacidae	89	12	13.48314607	0.5664	> 0.05
Scopidae	1	0	0	0.8643	> 0.05
Sittidae	27	4	14.81481481	0.5086	> 0.05
Spheniscidae	17	10	58.82352941	0.0000	<0.001
Steatornithidae	1	0	0	0.8643	> 0.05
Stercorariidae	8	0	0	0.3113	> 0.05
Strigidae	181	27	14.91712707	0.3296	> 0.05
Struthionidae	1	0	0	0.8643	> 0.05
Sturnidae	114	14	12.28070175	0.4073	> 0.05
Sulidae	10	2	20	0.4023	> 0.05
Tetraonidae	18	3	16.66666667	0.4498	> 0.05
Thinocoridae	4	0	0	0.5580	> 0.05
Threskiornithidae	36	9	25	0.0474	< 0.05
Tinamidae	49	8	16.32653061	0.3452	> 0.05
Todidae	5	0	0	0.4822	> 0.05
Trochilidae	333	30	9.009009009	0.0070	< 0.01
Troglodytidae	76	6	7.894736842	0.0947	> 0.05
Trogonidae	40	1	2.5	0.0213	< 0.05
Turnicidae	16	3	18.75	0.3727	> 0.05
Tyrannidae	408	27	6.617647059	0.0000	<0.001
Tytonidae	17	5	29.41176471	0.0698	> 0.05
Upupidae	3	1	33.33333333	0.3544	> 0.05
Vangidae	16	4	25	0.1625	> 0.05

Family	Number of species	Number threatened species	% threatened species	*p*-value	*p*-value class
Vireonidae	53	3	5.660377358	0.0588	> 0.05
Zosteropidae	100	24	24	0.0035	< 0.01

Appendix 3g.

Amphibian orders more or less threatened than expected, relative to the average for amphibians as a whole

Order	Number of species	Number threatened species	% threatened species	*p*-value	*p*-value class
Anura	5,067	1,653	32.622854	0.3284	>0.05
Caudata	508	234	46.062992	0.0000	<0.001
Gymnophiona	168	4	2.3809524	0.0000	<0.001

Appendix 3h.

Amphibian families more or less threatened than expected, relative to the average for amphibians as a whole

Family	Number of species	Number threatened species	% threatened species	*p*-value	*p*-value class
Allophrynidae	1	0	0	0.6707	>0.05
Ambystomatidae	29	13	44.8275862	0.1230	>0.05
Amphiumidae	3	0	0	0.3017	>0.05
Arthroleptidae	50	13	26	0.1873	>0.05
Ascaphidae	2	0	0	0.4499	>0.05
Astylosternidae	29	21	72.4137931	0.0000	<0.001
Bombinatoridae	10	5	50	0.2049	>0.05
Brachycephalidae	6	1	16.6666667	0.3592	>0.05
Bufonidae	461	210	45.5531453	0.0000	<0.001
Caeciliidae	109	2	1.83486239	0.0000	<0.001
Centrolenidae	138	51	36.9565217	0.1792	>0.05
Cryptobranchidae	3	1	33.3333333	0.6983	>0.05
Dendrobatidae	229	65	28.3842795	0.0806	>0.05
Dicamptodontidae	4	0	0	0.2024	>0.05
Discoglossidae	12	4	33.3333333	0.5952	>0.05
Heleophrynidae	6	2	33.3333333	0.6408	>0.05
Hemisotidae	9	1	11.1111111	0.1489	>0.05
Hylidae	857	211	24.6207701	0.0000	<0.001
Hynobiidae	44	27	61.3636364	0.0001	<0.001
Hyperoliidae	248	49	19.7580645	0.0000	<0.001
Ichthyophiidae	39	2	5.12820513	0.0000	<0.001

Family	Number of species	Number threatened species	% threatened species	*p*-value	*p*-value class
Leiopelmatidae	4	4	100	0.0118	<0.05
Leptodactylidae	1,124	529	47.0640569	0.0000	<0.001
Limnodynastidae	50	10	20	0.0325	<0.05
Mantellidae	156	35	22.4358974	0.0027	<0.01
Megophryidae	123	43	34.9593496	0.3472	>0.05
Microhylidae	413	71	17.1912833	0.0000	<0.001
Myobatrachidae	71	13	18.3098592	0.0047	<0.01
Nasikabatrachidae	1	1	100	0.3293	>0.05
Pelobatidae	4	1	25	0.5998	>0.05
Pelodytidae	3	0	0	0.3017	>0.05
Petropedetidae	102	24	23.5294118	0.0254	<0.05
Pipidae	30	3	10	0.0038	<0.01
Plethodontidae	348	169	48.5632184	0.0000	<0.001
Proteidae	6	2	33.3333333	0.6408	>0.05
Ranidae	650	165	25.3846154	0.0000	<0.001
Rhacophoridae	262	113	43.129771	0.0004	<0.001
Rheobatrachidae	2	2	100	0.1084	>0.05
Rhinatrematidae	9	0	0	0.0275	<0.05
Rhinodermatidae	2	2	100	0.1084	>0.05
Rhinophrynidae	1	0	0	0.6707	>0.05
Rhyacotritonidae	4	1	25	0.5998	>0.05
Salamandridae	63	21	33.3333333	0.5199	>0.05
Scaphiopodidae	7	0	0	0.0611	>0.05
Scolecomorphidae	6	0	0	0.0911	>0.05
Sirenidae	4	0	0	0.2024	>0.05
Sooglossidae	4	4	100	0.0118	<0.05
Uraeotyphlidae	5	0	0	0.1357	>0.05

Appendix 3i.

Changes in numbers of Extinct (EX) and Extinct in the Wild (EW) species by major taxonomic group since 1996 (1998 for plants)

	1996/98			2000			2004		
	EX	EW	Total	EX	EW	Total	EX	EW	Total
Mammals	86	3	89	83	4	87	73	4	77
Birds	104	4	108	128	3	131	129	4	133
Reptiles	20	1	21	21	1	22	21	1	22
Amphibians	5	0	5	5	0	5	34	1	35
Fish	81	11	92	81	11	92	81	12	93
Subtotal	**296**	**19**	**315**	**318**	**19**	**337**	**338**	**22**	**360**
Invertebrates									
Insects	72	1	73	72	1	73	59	1	60
Crustaceans	9	1	10	8	1	9	7	1	8
Molluscs	230	9	239	291	12	303	291	12	303
Other inverts	4	0	4	4	0	4	2	0	2
Subtotal	**315**	**11**	**326**	**375**	**14**	**389**	**359**	**14**	**373**
Plants									
Mosses	0	0	0	3	0	3	3	0	3
Ferns and allies	0	0	0	0	0	0	3	0	3
Gymnosperms	0	1	1	0	1	1	0	2	2
Dicotyledons	69	14	83	69	14	83	78	20	98
Monocotyledons	2	2	4	1	2	3	2	2	4
Subtotal	**71**	**17**	**88**	**73**	**17**	**90**	**86**	**24**	**110**
Protista									
Red algae	0	0	0	0	0	0	1	0	1
Subtotal	**0**	**0**	**0**	**0**	**0**	**0**	**1**	**0**	**1**
Total	**682**	**47**	**729**	**766**	**50**	**816**	**784**	**60**	**844**

Appendix 3j.

The numbers of threatened species present and threatened species endemic per country for mammals, birds, amphibians, turtles, chondrichthyan fishes (elasmobranches), conifers and cycads. The figures for threatened species present exclude uncertain occurrences and vagrants. These will therefore differ from figures obtained through a country search on the *2004 IUCN Red List of Threatened Species*™, which includes all countries listed within the species' range. Note also that the numbers of amphibians in Brazil are derived from a consistency check of the Global Amphibian Assessment results (see footnote to Table 2.1). The *IUCN Red List* web site, however, shows different numbers as agreement on the results of the consistency check has not yet been reached.

	Mammals		Birds		Amphibians		Turtles		Elasmobranchs		Conifers		Cycads	
	Present	Endemic	Present	Endemic	Present	Endemic	Present	Endemic	Present	Endemic	Present	Endemic	Present	Endemic
Afghanistan	15	0	14	0	1	1	1	0	0	0	0	0	0	0
Albania	2	0	5	0	2	0	3	0	8	0	0	0	0	0
Algeria	15	1	9	1	1	0	2	0	8	0	2	1	0	0
American Samoa	3	0	8	0	0	0	2	0	1	0	0	0	0	0
Andorra	1	0	0	0	0	0	0	0	0	0	0	0	0	0
Angola	13	0	16	7	0	0	3	0	6	0	0	0	0	0
Anguilla	0	0	0	0	0	0	2	0	2	0	0	0	0	0
Antarctica	0	0	5	0	0	0	0	0	0	0	0	0	0	0
Antigua and Barbuda	1	0	1	0	0	0	3	0	2	0	0	0	0	0
Argentina	33	5	49	0	30	24	2	0	8	0	7	0	0	0
Armenia	10	1	11	0	0	0	2	0	0	0	0	0	0	0
Aruba	1	0	1	0	0	0	2	0	2	0	0	0	0	0
Australia	65	56	50	23	47	47	10	4	32	7	10	10	18	18
Austria	6	0	5	0	0	0	0	0	0	0	0	0	0	0
Azerbaijan	11	0	10	0	0	0	2	0	0	0	0	0	0	0
Bahamas	4	3	7	0	0	0	4	0	3	0	1	0	0	0
Bahrain	2	0	4	0	0	0	4	0	5	0	0	0	0	0
Bangladesh	30	0	25	0	0	0	19	0	6	0	0	0	0	0
Barbados	0	0	2	0	0	0	3	0	2	0	0	0	0	0
Belarus	6	0	3	0	0	0	0	0	0	0	0	0	0	0
Belgium	8	0	1	0	0	0	0	0	4	0	0	0	0	0
Belize	5	0	3	0	6	0	4	0	2	0	1	0	2	1
Benin	9	0	2	0	0	0	0	0	5	0	0	0	1	0
Bermuda	2	0	2	1	0	0	1	0	3	0	1	1	0	0
Bhutan	22	0	15	0	1	0	0	0	0	0	1	0	0	0
Bolivia	26	6	30	7	21	17	2	0	0	0	0	0	0	0
Bosnia and Herzegovina	8	0	5	0	1	0	0	0	4	0	1	1	0	0
Botswana	7	0	7	0	0	0	0	0	0	0	0	0	0	0
Bouvet Island	0	0	2	0	0	0	0	0	0	0	0	0	0	0

	Mammals		Birds		Amphibians		Turtles		Elasmobranchs		Conifers		Cycads	
	Present	Endemic	Present	Endemic	Present	Endemic	Present	Endemic	Present	Endemic	Present	Endemic	Present	Endemic
Brazil	74	42	117	67	110	106	13	3	18	6	1	0	0	0
British Indian Ocean Territory	0	0	0	0	0	0	2	0	2	0	0	0	0	0
Brunei Darussalam	13	0	22	0	3	0	4	0	3	0	1	0	0	0
Bulgaria	13	0	11	0	0	0	1	0	0	0	0	0	0	0
Burkina Faso	7	0	2	0	0	0	0	0	0	0	0	0	0	0
Burundi	10	0	7	0	6	0	0	0	0	0	0	0	0	0
Cambodia	24	0	25	0	3	0	10	0	6	0	0	0	2	0
Cameroon	42	13	12	6	50	34	0	0	7	0	0	0	0	0
Canada	16	1	18	0	1	0	3	0	4	0	1	0	0	0
Cape Verde	3	0	3	2	0	0	0	0	9	0	0	0	0	0
Cayman Islands	0	0	1	0	0	0	3	0	1	0	0	0	0	0
Central African Republic	11	0	3	0	0	0	0	0	0	0	0	0	0	0
Chad	12	0	3	0	0	0	1	0	0	0	0	0	0	0
Chile	22	5	32	3	20	16	0	0	4	0	7	1	0	0
China	82	30	85	17	87	80	27	7	14	0	34	26	12	8
Christmas Island	0	0	5	3	0	0	1	0	1	0	0	0	0	0
Cocos (Keeling) Islands	0	0	0	0	0	0	1	0	0	0	0	0	0	0
Colombia	39	9	85	40	208	158	13	3	6	0	0	0	9	6
Comoros	2	1	9	6	0	0	2	0	1	0	0	0	0	0
Congo	14	0	3	0	0	0	0	0	7	0	0	0	0	0
Congo, The Democratic Republic of the	31	5	29	7	13	4	1	0	7	0	0	0	1	1
Cook Islands	1	0	15	5	0	0	2	0	1	0	0	0	0	0
Costa Rica	13	3	17	5	61	23	6	0	2	0	0	0	0	0
Côte d'Ivoire	24	1	11	0	14	5	1	0	8	0	0	0	0	0
Croatia	7	0	9	0	2	0	0	0	4	0	0	0	0	0
Cuba	11	8	19	10	47	47	4	0	7	0	4	2	2	1
Cyprus	4	0	4	0	0	0	3	0	5	0	1	1	0	0
Czech Republic	7	0	5	0	0	0	0	0	0	0	0	0	0	0
Denmark	3	0	1	0	0	0	0	0	4	0	0	0	0	0
Djibouti	6	0	5	1	0	0	0	0	6	0	0	0	0	0
Dominica	1	0	3	2	2	1	4	0	2	0	0	0	0	0
Dominican Republic	5	0	16	0	31	11	5	0	1	0	3	1	0	0
Ecuador	34	8	69	15	163	102	6	1	7	1	0	0	1	1
Egypt	12	0	9	0	0	0	7	0	10	0	0	0	0	0
El Salvador	4	0	3	0	8	0	2	0	3	0	2	0	1	0
Equatorial Guinea	17	2	6	3	5	0	2	0	4	0	0	0	0	0
Eritrea	12	0	5	0	0	0	6	0	7	0	0	0	0	0
Estonia	5	0	2	0	0	0	0	0	0	0	0	0	0	0
Ethiopia	37	20	19	10	9	9	1	0	0	0	0	0	0	0

Appendices

	Mammals		Birds		Amphibians		Turtles		Elasmobranchs		Conifers		Cycads	
	Present	Endemic	Present	Endemic	Present	Endemic	Present	Endemic	Present	Endemic	Present	Endemic	Present	Endemic
Falkland Islands (Malvinas)	4	0	11	1	0	0	0	0	1	0	0	0	0	0
Faroe Islands	3	0	0	0	0	0	0	0	4	0	0	0	0	0
Fiji	5	1	13	9	1	1	3	0	4	0	3	3	1	0
Finland	4	0	2	0	0	0	0	0	0	0	0	0	0	0
France	15	0	4	0	4	1	2	0	8	0	0	0	0	0
French Guiana	10	2	0	0	3	2	7	0	2	0	0	0	0	0
French Polynesia	3	0	31	17	0	0	1	0	1	0	0	0	0	0
French Southern Territories	2	0	14	1	0	0	0	0	0	0	0	0	0	0
Gabon	12	1	4	0	2	0	0	0	8	0	0	0	0	0
Gambia	8	0	2	0	0	0	0	0	7	0	0	0	0	0
Georgia	13	0	7	0	1	0	1	0	0	0	0	0	0	0
Germany	9	0	3	0	0	0	0	0	4	0	0	0	0	0
Ghana	17	0	6	0	10	1	1	0	5	0	0	0	1	0
Gibraltar	2	0	2	0	0	0	0	0	8	0	0	0	0	0
Greece	11	2	9	0	4	2	2	0	7	0	0	0	0	0
Greenland	7	0	0	0	0	0	0	0	0	0	0	0	0	0
Grenada	1	0	1	1	1	1	4	0	2	0	0	0	0	0
Guadeloupe	6	3	2	0	3	2	3	0	2	0	0	0	0	0
Guam	3	0	9	0	0	0	2	0	2	0	0	0	0	0
Guatemala	8	2	10	0	74	31	5	0	3	0	5	0	7	1
Guinea	19	1	10	0	5	1	0	0	4	0	0	0	0	0
Guinea-Bissau	7	0	0	0	0	0	0	0	6	0	0	0	0	0
Guyana	13	0	3	0	6	3	6	0	2	0	0	0	0	0
Haiti	4	0	15	0	46	26	5	0	1	0	3	0	0	0
Heard and McDonald Islands	0	0	12	0	0	0	0	0	0	0	0	0	0	0
Honduras	10	2	6	1	53	38	5	0	3	0	2	0	2	1
Hong Kong	1	0	15	0	5	2	1	0	3	0	0	0	0	0
Hungary	9	0	8	0	0	0	0	0	0	0	0	0	0	0
Iceland	6	0	0	0	0	0	0	0	4	0	0	0	0	0
India	90	30	76	16	66	63	23	3	20	1	2	1	2	1
Indonesia	146	88	119	69	33	23	24	4	23	0	3	0	0	0
Iran (Islamic Republic of)	25	5	15	0	4	3	5	0	6	0	0	0	0	0
Iraq	12	0	16	0	1	0	2	0	1	0	0	0	0	0
Ireland	3	0	1	0	0	0	0	0	5	0	0	0	0	0
Israel	15	3	10	0	0	0	5	0	9	0	0	0	0	0
Italy	12	0	6	0	7	3	3	0	8	0	1	1	0	0
Jamaica	5	2	12	6	17	17	4	0	2	0	1	0	1	0
Japan	38	22	39	7	20	19	8	1	12	0	5	5	0	0
Jordan	11	0	7	0	0	0	1	0	4	0	0	0	0	0

187

	Mammals		Birds		Amphibians		Turtles		Elasmobranchs		Conifers		Cycads	
	Present	Endemic	Present	Endemic	Present	Endemic	Present	Endemic	Present	Endemic	Present	Endemic	Present	Endemic
Kazakhstan	17	1	19	0	1	0	1	0	0	0	0	0	0	0
Kenya	33	6	27	8	5	4	5	1	8	0	0	0	1	1
Kiribati	0	0	5	0	0	0	1	0	1	0	0	0	0	0
Korea, Democratic People's Republic of	12	0	19	0	1	0	0	0	4	0	0	0	0	0
Korea, Republic of	11	0	27	0	1	0	0	0	7	0	0	0	0	0
Kuwait	4	0	7	0	0	0	1	0	6	0	0	0	0	0
Kyrgyzstan	9	1	4	0	0	0	1	0	0	0	0	0	0	0
Lao People's Democratic Republic	33	0	21	0	4	0	11	0	1	0	1	0	1	0
Latvia	5	0	3	0	0	0	0	0	0	0	0	0	0	0
Lebanon	9	0	5	0	0	0	0	0	7	0	0	0	0	0
Lesotho	4	0	5	0	0	0	0	0	0	0	0	0	0	0
Liberia	21	0	11	1	4	1	1	0	5	0	0	0	0	0
Libyan Arab Jamahiriya	9	0	3	0	0	0	3	0	7	0	0	0	0	0
Liechtenstein	2	0	0	0	0	0	0	0	0	0	0	0	0	0
Lithuania	6	0	3	0	0	0	0	0	0	0	0	0	0	0
Luxembourg	3	0	0	0	0	0	0	0	0	0	0	0	0	0
Macao	0	0	2	0	0	0	0	0	3	0	0	0	0	0
Macedonia, the former Yugoslav Republic of	9	0	9	0	0	0	1	0	0	0	0	0	0	0
Madagascar	49	43	36	27	55	55	10	4	10	0	0	0	0	0
Malawi	7	0	12	1	5	3	0	0	0	0	1	1	1	0
Malaysia	50	17	43	2	45	33	19	0	13	0	12	11	1	0
Maldives	0	0	0	0	0	0	2	0	5	0	0	0	0	0
Mali	13	0	3	0	0	0	1	0	1	0	0	0	0	0
Malta	1	0	2	0	0	0	0	0	9	0	0	0	0	0
Marshall Islands	1	0	2	0	0	0	2	0	4	0	0	0	0	0
Martinique	1	0	2	1	2	1	3	0	2	0	0	0	0	0
Mauritania	11	0	5	0	0	0	2	0	8	0	0	0	0	0
Mauritius	4	1	12	9	0	0	5	0	5	0	0	0	0	0
Mayotte	0	0	4	1	0	0	2	0	0	0	0	0	0	0
Mexico	73	53	58	24	191	156	15	4	7	0	16	10	38	32
Micronesia, Federated States of	6	3	8	4	0	0	2	0	2	0	0	0	0	0
Moldova, Republic of	5	0	8	0	0	0	1	0	0	0	0	0	0	0
Monaco	0	0	0	0	0	0	0	0	8	0	0	0	0	0
Mongolia	13	1	20	0	0	0	0	0	0	0	0	0	0	0
Montserrat	1	0	2	1	1	0	2	0	2	0	0	0	0	0
Morocco	17	1	9	0	2	1	2	0	7	0	1	0	0	0
Mozambique	13	1	22	1	3	0	5	0	13	0	0	0	10	2
Myanmar	40	2	40	1	0	0	21	5	5	0	4	1	1	0
Namibia	10	0	19	0	1	0	2	1	7	0	0	0	0	0

	Mammals		Birds		Amphibians		Turtles		Elasmobranchs		Conifers		Cycads	
	Present	Endemic	Present	Endemic	Present	Endemic	Present	Endemic	Present	Endemic	Present	Endemic	Present	Endemic
Nauru	0	0	2	1	0	0	0	0	1	0	0	0	0	0
Nepal	32	0	30	0	3	2	4	0	0	0	0	0	1	0
Netherlands	10	0	1	0	0	0	0	0	4	0	0	0	0	0
Netherlands Antilles	3	0	1	0	0	0	3	0	2	0	0	0	0	0
New Caledonia	6	3	15	7	1	0	2	0	6	1	15	15	1	0
New Zealand	8	4	70	43	6	4	1	0	5	0	1	1	0	0
Nicaragua	6	0	8	0	10	3	6	0	5	0	1	0	0	0
Niger	11	0	2	0	0	0	0	0	0	0	0	0	0	0
Nigeria	28	3	9	2	13	1	1	0	9	0	0	0	1	0
Niue	0	0	8	0	0	0	1	0	1	0	0	0	0	0
Norfolk Island	0	0	17	4	0	0	0	0	1	0	1	1	0	0
Northern Mariana Islands	2	0	13	5	0	0	2	0	2	0	0	0	0	0
Norway	9	0	1	0	0	0	0	0	4	0	0	0	0	0
Oman	12	2	8	0	0	0	4	0	12	0	0	0	0	0
Pakistan	22	2	26	0	0	0	7	0	11	0	0	0	0	0
Palau	3	0	1	0	0	0	2	0	3	0	0	0	0	0
Palestinian Authority Territories	0	0	3	0	0	0	0	0	0	0	0	0	0	0
Panama	17	5	20	4	52	14	6	0	4	0	1	0	3	3
Papua New Guinea	58	25	32	12	10	8	9	1	16	2	0	0	0	0
Paraguay	11	0	28	0	1	1	2	0	0	0	1	0	0	0
Peru	47	13	93	35	79	56	5	0	5	0	0	0	5	2
Philippines	50	46	67	56	48	48	6	1	14	1	4	1	1	1
Pitcairn	0	0	11	5	0	0	0	0	0	0	0	0	0	0
Poland	13	0	4	0	0	0	0	0	0	0	0	0	0	0
Portugal	15	1	7	1	0	0	0	0	10	0	2	1	0	0
Puerto Rico	3	0	12	4	13	12	4	0	1	0	0	0	2	1
Qatar	0	0	4	0	0	0	1	0	4	0	0	0	0	0
Réunion	4	0	6	3	0	0	4	0	3	0	0	0	0	0
Romania	15	0	11	0	0	0	1	0	0	0	0	0	0	0
Russian Federation	44	4	48	0	0	0	2	0	2	0	0	0	0	0
Rwanda	16	1	9	0	8	0	0	0	0	0	0	0	0	0
Saint Helena	1	0	19	7	0	0	1	0	0	0	0	0	0	0
Saint Kitts and Nevis	1	0	1	0	1	0	3	0	1	0	0	0	0	0
Saint Lucia	2	0	5	3	0	0	4	0	1	0	1	0	0	0
Saint Pierre and Miquelon	0	0	1	0	0	0	0	0	1	0	0	0	0	0
Saint Vincent and the Grenadines	2	1	2	2	1	1	3	0	2	0	0	0	0	0
Samoa	3	0	7	5	0	0	1	0	1	0	0	0	0	0
San Marino	0	0	0	0	0	0	0	0	0	0	0	0	0	0
São Tomé and Principe	3	3	10	9	3	3	1	0	4	0	1	1	0	0

	Mammals		Birds		Amphibians		Turtles		Elasmobranchs		Conifers		Cycads	
	Present	Endemic	Present	Endemic	Present	Endemic	Present	Endemic	Present	Endemic	Present	Endemic	Present	Endemic
Saudi Arabia	11	0	12	0	0	0	2	0	7	0	0	0	0	0
Senegal	13	0	5	0	0	0	5	0	13	0	0	0	0	0
Serbia and Montenegro	10	0	10	0	1	0	0	0	8	0	0	0	0	0
Seychelles	3	2	11	8	6	6	3	0	7	0	0	0	0	0
Sierra Leone	14	0	10	0	2	1	2	0	4	0	0	0	0	0
Singapore	5	0	13	0	0	0	4	0	6	0	0	0	0	0
Slovakia	9	0	8	0	0	0	0	0	0	0	0	0	0	0
Slovenia	7	0	2	0	2	0	0	0	6	0	0	0	0	0
Solomon Islands	20	12	22	8	2	0	3	0	2	0	0	0	0	0
Somalia	16	3	10	5	0	0	2	0	10	0	0	0	0	0
South Africa	30	11	34	3	21	20	4	1	18	1	2	2	26	20
South Georgia and the South Sandwich Islands	1	0	8	0	0	0	0	0	0	0	0	0	0	0
Spain	21	2	15	3	4	2	2	0	11	0	1	0	0	0
Sri Lanka	21	9	13	7	44	43	5	0	10	0	0	0	0	0
Sudan	18	0	10	0	0	0	2	0	7	0	0	0	0	0
Suriname	12	0	0	0	2	1	6	0	1	0	0	0	0	0
Svalbard and Jan Mayen	5	0	0	0	0	0	0	0	0	0	0	0	0	0
Swaziland	5	0	6	0	0	0	0	0	0	0	0	0	8	0
Sweden	5	0	2	0	0	0	0	0	3	0	0	0	0	0
Switzerland	4	0	2	0	1	0	0	0	0	0	0	0	0	0
Syrian Arab Republic	8	1	10	0	0	0	2	0	7	0	0	0	0	0
Taiwan, Province of China	13	4	20	1	9	7	8	0	9	0	10	6	1	1
Tajikistan	9	0	8	0	0	0	1	0	0	0	0	0	0	0
Tanzania, United Republic of	34	14	36	12	40	39	5	0	10	0	0	0	2	2
Thailand	38	3	44	1	3	2	21	0	17	0	2	0	6	3
Timor-Leste	0	0	7	0	0	0	1	0	1	0	0	0	0	0
Togo	9	0	1	0	3	0	1	0	5	0	0	0	1	0
Tokelau	0	0	1	0	0	0	2	0	1	0	0	0	0	0
Tonga	2	0	4	1	0	0	1	0	1	0	0	0	1	0
Trinidad and Tobago	1	0	2	1	9	6	5	0	3	0	0	0	0	0
Tunisia	13	0	6	0	0	0	2	0	7	0	0	0	0	0
Turkey	17	1	14	0	5	2	4	0	7	0	0	0	0	0
Turkmenistan	14	0	14	0	0	0	2	0	0	0	0	0	0	0
Turks and Caicos Islands	0	0	4	0	0	0	4	0	1	0	0	0	0	0
Tuvalu	0	0	1	0	0	0	1	0	2	0	0	0	0	0
Uganda	30	4	14	0	6	0	0	0	0	0	0	0	3	3
Ukraine	16	1	11	0	0	0	1	0	0	0	0	0	0	0
United Arab Emirates	6	0	7	0	0	0	1	0	5	0	0	0	0	0
United Kingdom	9	0	3	0	0	0	0	0	6	0	0	0	0	0

	Mammals		Birds		Amphibians		Turtles		Elasmobranchs		Conifers		Cycads	
	Present	Endemic	Present	Endemic	Present	Endemic	Present	Endemic	Present	Endemic	Present	Endemic	Present	Endemic
United States	42	18	76	31	51	46	21	8	10	0	13	11	0	0
United States Minor Outlying Islands	0	0	10	0	0	0	1	0	2	0	0	0	0	0
Uruguay	7	0	25	0	4	1	1	0	9	0	0	0	0	0
Uzbekistan	9	0	13	0	0	0	1	0	0	0	0	0	0	0
Vanuatu	5	1	8	5	0	0	2	0	2	0	1	1	1	0
Vatican City	0	0	0	0	0	0	0	0	0	0	0	0	0	0
Venezuela	26	4	25	12	68	61	10	1	2	0	0	0	0	0
Viet Nam	42	5	40	5	15	5	24	1	13	0	12	5	16	11
Virgin Islands, British	1	0	2	0	2	1	4	0	1	0	0	0	0	0
Virgin Islands, US	2	0	3	0	2	1	3	0	1	0	0	0	0	0
Wallis and Futuna Islands	0	0	9	0	0	0	0	0	1	0	0	0	0	0
Western Sahara	7	0	0	0	0	0	0	0	9	0	0	0	0	0
Yemen	8	0	12	2	1	1	2	0	10	1	0	0	0	0
Zambia	12	2	9	0	1	0	0	0	0	0	0	0	0	0
Zimbabwe	8	1	10	0	6	4	0	0	0	0	0	0	3	1